HARDBALL

THE EDUCATION
OF A BASEBALL
COMMISSIONER

BOWIE KUHN

EDITORIAL ASSISTANT: MARTIN APPEL

with a new afterword by the author

UNIVERSITY OF NEBRASKA PRESS

LINCOLN AND LONDON

♾ The paper in this book meets the minimum requirements of American National
Standard for Information Sciences—Permanence of Paper for Printed Library
Materials, ANSI Z39.48-1984.

First Bison Books printing: 1997
Most recent printing indicated by the last digit below:
10   9   8   7   6   5   4   3   2   1

Library of Congress Cataloging-in-Publication Data
Kuhn, Bowie, 1926–
Hardball: the education of a baseball commissioner / Bowie Kuhn; editorial
assistant, Martin Appel; with a new afterword by the author.
p.   cm.
Originally published: New York: Times Books, c1987
Includes index.
ISBN 0-8032-7784-9 (pa: alk. paper)
1. Kuhn, Bowie, 1926–   . 2. Baseball commissioners—United States—
Biography.   I. Appel, Martin.   II. Title.
GV865.K78K85   1997
796 357'092—dc21
[B]
97-6823   CIP

Reprinted from the original 1987 edition by Times Books, New York.

*To the ladies who have always inspired me—
my wife, Luisa, and my mother, Alice—and to my children
and their spouses, who have given my life meaning and
purpose—George and Carole, Paul, Alix and Stephen,
and Stephen*

Acknowledgments

M y struggles with this book would have been fruitless but for a group of friends who helped me along this difficult way. No one was more patient, supportive and understanding than Luisa. Marty Appel was my drill sergeant, fount of knowledge and faithful critic. Jonathan Segal kept me at my task, skillfully winnowed out the trivial and smoothed the balance. Peter Ueberroth gave me encouragement and Charlyne Sanders found needles in haystacks. Bill Adler made me believe this book could be written and that I had something to say. Sandy Hadden and Bob Wirz read much of the manuscript and gave me good counsel. Ruth Fecych, Ravin Korothy and Nancy Inglis straightened out the infinite details with skill and professionalism. My secretary Carmela Battaglino gracefully handled the logistics between me and all the others. Numerous others were kind enough to help. I thank them all.

Contents

HARDBALL

1

Voices
in the Night

According to legend, Rudy York, the Cherokee first baseman of the Detroit Tigers in the 1930s, was once hauled from a burning bed by an irate hotel manager who accused him of starting the fire by smoking. York's answer was a classic of innocent baseball dishonesty: "That bed was on fire when I got into it."

It is not dishonest to say that baseball was on fire when I became commissioner in 1969. While that fire had varied in ferocity during the ensuing years, never had it blazed more scorchingly than in June 1981. On June 12 the Major League Players Association blundered into a strike that would prove to be the worst in American sports history.

The Association had gravely miscalculated the stubbornness and determination of ownership on the issue that had precipitated the strike: whether or not the owners were entitled to increased compensation for players lost to free agency. While I had often disagreed with the owners' labor positions, I strongly favored increased compensation. These factors, taken together with the zealotry of Marvin Miller, the Association's leader, and his hatred of ownership provoked the darkest foreboding.

Somehow, I felt a lift when on the fifth day of the strike Baltimore Orioles owner Edward Bennett Williams called. Two of his players,

Mark Belanger and Doug DeCinces, were key figures in the Association. I knew he had kept the lines of communication open with them.

When I first met Ed in the early years of my commissionership he was president of the Washington Redskins. He was also one of the nation's best-known attorneys who moved easily in high political circles in Washington and was an adviser to presidents. Magnetic, animated and a man of prodigious ability, he was a marvelous companion, though I learned early on to be wary of his humor, which on occasion had the venom of a serpent. Years later, I helped set the stage for his entrance into baseball by suggesting his name as a possible Baltimore co-owner to Bill Simon, the former secretary of the treasury, who contemplated buying the club in 1979.

On this day, however, Williams's voice had an edge of urgency. He wanted to know if I was free to meet for dinner that evening; he would fly up from Washington to join me in New York.

We confirmed the arrangements, and several minutes later, as an afterthought, I telephoned Lee MacPhail and asked him to join us. MacPhail, the American League president, would be a good addition to the conversation. Highly regarded for his integrity and gentlemanly manner, he had played an active role in the negotiations to date. He had spent his entire career in baseball. His father was Hall of Famer Larry MacPhail, who at various times ran the Cincinnati Reds, the Brooklyn Dodgers and the New York Yankees.

We met Williams at Christ Cella, a restaurant on East Forty-sixth Street in Manhattan. Curiously, the conversation was strained and desultory. Ed's normal amiability was missing. I filled the conversational vacuum, talking more to MacPhail than to Williams. Both Lee and I sensed that Williams was annoyed because he had anticipated a private session with me.

MacPhail excused himself before coffee, leaving me alone with Williams, who came speedily to the point. Modulating his voice so that I could hear but neighboring patrons could not, he said, "This is the end of our friendship." It was dramatic, precisely as this most skillful actor intended it to be. His directness left me both silent and surprised.

With Shakespearean accents, he said, "I feel deep sorrow that this is necessary. I deplore it, I really deplore it. I'm really sorry about this. I'm so sorry that circumstances have brought our friendship to an end." Williams had seen my invitation to Lee as a lack of trust on my part, a need to have a witness present at our conversation.

Whatever brought him to New York for dinner that night, I never learned. While I told him that friendships were not things turned on and off with valves, an evaluation that proved to be correct regarding Williams and me, I believe that my reign as commissioner began to come apart irretrievably that night. I had hurt him and he would exact a price for it.

I would remain commissioner for more than three years, would in fact even see Williams support my reelection, but that evening had been a watershed.

Six months later, another unpredictable owner, Ted Turner, provided another curious twist.

I had never before missed a day of a baseball annual meeting, but the growing threat to the game being offered by cable television and its superstation suppliers of baseball telecasts convinced our Washington advisers that I should leave our December meeting in Hollywood, Florida, and fly up for a day to testify before Congressman Robert Kastenmeier's House subcommittee, which was holding hearings on pending cable-television bills. With some reluctance, I chartered a plane and flew to Washington. I was no stranger to congressional hearing rooms; neither was my fellow witness Ted Turner.

By 1976, when he wanted to buy the Atlanta Braves, Turner had for five years operated WTBS, an independent television station in Atlanta. We knew he was interested in making WTBS a superstation, potentially beaming its signal across the country by satellite. That meant carrying Braves baseball into other major-league markets. Because that could pose serious conflicts with existing TV contracts, we asked Bill Bartholomay, who wanted to sell the Braves to Turner, to get a letter reassuring us of Turner's intentions.

Turner complied with a letter to Bartholomay dated January 7, 1976, in which he said in part that "it is Turner Communications' and my personal intention to comply with the best interest of baseball in all matters including baseball's collective posting on cable television."

Lulled by Turner's assurance, the National League approved his purchase of the Braves. Later that year, the Federal Communications Commission approved an application by Southern Satellite Systems to carry the WTBS signal nationally. The nation's first superstation was born.

Had Ted been dishonest with us? He surely had, and he would later boast to me in my office that he had "pulled the wool over the eyes of the National League."

Turner and I had clashed many times in Congress because of my support of bills designed to protect baseball from the indiscriminate broadcasting of our games by cable television. The prime supplier of those games was Turner's WTBS, which had grown explosively to a point where it was feeding some twenty million cable homes. There was no secret to this success; without his 150 Braves games, WTBS would have been a cipher in the superstation marketplace.

Room 2226 of the Rayburn House Office Building was jammed with spectators and reporters. Turner was standing in front of the room surrounded by press. As I approached him, he launched into a remarkable and animated monologue intended as much for the press as it was for me, declaring, "Commissioner, I'm not signing any letter. I'm not planning to join those people who are out to get you! I know we've had our differences in the past, Commissioner, but I don't know where we'd ever get anybody as good as you, and I told those fellows I wouldn't go along with them."

I really had no idea what he was talking about, but it seemed clear enough that I was not going to like it when I knew more. Or was it just one of Turner's flights of fancy? I was in that room as the principal spokesman against his interests. Was he trying to soften me up? In any case, the hearing was being called to order, and there was no opportunity that day for me to ask him what he was talking about. As I flew back to Florida that evening, I wondered about the enigmatic Mr. Turner, and wondered if there was more to come.

That evening in the hotel, National League president Chub Feeney told me, "Something's up. I'm not sure what it is, but I don't like the tone of what I've been hearing." When my wife, Luisa, wondered about the significance of Feeney's remark, I told her about Turner's bizarre remarks in Washington. While I had great respect for Feeney's astute evaluation of baseball's Byzantine affairs, alarms of this kind had become too commonplace to have much effect on me.

I retired early that night, knowing I had a busy day ahead of me as baseball dealt with its poststrike affairs. At 3:00 A.M. the telephone rang. It was Peter O'Malley, owner of the Dodgers.

"I've got some bad news," he said. "Ballard Smith [president of the San Diego Padres] has just told me about a letter signed by nine owners calling for your resignation."

I asked for the names. He said, "There's Ballard himself and Steinbrenner [Yankees], McMullen, [Houston], Chiles [Texas], Busch [St. Louis], Doubleday [Mets], Argyros [Seattle], Bill Williams [Cincinnati] and Ed Williams. I've got to come up and see you."

I asked him to repeat the names and he did. I noted with interest that Turner, true to his word, had not signed. Four of them who did came as no surprise: George Steinbrenner, John McMullen, Nelson Doubleday and Eddie Chiles. What were the other five doing on that letter? Oddly enough, I still could not accept the defection of Ed Williams or think that an old baseball lion like Gussie Busch was off the reservation.

I told Luisa what the call was about and repeated the names for her. She reacted calmly, but not without some well-controlled passion. I slipped quickly into my running pants and pulled a sweater over my bare torso.

Next I awakened Sandy Hadden, baseball's general counsel, who was occupying another bedroom in our suite. Hadden was a loyalist. More a partner than a chief operating officer, he had shared the travails of the office with me since he left a distinguished career with the Cleveland law firm of Baker, Hostetler & Patterson and joined me in 1970 as the number two man in baseball. Unflappable and dead honest, Hadden had my total trust, and I fully appreciated his encyclopedic understanding of baseball's affairs and curious characters.

Our suite in the Diplomat Hotel was adorned with metallic silver-orange-purple wallpaper and maroon drapes. Its seraglio aspects were nicely complemented by the night's events and by the Arab sheik who occupied the entire floor below us. Each time the elevator stopped there, formidable armed guards would stare in to make sure that only the anointed got off. One began to hope that *certain* letter signers stumbled there by mistake.

Peter O'Malley arrived, businesslike and somber. I learned that Milwaukee Brewers owner Bud Selig had told him that night of the letter's existence. O'Malley promptly saw Ballard Smith and got the story. After talking to Lee MacPhail, he called me.

"I think we'd better get some of the guys up here and talk," he said. We went over names and he began making calls.

I mulled over the nine names on the letter. My battles with Steinbrenner were an everyday part of life. Doubleday, McMullen and Chiles were all "new breed" owners, lacking, in my opinion, any real sense of the game or appreciation of its verities rooted in the nineteenth century. Their hostility was transparent.

Bill Williams and Ballard Smith were men of different quality who did not belong in the group, nor did I believe they would stay. George Argyros, while new, seemed out of place. Logic suggested that Ed Williams belonged on the anti-Kuhn list going back to June. Still, because of my fondness for him, I was surprised.

Gussie Busch was the only veteran owner on the list. I liked Busch, for all his imperious and curmudgeonly ways. I do not know any owner who loved the game more. Since Anheuser-Busch had taken over the Cardinals in 1953, Busch had been by my standards a good owner. Even though we had collided on a number of issues, I felt he usually landed on the right side of the issues, after a certain amount of wandering in his own wilderness. But Busch could be unpredictable. He had once led an effort to dislodge Chub Feeney as National League president, only to place his name in nomination when the matter came to a vote. Nonetheless, my first reaction to learning that he was in the group of nine was that he could be turned around—a miscalculation.

Baseball executives in various states of dress and undress began arriving in my suite to assess the coup attempt. They came and went throughout the early morning hours. The garishly colored room was at odds with the gray mood of these men. Some sat at a large table in the center; others spoke softly in corners.

The group included O'Malley, Hadden, Bob Lurie of San Francisco, Selig of Milwaukee, Bill Giles of Philadelphia, Haywood Sullivan of Boston, John Fetzer of Detroit, John McHale of Montreal, Lou Hoynes of Willkie Farr & Gallagher, the National League attorney, Chub Feeney and MacPhail. In and out they came. Unseen but intently listening behind the drapes in the balcony bedroom above was Luisa.

O'Malley and Lurie, the most vocal, were outraged at the cloak-and-dagger approach of the signers, particularly their failure to bring up the matter with their brethren. The group shared their anger.

As I listened, I found myself detached, pensive, not as outraged as the others. The letter, as outlined by O'Malley, was polite enough. I wondered why they had not come to me if they really wanted a peaceful change. After thirteen years, I was far from certain that I wanted to continue. That is a long time to be chief executive of any business, especially one as turbulent as ours. I had said publicly that I might not continue.

While I thought their strategy was ill-conceived, their motive for proceeding as they had was clear enough. Since they did not, and could not, trust one another, their first priority was to lock fellow conspirators in place with the letter. The danger of that strategy was that their plan would leak. Virtually everything in baseball leaked. Now it had, and I saw it solidifying the other clubs. I saw it happening right in front of me.

The letter was the focal point of the discussion that night. Although a copy was not actually in the room, O'Malley knew what it said and gave its essence. Susman and Ed Williams were reported as the architects. Some time later, Smith gave me a copy. In full text, it read:

Members of the Executive Council:
The undersigned owners wish to be on record of their intent not to vote for the renewal of Commissioner Kuhn's employment contract.

It is the intent and desire of the undersigned that the Commissioner be afforded the courtesies and financial arrangements that are not only called for in the Agreement, but, if necessary, to go beyond the intent of those agreements to be sure that this matter is handled in a dignified and proper manner. We would be happy to discuss with the Executive Council or any representative our ideas as to the details of those arrangements.

Commissioner Kuhn is a fine man of great integrity and has given 100% in his efforts to lead us in the right direction. We would hope that when our action is conveyed to him that he would understand that this in no way reflects upon his fine characteristics. However, the time has come, in our opinion, for a new, dynamic and creative leadership for baseball, unencumbered with the burdens, scars and prejudices of the past.

In light of the developments of this letter, we would suggest that an "owners only" meeting be held as soon as possible on this very delicate subject.

As the small hours of the night wore away, a plan began to emerge. It focused on the National League, since five of the signers were from that league. Under the Major League Agreement, which contained the rules for reelection of the commissioner, a three-quarters vote of each league was required. Thus, four votes in the National League could block my reelection. On the face of things, they had those four votes and one more for good measure.

The three-quarters rule was a reflection of the owners' almost paranoid fear of the commissioner's role in baseball. The rule had been adopted after the death of the formidable Judge Kenesaw

Mountain Landis, who had often terrorized the owners during his twenty-four years as the game's first commissioner. It guaranteed that any commissioner who did his job correctly would have trouble getting reelected by owners on whose tender toes he was bound to have trampled. Only Commissioner Ford Frick, who was reelec ed in 1958, escaped the foolish machinations of the rule.

According to the plan, at the next morning's National League meeting, the nonsigners would excoriate the five signers and demand that the letter be withdrawn. While there had been some support for a more diplomatic approach, it was rejected. Diplomacy was not in vogue that night. The nonsigners thought that the moral outrage of the "good" owners would shake loose such obviously decent men as Bill Williams and Smith from the conspiracy. They were partly right.

Much of the conversation was given over to meandering evaluations of various owners. McMullen and Doubleday were mavericks. So was Chiles. While not an owner, Susman significantly influenced Busch. So, necessarily, did Anheuser-Busch. Ed Williams's involvement probably destroyed any hope he had of becoming a major baseball power broker. Steinbrenner's participation in the conspiracy undermined its effectiveness and credibility. Sullivan saw them all as "banana republic generals."

The meeting broke up about 8:00 A.M. Harry Gibbs, my director of security, and I went jogging through the streets of Hollywood. I had taken up running a few months before as a fifty-fifth-birthday present to myself. I liked to tell people I did it not to improve my cardiovascular system but strictly for self-defense. Gibbs and I laughed about that. In the years ahead, as the pressure increased, my running became an invaluable means of releasing stress. So I lengthened the distance and increased the regularity.

Luisa called our four children and my mother, alerting them to the breaking news. We did not want them to be caught by surprise. They took it in stride.

At the National League meeting, the letter was in fact withdrawn —even symbolically torn up by Susman right on the spot. But the philosophy behind the letter would not so easily evaporate, any more than testimony a jury is told to disregard evaporates. That was apparent soon enough.

The signers gathered in Busch's suite at lunch. Others, like eighty-year-old Fetzer, were invited. Fetzer belied the common and adverse view of baseball ownership. A philosopher, a Renaissance man, courtly, circumspect and decent, Fetzer had been in the game for twenty years and was a close friend of mine. He went straight from Busch's suite to mine, which was just down the hall.

Fetzer joined Lurie, O'Malley, Selig, Hadden and others who were gathering in my suite. Sitting on a sofa in the bright Florida sun, and for once looking his age, he said, "I cannot believe what I have just seen and heard. Busch screaming and yelling, pounding with his cane, demanding that Bowie get out. And some of the others were nearly as bad. It was irrational. It was madness. I think the time has come to get out. I don't want to be in the same business with those people. And, Bowie, if I were you, I'd walk out on them right now. You don't need this job."

Challenged by the "Kuhn loyalists," the conspirators had turned ugly and threatening. They had planned a negotiated victory and reaped a whirlwind. Now they would fight.

And I knew then that I was going to fight, too. Why, after thirteen often brutal seasons as commissioner, did I choose to fight it out? Why did I turn my back on the golden parachute dangling in front of me? Why did I elect to fight a group of tough, cunning, ruthless people with limitless financial resources?

The answer was simple enough. They were trying to shove me out. Fetzer's report of their meeting made that clear. You can reason with me about most things and, chances are, get somewhere. But I do not liked to be shoved. The more I heard, the more stubborn I became. And Luisa, who might have changed my view had she been so inclined, has even more mule in her genes than I do.

I was also stiffened by the quality of my supporters. They were the best in baseball. I admired them personally and professionally. Like Fetzer, they were vastly superior to the common press perception of "greedy owners." If they could put their trust and confidence in me, as they unceasingly had, I owed them the fight. And the fight, make no mistake, was viewed as a fight to save the game from a group of arrogant men who were scheming to use their minority position to control baseball for their own selfish purposes.

I also hated the thought of leaving the baseball people. We had gone through so much together in thirteen years. With obvious exceptions, they were good people—not saints, mind you, but not devils, either. They were dedicated to the game and bristled at newcomers who cared little for its traditions and rhythms. Clannish and fun-loving, their loyalty to their own was legendary, even to a fault—even to the commissioner.

2

Dad Was an Immigrant, Mother Liked the Senators

I imagine it will surprise some to know that my father was an immigrant, hardly the right ancestral background for the Ivy League–Wall Street "stuffed shirt" many people take me for.

Louis Charles Kuhn was the son of a farm family in the small Bavarian town of Ebenhausen. His mother, Marie, died twelve days after he was born in November 1893. Only three months earlier his father, Gottfried, then twenty years old, had come to the United States in search of the fabled American opportunity. The care of my father passed to his mother's older sister, Anna Lutz. Anna and my father left Germany on September 20, 1894, on the steamship *Elba* and arrived in Pittsburgh, Pennsylvania, eleven days later, joining Gottfried, who had settled there. Their timing was fortunate; the *Elba* sank two months later after colliding with a British ship. All hands were lost.

Within the month Anna married Gottfried at St. Leo's Catholic Church in Pittsburgh. She raised my father as her own; indeed, he did not know until much later in his life that she was not his mother.

The household was German-speaking, like that of Lou Gehrig in New York in the same period.

Like many immigrants, Louis Kuhn was an extraordinarily proud American. Nothing so dominated and motivated his life as his devotion to the United States. He enlisted in the American army on July 16, 1917, and served with the 28th "Keystone" Division of the Pennsylvania National Guard, participating in the Allied Expeditionary Force campaigns at Champagne-Marne, Aisne-Marne, Oise-Aisne and Meuse-Argonne. The ribbons for those campaigns were his battle laurels. Nothing he owned pleased him so much, even though two of his first cousins died fighting for the German army.

A year to the day after he was discharged from the army, he married my mother, Alice Waring Roberts, on May 20, 1920, in Nashville, Tennessee, where my mother was working on temporary assignment by the War Department. The ceremony was performed at Old St. Mary's Catholic Church. By all accounts, they were a very handsome couple. They settled in Washington, D.C., an area where my mother had deep ancestral roots. Her ancestors were immigrants, too, but arrived in Maryland in 1634 on the *Ark* and the *Dove,* 260 years before my father, sailing from Gravesend in the Stuart England of Charles I. My mother's ancestors included five governors and two United States senators, in addition to various congressmen, judges and lawyers. Distantly related, Jim Bowie was, of course, the inventor of the awesome Bowie knife and one of the heroes of the Alamo, where he died in 1836, no doubt knowing little and caring less about the game of baseball. (Shortly before I left office as commissioner, a friend generously gave me a Bowie knife —several years too late.)

Whatever the disparities of their immigrant backgrounds, my parents were a good match, both strong believers in education and the work ethic, both Catholics (though my father had dark nights of faith), both dedicated to family life and togetherness, both politically and culturally conservative, both highly patriotic. The American flag always flew at our house on national holidays.

My father was happy to leave Pittsburgh behind. He had never gotten along well with his tough Germanic father, who died during the great flu epidemic that swept the United States during the closing phase of the war. Nor had he been educated beyond the high school level. Fortunately he was endowed with the mind of an engineer, which grasped the workings of machinery and equipment at a glance. He loved automobiles, which he could dismantle and reassemble almost by instinct. Mentally quick and incisive, he was impatient with those who could not keep up with his pace. His formidable energies led him in time into the retail and industrial oil business, where, self-trained, he rose to head the Washington area office of the Petroleum Heat and Power Company. I often heard it said that nobody in Washington understood the industrial oil business better than my father. Valid as that point is, my father's lack of formal education pained him deeply throughout his life and inspired his vicarious satisfaction in whatever educational successes his children achieved. While it was often difficult for him to convey to us how deep that satisfaction was, we knew it was there abundantly.

My brother, Lou, was born in 1921 and my sister, Alice, in 1923, leaving me to be given names deeply steeped in my Maryland ancestry—Bowie Kent—when I was born on October 28, 1926.

I graduated in 1944 from Theodore Roosevelt High School in Washington, where at 6 feet 5 inches I was not only the tallest boy in the school, but also class president and a good student. My mother and father took enormous pride in the academic achievements of their children. Good report cards were received with jubilation, which inspired the student in us.

I played intramural sports as a member of the high school Cadet Corps football team, and thought myself an adequate passing tailback in the style, as I fantasized, of the Redskins' Sammy Baugh. The fantasy was exclusively mine. We held our own in scrimmages against the varsity second team, but as a memento I have a broken nose that to this day deviates to the east.

The only varsity sport I attempted was basketball. Roosevelt's coach during my senior year was a man with fiery red hair named Arnold Auerbach, better known today as Red Auerbach, the Hall of Fame coach and general manager of the Boston Celtics. Coach Auerbach stopped me in the hall one day, looked up and said, "Son, you're the tallest boy in the school. How come you're not out for the basketball team?"

"Because I'm a lousy player," I replied.

"You let me be the judge of that," he answered, and suited me up for a week of workouts under his guidance. After a week, he took me aside and said, "Son, you were right, and I was wrong. You won't have to come back tomorrow."

Shortly thereafter, Red left and was replaced by a kindly little coach who talked me back onto the team. Though I somehow survived the season and earned a varsity letter, Red was right, as usual.

While I was a passionate across-the-board sports fan, I was transcendently a baseball fan. I loved the Washington Senators, really loved them. I first remember them in 1933, when I was six years old. The town was electric because the Senators were winning the American League pennant. I had no awareness of the All-Star Game, held for the first time that year, or of Babe Ruth's winning it with a home run. In fact, I never saw Babe Ruth play. But I knew the Senators were winning the pennant. It was their third pennant and would prove to be their last. Manager and shortstop Joe Cronin became a hero for me then and still is.

The Senators played in beautiful Griffith Stadium, with its classic squared-off lines, its predominant green colors and its acres of grass. The left-field bleachers were almost unreachable, at least for the Senators, and the right-field wall was so high that few home runs were hit there. Griffith Stadium had character.

I have vivid recollections of that 1933 World Series, which Washington lost to the Giants in five games. All of Washington seemed caught up with names like Goose Goslin, Joe Kuhel, Ossie Bluege, Heinie Manush, Joe Cronin and "General" Alvin Crowder, heroes all. Fat Freddie Fitzsimmons was my favorite Giant—he was the only New York pitcher we managed to beat.

I have had only a few jobs in my life, but the best was scoreboard boy at Griffith Stadium. I managed to "inherit" the job from friends during my high school days. Though the old scoreboard in the right-center-field wall could be a brutal sweatbox on humid summer days and we were paid only a dollar a game, I never spent an unhappy day there. It was ecstasy. To this day I have a social security card in my wallet that shows my employer as Clark Griffith, the man who had owned the club since 1912. His nephew Calvin was my immediate boss.

The key to my interest in 1933 and thereafter was my mother. She was the baseball fan in our house. She cared and that care was as infectious as her interest in American history, the sonorities of the Catholic church, her family and its history, the study of language, English literature, horticulture and the old-fashioned virtues. She was an inspiration. When I was a little kid I played baseball feverishly on a church lot near our house with neighborhood kids and my sister, Alice. She was better than I was. In fact she was better than the other kids too.

The Catholicism that came to me from my parents, but particularly my mother, took hold and rooted. The rich traditions and mystery of the church deeply appealed to me. I believed in Jesus Christ and the message of salvation he preached. It should come as no surprise that my favorite autobiography is Thomas Merton's *Seven Storey Mountain,* the story of a Columbia University student's search for faith as a Trappist monk. I read it and reread it. The church's teaching on love of neighbor and fair play compelled me. All of this shaped my sense of morality as the years of my life went by.

After graduating from high school in June 1944, I entered the wartime naval V-12 program, which trained reserve officers. I was assigned first to Franklin and Marshall College in Pennsylvania and then to Princeton University in New Jersey during my two years of navy duty. My sixteen months at Franklin and Marshall (hardly a seaport, but a wonderful college) were highlighted by my failing to make the basketball team under yet another red-headed basketball coach, failing to make the baseball team as a pitcher for want of shoes big enough for my size 13 feet (I suspect the reason was politeness), failing to make the football team as an end, periodic near-drownings at the hands of a sadistic chief petty officer who regularly rat-raced us after breakfast, and being browbeaten by our commanding officer, Lloyd Jordan, who later became head football coach at Harvard. Perhaps it is a tribute to such methods that both the V-12 unit and the Harvard football team performed creditably under his guidance.

After the navy, I returned to Princeton and graduated in 1947 with an honors degree in economics. At Princeton I was too smart to try out for any teams, thus saving innumerable varsity coaches the task of devising reasons for dropping me off their squads.

My years at the University of Virginia law school completed my educational career. While I was enthusiastic at age twenty-three about facing the challenges and rigors of a legal career in New York, I left the academic world behind with a strong sense of regret. I loved education and the great institutions I had been fortunate to attend.

After traveling through Europe during the summer of 1950, I joined the New York City law firm of Willkie Owen Farr Gallagher & Walton in September. While I had received offers from various excellent law firms, there were two reasons that led me to Willkie Owen. The first was the name of Wendell Willkie. One of my political heroes, he had mounted a dramatic, though unsuccessful, campaign for the presidency against FDR in 1940. The drama of his dark-horse efforts and the "We Want Willkie" Philadelphia convention were still vivid in my memory nine years later. As a thirteen-year-old, I sat by my Philco radio and kept the tally of that convention, rooting for Willkie. His oil portrait hung in the Willkie Owen reception area the day I was interviewed in December 1949, as it does today in what is now Willkie Farr & Gallagher.

A second, and equally important, factor in my decision was that the firm's impressive roster of clients included the National League of Professional Baseball Clubs.

I was delighted to receive a starting salary of $4,000 a year, considered good by 1950 Wall Street standards, and took up residence in a bachelor apartment in Manhattan.

I met Luisa Degener in the Long Island seaside village of Quogue in the summer of 1955. We were married in October 1956. Nothing has so shaped and touched my life as Luisa and our four children: George, Paul, Alix and Stephen. Nothing having the slightest claim to merit that has occurred in my life since my marriage could have happened without their love, courage, patience and support. They are the surest sign of God's inexplicable goodness to me.

3

Commissioner
Landis Beckons

I have my own pantheon of lawyers. Its membership is small. Louis F. Carroll is there. In November 1950, I summoned up all my new-boy courage and knocked on his door. Bidden to enter, I brazenly suggested that I would like to work on baseball. It was rather like Oliver Twist's saying that he wanted more food at the orphanage.

Carroll, a senior partner in the firm, was a superior lawyer—meticulous, thoughtful, loyal, moral, unflappable. He had represented the National League since the mid-1930s, when the league came to former New York governor Nathan Miller of the firm seeking advice regarding the control of baseball radio broadcasts. He had also represented the All-America Football Conference until its merger with the National Football League in 1949. By 1950 he had become one of the most highly respected minds in baseball; properly so.

Within baseball circles, he came to be known as "The Wise Man." Baseball people would come to me in later years and ask, "What does The Wise Man say?" So great was baseball's respect for him that he almost certainly would have become commissioner if he had been interested in the job. He was not.

Carroll told me he would see what he could do about my request and sent me on my way. I was both ecstatic and surprised when a few weeks later he put me to work on some pending baseball antitrust cases.

In 1922 the United States Supreme Court, in a famous (some thought notorious) decision by Oliver Wendell Holmes, held that baseball was immune from federal antitrust laws. Nonetheless, periodic challenges arose. Prior to my joining the Willkie firm, Danny Gardella, a former New York Giant outfielder of modest talent but litigious instinct, had sued major-league baseball for thwarting his return to it after having jumped to the Mexican League.

Along with Gardella, other major leaguers, among them Mickey Owen, Sal Maglie and Junior Stephens, had succumbed to the financial blandishments of the Mexican Pasquel brothers. The Pasquels had embarked on an unprecedented, costly and ultimately unsuccessful effort to create a new major league outside the United States. In due time, the "Mexican Jumping Beans," as they inevitably came to be known, sought reinstatement in the majors. When this was denied, Gardella's lawsuit followed, asserting violations of the federal antitrust laws. While the case was settled before trial, an intermediate decision of the federal Second Circuit had referred to the 1922 Supreme Court decision as an "impotent zombie." This unhappy phraseology provoked a freshet of eight additional antitrust suits by the time Lou Carroll dropped me into the fray.

One of the suits involved George Toolson, a Yankee farmhand who had refused to accept a demotion from Newark to Binghamton. I worked on the Toolson case during its progress through the courts, counting myself fortunate to be dealing with a matter of such critical importance to the game. The case brought me into contact with Commissioner Ford Frick and the league presidents, Warren Giles of the National League and Will Harridge of the American League.

The Toolson case went to the United States Supreme Court, where on November 9, 1953, it was decided in baseball's favor. By a 7–2 vote, the Court upheld the original 1922 Holmes decision. Though we had won, the decision foreshadowed new problems for baseball. The Supreme Court in its short opinion said it was standing by Holmes only as a matter of precedent and that any change in baseball's status should come from Congress. Indeed, Congress was already taking a look.

Powerful Brooklyn Congressman Emanuel Celler, chairman of the House Subcommittee on Monopoly Power, had launched an investigation in July 1951 into baseball's antitrust immunity. The hearings produced a cavalcade of baseball stars and characters. The press loved it. So, I suspect, did Chairman Celler. I can assure you that I did. An aging Ty Cobb was first, followed by many others, until one memorable day Ted Williams, Mickey Mantle and Casey Stengel all testified, the latter in pure, classic "Stengelese," comprehensible to no one. Mantle followed with what has to be one of the great lines in congressional history: "My views are just about the same as Casey's." It was almost as much fun as being back in the Griffith Stadium scoreboard. And it was an extraordinary education in the history, people, philosophy and alleyways of baseball.

The Celler hearings also produced another member of my legal pantheon—Paul Porter. Baseball had retained Porter, of the law firm of Arnold, Fortas & Porter, to represent the cause in Washington. Porter had come to Washington as a young New Dealer out of his native Kentucky. Parlaying his Bluegrass charm, he became one of the capital's most famous and successful lawyers and a friend of presidents from FDR to Lyndon Johnson. Bon vivant and unexcelled raconteur, he achieved a popularity in the Washington community that transcended politics. My Washington mentor, he became that rarest of things in human relationships—a completely loyal friend. Paul did not live to see the battle for my commissionership that began in 1981. How he would have loved turning his Kentucky arsenal on the Kuhn antagonists. He died in 1975.

In 1952, the Celler subcommittee concluded that it would recommend no legislation, propelled to that judgment by a series of lawsuits then pending against baseball. Almost lost in the subcommittee's report was the observation that "the baseball map needs realignment." Imagine a Brooklyn congressman's putting such a thought into the fertile mind of Walter Francis O'Malley, owner of the Brooklyn Dodgers. As will be seen, the period of gestation from thought to action was five years.

Through the years, I continued to work on baseball matters. But I was also increasingly involved in the affairs of the Continental Can Company and its corporate acquisitions under the astute leadership of General Lucius Clay, hero of the Berlin airlift, as well as the corporate activities of the International Minerals and Metals Company and the Hygrade Food Products Corporation.

Then came a development that heightened my visibility in baseball and set in motion events that led ultimately to the commissioner's chair.

In 1964, the owners of the Milwaukee Braves decided to move their franchise to Atlanta. The proposal caused consternation in the press and among some in baseball circles. The Braves had left Boston only twelve seasons before. They had been a stunning success in Milwaukee, winning pennants in 1957 and 1958, coming close three other times and drawing over 2 million fans in four consecutive years. However, notwithstanding stars like Henry Aaron, Eddie Mathews, Joe Torre, Warren Spahn and Lew Burdette, attendance had been slipping rapidly, from a high of 2.2 million in 1957 to under 800,000 in 1962. By 1964 things were little better.

With their lease expiring in 1965, the Braves sought permission from the National League to move. From my vantage point on the sidelines, I was surprised to see the league agree, although the Braves were required by the league to complete their 1965 lease obligation. It was unprecedented for a club to play in three cities in thirteen years; it gave baseball an irresponsible, gypsy look. No one felt this more strongly than Commissioner Frick, who was in his last year in office. I believe he would have blocked the move had it come a year earlier.

It was no upset when the state of Wisconsin and the county of Milwaukee went to court to keep the Braves in Milwaukee. Because the National League was sued along with the Braves, Lou Carroll asked me to represent the league.

My heart and my responsibilities were not in the same place. I have always seen franchise movement as an absolute last resort. I hoped and expected that Milwaukee interests would come forward to purchase the Braves. It never happened.

The trial lasted over seven weeks in the Milwaukee County Court before Judge Elmer W. Roller, hardly a friendly venue. It soon became apparent to defense counsel that Judge Roller had no sympathy for anything we had to say. Inescapably, he became known in our private conferences as "Steam Roller," an appellation he reinforced with a decision enjoining the move of the Braves.

In point of fact, Judge Roller was a kindly and decent man, as I learned during our many conferences in his chambers. He did his best to persuade us to settle the case by granting Milwaukee an expansion franchise. This was unavailing; the National League opposed expansion and some members would not have been heartbroken had the Braves been forced to stay in Milwaukee.

The litigation did bring to the fore two estimable native sons in Ed Fitzgerald and Bud Selig, who headed a citizens' effort to save the Braves and who would play critical roles in the baseball future of Milwaukee and Bowie Kuhn.

A sidelight of the Milwaukee battle was the involvement of Red

Smith of the *New York Herald Tribune*. Not only had Milwaukee embarked on a court battle, they had also enlisted Ben Barkin, one of the country's best public relations men, in their cause. Barkin superbly organized a formidable press assault on baseball. Smith, a Wisconsin native, needed little encouragement. He denounced baseball for the "rape of Milwaukee." Smith and others heaped vilification upon vilification. Less stubborn folk than baseball owners might have faltered. One thing was sure: Smith never forgot the name of the lawyer who defended the National League.

We achieved an expedited appeal of Judge Roller's decision to the Wisconsin Supreme Court, and in the summer of 1966 I argued the antitrust issue on which the court ruled in our favor and vacated Judge Roller's injunction. I viewed the decision as a remarkably courageous act, given the fact that these judges were subject to popular election by an electorate that was plainly outraged by their determination. It was a gutsy demonstration of judicial responsibility.

If the Milwaukee move was a baseball mistake, an even greater one occurred in 1957. Walter O'Malley cannily moved the Brooklyn Dodgers to Los Angeles, carrying along his sidecar companion Horace Stoneham and the New York Giants for drop shipment at the Golden Gate. It was a blunder by the National League. Faced with growing competition in the entertainment field, particularly from other professional sports, and confronted by congressional pressure to amend its static ways, baseball should have expanded to the West Coast with brand-new teams. Instead, two of its most colorful and historic franchises went west. Gratifying as this may have been to the shade of Horace Greeley, it left behind an embittered generation of baseball fans in the media capital of the nation. Nearly three decades later, that bitterness still lurks along the Hudson and Gowanus.

I recall the day the moves were announced. In the stenography pool at the Willkie firm, women sat at their typewriters crying. People wept throughout the city. The cultural and social impact was seismic.

O'Malley and Stoneham argued with compelling logic that their ballparks, Ebbets Field and the Polo Grounds, were crumbling and that their respective neighborhoods were deteriorating along with the parks. They argued further that under the circumstances they could not compete with burgeoning new franchises like Milwaukee. What irony.

O'Malley offered to stay if the city would condemn land so that he could finance a new ballpark. Though this was practical and was indeed exactly what he proceeded to do in Los Angeles, the city said no, selling short both O'Malley's resourcefulness and his determination.

I imagine that with all of O'Malley's ability the moves might not have mustered the necessary votes but for the remarkable popularity of Horace Stoneham among baseball people. Inheriting the Giants from his father, Charles, in 1936, Horace may well have been the best-liked owner in baseball over the years I observed the game. Good-hearted to a fault, he and his endearing eccentricities gave rise to stories that even today delight baseball people. Like biblical scripture writers, our people live by stories.

In contrast to Stoneham, O'Malley would never be described as a beloved figure. He was too much the consummate businessman and never one of the boys. But he was remarkable. He dominated others more skillfully than anyone I have ever seen. He was a master of human relations. If he had decided to be king of Ireland, the Emerald Isle would be a monarchy today—and a profitable one at that.

O'Malley was both a lawyer and an engineer by education. His keenly intelligent eyes, behind thick glasses, were set in a face capable of myriad expressions. He had a great shock of dark hair, combed back, marvelous jowls and a bay window that was a work of art. His baritone voice showed the effects of years of cigar smoking, but he used it like a musical instrument. Like Orpheus, he could charm stones.

Did Walter O'Malley control Bowie Kuhn, as was often charged by the press during the decade before O'Malley's death in 1979? I imagine the fair answer is that I have always been too mulish to be controlled by anyone. By training, personal philosophy and nature, I believe I have always had good manners, which means I try, not with invariable success, to treat other people with respect. So it was with Walter. Old enough to be my father, he had not only my respect but my admiration and affection as well.

While he stood with John Fetzer as the best baseball executive I have seen, he could be selfish, narrow-minded and devious. Under the circumstances, conflict between us was inevitable. We battled on issues as varied as the designated hitter, interleague play, baseball in Washington, expansion, administrative restructuring, the Baseball Chapel, whether to oppose women reporters in clubhouses, cooperation between the two leagues and Howard Cosell. More often than not, I prevailed in these conflicts.

O'Malley was particularly resolute in his dislike of maverick American Leaguers like Bill Veeck, George Steinbrenner and Charlie Finley. For instance, any instinct he might have had to support the designated hitter was drowned in his detestation of Finley, who supported it. Interleague play disappeared in the same waters. Though he often could not accomplish what he wanted, he skillfully derailed proposals he opposed. This talent frustrated me on important issues like interleague play and Washington.

The major leagues had been giving thought to appointing a commissioner even before the knowledge of the Black Sox scandal, which broke in 1920. The National Commission rule under the two league presidents and a single club owner was clumsy and ineffective. The Black Sox finished it off. The game needed someone to restore integrity. A tough Chicago federal judge named Kenesaw Mountain Landis was the perfect choice.

Out of desperation more than desire, the owners let Landis define his own powers. He sped to the task and emerged as paterfamilias of the game, which he remained for twenty-four years. In many ways it was a good time to be commissioner. Americans tended to be less questioning of leadership at all levels in the twenties and thirties and during the war. There seemed to be more continuity, whether it was FDR in the White House, La Guardia in New York, Joe Louis in boxing or Landis in baseball.

The time in which Landis ruled was actually a rather peaceful time for baseball. Though he fussed with ownership over the farm system, released many players who exceeded the "under control" limits, and defeated Browns' owner Phil Ball in court over the commissioner's power to deny an option, he is still best remembered for his very first decision, banning the Black Sox players. He maintained his strong hold on the game until his death in 1944.

He always enjoyed public support. The public looked for strong leadership, and he provided it. He could be arbitrary, difficult, even capricious, but he established baseball's reputation for integrity. For that, he belonged in baseball's Hall of Fame.

Along with Babe Ruth, Landis snatched baseball from the disaster it faced with the Black Sox. Not a man for all seasons, but clearly the man for the season happy fate assigned him, he earned his reputation as the finest American sports commissioner. Still, things can go too far. One day in 1970 a reporter blasted me for my handling of the Denny McLain gambling case and extolled the late Judge Landis for the manner in which he surely would have handled it. One grew used to these extrapolations into the beyond. Charley Segar, who had been secretary-treasurer of the game under Ford Frick and Spike Eckert, and stayed on during my early years, came into my office carrying the story. Charley, one of the few people who has known all six baseball commissioners, eyes the baseball world with uncommon sagacity. He tapped the story and said, "If Landis read that, he'd sit up in his grave, shake his curly head and say 'Thank God Kuhn is stuck with the job today.'"

Albert B. Chandler, known as Happy, succeeded Landis. A sharper contrast can hardly be imagined. Happy is as warm-spirited as Landis was crusty; as homespun as Landis was profane; as much a teetotaler as Landis was a drinker; as much a Democrat as Landis was a Republican; as voluble as Landis was terse; as kindly as Landis was pugnacious. Yet they had in common intense dedication to the game. Both have plaques in Cooperstown.

Happy was a United States senator from Kentucky and a former governor when he was selected. His government experience was important as baseball faced the postwar uncertainties. Though he had an excellent reputation and solid values and had served on the critical Senate Military Affairs Committee, he was undoubtedly seen as a more malleable commodity than Landis, whose death had provoked many a dry eye among baseball executives. He took office on April 24, 1945, twelve days after Harry Truman succeeded FDR. Truman and Chandler, who had served together in the Senate, were both faced with the awesome task of replacing men seen by the public as giants.

With World War II about to end, America was destined for change. Old fences would be hauled down with few questions asked. Authority would be challenged.

After a quarter-century of pulling their forelocks to Landis, the baseball owners were ready to exert their influence. Senator Chandler, accustomed to the respect of high office, had no intention of accepting dictation from the ownership. Nor did he intend to dilute the role of the commissioner. Departing from the status quo posture of Landis, Chandler publicly supported the opening of baseball to black players. He thought the "Four Freedoms" meant what they said. In Brooklyn, Branch Rickey and Walter O'Malley, owners of the Dodgers, were taking that concept seriously, as time would show. In many other baseball front offices, Chandler's view was hardly a cause for rejoicing.

In April 1947, he suspended for a year the popular Brooklyn manager, Leo Durocher, for consorting with gamblers and conduct detrimental to baseball. The same month, he presided over Brooklyn's introduction of Jackie Robinson as the first black player in the major leagues. While the Dodgers' bold move could have ignited a revolution, it is to the credit of Chandler's administration that it did not, but instead permitted the brilliant matching of Rickey and Robinson to signal baseball's greatest moment.

He imposed five-year suspensions on players who had jumped to the Mexican League, but wisely lifted those suspensions when dissipation of the Mexican threat made it apparent that they had served their purpose. He was instrumental in establishing the first pension plan for players. Indeed, he came to be known as a "player's commissioner" because of his strong support of player causes. He was hardly proving to be the malleable commissioner many had wanted.

Had Al Smith not earned the title "Happy Warrior" a generation earlier in New York, it should have become Chandler's, blending as he did not only charm but a granite-hard tough streak.

While he served with distinction and dedication for almost seven baseball seasons, he was faced with the burden of needing 75 percent of the club votes for reelection. On July 15, 1951, he got a majority but fell short of the necessary 75 percent. Chandler was outraged, and he remains so to this day. Proud of the support he received from veteran owners like Connie Mack, Phil Wrigley, Clark Griffith and Tom Yawkey, he still feels he was sandbagged by a minority who opposed him for personal reasons, and he is unforgiving. Shedding his normal courtly style, he once vowed: "Pardner, I'm going to stay around until I have outlived every one of those SOBs."

Today, Happy Chandler, a vigorous eighty-eight, is relentlessly keeping that promise, and it isn't limited to baseball people.

Several years ago Luisa, Happy and I were having dinner together in St. Louis. Arriving moments behind them, I was stopped en route by a dignified old Kentucky politician who wished me well and asked that I remember him fondly to Happy. When I did so, Happy's eyes narrowed to slits, and he said, "Honey, that's one of those SOBs I'm still outliving." Happy's irrepressible dislike of those who have "done him wrong" is matched by only one other person I ever encountered—Howard Cosell. But I know of no two people more fiercely protective of their friends, either.

I first met Happy Chandler at the National League's seventy-fifth anniversary celebration, on February 2, 1951. It was held at the Broadway Central Hotel in Manhattan, which, as the Grand Central Hotel, had been the site of the birth of the league in 1876. The league began play in the same spring that Sitting Bull, Crazy Horse and their Sioux warriors were polishing off General George Armstrong Custer above the banks of the Little Big Horn. The spirit of massacre lives on to this day in baseball.

As a young lawyer accompanying Lou Carroll, I found the celebration a glamorous occasion, replete with such National League heroes as Kid Nichols, Fred Clarke, Mel Ott, Rogers Hornsby, Pie Traynor, Carl Hubbell and eighty-one-year-old John Heydler, who'd been National League president in 1909 and again from 1918 to 1934. The American League was in full force, too, with no less than Ty Cobb, Jimmie Foxx, Cy Young, George Sisler, Mickey Cochrane, Eddie Collins, Tris Speaker and Charlie Gehringer on hand.

Chandler came over to greet Lou, and joked about my being Lou's bodyguard, a reference to my size and age (twenty-four). The laughter that followed was uneasy. Chandler was unsure about Lou and more particularly about his client, National League president Ford Frick, a potential successor. I had a brief and unimportant private conversation with a very affable Happy, and would not see him again for more than eighteen years, during which time he languished in baseball oblivion. I had the wit to rescue him when I became commissioner in 1969. I consulted with him, invited him to baseball functions and made frequent references to him throughout my term.

Returning to his beloved "old Kentucky home," he found resilience in the Bluegrass State. He was duly reelected governor in 1954 by an electorate that, if it paid any attention at all, probably viewed his rejection by certain baseball owners as a form of endorsement. He remains a political force in Kentucky today.

With the departure of Chandler, baseball for the first time elected one of its own when National League president Ford Frick was named commissioner in September 1951. At fifty-six, he was the oldest of the six commissioners at the time of election. His league presidency began in 1934, following a career as a sportswriter and sportscaster in New York. For a time, he had even been a ghostwriter for Babe Ruth.

Neither as dramatic as Landis nor as colorful as Chandler, Frick understood the game and loved it. His testimony before Congress revealed an honest, protective passion for baseball. He was Big Daddy; everything would be all right.

Ford served at a time when harmony was needed. The battle over Chandler's reelection had worsened old enmities. On the surface, it was curious that a league president was selected. Neither before nor since has that happened. The hatred between the two major leagues was palpable, with roots in the last century, the hermetic world of baseball durably nourishing its feuds. But Ford was a peacemaker and was blessed for that quality with nearly fifteen years of owners' tranquility.

His was a time of geographic change in baseball. Since the turn of the century, the franchise map had been as static as Coleridge's "painted ship upon a painted ocean." No more. In 1953 the Boston Braves moved to Milwaukee, in 1954 the St. Louis Browns moved to Baltimore, in 1955 the Philadelphia Athletics moved to Kansas City, in 1957 the Dodgers and Giants left New York for Los Angeles and San Francisco, both leagues expanded by two clubs apiece in the early 1960s and in 1965 the Braves moved on to Atlanta. If he was not happy with all of these developments (as in the case of the 1965 Braves move), his helmsmanship was necessary to steer the now active baseball ship through these new waters.

Ultimately, Frick saw himself as the guardian of baseball's integrity. He repeatedly pounded that point home in conversations with me. In order to preserve his own integrity and the freedom to deal with owners as necessary, he avoided socializing with them, in contrast to Chandler and me. The everyday mechanics of the office were entrusted to crusty Charley Segar, an ex-newspaperman who served Ford as secretary-treasurer with dedication and uncompromising determination.

Frick, having been a league president himself, respected their autonomy and gave Will Harridge and Joe Cronin of the American League and Warren Giles of the National League leeway to do their jobs. At a time when the increasingly competitive National Football League was getting its administrative act together in the 1960s under a new and aggressive young commissioner named Pete Rozelle, Frick was put at some disadvantage in the eyes of the press. Though his press relations were generally good, the quality of that relationship diminished as his years in office lengthened.

In 1965, Frick, then seventy years old, had no desire to continue beyond the end of his second seven-year term. Nevertheless, he agreed to stay on until his successor could take over.

I vividly recall his last day in office: December 15, 1965. I called Mary Anargeros, his executive secretary, that morning to see if anything special was being done to celebrate a day that concluded thirty-one years of loving service to baseball. I was appalled to learn that there were no plans; so I quickly organized a private room at Delmonico's Restaurant on Beaver Street and invited a few of my law partners for a farewell lunch. Though it was only a fraction of what he deserved, Ford had several martinis, regaled us with baseball stories and put us at ease. He was a gracious man.

In an inexplicable move, baseball selected General William D. (Spike) Eckert as its fourth commissioner. Spike was a retired air force general without experience in sports administration and without any apparent qualifications for the job save one—he was dead honest.

I came to know Spike well, as lawyer and friend. He was a quality person, hardworking and motivated. But he was as mystified about his selection as was the sports world. At a time when baseball needed enhanced marketing and salesmanship to compete in an ever more competitive and, from baseball's point of view, threatening entertainment industry, Spike lacked marketing skills.

The theory was that his military background would give him a natural ability to command the fractious owners and that he could be backstopped by capable executives who would carry on the business of the office. In fact, Lee MacPhail and John McHale, both high-quality baseball executives, were brought in successively to act as Spike's chief administrative officer. Still, leadership had to come from the top and Spike could not provide it, lacking as he did any real feel for the game and its people.

I suspect that the Spike Eckert who arrived in baseball on December 15, 1965, was not the same man who had been an effective air force general. He died within twenty-six months of leaving office. It is not unlikely that his health was failing and that he simply did not have the mental and physical vigor he once had. From the very first it was plain he was struggling in every way. Sadly, he knew it, too.

It soon became apparent that a change had to be made. Several developments precipitated the change. First, in 1966 Marvin Miller was elected by the players to head their union. Miller was a consummate union professional. It was the lion and the lamb. He and Spike might lie down together, but there would be no lamb in the morning.

Second, Spike's press relations, never good, began to disintegrate. The press was unkind but not unfair to him; it was obvious to them Spike was losing the struggle. He simply could not, in press conferences or in individual meetings, deal with the topics of the baseball day. I saw veteran writers openly scoff at his efforts. The press cannot necessarily break a commissioner, but it can play a key role in breaking him. It did in Spike's case.

Third, baseball was losing its share of the entertainment market. Attendance and revenues were stagnant while other sports and entertainment forms were booming. More and more it was written that baseball was dying—it was just too slow for the fast-paced sixties. That was nonsense—baseball was never going to die—but it put an unfortunate gloss of pessimism on the game.

As the annual meetings of 1968 approached, change was in the wind, and I knew it. The meetings were held in San Francisco's Palace Hotel. As the final session concluded, Baltimore owner Jerry Hoffberger asked that all nonowners leave the room. That excluded General Eckert as well as Paul Porter and me, lawyers for the commissioner's office and the National League, respectively.

I had no stomach for lingering in the hotel, knowing what was happening behind those closed doors. Luisa and I and Porter drove to Cypress Point for a late lunch. For seventeen years, times full of laughter, storytelling and good fun, we had gotten along marvelously together. But there was little laughter this day, though Paul's unquenchable humor bobbed in and out. On the way back, we heard on the car radio that Eckert had resigned.

I learned later that at their closed-door meeting the owners had agreed to ask him to do so. A delegation having given him the bad news, he had gone into the meeting and graciously done as requested.

I went to Eckert's suite that evening. I told him that I was sorry, but that I really thought getting out of the job was personally the best thing for him. He was tearful but showed no resentment. And he told me, "You should be the next commissioner, Bowie."

A rather difficult moment was still ahead for Spike and me. After I became commissioner, I found that Spike had moved his belongings out of the commissioner's office and into an adjoining office. There he was, seated at his desk, prepared to fulfill the terms of his "consultant's" agreement, which was a way of rounding out the remaining four years on his contract. I knew this would not work, but I lacked the heart to say so right away. I hated the thought of hurting him even more. He was so straightforward, unpretentious and, now, vulnerable. I waited several days. Then one morning I dropped into his office. We discussed some transitional matters that he wanted to cover. Then I said, "Spike, I really don't think it will work having you here in the office. I'm a new boy and have to establish my own image for better or worse. I know I can call on you and get your advice but I can do that wherever you are. I'm sorry, but I really think this will be best."

I knew immediately that he was hurt, though I had spoken as gently as I knew how. But he looked me straight in the eye and said, "Of course, Bowie. I understand. I'll be gone today." And he was.

The general died in April 1971. He was buried at Arlington National Cemetery with full military honors. I gave the eulogy. I wish I could have said more.

In 1968, just after Spike resigned, baseball launched a search for a new commissioner, determined this time to find someone with experience in the game. None of the first four commissioners had been a club executive, but interestingly the early favorites for the job were all club executives: Lee MacPhail and John McHale, who had been Commissioner Eckert's administrators; Chub Feeney, vice president of the Giants; and Mike Burke, president of the Yankees.

MacPhail at this stage was the Yankees' general manager, while McHale had only recently become president and part-owner of the Montreal Expos, an expansion team scheduled to debut in April 1969.

I knew John McHale well, as we had been allies in the battle to move the Braves to Atlanta, John having run the Braves at that time. When he became administrator in Commissioner Eckert's office, we again worked together closely. He had the credentials to make an excellent commissioner, but he also had a keen sense of duty and obligation. By December 1968 he was the key figure of the Expos, who had yet to play a major-league game. They needed him desperately. Putting duty first, he took his name out of the race. Had he done otherwise and made it to Landis's chair, he would have been the first commissioner with major-league playing experience. He had a sixty-four game career with the Tigers during which he hit three home runs, two off sinker-ball pitcher Nelson Potter.

Feeney emerged as the leading candidate among the National League owners, with respectable American League support as well. Forty-seven years old and media-oriented, he was bright, witty and experienced, well-liked within the game, very much one of the clan.

A Giants executive since graduating from Fordham Law School in 1947, he was in fact owner Horace Stoneham's nephew, but was without prospects of moving higher, given Uncle Horace's vigor and enthusiasm. I had worked with Chub closely over the years, particularly in his role as an industry witness in various antitrust litigations in the 1950s.

Mike Burke had his support among American League club owners, who clearly recognized his potential in the areas of marketing and public relations. He was an "American Leaguer," not unimportant to a league that had felt during Frick's fifteen years that down deep he was really a "National Leaguer." Whether or not this was fair to Frick, and I think from first-hand observation it was not, the attitude toward him was real.

Burke was new to the baseball scene. He became president of the Yankees when CBS purchased the club in 1965. While the lordly Yankees had been a second-division club under his leadership, his considerable charm and enthusiasm brought warmth to the club's cold image, a necessity because the lovably inept, Stengel-storied Mets of the 1960s were winning the hearts of many fans in New York.

Burke certainly had a colorful background, having played varsity football at the University of Pennsylvania, and having had careers with the OSS, the CIA, Ringling Brothers and CBS before entering baseball. Like Feeney, he was popular with the media. Unlike Feeney, he could not by nature be one of the clan. There were deep-seated reservations about the "circus guy" throughout the National League. Though both Walter O'Malley and Burke were Penn graduates, Walter in particular wanted no part of his fellow Quaker alumnus. I had worked closely with Burke in the past year, the two of us having carpentered the Major League Baseball Promotion Corporation, a long-overdue attempt to market baseball promotions and trademarks on a national level.

The owners met at Chicago's O'Hare Inn on December 20, 1968, several weeks after Eckert's San Francisco resignation. In a memorable, marathon evening that did not adjourn until 4:55 A.M., they took nineteen ballots and came up dry. While the meeting was restricted to club executives, I wandered in and out. It was like a giant poker game played at a U-shaped table. As it became apparent that neither Burke nor Feeney would muster the necessary votes, owners warily dealt out new names. I got one name reconsidered. Finding myself seated next to Frank Dale, who represented the

Cincinnati Reds, I suggested Lee MacPhail to him as a man apt to surmount the medieval league politics. Lee's name had been considered but he was thought not to want the job. Frank, the able publisher of the *Cincinnati Enquirer* and new to the baseball scene, put MacPhail's name back into consideration. When doubts were again raised as to MacPhail's interest, I was asked to telephone him, though it was hours past midnight. I found Lee asleep but hardly befogged. Firmly yet graciously he declined. As commissioner, I would twice thereafter ask Lee to take major baseball posts; both times he said yes.

During the Christmas holidays, Luisa and the children and I spent a long weekend at Mary and George Degener's farm in Dutchess County, New York, where we had been married. George was the grandfather of our two older sons. He and Mary were as much like our own parents as anyone could be, and as treasured. While at the farm, I received a call from Mike Burke. He told me that he and Feeney were irretrievably deadlocked and that the owners had to go in another direction. "Would you be interested in the job?" he inquired. I was not surprised. Mike and I had been cordial and my partner, Lou Carroll, had been telling me to expect something like this. Lou could always see the trees bending before the wind blew.

I told Mike I was flattered but that I was not interested. I said, "Mike, I am a very private person and I like it that way and I want to leave it that way." I wished him a Merry Christmas and we hung up. I told Luisa and George about the call and added, "I'm guessing that will not be the last we'll hear on that subject."

The next owners' meeting was held on February 4, 1969, at the Americana Hotel in Bal Harbour, Florida. I was there with Sandy Hadden, the American League attorney, and John Gaherin, head of the Player Relations Committee. After some routine business, chaired by American League president Joe Cronin, the three of us left the room.

Sandy and I went to my room to work on collective bargaining matters that were then in negotiation. The telephone rang and I was asked to meet with a delegation of owners. I went immediately to the appointed room, where I found a group that included O'Malley, John Galbreath, John Fetzer, Bob Reynolds and Gabe Paul. They told me that the most important thing before baseball was a new proposal on restructuring. They needed a man to take charge of that vital task on an interim basis. After that, they could concentrate on getting a full-term commissioner.

The restructuring proposal, approved by the owners six weeks earlier in Chicago, stated:

RESOLVED, that it be declared the sense of this meeting that Baseball, through the new Commissioner and the organization of baseball, study and recommend action on any and all matters, without limitation, as may be deemed to be in the best interests of baseball, including such matters as

1. doing away with traditional procedures which now require separate League consideration of those matters which concern Baseball as a whole;
2. exploring ways to improve the presentation of the game;
3. developing a plan for the reorganization of the governing bodies of baseball and the revision of their constitutions; and
4. developing a plan for the consolidation of the office and staffs of the Commissioner and other officials of baseball.

They wanted me to take a one-year job as commissioner pro tempore. I was to be the restructuring boss. They said I would be a unanimous choice if I consented to take the job. The salary was $100,000—$35,000 more than Eckert had been paid.

I was not thrilled. It could be an ignominious interlude. I could be eased out if a golden vote-getter emerged. It reeked of compromise. I would have to withdraw from my law firm.

I told them I wanted to think about it and to make some calls. As they left, O'Malley became Delphic: "Be careful, Bowie. Baseball is a virus. Once you catch it, you never get well. Think about it."

Having no entrails to read, I called Lou Carroll in New York and explained the situation and my reservations. He would normally have been at this meeting, but his health was failing and his travel had been restricted. Like the wise man he was, he heard me out. Then he said, "Bowie, I don't think you have much choice. They're asking you as their lawyer to bail them temporarily out of a tough spot. From the firm's point of view, I hope you'll do it. Don't worry about the withdrawal-reentry problem with the firm. We'll work that out. Now, if you want my opinion as to what they're really doing, they're easing you in with a gimmick and you will end up the full-time Commissioner of Baseball. Don't say yes unless you're prepared for that possibility." His forecast proved unerring; I told him I would call Luisa. If she was agreeable, I would say yes.

I reached Luisa at our home in Ridgewood, New Jersey. I took her through it all, including Lou's reaction. Her recommendation: "I think you should take it. It could be exciting; it could be fun; what the heck." Luisa does not equivocate.

Luisa had always liked the baseball people and their conviviality. We talked at some length about the children, the travel obligations, our financial situation and Willkie Farr & Gallagher, which was encouraging a positive answer. Luisa was right; it could be fun.

I called the owner delegation back together and said I would take the job. They told me to sit tight; they would be right back.

Down they went to the Floridian Room. In short time they were back, this time representing a sort of honor guard to escort me downstairs. I entered the room and everyone stood and applauded. It was a nice moment.

With that, the doors were opened and the press was invited in. The owners, who normally do not attend a commissioner's press conference, could not resist this one. They wanted to see how the new fellow dealt with his baptism under fire.

It was an easy press conference. While the writers asked all the appropriate questions about the pending collective bargaining, restructuring and baseball's declining image, they had no expectation of definitive answers. They did find out that one of my boyhood heroes had been Kenesaw Mountain Landis and that I had once been a dollar-a-day scoreboard boy in Washington. Everybody laughed when I said, "I'm finally getting even with Calvin Griffith," well known for his tight-money operation.

I had dinner that evening with a large group of baseball people. It was a celebration, and I went to bed very late.

At 6:00 A.M., I was awakened by a telephone call. The machine-gun voice was familiar, if not welcome.

"Commissioner . . . this is Howard Cosell . . . congratulations . . . it is essential you appear on my television show in New York tonight." Pure, vintage irresistible Cosell. And of course I agreed.

When I arrived in New York, I went straight to Willkie Farr & Gallagher. After talking to my partners, my first call as commissioner went to Marvin Miller, the head of the Players Association. I had been heavily involved in baseball's dealings with Marvin and his lawyer, Dick Moss; nobody in the game knew them better than I.

I said, "Marvin, if you're going to be there for a while, I'd like to drop in, just so you can see how my new crown fits." Marvin, Dick and I spent an hour in their office in the Seagram Building on Park

Avenue and laughed a lot. For a serious, even reticent man, Marvin has a lively sense of humor. Unfortunately, the cordiality of that hour did not foreshadow the future.

Arriving home after doing the Cosell show, I was led blindfolded to the kitchen to behold a large banner made by my children proclaiming "WELCOME HOME, COMMISSIONER!"

The fun was only starting. So were the blindfolds.

4

The First Year

So far as I know, Ford Frick never uttered those famous words with which Louis XV predicted the French Revolution (*"Après moi, le déluge"*), but he clearly saw the upheavals to come in baseball and conveyed his concern to me. The problems were indeed there, and I had been too close to the game to miss them. Could something be done by a temporary commissioner to generate the proper concern?

It would not be easy. Baseball has always tended to complacency, to a belief that in the long sweep of time things work out. Baseball people were the descendants of Prime Minister Lord Salisbury of England, who once said, "Any change will be for the worse; therefore it is in our interest that there be as little change as possible." Put another way, baseball believes in the cyclical or merry-go-round approach: If something is amiss, sit tight; by the time the little bouncing horse comes around again, things will be all right.

Ben Fiery, a Cleveland lawyer, guided the legal fortunes of the American League as Lou Carroll had guided the National League. Ben was like a firecracker with a faulty fuse. You never knew when he was going to explode. A figure more colorful, sad to say, than the law normally provides, he had served in the Lafayette Escadrille in World War I, had been a principal aide to Newton Diehl Baker when Baker was secretary of war in the administration of Woodrow Wilson, and suffered fools, in particular verbose fools, badly—or more accurately, did not suffer them at all. In 1964 Ben told Lou Carroll he was turning over the representation of the American

League to his partner Sandy Hadden, explaining that he did not like the idiots who were coming into baseball and wanted no part of representing them in the troubles ahead. It is instructive to know that the model of what he could not abide was Charles O. Finley, then owner of the Kansas City A's. Ben detested Finley. Ben is in my pantheon.

The sports media could be as conservative as the baseball establishment, particularly the veteran writers. In response to the growing charge that baseball was dull, Red Smith wrote, "Only dull people believe that baseball is dull." The baseball establishment loved it. New-breed critics of the game's administration like Howard Cosell were put down as unworthy, or as shills for football, by old-line journalists. As much as anything, this kind of thinking stemmed from baseball's incredibly long run as the "national game." Nearly a century and a half of preeminence had made it the sanctum sanctorum of American sports. While I had a deeply rooted respect for baseball's traditions and had conservative inclinations in general, I would soon seem like a Bolshevik in a czarist state.

With football, basketball and hockey enjoying healthy growth and public esteem, baseball was faced with increasing competition in the sports field. In addition, the public was increasingly wooed by other forms of entertainment, including outdoor activities. Baseball could no longer just open the gates and expect the public to pour in. The country had become more susceptible to good marketing. If you asked an ordinary consumer whether he cared about the packaging of his breakfast cereal, he would more than likely say no. But the test came in the supermarket, where he reached for the colorful, graphically attractive box, rather than a plain-brown-wrapper brand. Baseball was taking on a plain-brown look.

Moreover, the constant repetition of the game's alleged woes certainly gave them verisimilitude. Baseball's style and stately cadences *seemed* more attuned to an era of royal minuets than to the rebellious sixties. Other sports were more dynamic, more violent. Psychologists and sociologists found baseball passé in a decade darkened by the war in Vietnam.

At the high school and college levels, football and basketball were more popular. Baseball, with its finely tuned skills, is difficult to present as attractively as other sports at that level. This has always been so, but at a time when baseball was already struggling, it stood out.

Too many of the major-league clubs lacked capable marketing

departments and skilled marketing executives. The Dodgers sparkled as an exception.

The game itself was dominated by pitching. In 1968, the National League hit .243 and the American League .230. There were only six .300 hitters in the majors, and Carl Yastrzemski, at .301, led the American League. The tenth best hitter in the American League, Rick Monday, batted .274.

Attendance was showing little long-term growth, and a short-term decline. Between 1962, the first year of twenty teams, and 1968, attendance had risen by only 1.7 million. Attendance of 23,102,745 in 1968 was down 1.2 million from 1967 and 2 million from 1966.

Our audience profile was too heavy on the middle-aged and older fans. Young fans were flocking to the other sports, where modern heroes like Joe Namath captured their fancy.

Our arrangements with television were not exciting. We had a national contract only with NBC, which presented our games on Saturday afternoons, a low-viewing period in summer months. We had pioneered the Monday-night concept under the guidance of John Fetzer of the Tigers, but the small number of games that NBC carried had modest ratings. Our broadcasting revenues compared poorly with those of professional football, which, following the NFL-AFL merger, was now on CBS and NBC and was preparing to add ABC in 1970 with a Monday-night game each week.

The teams in New York, Chicago and Los Angeles were not doing well, and this hurt because they were key media centers. The Yankees were in the midst of a long decline, and Mickey Mantle had retired after the 1968 season. The Mets had outgrown their colorful, Casey Stengel origins and had become just another last-place team. With Sandy Koufax retiring after the 1966 season, the Dodgers were a second-division club. The Angels were not much more than an expansion team. The White Sox had won only one pennant since 1919; the Cubs hadn't won at all since 1945.

Also, 1968 was the last year of ten-team leagues. With a new round of expansion taking place in 1969, baseball was forced to go to a two-division structure in both leagues with playoffs between the division winners. By hindsight, it is hard to believe that we had played through most of the sixties with deadly ten-team leagues, with only two teams eligible to go on to postseason play. There were indications that baseball was waking up. For 1969, the pitching mound was lowered from fifteen inches to ten inches and the strike zone was narrowed, both moves designed to ignite batting averages. And there was serious talk of a designated hitter for the pitcher.

Finally, baseball was faced with a players' union, militantly and skillfully led by Marvin Miller. There was talk of a strike as I took office. For months negotiations had stewed fruitlessly over a new benefits plan, but by February 1969, the parties were not even talking.

So the problems were painfully real, particularly given my temporary status. One decision I made at the outset was that I was not going to conduct myself like a "rental" commissioner. I was inclined to agree with Lou Carroll that the "temporary" label was a subterfuge and that key owners would maneuver to make it "full-term." I was also getting robust encouragement from the press and from most owners to take charge. "For God's sake, do something, even if it's wrong, just do something," Bob Reynolds, co-owner of the California Angels with Gene Autry, said to me. While at forty-two I was the youngest of the six baseball commissioners to date, I had been involved with the game's problems more than any new commissioner with the possible exception of Ford Frick.

The first thing to resolve was the problem of the stalled labor negotiations. I called Dick Meyer of the St. Louis Cardinals, who was the strongman of the owners' Player Relations Committee (PRC). Dick was also a ranking officer of Anheuser-Busch and one of the best executive talents in baseball, bright and practical. I told him this was no way for a new commissioner to start out. Unsympathetic as he was to Miller and the union's position in the negotiations, Dick agreed. We discussed several moves by the owners that could resolve the problem and agreed that we would authorize John Gaherin, director of the PRC, to use them. Dick said, "Okay, you'll have to get Miller back to the table." Neither of us thought that would be a problem.

I called Miller and asked him to resume bargaining. He responded warmly, pointing out that he had not favored the break-off in the first place. While Gaherin was not anxious to make further concessions to Miller, he was a good soldier and recognized the practical necessities. Negotiations were resumed and an agreement was promptly reached. The commissioner was widely commended. A major problem was gone—at least for the moment.

It was apparent at the outset that the commissioner's staff would have to be enhanced. It was a skeleton crew, a low-budget operation that reflected past commissioners' respect for parsimony but was hardly geared to the tasks that now lay ahead. I more than doubled the budget. With Charley Segar retiring as secretary-treasurer, I brought in Sandy Hadden to fill those jobs and made him general counsel as well. For the first time we had a law department. Not only was this good economics, it gave me a chance to stay close to the legal developments in the game.

The vacant job of administrator, held most recently by Montreal's John McHale, went to Johnny Johnson, an experienced vice president of the Yankees with excellent credentials in player development and minor-league affairs. Along with Johnny came George Pfister, a veteran Yankee executive and former catcher who would officially handle the multitude of details in Johnny's department. So excellent were Johnson's qualifications that in 1979 he became head of the minor leagues and has since led them to their greatest growth in decades.

I found Henry Fitzgibbon to head our enlarged security operations, an area of critical importance given the growth of illegal gambling. The discovery of Fitzgibbon came about under singular circumstances.

One of my first assignments as commissioner was a visit with J. Edgar Hoover at FBI headquarters in Washington. I was eager to get his thoughts on sports gambling and his recommendations for security personnel.

The meeting was remarkable. We talked about baseball past and present—just two fans talking about a game we both obviously loved. We talked about cooperation between the bureau and baseball going back to the days of Judge Landis, with emphasis on the threat that gambling posed to the game. Hoover made it clear that he viewed the relationship between the two institutions as special. He shared with me his frustrations over the restraints on law enforcement being imposed by court decisions.

We talked for three hours. Several weeks later, I received a letter from him with three names. One was Henry Fitzgibbon's.

Henry had retired as head of the administrative division of the FBI's New York office in 1966 and had become a commander of the metropolitan police department in St. Louis. He was a thorough professional who promptly developed contacts in all of our cities. He could run down an unsavory rumor in hours. His investigatory skills drew the ire of the Players Association, which usually put its perception of players' rights ahead of the long-term reputation and welfare of baseball. As a result, the Association's ever-alert efforts to hobble our investigations became a constant source of friction between our offices.

Baseball had never had a broadcasting expert on staff. Contracts with NBC had been negotiated by John Fetzer and Walter O'Malley, using California-based, former NBC sports executive Tom Gallery as a consultant. Clearly, we needed someone full time in that vital area and I hired Tom Dawson, former president of CBS Television, as director of broadcasting. Tom's task was threefold—to stimulate interest at ABC and CBS so that in the future we could add one or both as network partners along with NBC, to use network television more effectively to stimulate increased fan interest in baseball, and to increase the dollar value of network television. Tom was soon talking about the introduction of night games in the World Series as an approach to all three.

I inherited three staff members who remained with me throughout my sixteen years: Mary Anargeros, Joe Reichler and Monte Irvin.

Reichler was a highly regarded Associated Press sportswriter whom Spike Eckert had hired as public relations director. Joe had more baseball history in his head than most of us could find in encyclopedias. Deeply dedicated to the game and to me, in 1974 he moved his skills to our nascent film operations, where his baseball knowledge was invaluable.

Hall of Famer Monte Irvin, also hired by Eckert, was a special assistant to the commissioner. Monte was superior on special assignments, especially as a pinch hitter for the commissioner. He flawlessly handled speaking engagements and other appearances I could not make, courted amateur players torn between baseball and other sports, maintained liaison between our office and major-league players, smoothed out public relations problems and battled with critics of the commissioner. Needless to say, the last task could have occupied an entire department.

Mary Anargeros, known by her maiden name of Mary Sotos to everyone in baseball, had an uncommon career. She had been hired in 1936, at age nineteen, by National League president Ford Frick as his secretary. When he was elected commissioner in 1951, she moved with him. Upon Frick's retirement, she served General Eckert for his three-year term. She stayed on to be my executive secretary for sixteen years, wrapping everything up by working one day for Peter Ueberroth before her own retirement in 1984. During a period of forty-eight years she had served four of the six baseball commissioners and one league president. Remarkably enough, she departed in a state of complete sanity.

Mary was far more than a secretary. Within baseball, it was often remarked that she was the "real" commissioner. In my own view, that was a toss-up between her and Luisa. Mary was an executive assistant, a friend and a counselor with great common sense. For instance, it was her job to screen my calls. With little or no guidance from me, she selected those that got through. Owners in ornery moods might well not make it. She could fence with an angry fan or charm George Steinbrenner. While I thought I was hardly transparent, I was a pane of glass to Mary, who could anticipate my reactions. She was a bulwark in the hard times and a joy in all seasons.

Mary, Monte and I, having traveled together for sixteen years, went through the exit door at the same time. I can't think of a better way to go.

Having made up my mind that I was going to behave like a full-time commissioner, I decided to go on tour, starting with spring training 1969. I was not going to be Bowie "Who He?" for long. I had discussed with Luisa the endless travel that is so much a part of professional sports. I would become the "travelingest" commissioner any sport had ever seen. I started with Florida and Arizona, where I hit almost every spring training camp and talked to all the players. The few I missed I caught up with in the early part of the regular season.

I spoke to the players about our need to work together to promote the game in every way we could. I reminded them of the strong competition we faced and of the need to be good to the fans. I reminded them that the integrity of baseball was a paramount concern. If the game had a good reputation they would profit from it; if not, they would surely suffer. I urged them to use our security department if they had any concerns about their personal business ventures or associations. I told them they must stay away from gamblers and undesirables and that Major League Rule 21, which provided for lifetime suspensions for throwing games, meant what it said.

I had asked Johnny Johnson and Monte Irvin to begin a job-placement program for players nearing the ends of their careers. I encouraged the players to use it and to follow up with calls to John and Monte. Finally, I told them I wanted an open-door administration, and I encouraged them to call me with any questions they might have. I was warmly and attentively received, usually with applause. I was encouraged.

I had put my heart into those talks. I wanted to reach the players because they were important, but more poignantly, because I admired them. No matter the problems of later years, no matter the union's policy of making the commissioner appear to be a Wall Street satan, I would always be the little kid on the curb watching the parade of stars march by.

One of the joys of travel for me was the minor-league ballparks and people. I always felt that the heart of baseball was in those nostalgia-laden bandboxes and hard-striving people. There was a rich-textured, profound feel of the game in the minors that I found nowhere else, something closer to the game I first knew as a lad in Griffith Stadium and Forbes Field. So I beat my way across the minors from the Carolinas to Oregon, from Connecticut to West Texas, and I ate their hot dogs, savored their hospitality, and told them how much I cherished them. There was jubilation in my shop as the minors soared in popularity during my time in office.

The press presented a special challenge. Every commissioner since Landis had felt its rage. At the urging of Joe Reichler, I was determined that inaccessibility was not going to be my problem. I held press conferences wherever I went. I faithfully visited press boxes in all ballparks. I gave interviews and went on radio and television. I even went on CBS's *Face the Nation* on my first Easter Sunday as commissioner. I imagine that I ultimately gave more press conferences and interviews in more cities large and small around this country, and indeed the world, than all of my predecessors combined.

Looking back, it is hard to believe how well I was received and dealt with by the press during my first year. Jerome Holtzman, of the *Chicago Sun-Times,* exemplified that attitude in the Official Baseball Guide: ". . . Commissioner Kuhn had proven to all—fans and insiders alike—that he possessed the qualifications for baseball's top position." What a contrast with things to come.

With the opening of the 1969 season, Luisa and I "flew the flag" more vigorously than ever by attending seven opening games. I saw thirteen games in the season's first seventeen days. When our plane arrived in San Diego, we were enchanted to look out the windows and see a large military band and officials lined up to greet us. Imagine our chagrin when we discovered that the Spanish ambassador, who was deplaning just behind us, was the actual object of all this ceremony.

While there may have been a bobble here and there, I was shaking things up. The impression of an activist commissioner who was not afraid to take on challenges was emerging and coming through to the public, in part because of the circumstances.

A major issue started innocently enough, when Donn Clendenon announced his retirement from baseball on February 28, 1969. A month earlier, he and Jesus Alou had been dealt to Houston by the fledgling Montreal Expos. Donn had gone to Houston for a press conference, which the Astros decided was urgent, since the consideration for the two new players had been none other than their greatest star, Rusty Staub. In Montreal, the orange-haired Staub was seen as a player of heroic proportions who could win the hearts of the French-Canadians and give the Expos a major star in their first season. He was tabbed "Le Grand Orange."

The Clendenon retirement, surprising as it was, seemingly canceled the trade under Major League Rule 12(f), which stated, "In the event of a bonafide retirement of a player from the game during the interval following assignment of his contract and thirty days of the assignee club's officially scheduled season . . . the agreement . . . shall be void and the consideration returned to the assignee club, unless the player shall have reported to the assignee club within such an interval." For my part, I was not so sure and said I would take a look at the situation, even though commissioners had infrequently involved themselves in owners' trades, certainly not in recent decades. Besides, I didn't want the deal to fall apart. Staub was important to the new Montreal franchise.

Judge Roy Hofheinz, who had owned the Astros (née Colt .45s) since their birth in 1960, was furious at my threatened meddling and determined to persuade me to nullify the trade. Charles Bronfman and John McHale of the Expos, like Brer Rabbit, were "laying low," professing their willingness to abide by whatever decision I thought appropriate.

I met with both Clendenon and Staub during my travels through Florida. At these further signs of my involvement, the Judge was even more furious and the Expos were laying lower. Donn, whom I have liked from our first encounter, was straight-talking. He said he had made up his mind to quit. At age thirty-three he had an opportunity to take an executive position with Scripto Pen and thought he ought to grab it.

Rusty hoped that somehow the trade could still go through. He was anxious to join the Expos and begin his new career in Montreal. Rusty was even then viewed as a skillful pleader, an opinion that has been reinforced over the years as I have watched his work as a major figure in the Players Association. Rumors began to filter through to me that baseball executives thought the commissioner was paying too much attention to player views.

In several Florida meetings with him, Judge Hofheinz made it clear to me that that was how he felt. Big and heavyset, he was a formidable character for a rookie commissioner to confront. While he could be threatening and bombastic, he could also be a tenacious persuader, given to florid but effective surges of Texas oratory. There was no selling short his ability to get things done, the Astrodome, of course, being his supreme achievement. Its executive suites would have shamed a Chinese emperor, manifesting an exotic flair totally at odds with his unpretentious personal appearance. He was by all odds one of the most remarkable people I have ever encountered. And one of the most difficult.

I told him I might indeed nullify the trade but that I was also considering having Montreal provide additional players as compensation for Clendenon. This did not please him at all, for it was Clendenon he sought for the long ball and to fill in at first for a couple of years until a youngster named John Mayberry was ready. He argued that an expansion franchise like Montreal did not have the necessary prospects to restructure the deal. He wanted the deal off and Staub back. In any event, he challenged my power under the rules to order a restructure and told me that my old mentor, Lou Carroll, agreed with him.

I called Lou, who said he had advised the Judge that Major League Rule 12(f) would seem to require me to nullify the trade. I replied, "Maybe so, but as I understand the law and the history of baseball, the commissioner also has the broad power to override the rules and do what he thinks is best for the game. I think this is a case to override." Lou conceded that the broad power existed but cautioned that if I went that route I was going to make a lot of baseball owners angry. He was right, but that was a risk I was prepared to run. If I was going to do the job right, I had to stand up and be the paterfamilias every now and again.

So I did. I ordered the trade to stand, Staub and Alou to suit up and the Astros and the Expos to restructure the deal.

Hofheinz went wild. He filed suit in Texas and released a statement saying, "This Johnny-come-lately has done more to destroy baseball in the last six weeks than all of its enemies have done in the past one hundred years." Referring to me as "Blewie Kuhn," as in "he blew it," he went on to say, "I don't propose to stand by and see a franchise destroyed and the National League ruined by a temporary interim commissioner."

Well, this Johnny-come-lately, who had worked hard in baseball for nineteen years, was not going to let the Judge, a mere novice with seven years under his belt, insult the office of the commissioner, or its occupant. As fast as his contemptuous quotes rolled off our wire reports, I teletyped them right back to the Judge asking him to immediately confirm or deny their accuracy. I promptly received a call from his lawyer, asking if he could come to see me. Arriving that same evening, he minced no words. He said the Judge was sorry for what he had said and was prepared to issue a public apology; of course, the Judge would drop his lawsuit.

"Fine," I said, "don't go anywhere. I'm going to write an apology for him myself." The Judge issued the apology just as I wrote it.

The Staub case was important. It confirmed the broad, flexible power base of the commissioner and his willingness to use it. It also demonstrated the commissioner's willingness to face a showdown with one of the toughest and most formidable owners. Though I had tried to handle the problem with quiet diplomacy, the fire fight that the Judge provoked had worked to my benefit. (The Judge and I never had another problem and got along commendably. He supported my election later in 1969 and in 1975.)

As for the rest of the deal, Houston finally agreed to take two pitchers as replacement for Clendenon, one of whom, Jack Billingham, went on to become a solid member of those Big Red Cincinnati machines of the seventies.

The saga of Judge Hofheinz thereafter was not a happy one. He was crippled by a stroke in 1975, which left him in a wheelchair for the rest of his life. His *Astrodomain* complex, of which the club was a part, fell on evil financial days and was operated by its creditors until it was sold to John McMullen's group in 1979. The soaring imagination that continued to dream such dreams as doming the Roman Coliseum for the circus and baseball disappeared only upon the Judge's death in 1982.

The Staub decision had been an anguishing one for me. Indeed, baseball people almost uniformly thought it was wrong under the rules. In my own office, and among my own advisers, only one spoke up strongly for the decision I reached. That was Jimmy Gallagher, a Damon Runyon–like character who had been general manager of the Cubs and who was responsible for the supervision of playing

rules and amateur baseball. Jimmy argued that the overriding concern for the good of the game should prevail.

Jimmy Gallagher was a baseball classic. A onetime Chicago sportswriter, he had been elevated to the general managership of the
Cubs when owner Philip K. Wrigley wearied of press criticism of the
club's operation. As a young lawyer in the early 1950s, I first met
Jimmy as his guest at a Cubs-Cardinals game in Wrigley Field. When
the Cardinals' fire-eating outfielder Enos Slaughter devastated Cubs
catcher Harry Chiti with a sliding assault at the plate, Chiti miraculously held on to the ball for the out. I turned to Jimmy and said,
"What a fantastic play by Chiti." His reply was, "That's what we pay
the dumb SOB to do." I am sure Jimmy appreciated Chiti's play as
much as I did, but he had come by an honest reputation for crusti-
ness.

Not surprisingly, I included Montreal among my flurry of opening
days in 1969. On April 14, Luisa (whose mother was Canadian) and
I were seated in beautiful little Jarry Park awaiting the first official
major-league baseball game ever played outside of the United
States. It was an exciting and emotional day. The brilliant sun was
countered by a flag-snapping wind, and there was enough snow
piled behind the right-field fence to suggest that Mount Tremblant
had found its way into the parking lot. The sound of baseball terms
in French, words such as "lanceur" and "frappeur," added new
romance to the game.

Just the previous summer all had appeared lost for the city of
Montreal. Although the Charles Bronfman group had been awarded
the franchise as part of the National League expansion plan, the
award was contingent on a suitable stadium's being provided. By
August 1968, there was still no stadium and the league was faced
with going elsewhere.

As National League attorney, I had flown there with league president Warren Giles to see what could be done. At dinner with Mayor
Jean Baptiste Drapeau, Expos president John McHale and various
officials, it became apparent that hopes were slim for a suitable
playing field. But the irrepressibly optimistic mayor was resolute.
"There are no problems," he insisted, "only solutions." Several times
the discussion turned to a small, city-owned amateur stadium in
Jarry Park. Each time it was put aside for various inadequacies.
Finally, it seemed the only hope, and Mayor Drapeau, having called
ahead to have the lights turned on, headed a cavalcade to the park.

There it was in all its honest, amateur simplicity. But the mayor conjured up visions of a beautiful park that would surely suffice until a permanent stadium could be built. The more Giles and McHale looked, the more it seemed the mayor's vision could be realized. It was.

Five days after the Montreal opener, Boston traded Ken "Hawk" Harrelson to Cleveland, and another rhubarb dropped into my lap. It was a six-player deal, but the flamboyant, self-proclaimed "Hawk" was the big name. In the sixties, he had brought to the game his brand of swagger, a series of embellishments that caught on with other players. He was the first player to wear a golf glove regularly, the first to wear wristbands, the first to paint lampblack under his eyes. Stylish and outspoken, the Hawk had so enraged Charlie Finley in Kansas City in 1967 that Finley, who rarely gave anything away, released him. A free agent in midseason, Harrelson was grabbed by the Red Sox with a bonus and salary increase and became a key figure in the Boston pennant drive. In 1968, he led the league with 109 runs batted in and was named American League Player of the Year by *The Sporting News.* He was at the pinnacle of his career. Not that he was a great talent, mind you; he was a lifetime .239 hitter. But the Hawk had flair and the crowds loved him. His personal charm did nothing to hurt his cause.

So it came as a surprise when the Hawk announced he was going to retire because he did not want to leave his business interests in Boston. On reflection, it was not really surprising. He and his lawyer, Bob Woolf, had obviously gone to school on the Clendenon retirement and were putting some pressure on Cleveland Indians president Gabe Paul and, I suppose, hoping that the commissioner would wade into the transaction and add to their leverage.

I talked to Gabe, who was anxious to see the deal completed because Cleveland needed a colorful character like the Hawk. We both speculated that the retirement threat was part of a chess game Woolf was orchestrating where the object was not the opponent's king, but Gabe's dollars. There was nothing wrong with that except that the six players were momentarily homeless, dangling between Boston and Cleveland. Whether the deal was going through or was canceled, action was needed promptly; so I called the key actors to New York—Dick O'Connell of the Red Sox, Harrelson, Woolf, Gabe Paul and the American League president, Joe Cronin.

This was not typical of past commissioner practice, which would have left this matter to the American League to resolve. I was impatient with that approach. The commissioner had more clout than anybody and ought to use it. Certainly allied in this view was Cronin, who had a high, traditional respect for the commissioner's authority.

The meeting was essentially a formality. After some initial posturing by all concerned, where the predictable positions were stated in ceremonious fashion, I suggested that Paul, Woolf and Harrelson talk privately. So they withdrew to another room and, sure enough, the Hawk emerged with a rare two-year contract, calling for $100,000 per season to play for the Indians.

The Hawk, mod and splendid in puffed sleeves, a scarf, flared trousers, a pullover vest and an early-Beatles haircut, greeted the huge press contingent in our lobby. He spoke of how much he looked forward to playing for Gabe and the Indians, and how happy he was about the way things worked out. Now papered with wampum, the previously unappealing shores of Lake Erie had become Eden.

The press was supportive of me. The more I disturbed the status quo, the more they seemed to applaud. The clucking in the background was the sound of worried owners, noting that the commissioner's interference had resulted in a pay raise for a player already under contract for 1969. In both the Staub and Harrelson cases, I was seen to have behaved like a "players' commissioner." Marvin Miller and the Players Association were watching but silent. In later years, *any* move by the commissioner that affected a player was apt to draw criticism or attack from Miller, but for now, still consolidating his power, he watched and perhaps worried. The last thing he wanted to see was a commissioner exercising power over clubs and players with press approbation in the bargain.

In June came a significant issue concerning the involvement of club owners in Parvin-Dohrmann Company, which owned and operated three gambling casinos in Las Vegas—the Fremont, the Stardust and the Aladdin. Three directors of the Atlanta Braves—Bill Bartholomay, John Louis and Del Coleman—were directors of Parvin-Dohrmann, and Oakland's Charlie Finley was a stockholder.

I called the group together in New York and explained that, while they were guilty of no wrongdoing, they should not be involved with a casino operation. This was the first of many occasions when I would direct baseball people to keep their distance from gambling activities. There were people inside and outside the game who saw the 1919 Black Sox scandal as ancient history. I did not. I was convinced that the gambling danger was as great fifty years later, and was supported in that view by the enormous growth in illegal wagering on American sports. Nor was I unaware of the gambling scandals that had struck college basketball and professional football in more recent times. There was no reason to think baseball was immune. People at all levels of the game had to understand that baseball administration was going to be tough on gambling questions. I wanted no false signals given. Critics then and now would decry my concerns as image making. I was convinced that I knew more about the danger than they possibly could.

The gentlemen before me argued that their Parvin-Dohrmann interests presented no real threat to baseball and that my concerns were unfounded. I felt otherwise. Chip away at your integrity and in time you had none. What law had they broken? What crime had they committed? The answer was none. Finley correctly argued that his Parvin-Dohrmann stock did not amount to 1 percent of the company. It came down to a question of judgment; there was no nice, tidy road map to steer me to an answer. But the answer was negative. They had the choice of staying with either their baseball or their Parvin-Dohrmann interests. I gave them all a reasonable amount of time to terminate their Parvin-Dohrmann interests if they elected that route. Only Coleman opted for Parvin-Dohrmann. He said he would resign from the Braves' board of directors and continue as chairman of the Parvin-Dohrmann board.

This story was long forgotten when I made the Willie Mays (1979) and Mickey Mantle (1983) decisions, giving them the choice of working either for New Jersey casinos or baseball, but not both. But I had followed the Finley-Braves precedent. The press and public can be fickle. They thought it was perfectly acceptable to box the ears of an owner, but quite another thing where popular players were involved. As commissioner, I could not indulge in such emotional inconsistencies.

The problems coming over the transom brought a healthy whir of activity to the commissioner's office, but far more important were plans to get the sport dynamically on the move and to fight for its rightful place in the burgeoning entertainment marketplace.

We brought in Tom Villante, senior vice president of BBD & O Advertising, as a consultant on marketing matters and to handle our centennial celebration, the first professional baseball team having been the undefeated Cincinnati Red Stockings in 1869. Tom, effervescent and energetic, was a former Yankees batboy and had helped both the Dodgers and Yankees over the years by running the accounts of their major beer sponsors. He was not only a superior marketing talent but had close ties to baseball and a keen knowledge of the game. Some years later, when the opportunity presented itself, I brought Tommy into baseball as our director of broadcasting and marketing.

Hundreds of marketing ideas bounced onto my desk from all sources: fans, media, club executives, sponsors and staff. The marketing projects taken together with all the other activities made me thankful for the intensive work habits I had developed in two decades as a lawyer. I now moved into a regular schedule of rising at 5:00 A.M. and working into the evenings. I immersed myself in matters large and small.

As a fan, I had felt that baseball was happy to have us in the audience but did little to give us a sense of participation in the game we loved. Operating on the theory that other fans were similarly minded, we concentrated on fan involvement through voting. The centennial was an ideal vehicle. Tom Villante and Joe Reichler suggested having the fans in each major-league city select their local greatest team of all time, followed by run-off national selections of the greatest team overall and greatest living team. The elections were a striking success, generating national debate and enthusiasm, and capitalizing on fans' enduring sentimentality about the game, its history and its stars. Was Speaker better than DiMaggio or Wagner superior to Cronin? No matter, baseball was the clear winner.

The final poll judged Babe Ruth the greatest player ever and Joe DiMaggio the greatest living player.

In 1969 the All-Star starting lineups were to be selected by the major-league players, coaches and managers, as they had been since 1958. Apart from the fact that the fans had no vote, no one could find fault with the validity of the system that Ford Frick had installed after a fan-voting method based on newspaper ballots had gone awry in 1957, resulting in the election of a National League starting lineup of seven Cincinnati players to the exclusion of obvious All Stars like Willie Mays, Henry Aaron, Ernie Banks and Eddie Mathews. Having dictated the changes necessary to realign the National League team, Frick abandoned fan voting.

While it was too late to change the system for 1969, I was determined to give the voting back to the fans in 1970. There would be some howls, but fan voting made too much marketing sense to ignore. Indeed, that had been the original concept when sports editor Arch Ward of the *Chicago Tribune* conceived the first "fans dream game" in 1933, and used a newspaper ballot to get the fans to vote. (The fans that season picked an aging Babe Ruth to start for the American League, and he responded with the first All-Star Game home run, driving in what proved to be the winning run.) As I saw it, this was still a game for the fans. We should not tell them whether or not to select players with hot starts that season, big years the previous year or great careers. It was their game and each fan could decide what the criteria should be.

Working with the Gillette company, whose sponsorship of baseball covered more than half a century, we devised a system utilizing a computerized ballot, wide national distribution of over twenty million ballots and centralized, automated counting. The system's complexities made it expensive but also gave assurance against such vote-tilting results as we had experienced in 1957. I knew the concept was right, I knew it promised major promotional and marketing gains for baseball, but I certainly did not have access to the money necessary to finance the high-road system we were contemplating. Gillette agreed to cover the cost. I was ecstatic.

When a Gillette representative and I made a joint announcement that we were renewing fan voting in 1970, I was accused of selling out the integrity of the selection process to Gillette. We were told the fans could not do as good a job as player-manager-coach voting was doing now. But I was sure we were right because we were serving the fans. That was the touchstone, and it was one I would use in future marketing decisions.

The new All-Star voting system had a number of kinks that, far from damaging the process, fostered fierce debates and actually popularized the new voting; one thing of which the baseball world never wearies is a hot debate. Year by year we corrected, adjusted and did the most scrupulous staff work in an effort to achieve the perfect system. But it always evaded us, because baseball, like a cage of squirrels, is constantly in flux and cannot be caught in a single pose. The downside of the kinks was the annual rite of pounding the commissioner for some new "stupidity" that had crept into the system. Some April "flash" had been omitted from the ballot; some April-traded player was now in the other league, or was being played in the outfield by his new club though listed at third base on the ballot. I developed an almost totally successful cure for this pain: I "forgot" to read the newspapers every year when the ballots were distributed.

While I was shaking things up, I wanted to take a look not only at the playing rules but also the liveliness of the balls then in use. I was far from sure that any of this needed changing but I wanted us to be seen as willing to consider innovation. So when Johnny Murphy of the Mets came to me in February 1969 with juiced-up baseballs, having 5 percent more core resiliency than the existing balls, and wanted to experiment with them in spring training, he got my enthusiastic support. These so-called 5X baseballs were used a few times that spring with inconclusive results.

We tried a 10X ball the following spring. I went to Phoenix to watch the Giants use it in a game. Bobby Bonds hit two balls over the left-field fence, doubled one to the center-field fence and drove a fourth to the wall. After the game, I asked him if he had seen a difference in the balls.

"No," he said. "I just got hold of them good."

In 1970, we tried flared foul lines (pivoted outward a few degrees at first and third) at one field in the Gulf Coast Rookie League. It was a bad idea and one for which I must confess I was responsible. One such experiment was enough.

Charlie Finley was hooked on the periodically popular notion that the game had to be speeded up. While he and Judge Roy Hofheinz were both innovators, they came to opposite conclusions on how to invigorate the game. The Judge was convinced that the game had natural cadences that you changed at your peril and that game length was no problem if the fans were given a polished and entertaining setting like the Astrodome. Charlie wanted to change that cadence by going to a three-ball walk and two-strike strikeout. Wild as this notion was, we allowed the A's to play one such game in spring training. It produced eighteen walks and was ridiculously long and dull. At least we took a look.

Suggestions to speed up the game came like unwelcome relatives over the years; I found myself in the Hofheinz camp. We should not tinker with the game's natural flow. Very rarely is the subject broached today, even with games getting progressively longer.

Finley also lobbied for the use of orange baseballs, and we gave them a showcase in an exhibition game. Indeed, it was not the worst idea ever proposed: Tennis had gone almost entirely to yellow or orange balls on the theory that they have better visibility than white ones. Still, it was hard to demonstrate a dramatic difference, and Finley's support undermined the cause in any event. Anything Finley touched automatically drew opposition from baseball people. Well, we tried it once.

As to the playing rules, baseball had been loath to make major changes. There had been no major change since 1901, when the National League provided that a foul on a two-strike count would not result in a strikeout. The American League followed in 1903. My respect for the wisdom of this restraint did not deter me from wondering if the designated hitter concept could help baseball out of its hitting doldrums. The consideration of such a change was certainly very much in our interest, if only to demonstrate that we had some oil lubricating our imaginations. I freely talked in press conferences about the hitting problem and the possibilities of the DH. On more than a few occasions, owners asked if I could avoid public discussions of our problems. My answer was that I was not going to isolate myself from the public and press. That meant I was going to have to answer questions and my answers would be honest. We were not going to solve our problems by the ludicrous pretense that they did not exist.

The DH debate we stirred up in 1969 was altogether healthy. Meanwhile, five of our minor leagues were experimenting with different versions of the DH rule. I think the public was beginning to believe we were finally awake. Executives like Lee MacPhail of the Yankees believed in the DH and were beginning to make some progress in the American League. Certainly, if change in any area was coming, the more venturesome American League would be the place for me to seek allies. They had precipitated expansion in 1961 and 1969, forcing the reluctant National Leaguers to follow suit both times.

In all fairness, it should be noted that on both occasions the American League had itself been shoved by external forces—in 1961 by the threat that Branch Rickey's Continental League would become a reality, and in 1969 by Missouri senator Stuart Symington's rage over the league's preposterous 1967 decision to move the Kansas City A's to Oakland. In one muddle-headed disaster, the league left the excellent Kansas City area and doomed the Bay Area to mediocrity by putting a second club there—all to accommodate their archvillain, owner Charlie Finley!

But the fact remained that I looked to the American League for support. Whether I talked about the DH, experimental rules, interleague play or other novelties, someone there was always listening. The practical fact was that on any major change, of whatever kind, the commissioner could not successfully buck the opposition of both leagues. He needed an ally. The ultimate test of this axiom would come some years later, when the American League expanded into Toronto, provoking a major crisis.

One change that got increasing attention in my staff meetings was playing night games in the World Series. The marketing potential was dramatic. We were hiding too much of our showcase event on weekday afternoons when few people could see it. In 1968, the All-Star Game was played at night. Why not the World Series, at least on weekdays? The answer was obviously tradition, while I was not at all sure it was right. I wanted a full evaluation.

Washington was another area in which I wanted to increase the commissioner's activities. In the past, we had left political matters largely to our capable lawyers, but I decided to make Washington a regular part of my beat. As a native, I felt a great sentimental attachment to the area. Perhaps such factors should not motivate chief executives, but precious few avoid them. Moreover, I enjoyed politics and politicians. Like it or not, the commissioner's job was highly political and was becoming more so. Besides, Bob Short, the Washington Senators' new owner, had done a wondrous thing by enticing Ted Williams to become manager in 1969. For me, Williams was the greatest personality in the game, outranking even Casey Stengel. I managed to squeeze a healthy number of Washington games into my schedule.

The first was opening day 1969. President and Mrs. Nixon were there, and sat with Luisa and me. He, of course, was renewing the tradition of the "Presidential Opener," which went back to President William Howard Taft in 1910. Taft had had such generous physical dimensions that it was necessary to unscrew a row of permanent seats in his box and replace them with a sofa. President Nixon fit tidily into his seat beside me. He thoroughly understood the game and took a sharp, perceptive interest in all its aspects. He talked easily about current and past players. A special favorite we both shared was Bobo Newsom, a talented eccentric who was acquired five times by the Washington club. The president was also an attentive listener and got the benefit, doubtful though it may have been, of my baseball stories, trivia and statistics.

On this opening day, I promptly gave him some information of the doubtful variety. I explained that Ted Williams had worked in spring training to convince his giant slugger, Frank Howard, to avoid swinging at bad balls. As the game's greatest hitter, Williams hated bad balls the way saints must hate the works of the devil. Ted had told me that very afternoon that Howard had gotten the message and that we would see him get more bases on balls and more good pitches to line out of the park. The president listened. On Howard's first time at bat, Mel Stottlemyre threw him a curve that landed two feet in front of the plate. Howard swung and missed. The president, laughing, turned and said, "Thanks a lot, Bowie, for the inside dope."

During those days, my Washington lawyer, Paul Porter, and I made courtesy calls on many of the key figures in Congress. I was naive enough to be surprised at how easily this was accomplished. I did not yet understand the respect people at all levels have for the office of commissioner of baseball. But I was learning.

As I remember, Paul and I made our first call on Senator Everett McKinley Dirksen of Illinois. It was an inspired beginning. The Congress has produced a great many colorful characters, but few to top this senator. In his outer office was a group of schoolchildren from back home. Their spontaneous arrival immediately displaced us and we watched as they chattered their way within. As they chattered back out, they had the senator, who was benignly dispensing smiles and felicitations, in their midst. With a wink, he led us into his office. All rumpled charm, he opened with a line I will never forget, "What mischief have you brought me today?" He seemed genuinely crestfallen when Paul said we had only come to say hello. While it would have been easy to dismiss the senator as an old humbug, an impression that I think he enjoyed conveying, I learned that he was a marvelously shrewd and kindly man whose death later that year deprived the Senate of a great legislator.

One of the senators I admired most was Phil Hart of Michigan. I admired him as much as anyone I had known in the Congress. I called on him occasionally, looking for help on some important issue. He always had time for me, if only a few minutes in the back of a hearing room, listened like a priest to a penitent, dispensed wisdom in such a self-effacing way that you felt it was your own, told you something funny that tickled you for days and sent you away refreshed and brightened. When he died in December of 1977, I went to his funeral mass at St. Matthew's Cathedral in Washington. I sat in the back row. His simple pine box was draped with an American flag. A string quartet played at the altar. It was just right. I went home and told Luisa, "When the time comes, please send me packing the same way."

Porter and I covered a lot of congressional marble in those days and, I think, created a good atmosphere for baseball. That would be important in the years ahead.

In the summer of 1969, Speaker of the House John McCormack

and I attended the congressional baseball game between the Republicans and the Democrats. Played at RFK Stadium in Washington, it was the first of many congressional games I watched. I actually climbed into umpire's gear and handled the first inning behind the plate. I was glad that the six outs accumulated neatly, with the teams playing with considerable skill and fervor. I was applauded for correctly calling a balk. Pure luck. The lively rivalry flowed into an annual postgame party, where I learned the important lesson that behind the surface conflicts were warm friendships that defied party labels. My own affection grew for men like Silvio Conte, who managed the GOP team, and Bill Chappell, who did the honors for the Democrats.

The highlight of our centennial celebration was a banquet on July 21 at Washington's Sheraton Park Hotel during which we announced the greatest all-time teams. This was the culmination of Tom Villante's planning and was the finest sports banquet I have ever seen. NBC's Curt Gowdy was a superb master of ceremonies, although a burned retina, caused earlier by experimental television lights, nearly knocked him out. Only his high sense of professionalism carried him half-blind through the evening.

The next afternoon President Nixon held a centennial reception in the White House as a prelude to the All-Star Game at RFK Stadium. All of the "greatest living players" were there, as were scores of baseball officials, players and the media. In a receiving line in the East Room, I introduced all the guests individually to the president. He gave a bravura performance, with an appropriate comment for almost everyone. He had memories to share with the old-timers, topical comments and advice for those now in the game and pertinent observations for many of the sportswriters and broadcasters. As the line thinned, the president suggested that I turn around and look out the window. To my horror, a torrential cloudburst was drowning Washington. He said, "Try to get the game in, because I'd like to be there and can't make it tomorrow." Our Apollo 11 astronauts, who had landed on the moon two days before, were soon splashing down in the Pacific, and Nixon was leaving to welcome them back.

Before the receiving line began, the guests were permitted to wander freely through the first floor of the White House. I remember my shock upon finding Lefty Grove in the Red Room, seated on one antique with his feet propped up on another. "Old Mose," who terrorized opposing batters, was now doing a pretty good job on the commissioner. I shook his hand, which got him up. I was afraid to look back as I left the room.

I really did want to play the game that night. This marked our third foray into night baseball for the All-Star Game. In 1967, our 4:15 start in Anaheim, California, which was prime time in the East, produced 55 million viewers, a huge increase over prior daytime All-Star games. In 1968, for a night game in the Houston Astrodome, we had 60 million viewers. We expected to do even better in 1969 with the centennial excitement.

Bess Abell, who was Lady Bird Johnson's social secretary in the Johnson White House, had been brought in to organize a festive pregame party. And that she did. Tents worthy of the dreams of a Persian potentate had sprung up on the grounds of the D.C. Armory, next to the stadium. Within, all manner of carnival luxuries awaited the invited guests, who included the entire United States Congress. Ragtime music and calliopes gave a vintage touch.

But the deluge I had first observed an hour earlier at the White House continued unabated. Water was everywhere. Luisa and I welcomed the guests standing in running water up to our ankles. When diminutive Majority Leader Carl Albert arrived bearing an embossed congressional resolution saluting our centennial, I was afraid he would be swept away in the current.

So formidable was the storm that some guests were stranded in their buses. I can remember Casey Stengel howling to my sons George and Paul to bring drinks through the downpour to the bus he would not leave. Meanwhile, I was making periodic dashes into Dutch Bergman's office in the Armory to talk to my staff in the stadium about field conditions and to reassure the White House that we would not call the game under any circumstances before eight o'clock that evening. However, when my staff told me that the water in the dugouts was so deep it was flowing out onto the field, I gave up and called the game. It was just about eight o'clock.

Water was building up in ominously large pockets on top of the tents. Our attendants and my sons were everywhere, pushing chairs up into the pockets in an effort to disperse them. But it was too few fingers in the dike and the tents began to collapse. Guests fled into the nearby Armory. Hours later, when all the guests had paddled away, a small group of survivors stood around a lonely bar in the center of the cavernous Armory building: Luisa and I, Judge Sam Sterrett and his wife Jeane, Senator Harrison Williams and Ann Christmas, a society columnist for the Washington *Star*. With that, a leak sprung in the Armory roof and water cascaded down on us all. So ended my first attempt to play one of our crown-jewel events in prime time.

By the next day, the waters had receded sufficiently to play the All-Star Game on a sunlit afternoon. Vice President Spiro Agnew represented the president, Willie McCovey belted two awesome home runs and the National League won 9–3. One way or another, it was a centennial celebration that no one would ever forget.

Our summer meetings in 1969 were set in Seattle in honor of that city's first year in major-league baseball. By the time of the meetings (August 13), I would have logged in something over six months of my one-year term. Early in the summer, John Fetzer and Walter O'Malley suggested I consider election to a full seven-year term. If I were agreeable, they wanted to sound out their leagues and "make sure the votes were there," to use a phrase popular with Walter.

The general feeling that the votes were indeed there filtered back to me from various owners. While I had made decisions that did not sit well with many of our clubs and had taken a more activist view of the job than many had expected, on balance the owners were pleased with my leadership. Reluctant as some may have been to strengthen the hand of the commissioner, there was really little alternative. The press was widely supportive. Even the Players Association had found little exposed freeboard at which to unload broadsides.

I also believe that another reason prompted the clubs to give me a full term. They had elected me in February on a restructuring platform. To be sure, some of the owners—Jerry Hoffberger in Baltimore, Mike Burke in New York and Dick Meyer in St. Louis—genuinely believed in restructuring. But the rank and file would just as soon have played with rattlesnakes as restructuring. They saw a commissioner taking his one-year election platform seriously. He had a study committee that was actually meeting and had hired the University of Pennsylvania's Wharton School to make a study and draw up recommendations. I think some owners believed that if the commissioner were just given a full seven-year term, perhaps the whole restructuring idea would slither away. By January 1970, I would see developments that dramatically supported, if not proved, this conjecture. Unfortunately, in August 1969, I was caught napping.

As much as I had enjoyed my six months as commissioner, the full seven-year commitment required thought. I had four young children at home. Much time would be spent on the road. I thought about the prolonged interruption of my legal career. But Luisa and the kids were enthusiastic about my continuing. I had made it a habit to take them with me whenever possible; if I traveled alone, I would always try to fly home the same night. I had also become a regular on the west-to-east red-eye flights from Los Angeles and San Francisco. Willkie Farr & Gallagher made it clear there would always be a "candle burning in the window" (sixteen years later, it was still there). Taking almost paternal pride in my activities as commissioner, Lou Carroll felt I owed it to myself to continue. He told me, "Nobody is going to make you stay if you get disenchanted. And the firm will always be here." In addition, my young partner, Lou Hoynes, was already developing a wide respect among baseball people and was more than able to pick up my work at the firm.

So I put the matter to my Executive Council, the equivalent of a board of directors, consisting of Warren Giles, Joe Cronin, Walter O'Malley and Gabe Paul. I told them that if they wanted to nominate me, I would continue. And at the summer meetings in Seattle, I was unanimously elected to a full seven-year term to run through August 1976.

With hindsight, I wish I had hinged that election on the adoption of meaningful restructuring and the elimination of the three-quarters rule for reelection of the commissioner. Beguiled by the seductive cooperation I was finding on every side and by the sweet ease of the election process, I simply did not worry about where the votes might be in the future if they were needed on restructuring or reelection. All things seemed possible that August. At least I learned enough later to correctly counsel Peter Ueberroth in 1984 to use the crest of the Olympic wave he was riding to demand necessary changes before he would accept the office.

I should have paid more attention to a radio interview featuring Frank Slocum that I heard earlier in 1969. Frank had been a special assistant to Commissioner Frick and has always had a rather special and bemused understanding of the game. "Don't be misled by all the support Kuhn is getting now," he said. "Sooner or later, they'll get him." Coincidentally, I ran into Frank shortly after the interview; I asked what his ominous remarks meant. He laughed and said, "Nothing against you; you're doing great. But down the line somewhere, those owners just aren't going to let you continue to run the show and be that powerful. One Landis was enough."

.   .   .

Our first season of division play produced Baltimore and Minnesota as American League divisional champions, and Atlanta and the Amazin' New York Mets in the National League. We had no idea what to expect from the first League Championship Series (LCS), which fans then preferred to call "the playoffs," as many still do today. There was no precedent on which to predict attendance; moreover, the games were all to be played in the afternoon with no local blackouts. We expected 25,000 per game.

The Mets-Braves series, swept by the Mets, played to three sell-outs of over 50,000 each, two in Atlanta and the finale in New York. Things were not as good in the American League, where the Orioles-Twins series, swept by the Orioles, played to 39,324 and 41,704 in Baltimore and 32,735 in Minnesota. We did better than we had anticipated and we knew the LCS needed time to develop. Not until 1971 did we even manage to get a fourth game played in an LCS, five of the first six series having been sweeps. In 1972, both series finally went the distance. By then, the LCS was coming into its own and moving toward consistent sell-outs.

The New York Mets' five-game victory in the 1969 World Series was a storybook climax to my first season as commissioner. The Mets had become a national joke. They were ninth in 1968, and even astute followers had failed to see the championship pieces slipping into place.

Looking back, the Mets did have some fabulous young arms in Tom Seaver, Jerry Koosman, Tug McGraw, Gary Gentry and Nolan Ryan. But consider some of the other names on that 1969 team: Al Weis, J. C. Martin, Rod Gaspar, Duffy Dyer, Jim McAndrew, Cal Koonce, Wayne Garrett, Bobby Pfeil, Don Cardwell and Jack DiLauro. Every pennant winner has some average players, lucky to be part of a star-bound club, but the Mets had many average players who excelled. Gil Hodges was superb and might have become one of the game's great managers had he not died suddenly in 1972.

I was delighted for that classy lady Joan Payson, who was much respected as the principal owner of the Mets, and who along with Donald Grant and Bill Shea had played a critical role in bringing National League baseball back to New York. Don liked to say that baseball should be fun, and the Grants made it fun for the hosts of visitors who poured through the Shea Stadium board room.

5

The End of
the Honeymoon

We almost managed to lose Joe DiMaggio over the Cambodian border during a 1969 USO tour.

After the 1969 season, the USO, working through our office, put together a small tour of Vietnam to include Joe and players Mudcat Grant, Milt Pappas and Ron Swoboda, fresh from his World Series heroics, and me.

Just prior to the tour's departure, Luisa and I were invited to have lunch with Terence Cardinal Cooke at his residence near St. Patrick's Cathedral in Manhattan. Luisa, an Episcopalian, asked if we would have to fall on our knees there. I assured her we would not. But as we were departing, my Vietnam trip came to mind and I spontaneously asked the cardinal for his blessing.

"Certainly," he said; whereupon I dropped to my knees. From that position I am not sure which was more inspiring, the beatific countenance of the cardinal or the visual daggers being fired at me by my wife. Both were memorable.

We departed from Travis Air Force Base in San Francisco just a few weeks after the World Series and spent our first night in Vietnam having dinner with the American commander, General Creighton Abrams, at his bunkered headquarters at Tan Son Nhut. In accordance with a decision our group had made, we urged the general to put us to work beyond the customary safe zones, and he complied by changing our orders on the spot. He was a superior host during a long and relaxing evening. Having discovered a mutual affection for opera, he and I wound down the evening in a separate room, where he played taped selections of my choice from an impressive operatic collection. The paradox of our commanding general's entertaining me with Puccini's "Che Gelida Manina" in this martial setting was hard to escape.

Outfitted in khaki uniforms, boots and USO caps, we were soon bound for the Cambodian border. After lunch with an American unit, we were put in two large armored helicopters for a trip to American fire bases in the Fish Hook border region. As either helicopter could easily have handled our whole group, I asked the colonel in charge why there were two. He said, "We improve the odds of getting some of you back."

Seated after takeoff facing DiMaggio I heard the sound of gunfire. It became louder. We realized that we were being fired at from the jungle below and that our helicopter gunners were returning the fire. DiMaggio and I exchanged a long, pregnant stare. Then he said, "What the hell are we doing here?" I thought it was an excellent question. We had several similar brushes during the week I was in Vietnam.

We traveled from Saigon to Cambodia to the Delta and back. We talked to thousands of American kids stuck in that ugly war. What most impressed them was that we were there voluntarily. It was inconceivable to them that anyone would do such a thing. My baseball comrades were marvelous, none more so than the normally retiring DiMaggio, who was fabulously popular. He was outgoing and gracious. Diplomacy not being in vogue on battlefields, we were asked all manner of questions, but our fellows handled it all with good humor, candor and style. Talking with young soldiers who might not live another hour would have been inspiring to even the dourest personality.

There was a hospital at Tan Son Nhut where the most grievously wounded were brought to the intensive care unit by helicopter from the battlefield. We went there, too. Nothing I had ever experienced prepared me for that. The doctors told us some were dying and asked us to talk to them. I wondered dumbly, "What do we say?" They told us to smile, say something nice and tell them who we were. It might help them a little. "For God's sake, smile." So we tried. "Hi, I'm Bowie Kuhn . . . you know, from baseball. I know you're gonna be okay." Maybe it helped. I'm not sure. But I will never forget those beautiful, wounded kids trying to smile back.

When I took office, I had been given a mandate in the resolution the owners adopted in December 1968 to do something about restructuring, consolidating and streamlining the administration of baseball. I promptly galvanized a major attack on the worn-out administrative procedures of the game by putting to work the five-man committee that had been created to study the subject. The committee had promise in four members who believed in restructuring: Mike Burke (Yankees), Jerry Hoffberger (Orioles), Dick Meyer (Cardinals) and Phil Wrigley (Cubs). They were men of great capability. By baseball standards, Phil Wrigley was a visionary. Years earlier he had urged that baseball voluntarily liberalize its reserve system, under which the owners were given complete control of their players. Phil also refused to play night baseball or to sell out his park in advance. Needless to say, most owners considered Phil a crackpot—wayward but lovable.

The fifth member of the committee was Chub Feeney of the Giants. Chub was a lost cause. He totally opposed restructuring and dreaded the thought of a closer alliance with the "wildmen" of the American League—Charlie Finley, Arthur Allyn (White Sox), Jerry Hoffberger, and Bob Short, the new owner of the Washington Senators. Chub made it plain that he would oppose restructuring and lobby against it. And he did. Since he was the heir apparent to Warren Giles, who was in his last year as National League president, Chub was a formidable opponent.

But the rest of us were committed. We retained the University of Pennsylvania's Wharton School to analyze baseball's administration and make recommendations. The Wharton professors interviewed every major-league club. Draft reports were prepared, discussed and modified. The committee was sensitive to the need to preserve reasonable autonomy at the club and league levels. These concerns had to be balanced against the need to enhance the powers of the commissioner so that we could have centralized leadership. Schematic diagrams of the administrative structure were prepared showing the reporting responsibilities of our various departments and functions. One depicted the commissioner as if he were a sun giving off brilliant rays, with the clubs, leagues and departments spinning obediently in orbit around him. Sandy Hadden and I dubbed it the

"Sun King" in honor of the title reverently given to Louis XIV by the French.

A special major-league meeting to present the report to the clubs was set for January 1970, since the report would not be ready in time for our December annual meetings. In December, our recalcitrant committee member Chub Feeney was elected president of the National League. I was not happy about that as I had asked the league to continue Giles until the restructuring matter was resolved. To make matters worse, the league agreed that Feeney could move the league office to San Francisco because he lived there. This was utter nonsense. We were going backward. I began to wonder how much of a mandate we really had to restructure baseball.

The final report was presented on schedule in January. It made sweeping recommendations calling for major changes in baseball administration. Among them were provisions calling for the league presidents, the Player Relations Committee and the Major League Baseball Promotion Corporation to report to the commissioner; streamlined voting for changing rules and electing commissioners; and expansion of the Executive Council from five to eleven members.

As a representative of the Wharton School delivered the report, I watched the reactions. It was obvious that the report was going down the drain. After a few polite questions, the owners said they would like time to study it further. "Commissioner, if this gets adopted," John Galbreath of the Pirates said to me after the meeting, "it would eliminate control by the owner over his own franchise. I might as well sell the club."

There was not a more sincere or decent man in baseball than John. But I could see that his mind was closed on the subject. The sad part was that his interpretation of the report was wrong. We had been careful to protect club autonomy. This was an early and dramatic example of how effectively baseball owners could be lobbied by conservative obstructionists. As most of our owners have little time for even the most important subjects, they are easily tilted by whoever gets there first with some adroit factual embroidery.

There was a second message that in a sense was more troublesome. Walter O'Malley exemplified it when he told me, "All this restructuring isn't necessary with you as commissioner. You've already got plenty of power as things stand and you're showing you know how to use it." Bob Carpenter of the Phillies gave it another dimension when he told me that evening, "Don't worry, sooner or later you'll get everything you want. They're just not in a giving mood right now. Be patient."

The report was not adopted, but over the years significant elements of it were adopted, and I had already accomplished a lot by enlarging the functions and increasing the personnel of the commissioner's office. The Executive Council was promptly enlarged to seven and later to eleven. Lee MacPhail's election as American League president in 1973 was a step toward consolidation, as the league office came from Boston to New York the following year. Feeney and the National League came east from San Francisco in 1976. By 1983, we were at last all together under one roof. In 1983, the Player Relations Committee and the Promotion Corporation were required to report to the commissioner. So things happened, but not on the timetable I had in mind.

For me, this was a philosophical crisis. By balking at my reasonable restructuring plan, the owners had gone back on the mandate they gave me when I was elected; implicit in that mandate was a promise to restructure. I was angered by that backtracking. On the other hand, the proponents of restructuring were guilty of contributory negligence. We had let the opposition out-lobby us. I also had confidence in my ability to sell restructuring in substantial pieces, if not wholesale. That in fact happened. And as O'Malley argued, restructuring in some ways was more psychological than real. Barring the opposition of a great majority of clubs, there was very little the commissioner could not accomplish if he set his mind to the task. And he had enormous power to prevent things he thought were bad for the game.

At about the time restructuring was sputtering into gradualism, Jim Campbell, the Tigers' general manager, called to report that his star pitcher, Denny McLain, was developing financial problems and was getting behind on paying his bills. Jim was uneasy and wanted me to know about the situation. There was nothing remarkable in this, but I told him I would ask our security director, Henry Fitzgibbon, to keep his ear to the ground in Detroit.

We soon learned that a Detroit grand jury was investigating some aspect of McLain's financial affairs. In addition, we had learned that *Sports Illustrated* was developing a major story that would link McLain with gamblers.

McLain, twenty-five, was the best pitcher in the American League. He won the Cy Young Award in 1968 with an incredible 31–6 record, and he shared it in 1969 with Mike Cuellar of Baltimore when he went 24–9. His 31-win season in 1968 had been the first in the American League since Lefty Grove's in 1931. He was a national celebrity and had married the daughter of the great former short-stop and manager Lou Boudreau. He was also an accomplished organist.

None of his celebrated flamboyance was in evidence, however, when he arrived at my office on February 13 with his young attor-ney, Bill Aikens. Denny was polite, cooperative and a little fright-ened. His characteristic brashness was pretty well bottled up, although a little poured out every now and again. Obviously, I wanted to know what the grand jury was investigating and what, if any, involvement he had ever had with gamblers. He told us about a bar in Flint, Michigan, he had frequented in 1967 that also hap-pened to house a bookmaking operation. He said he had been talked into investing $5,700 in the bookmaking operation and thought he had been made a partner.

He said the operation had handled football and basketball betting only and had not touched baseball. This was a vital point on which I was determined to get the facts. If betting on baseball had taken place, McLain could well face a minimum suspension of one year— or even a permanent suspension, if Tigers games were involved.

McLain was contrite. He knew he had no business being con-nected with any kind of gambling operation, whether or not base-ball was involved. "Commissioner, we're wholly at your mercy," Aikens said. "Whatever you decide, we'll abide by it. We're giving you all the facts and hoping for the best. This is between you and us. We don't want Marvin Miller or the Players Association in-volved." I told them I was going to investigate every aspect of the case and the meeting ended.

Four days later, on February 17, the *Sports Illustrated* story broke, with McLain's picture on the cover and the headline DENNY MCLAIN AND THE MOB: BASEBALL'S BIG SCANDAL. The story in-sinuated the mob's involvement with McLain, but lacked any solid foundation. The reaction in the press was mixed. Nevertheless, I told Fitzgibbon I wanted every rumor and every detail checked out. I wanted particular attention paid to whether the Flint operation handled baseball bets. Fitzgibbon was a pro and knew how to get answers.

With the Tigers' spring training camp about to open, I called McLain and Aikens in again on February 19 and informed them that I was suspending McLain indefinitely while I completed my investigation. This meant that he could not go to spring training. McLain and Aikens agreed to cooperate, but McLain was unhappy.

As his fate hung in limbo, my own honeymoon with the press was coming apart. It had been supportive and enthusiastic throughout my first year. Roger Angell, the gifted baseball essayist, had written, "[Kuhn's] operations have shown more sure-handedness, intelligence, and courage than have been customarily visible in the Commissioner's office in recent decades . . . [he] looks to be the kind of Commissioner who will support baseball's younger executives and thus at last force the game's Cro-Magnons into common sense planning and a grudging contemporaneity."

But now, the explosive importance of the McLain story required the press to get answers. They wanted to know what my investigation was revealing. I had to forgo my usual policy of openness and cooperation and say that I simply could not comment on a pending investigation. However rational and necessary, this action produced frustration and resentment. Unfortunately, this was not the type of investigation that could be rushed. The grand jury process was grinding ahead and we had to operate in its wake. Definitive answers were difficult to get. I was not going to either clear or condemn McLain, let alone give half-baked answers about what was developing, until I knew more. I was prepared to take the heat as long as I was confident that we were proceeding in a fair and thorough way.

Throughout March the investigation dragged on. Many in the press were becoming convinced that McLain had been guilty somehow of involvement in baseball betting. There was wide speculation that he would get a year's suspension.

On April 1, I announced that I was suspending McLain until July 1 and putting him on probation. So far as we could determine, the grand jury had developed no evidence that McLain had been involved in baseball betting, directly or indirectly. Nor had we. He was plainly at fault in his endeavors to become a partner in the Flint bookmaking operation and in his associations with the operation's criminal element. But the evidence strongly suggested that he was more a dupe than anything else. For his stupidity and greed, and for the harm he had done to public confidence in baseball, he clearly deserved a suspension, but I could not find justification for a full-season suspension, let alone a longer one.

At a press conference on April 1 at Manhattan's Americana Hotel, I faced my first hostile encounter with the media. Since many of these people had become convinced that McLain was guilty of serious wrongdoing, they felt my penalty was inadequate. Others felt the penalty was excessive in the absence of baseball gambling. In response to a question, I revealed that President Nixon had inquired the day before about the case and supported the decision as a compassionate one. It was a tough press conference, something of a revelation in terms of the intensity of feeling in the room. Most of these fellows had already taken positions on which decision I should make. Unfortunately, my decision did not confirm their forecasts.

In retrospect, the McLain case was a public relations debacle. Would I have been shrewder if I had made a final decision early in the process without waiting for a thorough investigation? Would I have been shrewder if I had imposed a suspension of at least a year? Those steps would have been popular and made the commissioner look strong and decisive. To do so would also have been morally wrong and selfish. The decision I made was fair; I have never wavered in that judgment over the years, not even when McLain was sentenced in Florida in 1985 to twenty-three years in jail on drug, extortion and related charges. In the final analysis, I felt that the commissioner's obligation was to do the fair thing, not the popular thing. Because I stuck rather doggedly to that philosophy while in office, I gave myself a lot of grief—but I never had a bad conscience.

Not long after the McLain decision, I had lunch with a prominent federal judge. He asked what was the hardest aspect of being commissioner. I replied that it was trying to find fair answers to the host of tough questions that piled up daily on my desk. I will never forget his advice: "Screw fair. Do what you think is right for baseball." I equated fair and right for baseball; he did not. I am sure a lot of people who prefer the hardball approach in business would agree with the learned judge.

Paul Porter, our Washington lawyer, was with me at the press conference. He had a driver and limousine taking him back to Washington. He persuaded me to drive back with him and get away from the telephone and tempest in New York. As we slid south on the New Jersey Turnpike, Paul said I had made a courageous decision in the face of fully anticipated criticism, but wondered why I "always had to strike such a high moral tone." Paul recognized the modern press aversion to moralizing. I knew it was practical and sensible advice. I gave Paul the answer from my heart: "I think it's the commissioner's job to strike a high moral tone, come what may."

Jerry Hoffberger of the Orioles called the next day, puzzled. He said that he felt I should have given McLain a longer suspension, or nothing at all, and that I had wandered into no-man's land. Mike Burke of the Yankees was quoted in the New York press as characterizing my decision as "ghastly!" That drew a letter from me asking for confirmation and suggesting that criticism should be made privately.

Buzzie Bavasi of San Diego called and said my decision had taken a lot of guts. He advised me, "Once you make a decision, don't bother explaining it. You don't have to, you're the commissioner." Buzzie was one of baseball's free spirits. He had a catlike ability to spring over, around and under our rules. He knew where all the bodies were buried, and more often than not, who had put them there. He spoke his piece on all subjects, sometimes not wisely. And he had a lot of heart and it was in the right place.

The press criticism was painful, but I dutifully read it as part of my education. Looking back, I am reminded of advice given to me by Vice President Nelson Rockefeller in the White House some years later. We chatted about press criticism. "You don't really read that stuff, do you?" he asked in his distinctive laughing style. "That's foolishness. You know more about what's right than your critics! Don't read the stuff. I learned that when I was in Albany."

I never fully accepted his advice, although as time passed I did tune out the writers whose consistent criticism made me question their fairness and honesty. Well, there was one exception—I could not resist Red Smith, no matter how often he shredded me. He wrote so beautifully.

To great fanfare, McLain returned to the Tigers on July 1. But something was wrong. His performance on the mound made you wonder if this was the same man who had won fifty-five games in the previous two years. Moreover, McLain began to act as though he was looking for trouble, which was not too smart for a man on probation.

He threatened a parking-lot attendant over a parking space in Anaheim. On August 28 in Tiger Stadium, in what he tried to characterize as a harmless prank, he called sportswriters Jim Hawkins and Watson Spoelstra over to his locker and doused them in separate incidents with buckets of ice water. Hawkins was willing to go along with it as a gag. But Spoelstra went to the Tiger management and demanded action. I immediately got a call from Jim Campbell. He told me he wanted to suspend McLain indefinitely. I concurred.

During that suspension, I learned that McLain had been carrying a gun on a scheduled airline flight and had in fact displayed it at a restaurant in Chicago. Carrying a gun on a commercial airplane was a federal crime even then.

With the Tigers coming to New York on September 9, I had McLain in for another session in my office. He admitted to carrying the gun. For two hours we reviewed his conduct since his first suspension.

I suspended him again, this time for the rest of the season. It was his third suspension of the year, and left this once-great right-hander with a 3–5 record and a 4.65 ERA for 1970.

His bizarre behavior bothered me. I suggested to Aikens and Campbell that McLain undergo a psychiatric examination. This he did, at the Ford Clinic in Detroit. The medical report concluded that McLain "is not mentally ill and not in need of such service."

A few days before the opening of the 1970 Reds-Orioles World Series, Campbell asked to see me and Joe Cronin in my suite in Baltimore. Campbell told me he had worked out a deal with Bob Short of the Washington Senators to send them McLain, Don Wert, Elliott Maddox and Norm McRae in exchange for Ed Brinkman, Joe Coleman, Aurelio Rodriguez and Jim Hannan. Since McLain was a suspended player, and suspended players could not be traded, Campbell asked if I would approve the deal.

Cronin and I looked at each other. We had Campbell repeat the names of the players. We were flabbergasted. We could not believe that Short would make such a deal. Campbell was trying not to smile but did so in spite of himself. He hoped we would not share our evaluation with Short.

The Tigers were getting the excellent starting left side of the Washington infield in Brinkman and Rodriguez and a fine starting pitcher in Coleman in return for much less. Short was gambling that McLain could come back. As an old Senator fan, I was appalled by Short's foolish gamble, but I decided to let the trade go through, since McLain was due to have his suspension lifted.

I hated to upstage the start of the World Series, but too many people were involved in this to keep it quiet. And so, we met the press that had gathered for the Series, and I announced the trade in order to explain the lifting of McLain's suspension. It was proba- bly the only time a commissioner ever announced a trade. It was an honor I would just as soon have passed up.

McLain led the American League with twenty-two losses in 1971 for the Senators. In 1972 he went to Oakland, then Atlanta and was through at the age of twenty-eight. In 1968, the year of his glory in Detroit, a song was composed with the lyrics "There's never been any like Denny McLain." How right they were.

While McLain was sitting out his suspension in 1970, an issue involving another pitcher captured national headlines. Jim Bouton, a journeyman pitcher who had faded from fastballs to knuckleballs after two good seasons with the Yankees in the early sixties, wrote a book that was excerpted in *Look* magazine in May. He purported to reveal the confidential clubhouse conversations and nocturnal habits of his teammates. It struck me as not very credible stuff.

American League president Joe Cronin thought the excerpts were unforgivable and suggested I talk to Bouton. I asked Bouton, who was then with the Houston Astros, to see me on June 1, when his team was in town. He arrived accompanied by a representative of his publisher and by Marvin Miller and Dick Moss of the Players Association.

In a short meeting I expressed my concerns about the credibility of the excerpts and discussed baseball's unwritten code about the confidentiality of the clubhouse. Bouton, Miller and Moss argued that he had the right to write as he wished.

Unfortunately, my meeting with Bouton was used by his publisher to make it appear as though I was trying to ban the book, which, while untrue, was an effective sales strategy. I would have been better off ignoring both the book and Bouton. Mickey Mantle handled it better than I did. When the press asked for his reaction to the book, he said, "Jim who?"

6

Curt Flood, Meet Marvin Miller

On October 8, 1969, two days after the Mets won the National League pennant, the St. Louis Cardinals traded Tim McCarver, Joe Hoerner, Byron Browne and Curt Flood to the Philadelphia Phillies for Richie Allen, Cookie Rojas and Jerry Johnson. Curt Flood decided he was not going.

Curt Flood had been an outstanding center fielder for the Cardinals for twelve years, his very initials indicating a position he seemed born to play. He had helped the Cardinals win three pennants during the sixties, most recently in 1968.

Not long after the trade, he met with Marvin Miller, executive director of the Players Association. Miller had become head of the Players Association in the spring of 1966, after the players decided to set up an office in Chicago or New York. His predecessor, Robert Cannon, an active county judge in Milwaukee, was not in a position to move. (Judge Cannon's father had been counsel for the Black Sox players in the Illinois criminal proceedings against them.)

A four-player committee consisting of Robin Roberts, Bob Friend, Harvey Kuenn and Jim Bunning was formed to search for a leader for the players. Roberts asked George William Taylor, a professor at the Wharton School, to recommend a possible successor to Cannon. Miller, until 1966 an economist with the United Steelworkers of

America, was Taylor's recommendation. He was available because his boss, David McDonald, had lost the union presidency to I. W. Abel. Miller traveled to the various major-league cities, winning the support of most, if not all, of the players.

I first met Miller in December of that year at the major-league meetings in Pittsburgh, where I had gone because of Lou Carroll's illness. An embryonic Player Relations Committee with Joe Cronin as chairman had a short meeting with Miller and his counsel, Dick Moss. I was present as National League counsel. Miller was at his disarming best, which could be very good indeed. He was all low-key charm. There were no threats or demands. It served his purpose to create as little problem as possible with management. He was far more preoccupied with solidifying his position among the players and heading off any challenges from other unions. My first impression of Miller was favorable. Neither pussycat nor radical, he gave every appearance of wanting to deal with matters in a reasonable way. Or so I thought.

That evening, Sandy Hadden, then American League counsel, and I met into the night with Miller, Moss and a group of players, including Jim Bunning, Tom Haller and Dick Hall, to work out a funding arrangement for the players' benefits plan. The question was whether a funding percentage formula (based on World Series radio-TV revenue and All-Star Game revenue) should be continued or whether there should be a flat funding sum agreed to by negotiation at the end of each agreement. The clubs preferred the latter approach, since funding based on a percentage of television revenues could in time produce amounts much in excess of any legitimate need of the benefits plan. After many hours of bargaining, it was agreed to abandon the percentage approach. Miller insisted on some face-saving language that he felt would permit him to ride both the percentage and flat-sum horses in the future. He is still straining to keep his feet on both to this day, demonstrating persistence, if not logic.

As part of that evening's agreement, the clubs committed to pay $4.1 million annually to fund the benefits plan, doubling pension benefits and increasing the owners' contribution from $2.85 million. Was Miller wise in giving up a percentage formula in favor of a $1.25 million annual increase? The owners were elated. Retired star Bob Feller was outraged. Feller, who had been a player leader on benefits plan matters for many years, had been involved in the search for a man to head the Players Association in 1966. Indeed, he had talked to Richard Nixon, then a private citizen, about taking the job before Miller was hired. Nixon declined, suggesting that the choice be a prominent player. As to Miller's surrender of the percentage formula, Feller argued that retention of the formula would have guaranteed the players much larger benefits plan contributions than they could subsequently achieve by bargaining. While the question is debatable, I shared Feller's surprise at Miller's strategy. In Miller's defense, he was new at the job and lacked the strength to galvanize the players into a major resistance to the owners and their offer to increase their annual contribution by more than a million dollars.

The Miller I saw in Pittsburgh gave no strong grounds for alarm, but he showed an early tendency to be pedantic, fussy over details and unwilling to deal straightforwardly with issues. At first blush, this seemed just an annoying matter of style. It was more than that. It appeared to be a calculated strategy to plant ambiguity in negotiations, discussions, letters and agreements. Those ambiguities might seem harmless at planting time, but to them he later would ascribe whatever meaning suited his current purpose. These later meanings were usually self-serving inventions, inconsistent with the previous understanding of the parties. The result was a never-ending game of cat and mouse in which Miller conducted union affairs with such endless slyness that he soured the relations between clubs and players. That was a misfortune for the game.

I saw a lot of Miller in 1967 and 1968. Pending the hiring of someone to head the Player Relations Committee, the clubs asked me to be their spokesman in dealing with union matters. We launched negotiations on a new minimum-salary structure, completed the details of the new benefits plan agreement, handled routine club-player questions and talked about a great variety of subjects, many of which had nothing to do with baseball. Miller never professed to be a baseball fan and was not comfortable with the garrulous baseball talk of team analysis, player comparisons, trivia games and discussions of players of the past. When it came to small talk, he preferred politics, current events and his own tennis game. He did like to tell anecdotes about baseball, but the stories were usually about management scoundrels and their incorrigible ways. He particularly liked to run his pitchfork through Paul Richards of the Braves and Buzzie Bavasi of the Padres, thereby making them folk heroes among their peers. For his own part, Richards publicly called Miller "a mustachioed four-flusher."

Miller was overall a knowledgeable and interesting man, a good listener, restrained and courteous in social settings. His left-of-center views were deep-seated and pervasive but not unpleasantly presented. But these views were at the core of his difficulty in dealing with baseball people. They were highly establishmentarian in their attitudes and as a group were as far right of the political center as Miller was left. I used to chuckle over Walter O'Malley's accusing Philadelphia's Bob Carpenter of being "the last American royalist." Essentially, it seemed to me, Miller had a deep hatred and suspicion of the American right and of American capitalism. And what could be more the prototype of what he hated than professional baseball, with its rich, lordly owners and its players shackled by the reserve system. One did not have to be a prophet to see the coming problems.

As the months went by, and I observed Miller on a daily basis, his real feelings became apparent. No matter how understated his style, I began to realize that we had before us an old-fashioned, nineteenth-century trade unionist who hated management generally and the management of baseball specifically. Deep inside, he harbored a suspicion of most institutions, which included the AFL-CIO and its leader, George Meany, who had the temerity, as Miller saw it, to say publicly that the baseball players did not need a union, and the Teamsters Union, which for a while flirted with the notion of organizing the players itself. Miller had nothing but scorn for the Teamsters in his discussions with me. Indeed, my advice to ownership was that we were better off with Miller and Dick Moss than we would be with the Teamsters. There was some dissent on that question, but it was minimal. The essence of the dissent was that Miller, who had served as economist for the Steelworkers, was not in fact an experienced negotiator and would lack practicality in dealing with a business as foreign to him as baseball. In time it would be shown that there was some merit to that point of view.

There was about Miller the wariness one would find in an abused animal. It precluded trust or affection. It set up a wall against any kind of close approach. I doubt that St. Francis could have surmounted the barrier. Certainly the picaresque characters of baseball could not. If they inspired anything in Miller as his experience with them grew, it was the building of higher earthworks. The fact that we had some rogues in our business only heightened the alarm in a mind already predisposed to distrust.

The barriers took an odd turn in my case. Both before and after I became commissioner, I invited Miller to lunches, dinners, games and other social events. Some he accepted, some not. Never once was the courtesy returned. Nor, incidentally, rarely if ever did I see him pick up a check, but I viewed that more as an understandable form of collective bargaining.

Miller's lawyer, Dick Moss, provided something of a counterbalance. In the first place, he was a real baseball fan (Pittsburgh Pirates) and liked to talk about the game. He really cared about baseball. He was neither a philosopher nor a zealot, as Miller was. Practical, irreverent and sassy, he had a better sense of marketplace realities. He was also a personality you could touch. By way of example, he came to me after a 1968 collective bargaining session during which I had been demonstrably angered by some typical Moss wisecrack. He apologized, saying, "I don't know why you got so mad but maybe I was wrong. Can we forget it?" Under no circumstances could I imagine Miller's saying anything like that. I *never* heard him admit he was wrong.

Unfortunately, Moss was the second banana and Marvin was the boss. Some years later, when Moss went out on his own as a player agent, he drew me aside at an All-Star Game party and said a remarkable thing: "Bowie, you know I'm leaving Marvin, and I just wanted to tell you some things. You've been wonderful to work with over these years. You've always been honest and decent, and frankly, I think we've screwed you from time to time. Look, the labor business is a dirty business. You have to do things you don't like, but everyone does it. I know I did and said things at times that were unfair to you, and I want to tell you I'm sorry about that. It was all in that context. I have the highest regard for you and I hope we'll be friends."

As Miller became more entrenched and secure over the years, and as more press flattery was heaped upon him, I rather hoped we would see some sense of statesmanship begin to emerge in him. It never happened.

Douglas Fraser of the United Auto Workers could work with Chrysler toward the salvation of the company by agreeing to "give-backs" and forgoing huge wage increases to save jobs and help get the company through hard times. It is inconceivable to me that Miller would do the same. Owners were bad and should be brought to heel, not cooperated with, not helped. How could you help people who had imposed a reserve system? They were scoundrels. They were as much tyrants as their management predecessors a hundred years before who had suppressed the rightful interests of American labor.

Though he was much respected over time in the eyes of the players and the press, I rarely observed anyone who regarded him with warmth or affection. Ownership regarded him with anything but affection. Some writers made it clear in private asides to me that, though they respected him for his skill in dealing with management, they clearly saw his cold, lonely, calculating side and his indifference to the game itself.

Still, his ability to cultivate the press was perhaps his greatest talent. He had some built-in advantages. Many writers, of course, were union people and no strangers to confrontations with management; so he found a naturally sympathetic ear. Most of the press also had no inherent sympathy for millionaire owners with elitist personalities. Miller's egalitarian pose was an effective counterpoint to the ownership. Miller was ever ready to give the press the kind of controversial, often exaggerated, stories that made news while his counterparts were rightfully hobbled by management policies requiring more attention to accuracy and less stirring up of public controversy. The clubs were also reluctant to criticize the players, given the fact that the players were their key asset. Management's primly correct approach resulted all too often in a vacuum of press information from their spokesmen while Miller was flooding the media with his propaganda. Starved for information, the media people were apt to give Miller's stories more credence than they deserved. Considering the limitations of his staff, it was a tour de force on Miller's part.

Laying aside any ethical judgment, Miller was a superior communicator, as effective with the media as anyone I have seen in the sports field and close to being a match for the best elsewhere. It was his greatest skill. It was the only area where he was better than John Gaherin and Ray Grebey, who successively directed the Player Relations Committee during his tenure. Had their roles been reversed, I am satisfied that either Gaherin or Grebey could have achieved as much for the players, given the trump cards Miller had been dealt. It was Miller's good fortune to inherit those advantages. To his credit, he knew what to do with them.

Miller's adversaries privately commented on his communication style. They even mocked it. Its most memorable aspects were deep, wrenching sighs; a funereal, ever-shaking visage; occasional mournful smiles and a wide-eyed, long-suffering, incredulous perplexity about the never-ending chicanery of management. These performances were delivered with such singular brilliance that only a cad would have insisted on seeing the hypocrisy within. For pure acting luster, they approached the skills of the illustrious John L. Lewis of the United Mine Workers.

Nowhere did Miller use his communication skills more effectively than with *The New York Times*. Since the public relations aspects of labor-management debates can play a critical role, the support of the nationally prestigious *Times* was an asset of incalculable value to Miller. His philosophy and version of facts were run more consistently by Red Smith, Murray Chass and Dave Anderson of *The Times* than by any other publication. Chass has been the principal *Times* writer on baseball labor matters since 1976. Smith wrote columns for *The Times* from 1971 to his death in 1982. Anderson has been writing columns for *The Times* since 1971. There was a standing, if unhappy, joke among club people about how long it would take before any new Miller point of view would show up unattributed to Miller in the writing of Smith or Chass. All too frequently, it was pretty fast.

This was the Marvin Miller to whom Curt Flood turned in October 1969, the Miller who detested the owners' reserve system and thought it both illegal and immoral. Here was a talented, respected and sincere veteran player willing to challenge that system.

By December 1969, Miller had Curt Flood well along the road to litigation against baseball. Lawyers had been consulted and what remained was to bring the matter before the Executive Committee of the union. These internal procedures were not known to me when I contacted Miller about my desire to attend the committee's meeting in San Juan. In an effort to cut what he saw as an umbilical cord linking the clubs and players, Miller for the first time had moved the players' meeting to a location different from that of the clubs' annual meeting. Miller's response to my request was a sure indication that he wanted an adversary relationship with the commissioner. He wondered with obvious suspicion what purpose would be served by my coming and what I wanted to talk about. Obviously, he was reluctant to have me there. But I persisted, and he finally agreed that I could have a slot on the agenda.

Miller's approach to my San Juan visit was far different from his successor Don Fehr's handling of Peter Ueberroth's visit to the Players Executive Committee meeting in Las Vegas in 1985. Fehr made the new commissioner welcome, and the press extolled Peter for this unprecedented gesture of goodwill toward the players. The press had a bad memory: I visited Miller's office in 1969 on my second day as commissioner and addressed the Players Association Executive Committee on several occasions, until discouraged by

Miller from doing so. Perhaps the union had gained enough sense of security in sixteen years to feel unthreatened by the appearance of a commissioner.

Arriving in San Juan, I did not feel like an adversary, despite Miller's cool reception. My relations with players had been cordial during spring training and throughout the season. In a spirit of cooperation with their association, I had taken the unusual step of sending Marvin a draft of the important Wharton Report, which dealt with baseball's administrative restructuring. I was genuinely seeking a good working relationship.

Appearing before the players' meeting, I began by expressing my disappointment with their decision to meet apart from baseball's annual meeting. I passed along the baseball writers' request that in the future the players' meeting not operate in a press vacuum. I explained my plans for fan voting on All-Star teams and my desire to make earflaps on helmets mandatory as a safety measure. I talked about the Wharton Report and touched on the state of the current collective bargaining, expressing the hope that divisiveness would be kept to a minimum at a time of increasing competition from other sports.

Miller then spoke. He explained why the players had chosen to meet separately from the annual meeting, describing "cold receptions" the union had received from baseball management in the past. He expressed some displeasure that players had not sufficiently participated in the decisions regarding All-Star voting and earflaps.

Then players asked me questions. Tom Haller asked about shortening the season, citing public opinion in favor of doing so. Mike McCormick discussed players' concerns about artificial surfaces. A number of players, including Jim Bunning, Ed Kranepool, Brooks Robinson, Bob Locker and Max Alvis, expressed their concerns about the injury factor on artificial surfaces. I told them that the surfaces would be removed if we saw them causing injuries. Phil Regan encouraged player autographings before games, and I agreed that we should encourage it rather than tighten rules against fans. Locker expressed the hope than an early agreement could be reached with the Player Relations Committee. Miller agreed. I then mentioned my trip to Vietnam and urged the players to participate in such tours if they had the opportunity. And that was it. I thought it odd that not a single question had been raised about Curt Flood or the reserve system. Since I had placed no limits whatsoever on our discussion, the opportunity clearly had been there.

I was shocked to learn later that Flood had appeared at the meeting the day before me. At that time, he had been thoroughly grilled by the players, who were testing his sincerity in stating that he was willing to go to court and sit out the season. When they were convinced of his desire, they voted to fund his litigation and to hire Arthur J. Goldberg as his attorney. Goldberg had been general counsel to the AFL-CIO, secretary of labor in the Kennedy administration, the American ambassador to the United Nations and a Supreme Court justice.

I was not aware of any of this when I addressed the meeting, but given the total absence of questions on a subject of immediate and intense interest to the players, the inescapable conclusion was that Miller had carefully wired the situation so as to avoid any discussion of Flood and the reserve system. I later learned that he had told the players the matter was too sensitive to bring up in such a forum with me.

Obviously, he was not looking for compromise. In hindsight, I can only assume that he decided to go the litigation route. Any discussion with me might produce something conciliatory, perhaps even take the spirit out of the Executive Committee, which had just voted to back Flood. So Miller kept the players silent on the issue. No wonder he had not wanted me in San Juan.

I left San Juan feeling I had made progress. I liked the give and take with the players and their attitude. I was optimistic about improving club-player relations, despite Miller's apparent lack of interest in having me there.

A year later, I made another attempt to meet with the Players Association, this time at their meeting in Miami. Miller told me he saw no point in my being there, but at the suggestion of Jim Bunning I persisted, and Miller reluctantly acquiesced. They let me cool my heels in my hotel room for hours before calling me, and then the questions were so perfunctory it was obvious that Miller wanted to make my appearance a futile exercise. I never tried again.

Why was Miller so uneasy about my attending player meetings? I can only speculate. Miller believed I was genuinely trying to create a commissionership the players could trust. Certainly, that was the track record of my first year in office. Miller wanted no part of that, since his goal was to break the paternalistic link between the players and the clubs, and if a wedge of ill will came between the players and both the commissioner and the clubs, so be it. It was essential to his long-term success that the players become reliant on the union. Nobody drove wedges better than Marvin.

Just after Christmas, I received a letter from Curt Flood.

Dear Mr. Kuhn:
After 12 years in the major leagues, I do not feel that I am a piece of property to be bought and sold irrespective of my wishes. I believe that any system that produces that result violates my basic rights as a citizen and is inconsistent with the laws of the United States and of several states.

It is my desire to play baseball in 1970 and I am capable of playing. I have received a contract from the Philadelphia club, but I believe I have the right to reconsider offers from other clubs before making any decisions. I, therefore, request that you make known to all the major league clubs my feelings in this matter, and advise them of my availability for the 1970 season.
Curt Flood

Thereafter, I had my first of several meetings with Arthur Goldberg. He was accompanied by Miller, Dick Moss and Jay Topkis of Goldberg's firm. Goldberg, an able lawyer, would work directly on Flood's case. Goldberg, who did most of the talking, took an inflexible position, asserting Flood's "right" to deal with clubs other than the Phillies. He swept aside my observation that Flood's contract did not permit negotiations with other clubs. He saw that as irrelevant, since the contract was "illegal." Though I had not expected much from the meeting, it was still a disappointment. I could not communicate with Goldberg, whose starchy, formalistic assertions left little room for even polite conversation. I almost wished everybody would go away and let me talk to Miller. Mr. Justice Goldberg sailed off, leaving me to wonder if he had not somehow managed to top even my well-honed reputation for pomposity.

On December 30, I sent the following reply to Flood:

Dear Curt:
This will acknowledge your letter of December 24, which I found on returning to my office yesterday.

I certainly agree with you that you, as a human being, are not a piece of property to be bought and sold. That is fundamental in our society and I think obvious. However, I cannot see its applicability to the situation at hand.

You have entered into a current playing contract with the St. Louis club, which has the same assignment provision as those in your annual major league contracts since 1956. Your present contract has been assigned in accordance with its provisions by the St. Louis club to the Philadelphia club. The provisions of the playing contract have been negotiated over the years between the clubs and the players, most recently when the present basic agreement was negotiated two years ago between the clubs and the Players' Association.

If you have any specific objection to the propriety of the assignment, I would appreciate your specifying the objection. Under the circumstances, and pending any further information from you, I do not see what action I can take and cannot comply with the request contained in the second paragraph of your letter.

I am pleased to see your statement that you desire to play baseball in 1970. I take it this puts to rest any thought, as reported earlier in the press, that you were considering retirement.

> Sincerely yours,
> Bowie Kuhn

The third paragraph of my letter focused on a subject that was not palatable to Miller, namely, that the union had negotiated a basic agreement with the clubs in 1967 and that they had to live with it. If they wanted to change the reserve system, they should have done it then. In effect, the union was trying to take two bites of the apple, one in negotiation and another in litigation. Miller tried to avoid this argument by contending that Flood was strictly on his own and that the union was not responsible for Flood's lawsuit.

More fundamentally, Miller had despaired of trying to negotiate a change in the reserve system. He saw the clubs as too adamant on the subject and he obviously doubted his ability to mount a strike of sufficient duration to force a change. Faced with this dilemma, it is not hard to understand why he viewed Curt Flood as a godsend. In fact, I think he took too pessimistic a view. There were club executives who would have considered negotiated approaches to some form of free agency, and their numbers, though limited, were bound to increase as new and younger ownership appeared in the game. The Flood lawsuit was a mistake both because its prospects were poor and because it soured the potential for negotiation in the years ahead.

As would come out later, the Players Association did not like any part of my letter, beginning with "Dear Curt," which was categorized as a symbol of the same old "plantation mentality" that they found so patronizing. Since I did not know Flood personally, I was supposed to call him Mr. Flood.

In response, Goldberg filed a lawsuit on January 16 in New York Federal Court seeking $1 million damages. I made no comment at the time, but the two league presidents issued a joint statement saying that "professional baseball would simply cease to exist" if the reserve system were abolished.

Before the trial began, I asked my special assistant, Monte Irvin, to contact Flood and see if he could meet with me in Los Angeles, where I was to attend a benefit-exhibition game in Dr. Martin Luther King Jr.'s memory. I felt that a little diplomacy might get Flood suited up for the 1970 season and help find a solution to his concerns. Similar efforts had worked in the Staub and Clendenon matter.

Curt told Monte that he would not see me. On April 2, 1970, I sent him a telegram:

AM DISAPPOINTED YOU DECLINED MY INVITATION FOR A PERSONAL CONFERENCE IN LOS ANGELES ON FRIDAY. I DESIRED AN OPPORTUNITY TO DISCUSS WITH YOU PERSONALLY YOUR BASEBALL CAREER WITHOUT PREJUDICE TO THE BASIC ISSUES INVOLVED IN THE PENDING LITIGATION. MY COUNSEL HAS ASCERTAINED FROM YOUR COUNSEL THAT THE LATTER HAD NO OBJECTIONS TO SUCH A CONFERENCE WITH THE EXPLICIT CONDITION THAT HE WAS NOT RECOMMENDING THAT YOU ASSENT OR DECLINE. THIS IS TO ADVISE YOU THAT IF YOU RECONSIDER I WILL CONTINUE TO BE AVAILABLE.

BOWIE KUHN

We never had the meeting. All avenues toward conciliation appeared somehow to be foreclosed.

The trial was held before Judge Irving Ben Cooper from May 19 to June 10. By now, Goldberg had launched a political campaign to run against Nelson Rockefeller as the Democratic candidate for governor of New York. Probably because his political obligations were in conflict with his court schedule, he, on several occasions, kept everyone, including Judge Cooper, waiting until he arrived. It was not good strategy.

Twenty-two witnesses testified; eleven for each side. I was on the stand for two days, evaluating the reserve system and tracing its history. I noted the chaos that existed between 1871 and 1879 when there was no reserve system. I set four tests by which I would measure the efficacy of any proposed reserve system and evaluated the systems proposed by Flood's witnesses. The tests were integrity, economic effect, mechanical workability and the effect on equalization of team strength.

There was one moment of good humor. Flood's lawyer, Jay Topkis, said to me, "You are trained as an economist, you told us yesterday."

"Thank you for the concession," I said. "I didn't realize I had said that."

"I thought you told us that you took a degree in economics at Princeton," Topkis continued.

"I did," said I. "That's not quite saying you are trained as an economist."

Whereupon my lawyer, Victor Kramer, suddenly leaped to his feet and interjected, "As a Harvard man, I would agree with that last statement."

I concluded that it would be "impossible to maintain the integrity of the game and maintain honesty among clubs and players" without a reserve system. Other defense witnesses who supported the need for a reserve system were Joe Cronin, Chub Feeney, John McHale, Bob Reynolds, Frank Dale, Ewing Kauffman, Bing Devine, economist John Clark, Jr., Joe Garagiola and John Gaherin.

Flood's case was supported by testimony from Hall of Famers Jackie Robinson and Hank Greenberg, as well as by Bill Veeck, economist Robert Nathan, Alan Eagleson of the NHL Players Association, former pitcher Jim Brosnan and Marvin Miller. Flood's lawyers also called three other sports commissioners, who were asked about the mechanics of their reserve systems: Pete Rozelle of the NFL, Walter Kennedy of the NBA and Clarence Campbell of the NHL.

Robinson said, "I can't see how modifying the reserve clause in any way could affect the game in a derogatory manner. I think it would improve in terms of the relationship between owners and players and I think basically this is what we are after: to have a better relationship between management and players if you are to have a great game."

Basically, the trial pitted me against Marvin Miller. We were the key witnesses for the two sides. Miller asserted that "the reserve rule system is illegal, and by virtue of that feeling we do not feel that it is in the same category as any other bargainable subject.

"It is unnecessary and unduly restrictive. I do not believe that you can operate without rules. It is quite clear that you need rules and you need rules relating to the contracting of players with employer clubs, but I do believe that the set of very tight restrictive provisions which currently exists is unnecessary, can be modified in a manner that you preserve the interest of the club owners, the players, and the fans."

The trial concluded on June 10. On August 12, Judge Cooper ruled in favor of baseball.

"Clearly," he wrote, "the preponderance of credible proof does not favor elimination of the reserve system."

He said he was impressed by Flood's arguments and thought that perhaps arbitration or negotiation might bring satisfaction to both parties, but said that only Congress or the Supreme Court could change baseball's antitrust immunity.

In a statement after the decision, I said, "I share Judge Cooper's conclusion that any change necessary in the reserve system can be achieved by bargaining."

The United States Court of Appeals upheld Judge Cooper on April 7, 1971, and the Supreme Court, on October 11, 1971, agreed to hear the case. We would have been much happier to see the Supreme Court decline to review. The decision to review meant that at least four justices had some question about the lower court decisions—hardly a good sign.

Meanwhile, we got Flood back in uniform. After sitting out the entire 1970 season, he was traded by the Phillies to the Washington Senators on November 3, 1970, less than a month after Bob Short had obtained Denny McLain. Poor Short seemed to be collecting everybody's problems. Predictably, the Senators were dubbed "halfway house" by the press.

Flood played poorly. In thirteen games, he managed to bat only .200, with seven singles and two runs batted in. At age thirty-three, twenty days after the adverse Court of Appeals decision in *Flood* v. *Kuhn,* he jumped the club, taking with him half a season's salary, some $55,000. He wired Short:

I TRIED. A YEAR AND A HALF IS TOO MUCH. VERY SERIOUS PROBLEMS MOUNTING EVERY DAY. THANKS FOR YOUR CONFIDENCE AND UNDERSTANDING.

. . .

Short, who had trusted Flood, would probably have preferred a money order for the unearned salary. Thus ended Curt Flood's playing career. Eleven months later, on March 20, 1972, the Supreme Court heard the arguments in *Flood* v. *Kuhn*. We were now in the courtroom where the original antitrust immunity had been granted in an Oliver Wendell Holmes decision a half century earlier. The court that had granted it could certainly now take it away. I thought it would not, but no one could be sure.

For Arthur Goldberg, who had lost his New York gubernatorial race to Nelson Rockefeller in November 1970, it marked his first appearance before the Supreme Court since he had left it in 1965. He argued the case like a man preoccupied. Paul Porter opened baseball's argument with an expert statement of preliminary aspects. I selected Lou Hoynes, who had succeeded me as National League attorney, to make the main presentation. I imagine that selection was theoretically something of a gamble, since Lou was a young lawyer who had never argued before the Supreme Court, a forum that has been known to petrify attorneys of great experience. Indeed, Walter O'Malley had urged me to argue the case myself. While I would have loved the challenge, I knew perfectly well that my executive responsibilities precluded me from giving the matter the kind of single-minded dedication it required. And I knew Hoynes's wide-ranging talents made him ideal. He carried the day by a wide margin. We were hopeful.

Three months later, on June 19, the decision was announced. By a 5–3 vote, with Justice Powell not participating, the court upheld baseball. Justice Harry Blackmun, a great baseball fan, wrote the majority decision. It must be one of the court's most remarkable.

He opened with a five-paragraph review of the history of baseball and the reserve system. Then he said, "Then there are the many names, celebrated for one reason or another, that have sparked the diamond and its environs and that have provided tinder for recaptured thrills, for reminiscence and comparisons, and for conversation and anticipation in-season and off-season: Ty Cobb, Babe Ruth, Tris Speaker, Walter Johnson, Henry Chadwick, Eddie Collins . . ." On and on went Justice Blackmun, totaling in the end eighty-seven names.*

*Justice Blackmun's complete listing: Ty Cobb, Babe Ruth, Tris Speaker, Walter Johnson, Henry Chadwick, Eddie Collins, Lou Gehrig, Grover Cleveland Alex-

The decision was hailed by many as a great victory for baseball, but it carried another message—that the immunity was "an aberration," and that it would be Congress's job, not the Court's, to correct it. I called the decision "constructive," and said, "It opens the way for renewed collective bargaining on the reserve system after the 1972 season. I am confident that the players and the clubs are in the best position to determine for themselves what the form of the reserve system should be and that they will both take a most responsible view of the respective obligations to the public and to the game." Far from claiming victory, I was espousing collective bargaining as the road for change in the reserve system. The last thing I wanted was the clubs to view the Flood decision as an excuse for doing nothing. Change was in the wind. Other sports were changing; we could not sensibly sit still. All we had was breathing time. I heard a lot of congratulations but not much heavy breathing.

In 1973, Ed Fitzgerald of the Brewers became head of the Player Relations Committee. He was also the CEO of Cutler-Hammer and one of the country's best executives. The company's success was in large measure attributable to his outstanding Marine Corps–bred leadership. And no wonder; Ed had brains, depth and courage, and combined executive talent and ethics as gracefully and naturally as any executive I knew. One of baseball's luckiest moments was the emergence of Fitzgerald and Bud Selig in the Milwaukee ruins left by the flight of the Braves to Atlanta.

Ed and I talked about the necessity for throwing open baseball's windows to the idea of free agency. He understood that the Flood decision was only a way station on a course that inevitably would

---

ander, Rogers Hornsby, Harry Hooper, Goose Goslin, Jackie Robinson, Honus Wagner, Joe McCarthy, John McGraw, Deacon Phillippe, Rube Marquard, Christy Mathewson, Tommy Leach, Big Ed Delahanty, Davy Jones, Germany Schaefer, King Kelly, Big Dan Brouthers, Wahoo Sam Crawford, Wee Willie Keeler, Big Ed Walsh, Jimmy Austin, Fred Snodgrass, Satchel Paige, Hugh Jennings, Fred Merkle, Iron Man McGinnity, Three-Finger Brown, Harry and Stan Coveleski, Connie Mack, Al Bridwell, Red Ruffing, Amos Rusie, Cy Young, Smokey Joe Wood, Chief Meyers, Chief Bender, Bill Klem, Hans Lobert, Johnny Evers, Joe Tinker, Roy Campanella, Miller Huggins, Rube Bressler, Dazzy Vance, Edd Roush, Bill Wambsganss, Clark Griffith, Branch Rickey, Frank Chance, Cap Anson, Nap Lajoie, Sad Sam Jones, Bob O'Farrell, Lefty O'Doul, Bobby Veach, Willie Kamm, Heinie Groh, Lloyd and Paul Waner, Stuffy McGinnis, Charles Comiskey, Roger Bresnahan, Bill Dickey, Zach Wheat, George Sisler, Charlie Gehringer, Eppa Rixey, Harry Heilmann, Fred Clarke, Dizzy Dean, Hank Greenberg, Pie Traynor, Rube Waddell, Bill Terry, Carl Hubbell, Old Hoss Radbourn, Moe Berg, Rabbit Maranville, Lefty Grove.

have other stops down the line. But was anyone else listening? Chicago's Phil Wrigley certainly was. Beyond him, Frank Dale at Cincinnati was flexible and had leadership potential. We knew we could count on Ed's partner, Bud Selig, and probably Charles Bronfman of Montreal. But overall, we did not think the outlook was encouraging. The more we talked, the more our soundings showed that the clubs were not in a mood to negotiate free-agency changes in the reserve system, barring a major development that would force their hand. A determined strike could have been such a development, but Marvin Miller never elected—or was never able—to go that route on the reserve-system issue, even though it took him a full decade to punch a fatal hole in the system. It was like guerrilla warfare: feints and skirmishes but no major engagements. So the leverage was not there for change; too bad, because the Flood decision provided an ideal climate within which to negotiate a free-agency system that would have better served baseball and its fans for the long term than the system that ultimately developed.

Eight years of dust had gathered on my bound volumes of *Flood* v. *Kuhn* when I walked into a Yankee Stadium pregame party in George Steinbrenner's office and saw Curt Flood. He was working for the Oakland A's as a broadcaster. He came across the room, put out his hand and said, "I'll bet you don't know who I am." I told him I certainly did.

"Well, I suppose I'm not one of your real favorites," he said with a smile. I told him there were no bad feelings because I had never questioned his sincerity. He looked well. We talked about his broadcasting career and what he had done over the last eight years. Finally, the old schoolteacher inside me said, "But you were wrong to walk out on Bob Short in 1971 after taking his money."

7

The Struggle to Save the Senators

The Seattle Pilots, an American League expansion team in 1969, played their games in Sicks Stadium, an appropriate name for a facility that was anything but major league. I went there on April 11 for the opening game and found carpenters still hammering and sawing the old stadium into shape. It turned out to be a festive occasion nonetheless, highlighted by the presence of United States senators Scoop Jackson and Warren Magnuson, and by Gary Bell's pitching the Pilots to a 7–0 victory over Chicago. Notwithstanding the poor ballpark, I was enthusiastic about the prospect of baseball in the growing northwest corner of the United States, a prospect that was brightened by the community's commitment to a domed stadium in the future.

Unfortunately the Pilots peaked on opening day. They soon settled into last place and drew a poor season attendance of 678,000. Principal owner William Daley became disillusioned and decided to sell the club.

As it developed, the leading bidder for the Pilots was a Milwaukee group headed by Bud Selig and Ed Fitzgerald. They were offering a very attractive $10.8 million. Although I was sympathetic to Milwaukee, I liked having major-league baseball in the Northwest and was troubled by the possibility of its leaving after one season.

In an effort to find a local buyer for the Pilots, Joe Cronin and I made a number of trips to Seattle, meeting with local bankers and businessmen. It was a discouraging exercise. The business community was not nearly as enthusiastic about the future of baseball in the Northwest as Joe and I were. And they certainly lacked the enthusiasm of the Milwaukee interests. Finally Ed Carlson, chairman of the board of Western Hotels, came forward with a plan to turn the Pilots into a nonprofit, community-owned franchise. While community ownership had worked with the Green Bay Packers of the NFL, it was unprecedented in baseball's more complex operations. I had reservations, but I preferred the Carlson plan to losing the franchise altogether. So I supported it.

On February 11, with the Pilots $3.5 million in debt and 1970 spring training about to begin, the American League met in Chicago to consider Carlson's proposal. Needing nine votes to meet the three-quarters requirement for new ownership, the proposal got eight. It was not the last time I would be frustrated by narrow defeat under the three-quarters rule.

I told Joe Cronin how I felt about one-vote margins. "When you get eight votes, you can always find a ninth," I said. "At least we ought to try. I'll bet we can turn a club or two around."

I called Carlson to tell him not to be discouraged, that we could still get the votes. Carlson told me it was too late. He said he had now released his group and, like Humpty Dumpty, it could not be put together again. I suspect the group did not have much enthusiasm in the first place and had gone along more because of Carlson than anything else. When Carlson told me it was dead, I knew it was; he was very reliable.

Now events unfolded quickly. We had no local buyers to turn to. The American League advanced the Pilots $650,000 to keep the club afloat and appointed Roy Hamey, the retired general manager of the Phillies and Yankees, as caretaker. But the club soon slipped out of our hands and into the hands of the bankruptcy court.

On March 17, the American League, faced with a thickening plot of lawsuits, met and issued a statement saying it was unable to continue operations in Seattle and must search for a proper and legal way to transfer the franchise. On March 31, with opening day a week away, a bankruptcy referee determined that the Pilots should accept the Milwaukee offer, as the club no longer had any funds with which to operate. And so, on April 1, the Seattle Pilots became the Milwaukee Brewers at a purchase price of $10.8 million.

A tailor worked furiously to remove P-I-L-O-T-S from the club's flannel uniforms and replace it with B-R-E-W-E-R-S in time for opening day. If you looked carefully, you could see the outline of the old name on the Milwaukee uniforms. Baseball people were delighted that Milwaukee had reacquired a franchise. The Selig-Fitzgerald ownership group added luster to our executive ranks, though nothing could dress up the sorry team they had bought. In time they would take care of that, too.

On the negative side, the Seattle episode was a bad chapter for baseball. We had been forced out of the Northwest after one futile season. We had seen a major-league club fall into bankruptcy. We had left with a lawsuit against us and a legacy of ill will among fans and politicians that still lingers. Some baseball people came in time to conclude that Seattle was a "bad baseball town." I do not think that is a correct assessment of Seattle or that there is any such thing in North America. Ineffective ownership is usually the problem in places where baseball struggles.

Seattle was only a warm-up for the problems that followed seventeen months later, when we lost the Washington Senators.

Bob Short had purchased the Senators in 1968 from James H. Lemon and the estate of James M. Johnston. In paying $9.4 million, he prevailed over the efforts of Bob Hope to acquire the club. Short had no real ties to Washington, an ominous sign that augured badly for the struggling expansion franchise, which had come into existence in 1961 to replace the original Senators, who had become the Minnesota Twins. It was a measure of the difficulty into which baseball had fallen in the late 1960s that local ownership in Washington and Seattle did not come forward to take over those franchises. Long-suffering Washington fans took little cheer from the fact that Short had previously owned the Minneapolis Lakers of the National Basketball Association, only to sell them to Los Angeles.

Short, a former treasurer of the Democratic National Committee, lived in Minneapolis, where he owned the Leamington Hotel, frequented by visiting American League clubs, and a trucking business. In many ways, he neatly fit the baseball-owner mold—flamboyant, opinionated, loquacious and publicity-oriented.

Inauspicious as his qualifications for Washington may have been, he promptly brought some excitement to the scene by hiring Ted Williams as manager. His 1969 Senators won eighty-six games and finished fourth in the eastern division, just a game behind Boston and four games out of second. Williams was named Manager of the

Year and the club drew 918,000 fans, up some 350,000 from the previous year.

But there were early signs that Short was not happy in Washington. He talked to me about helping him get a better stadium lease for RFK Stadium. But in the process, he so belabored Washington's alleged inadequacies that it was hard not to conclude that his real goal was to move the club. He certainly did not like my congressional testimony, in which I made it clear that I would take a dim view of any effort to move the franchise. All the same, I did support his efforts to get a better lease.

Both attendance and the ballclub slumped in 1970, dooming Washington in Short's eyes. By early April 1971, Short made it clear to me in a long, rambling, emotional late-night telephone conversation that he was not staying in Washington. "No one can keep me in Washington, not Nixon, not Cronin, not Kuhn," he said. "I will cannibalize the club if necessary. I own it and I will take it to St. Paul if I want. I have lawyers too. I will move wherever I want. Congress will not help me because of your position. I don't give a goddamn if they stick you with the antitrust laws. I'll go to St. Paul, Dallas or Toronto. Goldberg is my lawyer and I'll go the whole goddamn distance with you. Hoffberger is a genius. Let him figure it out. Or let Walter O'Malley and his National League friends help out. No place in Washington is safe at night and Nixon can't do anything about it. I may sell Ted Williams to Boston or Knowles, or Howard or Epstein. Ted says Washington is a horseshit town and I've gotta get out. I'll go elsewhere before I'm forced into bankruptcy like Seattle. I know I had my eyes wide open when I went to Washington, but I told the American League I wouldn't keep it there forever. If we're to save Washington, everybody has to give something: me, the players, TV and the federal government. Even the Humphrey Democrats are now hitting me. Maybe things will work out in a Cinderella way, but that's not likely."

That monologue perfectly catches the essence of Short and his wild, flailing style, his penchant for lashing out at everybody. There was little doubt in my mind that his goal was Arlington, Texas, between Dallas and Fort Worth.

Arlington's mayor, Tom Vandergriff, had been meeting with Short and was prepared to make it attractive for the club to go there.

Clearly, Dallas–Fort Worth belonged in the major leagues. It was included in Branch Rickey's drawing-board Continental League, the threat of which had inspired baseball's expansion of 1961/62. It would have made it into the National League ahead of San Diego in 1969 had it not been blocked by Judge Roy Hofheinz of Houston.

Dallas–Fort Worth belonged, but not at the cost of a second Washington franchise. If baseball was going to repair its wounded image, the time had come to stop moving franchises. We had moved enough of them in the last two decades to make a troop of gypsies jealous. If the fans were going to start believing in us again, they had to be convinced we were intent upon franchise stability. Nor did it make any sense to leave a major growth area like Washington and the surrounding Maryland-Virginia suburbs. The area had not failed; management had failed to provide attractive baseball. Finally, it made no sense to leave the nation's capital and to run the risk of antagonizing the government establishment to which we looked for legislative and administrative support.

Some people inside and outside baseball felt my views were biased by my personal history as a Washingtonian. I can honestly say my history was not a factor. There were persuasive reasons for staying in Washington that had nothing to do with sentiment.

On June 30, 1971, the American League held a meeting at the Metropolitan Airport Hotel in Detroit to discuss the issue. While I seldom attended league meetings, I made a point of attending this one. Short clearly resented my presence. By this time, it was clear to him that he and I were on a collision course. This baffled and upset him, as he never could grasp the concept that a commissioner had to have a broader perspective than the parochial view of a given owner. Short was typical of new owners we would see during my tenure, owners who lacked any true affection for baseball but saw the game and the commissioner as devices to further their own business interests. It was inconceivable to Bob that a commissioner whose salary he helped pay could be marching to some different drummer.

Short pleaded his case before the other eleven owners. He said there was no industry in Washington to buy season tickets and provide advertising revenue. He said it was impossible to get a good broadcasting contract, that the government was not a ticket-buying community and that Washington's population was transient and unreliable, with a long history of nonsupport. Short was eloquent. He was skillful on his feet, reflecting his legal training and his own homemade evangelical style. He made an impact on his audience, which already had a disposition toward the Lone Star State.

Joe Cronin, who had managed and played All-Star shortstop for

Washington's last pennant-winning team in 1933, offered me the floor. I noted the reasons I felt a team in Washington was so important. I made it plain that I would not let this be another Seattle if we could find a buyer for Short in Washington. Seeing that I was entrenched on this issue, the league decided to appoint a three-man committee to see if a buyer could be found in Washington.

The committee however, included Cronin, Short and me. Short obviously had no interest in finding a Washington buyer, for he stood to do much better financially in Texas. Cronin, while an ally at heart, was torn on this issue, knowing that the majority of the owners in his league were sympathetic with Short. He also felt that the American League was at a serious disadvantage compared with the more successful National League and therefore needed a move to the populous and growing Dallas-Fort Worth area. A lot of people in the American League agreed with that analysis.

Thus began a miserable summer. I knocked on doors, looked for new owners, looked for people who might suggest owners and gave newspaper interviews that were virtual advertisements for owners.

On the local scene, I tried Willard Marriott of the hotel chain, the *Washington Post* and the Washington *Star.* They had no interest in buying. Through my friend Judge Sam Sterrett I checked out a variety of local individuals with substantial fortunes but came up empty-handed. On the national level, I romanced General Motors, Chrysler, Ford, NBC, ABC, Coca Cola, Pepsico, Philip Morris, Gillette, World Airways and Kinney National, among others. I got interest here and there, but nothing more. I talked to Bob Hope several times, trying to rejuvenate his 1968 interest when he lost out to Short, but his earlier enthusiasm had waned. I worked hard on my friend Sonny Werblin, whose genius had made the New York Jets and with them the American Football League, but that too failed. I talked to bankers and congressmen looking for help. I got a lot of encouragement. I felt like a thousand pitchers visited by managers: I was getting plenty of pats on the rump. "You're goin' great, just keep throwin' hard."

One good soul emerged: Joe Danzansky, head of the Giant supermarket chain in Washington. It was an odd twist that Danzansky and I were put together by Baltimore's Jerry Hoffberger, who would hardly be benefited by Danzansky's saving the Senators. Danzansky was interested but was not a man of significant net worth. He found two partners, Marvin Willig and Dr. Robert Schattner, the inventor of Chloraseptic, the medicinal mouthwash, and began to put his financing together.

I warned Danzansky that he had to have an assured source of $9.4 million either from his partners or banks, or a combination of the two. As to banks, he must have written commitments. He said that would not be a problem. It was a relief to find someone like Danzansky, a highly respected member of the Washington business community and a man of charm and ability. At last, it seemed, we had found the right answer.

The American League scheduled a meeting for Boston on September 21 to resolve the issue. To my surprise, I read in the *Washington Post* on the eve of the meeting that President Nixon "had spoken with Short, and while dismayed about the prospects of losing the franchise, fully understood the circumstances and supported him."

Then came the real blow. Because of the Jewish holidays, Danzansky told me, he would not have his financing fully in place when the American League owners convened on the twenty-first. At the Boston meeting, Danzansky told the owners that there was "no problem; it can be done. . . . I just need a little more time." As he left the room, I knew we were doomed. I had worked all summer and had unearthed only one group. And they needed more time. That news settled like desolation on the American League. Short, catching the mood, pounded home the point that Washington was so bad that no businessman in his right mind wanted to operate a baseball club there. Mayor Vandergriff and Short made a skillful presentation, which included a guarantee by Arlington, Texas, that it would hold the league harmless against any claims that might arise from moving the club. The way was greased for the move.

Hoffberger spoke in favor of staying in Washington. I renewed my arguments about the foolishness of abandoning Washington, all of which, while valid, had a hollow ring in the absence of any owner ready to buy Short out there and then. Ominously, no one else came to Washington's defense. Short, now sensing victory, was going for the kill. "He's a working stiff, not an owner," Short shouted, pointing at me. "He has no investment in our game. You might all be in my position tomorrow!"

They went around the room and voted. I felt like Caesar staring at Brutus when I saw Milwaukee, which itself had lost out to Atlanta only six years earlier, vote for the move.

The first vote was 8–2, with Baltimore and Chicago opposed and California and Oakland abstaining. The move was one vote shy of approval.

Gene Autry of California was undergoing eye surgery a few miles away at Boston's Leahy Clinic. He and his club president, Bob Reynolds, had agreed to vote no. Reynolds took advantage of a recess to visit Autry and tell him of the news about Danzansky. Oakland's Finley in the meantime was trying to get his friend Ed Daly, chairman of the board of World Airways, to come through at the last minute and buy the club to keep it in Washington. But Daly, a man whom I had already canvassed, was not prepared to act on such short notice.

Another ballot was taken and approval was given by a 10–2 vote, with California and Oakland putting it over the top. The room was silent. Joe Cronin looked at me and said, "Commissioner, will you now approve or disapprove of this action?" I asked for a recess. The room emptied, leaving me sitting alone with Paul Porter and Sandy Hadden. Paul, as dedicated to Washington as I, said, "Bowie, I don't think you have any alternative but to go along." I ruminated about holding the issue up longer but I knew that was futile. I had no decent basis for a delay or veto. I reflected on the fact that no Washington leader had come forward offering any alternative. Did anybody care? I believe we all have moments in our lives when we see something clearly but nobody else cares. This was such a moment for me. So I said, "Yes, Paul. I have no alternative. I have no damned alternative."

The meeting reconvened: the heavy silence returned. I found it hard to speak. This was an emotional situation for me and my usually sure voice had no resolve. There was so much I wanted to say, but what was the point? So I simply said, "I wish the American League well in Texas." An old scoreboard boy from Griffith Stadium had in a sense been the Washington Senators' executioner—however unwillingly. Never good at concealing disappointment or putting a bright face on defeat, I was bitterly and visibly upset. As the club executives left, I stayed at my seat with Hadden and Porter until only Gabe Paul remained. He put his hand consolingly on my shoulder and said, "Bowie, I've never seen you look so sad." Tears were glistening in my eyes. I felt so bad for the fans of Washington, who had been dealt such inept teams for so long. The fan support was better than baseball deserved. We never gave the fans a fair chance.

So the Senators were gone, but the issue of baseball in Washington was not. To this day, it has haunted baseball like a bad conscience. The foremost nagger of that conscience proved to be Congressman Bernie Sisk of Fresno, California. Bernie was a superior legislator, as popular with the California grape district voters who biennially clicked off huge pluralities in his favor as he was with his fellow legislators on both sides of the aisle. He also exemplified the qualities that have given me an uncritical affection for politicians. Most of us have blind sides. One of mine is politicians. I am unable to explain that affection rationally. I just like them, if not exactly uniformly, then something pretty close to it. I have always forgiven them their faults, their fits of wiliness, their tendency to melt away when unpopular public stands are needed. I never expect them to be any better than the rest of us. I love their conviviality and by and large respect their ability at the congressional level, which is far greater than the public press would have it.

I liked Sisk, and that affection wasn't diminished when Bernie and Congressman Frank Horton of Rochester, New York, headed a Washington delegation that descended on our Phoenix annual meeting on December 1, 1971. Frank was another exemplar of congressional talent, and a former president of the Rochester Red Wings of the International League. The rest of their Washington group (which numbered ten) included Jack Kauffman, owner of the Washington *Star*, Congressmen Joel Broyhill and Mel Price, Mayor Walter Washington and his economic development director Julian Dugas, Gilbert Hahn, chairman of the D.C. City Council, Joe Danzansky and Tony Coehlo, administrative assistant to Bernie Sisk and later his successor. I thought it was about time Washington went on the attack. I am afraid they had looked to me as the man who during the summer of 1971 would pull the rabbit out of the hat. Unfortunately, we had all discovered there was no rabbit in my hat.

They arrived in the evening, exhausted and cranky after a long flight, interrupted by bad weather. There ensued a long, impassioned debate in my suite that lasted into the small hours. Knowing full well that my sympathies lay with them, they angrily poured out their unhappiness with baseball. They left no doubt that they felt a treasure had been stolen from them. Both Sisk and Horton were real baseball fans, so their views had the fervor of the true believer. In reply, I drove home the point that I had kept the door open to Washington through the entire summer of 1971 and no one had come through; only Joe Danzansky had tried. I said the failure was not so much baseball's as Washington's, and if they were realistic they would recognize that. I urged them to present a positive program to the ownership the next morning explaining why a way should be found to return baseball to Washington. I further urged that there be no threats of a legislative removal of baseball's antitrust immunity, as this technique would backfire. By the time we went to bed, we were all exhausted.

The Washington group appeared the next morning at the major-league meeting. Frank Lloyd Wright's architectural beauty, the Arizona Biltmore Hotel, was the site of the meeting. We met in a separate building called La Colina Solana, which had once been the palatial home of Cubs owner Phil Wrigley's parents. How often the trappings of economic royalty surround the "people's game" of baseball! Congressmen Sisk and Horton were splendid. The frustrated wrath of the night before had resolved into reason. They said they were prepared to offer the best lease in baseball to get a club back into RFK Stadium. They pledged to do all they could to support baseball there. It was a persuasive presentation.

After their departure, I discussed the matter with my Executive Council. They were impressed by what they had heard and by my argument that baseball should make some meaningful commitment to Washington. We agreed that I should inform the Washington group that "there would be no further expansion or franchise movement without Washington being accommodated."

The Washington group was pleased with that assurance. I myself was pleased by such a positive step, coming so soon after the Senators' departure. My pleasure might have been diminished had I foreseen the headaches and heartaches the Washington commitment would produce in the years ahead.

I went right to work on Jerry Hoffberger, owner of the Orioles. The Orioles had put outstanding ballclubs on the field but had drawn poorly. Indeed, the seventh game of the exciting 1971 World Series, played in Baltimore, had an embarrassing ten thousand empty seats. I thought Hoffberger could be persuaded to play some of his home games in RFK. It was not unprecedented. The Dodgers had played home games in Jersey City while based in Brooklyn; the White Sox had played home games in vacant Milwaukee County Stadium after the Braves moved to Atlanta.

There were times when I thought I had convinced Jerry that this was a good course of action. During my first three years as commissioner he had given me strong support, which gave me confidence that he would seriously consider my position. While he was willing to listen, it became clear to me that he had a low regard for Washington as a sports town and that in any event he would not want to play games there unless he was protected against a National League club's going into Washington. There was no way I would accept that condition.

While the matter was under discussion, I informed the clubs by bulletin that I had given the Executive Council's assurance to the Washington congressional group that Washington would be accommodated in the future. Hoffberger was furious. He said I had no authority to make any such commitment.

From that point on, our relationship disintegrated. Obviously, Jerry saw the salvation of the Baltimore franchise hinged to a baseball vacuum in Washington, which the Orioles would fill. I felt the overriding interests of baseball were more important than any one franchise. A Washington franchise was important for preserving our relationship with the federal government, maintaining traditions that went back to the origin of the American League, and preventing the abandonment of an important growth area to the National Football League. Jerry and I may both have been right when judged by our respective responsibilities. The collision was a sad one for me because I liked Jerry. He was basically a decent man with a record for philanthropy that would shame most Americans. But if you crossed him, he was unforgiving. I had crossed him.

In 1973, an opportunity arose to get baseball back to the capital. The San Diego Padres, in four seasons as an expansion team, had shown none of the attendance magic of their National League neighbors to the north, the Dodgers. Their best showing was 644,000, despite a beautiful new stadium. C. Arnholdt Smith, the club's owner, had been indicted for tax evasion. I advised him to sell the club and he agreed. Unfortunately, there were no buyers in San Diego.

Marge Everett, principal owner of Hollywood Park Race Track in Inglewood, California, was interested. However, her involvement in an Illinois scandal over the fixing of race dates (which led to the conviction of ex-Governor Kerner) put a cloud over her aspirations. Meanwhile, Joe Danzansky reappeared and sought to buy the Padres for Washington. He made rapid progress and, on December 6, 1973, the National League voted to transfer the club to Washington. Shirley Povich, who had been writing sports for the *Washington Post* since the Harding administration and whose columns had enchanted me as a man and a boy, sent me a two-word telegram: MAZEL TOV. Peter Bavasi, son of the Padres' Buzzie, was shuttling to Washington, preparing to take over as general manager. The National League did impose conditions, including a requirement that the Danzansky group indemnify the league against any claims and setting a deadline of December 21 to complete the deal.

I was delighted. Once I realized there were no qualified buyers emerging in San Diego, which should have retained its franchise if there were, I saw that here was the perfect opportunity to keep the commitment baseball had made to Washington. I was pushing hard for this result and in turn felt strong winds of encouragement blowing off Capitol Hill. Congressmen Sisk and Horton had now been joined in their efforts by an impressive bipartisan coalition that included Mel Price, chairman of the House Armed Services Committee, John Rhodes, House minority leader, and Michigan's Jerry Ford, whom history was positioning for dramatically new responsibilities in 1973 and 1974 as the problems of Vice President Spiro Agnew and Watergate worsened. I had seen a lot of these men in Washington and knew their views.

But there were ominous signs. Chub Feeney told me privately that he had real doubts if the "conditioned" transfer to Washington would go through. Chub's gift of baseball prophecy was formidable. When he felt things "in his bones," you paid attention. Walter O'-Malley of the Dodgers had gone along with the Washington vote at my urging, but was reluctant. He did not admire Danzansky, whom he picked apart behind the scenes, and had little faith in Washington as the site of a National League club. A reluctant Walter could be a problem, given his enormous influence in the league. Furthermore, I heard from league attorney Lou Hoynes that the negotiations with Danzansky were not going smoothly. There was a problem getting insurance to back the indemnity required by the league. Danzansky was doing his best, but time was running out on the league's fifteen-day time limit, which put an exceedingly short tether on Danzansky. When the time limit expired, the league was free to make a different move if it wished.

How much more time Danzansky might have been given became irrelevant when, in January 1974, a surprise figure entered the picture. His name was Ray Kroc, and he was one of the wealthiest men in America. He had rewritten the book on Horatio Alger when, at age fifty-two and down on his luck, he bought a hamburger operation called McDonald's and proceeded to write American business history in franchised fast food. A Chicago native with a lifelong passion for the Cubs and Bears, he stepped forward and offered $12 million for the Padres. He would have preferred to buy the Cubs or Bears, but neither was available. He also promised to keep the team in San Diego until at least 1980, perhaps forever. The National League promptly approved the deal.

So Ray Kroc got the Padres as spring training approached and

Washington's window of hope closed again. There would be only robins and Redskins at RFK Stadium.

The impetuous quality of Ray's enthusiasm as a fan was soon evident. On opening day in San Diego, with his club being shut out 8–0, he went to the public address mike and spoke to the crowd: "Ladies and gentlemen, I suffer with you. I've never seen such stupid ballplaying in my life."

While that may have been true (the Padres were outscored 52–9 in their first six games), it was a completely unprofessional and unacceptable performance on his part. I ordered an apology, which only magnified his popularity with the San Diego fans. Ray had pulled off an instinctive marketing coup. From then on, San Diego believed in Ray Kroc and gave him remarkable support. In Ray's first year the Padres drew a million fans for the first time, though they finished last.

Shortly thereafter, Ray and I met on his opulent yacht in Fort Lauderdale. I knew right away we had another fascinating egocentric in the world of baseball. Though he exuded confidence, he was disarmingly frank about his financial struggles before acquiring McDonald's and his career as a piano player. He was also a good listener and probed for my ideas about improving the Padres' popularity. I told him baseball was too conservative about marketing its product and urged him to try new things, but preferably not on the PA system. I even spoke favorably of Boston's occasional split-doubleheader, with one game in the morning and one at night. Not long afterward, Padres president Buzzie Bavasi called. "I don't mind your scolding Ray," he said, "but quit telling him to play baseball in the morning!" They never did.

8

The Strike of '72

On the labor front, Marvin Miller was confronted by management's John Gaherin, a veteran labor negotiator who had been hired in 1967. For a brief period that year, I, in my role as National League attorney, had filled the post, but a full-time man was needed. No one more enthusiastically supported that idea than I, as I had absolutely no desire to be locked into labor negotiations and administration.

There were two schools of thought on the selection: One group, which included Professor Jim Healy of the Harvard Business School, whom I had brought in as a consultant at the suggestion of Joe Cronin, favored the selection of a baseball man rather than a professional labor negotiator. The theory was that a baseball man would be less likely to provoke confrontation with the union; a professional would invite that.

Cronin, chairman of the Player Relations Committee (PRC), favored the baseball-man approach. So did I, and we canvassed the possibilities. I believe either Chub Feeney or the former Cleveland third baseman Al Rosen, who was in the financial-services business in Cleveland, could have had the job if they had been available, but neither was. So the sentiment shifted toward hiring a professional, the second school of thought, in order to face a professional with the same breed.

I have asked myself what might have happened had baseball gone the other way, as indeed happened in 1983 when a baseball man, Lee MacPhail, did take the post. My answer is that nothing very different would have happened. The key factor in negotiations has not been so much the bargaining leader on either side as it has been the ability of the respective sides to be cohesive. The players, young and less experienced, have been much more easily led and thus have stuck together. The owners, proud and opinionated, have always come asunder under pressure.

Our search produced one top candidate, John Gaherin, who had a long history of tough battles in the airline and New York newspaper industries. He knew the grueling work in the labor trenches.

I called Punch Sulzberger, the publisher of *The New York Times*, for a recommendation and got a strong one. American League attorney Jim Garner, who had represented Scripps-Howard interests, supported John. Harvard's Jim Healy went along, although reluctantly, preferring the baseball-man approach.

I recall an evening meeting in Washington at which I was to introduce Gaherin to the owners and present his credentials. As I was speaking, the Giants' Horace Stoneham crouched on the rostrum steps near my feet. As sometimes happened in those days before Horace mercifully took the pledge, he was several cups further into the refreshments than necessary. He punctuated my remarks with bellows of, "Where the hell is Lou Carroll?" Lou, of course, was my senior partner. When I plugged doggedly ahead, Horace began firing off one-word commentaries of "bullshit." Somehow we got Gaherin approved that night.

Gaherin set up shop in the Lincoln Building on Manhattan's Forty-second Street with legal counsel Barry Rona from my law firm and a secretary, Betty O'Connor, a great woman who had worked with John before. The PRC was now a full-time operation.

Gaherin was a character, although his public image was one of tight-lipped reserve. Like Miller, he professed little fan interest in baseball and found the rules complex, the personalities difficult. He had a store of jokes and Irish wisdom gleaned from his father. Many tense backroom moments were relieved by John's stories and his trenchant comments on the game's characters. He was an excellent student of human nature, as befitted a labor relations expert, and soon and accurately sorted out the good guys from the bad. Unfortunately, he developed some enemies early on, most notably Baltimore's Jerry Hoffberger, a PRC member. They had ugly confrontations, with Jerry more than once threatening to have John fired. The relationship with Jerry slowly induced in John a defensive attitude that adversely affected his effectiveness with the owners.

Miller's superiority with the press was also a major problem for John. Gaherin was never really successful with the press, though he worked at it. His snappingly effective backroom humor never translated publicly. Still, John was a skilled professional.

The benefits plan agreement we settled in my first month as commissioner was being renegotiated as Miller toured the spring training camps in 1972. At issue were highly technical questions involving asset gains and unfunded liability. Miller was scrapping for increased benefits beyond what the owners were willing to do, with the dreary result that we were well along in spring training with no agreement and no prospect of one.

Miller began polling the players in their spring camps for a strike authorization. Although there were some defections as the polling went on, particularly on the Red Sox, he eventually managed to collect an overwhelming majority for a strike, although this was hardly a strike issue. Why the strike vote? Either Miller's inexperience as a bargainer was showing and he was having difficulty knowing when to close a deal or he had decided to precipitate a strike as part of a strategy to intimidate the owners in the following year's negotiations on the basic agreement, which included the reserve system. By this point, having lost the Flood case on two judicial levels, and certainly with no reason to feel optimistic about the Supreme Court, after the oral argument there on March 20, it could have made sense to lay groundwork for the future. Either answer is plausible, and indeed both might have been correct. Still, I am inclined to think he was trying to deliver a message for the future.

The PRC strategy was to stand fast on what it felt was a fair offer. Among the club executives there was a divided view as to whether Miller was bluffing. Some felt that if Miller called a strike their players would not comply. They were in for a nasty lesson.

On April 1, with the season approaching, Miller called a strike and the training camps shut down. It was the first general strike in American sports history.

Unhappy as I was with a strike, I did not believe it would be a long one. If it was a show of strength, a demonstration that he could get the players to strike even on an issue of no great consequence, it would soon be over.

The PRC was in no mood to surrender to Miller, but I was careful to monitor the progress daily through Gaherin and the league presidents. I was confident that the clubs' position was fair and that there was a willingness to bargain in good faith.

Interestingly, Miller was getting roughed up in the press, a situation I watched very carefully. If Miller was getting hammered today, it could very well be the players tomorrow and the image of the players in the eyes of the fans was our most important asset.

The PRC had able owner-members working toward a resolution along with our capable bargaining team. They were Dick Meyer, Jerry Hoffberger, Frank Dale, Ewing Kauffman and Donald Grant. I was confident the strike would be controllable.

Finally, after thirteen days and eighty-six games, the strike was settled. The clubs agreed to contribute an additional $490,000 to the benefit plan in 1972, and to use $500,000 of the plan's profits for additional benefits. Miller called it an "honorable agreement." He said it was a matter of "human dignity."

"Ironically," he said, "this should bring the players and owners closer together. You don't have a good relationship when there are a superior and an inferior working under peaceful conditions." Miller's quote was quite consistent with my analysis of his motive in calling the strike: He had demonstrated that the players had the guts to strike. The "human dignity" talk was just familiar Miller rhetoric.

I held a press conference at which I said, "I think the players should have a players association and a capable leader of that association. I think Marvin Miller has done many beneficial things for the players—and I have told him so. But one of our mistakes was that both sides allowed too many people to talk for them.

"I hope we have all learned a lesson and I will work with people in baseball to institute procedures to prevent this sort of thing in the future."

That July we reduced the PRC from ten to six voting members and changed the voting rule for player matters to a simple majority of all the major-league clubs rather than a majority of each league. In 1973, we persuaded Milwaukee's Ed Fitzgerald to become PRC chairman. It was an important move. Widely respected within the game, he gave the PRC greater prestige among the clubs and provided Gaherin with the kind of constructive leadership that was needed in labor relations. He also brought a more modern and flexible attitude to baseball's player relations. That, too, was needed.

As for the 1972 season itself, attendance fell only by what could have been mathematically projected for the lost eighty-six games; there was no sign of fan discontent. Since the games were not made up, teams played different numbers of games for the season, leading to Detroit's edging Boston to win the American League's eastern division by a half game.

Having shown the owners in 1972 that he could lead his players into a strike, Miller was able to negotiate two significant modifications of the reserve system in 1973. He got the so-called ten-and-five rule, which meant that any ten-year veteran who had been with his club for the last five years could not be traded without his permission. He also got salary arbitration for the players. These would prove to be major achievements for the Players Association.

How was Miller able to achieve such improvements in the reserve system? Certainly, the 1972 strike had sent a message that was not lost on the owners a year later. Far more important was a more flexible management attitude as personified by Ed Fitzgerald. Ed viewed the baseball world with none of the biases that had previously hampered our labor relations. His outlook was completely practical and fair-minded. To the chagrin of some of our more traditional types, he saw no problem in modifying the reserve system if fairness required it. His views closely coincided with my own, which led to an easy and cordial alliance. Indeed, it transcended labor relations and developed into a broad working and personal relationship that was probably the most important I had with any owner.

Both Ed and I also well understood that the change was needed in baseball, was coming throughout professional sports and was required in baseball as a simple matter of equity, if nothing else. The changes adopted in 1973 proved to be more than fair. They also established the ability of the Association to achieve significant improvements in the reserve system by collective bargaining.

9

The Legacy of
Jackie Robinson

B y the time I became commissioner in 1969, a lively debate was percolating over whether stars of the old Negro Leagues, particularly Satchel Paige and Josh Gibson, should be considered for the Hall of Fame. Dick Young, the influential New York *Daily News* columnist and an activist in the affairs of the Baseball Writers Association of America, was behind the drive. It caught both my attention and sympathy.

In 1970, the first extensively researched history of the Negro Leagues, *Only the Ball Was White* by Robert Peterson, focused greater attention on the accomplishments of Negro League players.

I found unpersuasive and unimpressive the argument that the Hall of Fame would be "watered down" if men who had not played in the majors were admitted. "The rules are clear," said my opponents. "You need ten years of major-league service. Moreover, where are the statistics to support them? There was only sketchy and sloppy record keeping in the Negro Leagues."

I thought these arguments were much too technical under the circumstances. Through no fault of their own, the black players had been barred from the majors until 1947. Had they not been barred, there would have been great major-league players, and certainly Hall of Famers, among them. What applied after 1947 would have obviously applied before. This was precisely the kind of situation that required the bending of rules.

In early 1970, I held a meeting in my office to discuss our options. Ford Frick, who as National League president had been virtually the father of the Hall of Fame, was present and adamant against admitting the Negro Leaguers. Also present were Paul Kerr, the Hall of Fame president; Charley Segar, Joe Reichler and Monte Irvin, all three from my office; and Young and Jack Lang, representing the Baseball Writers Association.

The meeting was heated and unpleasant. Frick and Kerr took the negative position. Young was passionate and unrelenting in support of admitting black players. Though I categorically agreed with his arguments, I was offended by his rudeness to Frick. Wrong though Frick may have been on this issue, no one could challenge his honesty, genuineness or decency. Oddly enough, as a result Young and I, who were allies, had the most heated words of all. Nonetheless, out of that stormy little meeting grew a committee and a plan. It seemed obvious to me that the opposition was too formidable, at least for the time being. I certainly did not have the votes on the Hall of Fame's board of directors. So I decided to slip around their flank and look for an opening. In February 1971 I created a committee of Negro League experts whose assignment it was to determine the greatest players of the Negro Leagues. Once identified, these players would be honored with a display at the Baseball Museum at Cooperstown.

A predictable furor ensued. Cries of "Jim Crow" were heard; we were again treating these players separately, putting them through a back door in Cooperstown. Jackie Robinson, the NAACP and all sorts of activist groups spoke out in protest. I was placed under personal attack for putting forth the idea.

I knew that the furor would be heard by the board of directors and that the public outcry would be hard to resist. That is exactly what happened. By 1971, the board decided to give our committee the power to vote in members on a full and equal footing with everyone else. Satchel Paige, named in February as the first "honoree," was now made a full-fledged member.

The committee consisted of ex-players Roy Campanella, Bill Yancey, Eppie Barnes, Judy Johnson and Monte Irvin, writers Sam Lacy and Wendell Smith, and organizers Eddie Gottlieb, Frank Forbes and Alex Pompez. Dick Young and Joe Reichler were nonvoting members.

Satchel Paige was spirited into New York under the guise of receiving an award, but when he arrived he was told he was to be the first Hall of Fame inductee from the Negro Leagues. At the press conference that followed he was superb: colorful, witty, discursive and just pure Satchel. If he was bitter, he gave very little sign of it. And he was touched. That was the lovely part of it for me. This marvelous, zany character, who may have been the greatest pitcher of all time, was touched. Moments like that made the job of commissioner very worthwhile.

A by-product of Paige's election was his feeling that one of the perquisites of Hall of Fame membership was using the commissioner as a personal complaint department. Over the years, until his death in 1982, I had many calls from Satch grumbling about transportation and expense arrangements and other miscellaneous problems. While these often involved events foreign to my office, I always found some solution. I doubt that it ever occurred to Satch that there was anything out of the ordinary about this procedure, and somehow I rather enjoyed it. It kept us in touch.

In 1972 Josh Gibson and Buck Leonard were inducted. They were followed by Monte Irvin in 1973, Cool Papa Bell in 1974, Judy Johnson in 1975, Oscar Charleston in 1976 and Martin Dihigo and Pop Lloyd in 1977. Leonard, Irvin, Johnson and Bell were all living. They may be the most gracious group of athletes I have seen.

After 1977, the committee informed the Hall of Fame directors that their work was done and they thought they should disband. There came yet another cry from some segments of the public saying that it was an injustice to end the work of this committee. But as the idea had come from the committee itself, I found no fault with the decision. Further, we expanded the powers of the Hall of Fame Veterans Committee to include Negro League players in future considerations. They selected Rube Foster in 1981 and will doubtless select others.

Each year at Cooperstown, in a dinner preceding the induction ceremony, the league presidents award Hall of Fame rings to new members associated with their respective leagues. As there was no league president around for the Negro Leagues, the honor fell to me, and the Negro League players became "my" players. The relationship that grew with these men was warm and special; we made it a tradition to pose for a "team picture" each year, just me and "my guys." When Happy Chandler became a Hall of Famer in 1982 he joined our group, as he had been the commissioner when the color line was broken.

The Negro League players I came to know (and they included

more than the Hall of Famers) were among my favorite people, real salt-of-the-earth men. Rather than expressing any bitterness over having been denied access to the major leagues, these men had a genuine and infectious fondness for baseball and the old days of the Negro Leagues. The old broken-down buses, the missed paychecks, the lousy facilities, the games against white major-league barnstorming teams, the camaraderie, all were the sources of wonderful tales of a time when men had great fun playing baseball, sadly, an observation made less and less these days.

In later years, I became a supporter of plans to develop a Negro Baseball Hall of History in Ashland, Kentucky, where an annual reunion of former players was held beginning in 1979. Monte Irvin represented me at these reunions except in 1983, when I attended myself. I doubt that I ever enjoyed a baseball event more. Though we were unable to raise adequate financing to create the Ashland museum, a better solution was found in 1985 when the Cooperstown Hall of Fame agreed to take charge of the Negro League artifacts and display them in Cooperstown. This display will in time be seen as a real treasure, since the day is coming when we will have no one left to attend those reunions and tell the wonderful tales of the Negro Leagues.

Jackie Robinson, who played in the Negro Leagues in 1945, was the first black player to make the Hall of Fame. He was the most exciting player I have ever seen. Having come to New York in 1950, I had many opportunities to watch him in person at Ebbets Field and the Polo Grounds, and at Yankee Stadium in October. Perhaps there has never been anything so exciting in baseball as Jackie Robinson caught in a rundown. He was the most electrifying player of my time, full of the unexpected. The memories are indelible: Jackie the hitter, bat poised high; Jackie the runner, forcing pickoff throws to first, moving that large body with incredible quickness; Jackie with that proud bearing, giving no ground to anyone.

He would steal the big base—not marginally important ones, but big ones—with games on the line, like his steal of home in the 1955 World Series. Although Yogi Berra still swears he tagged him in time, Robinson was a winner, and maybe aggressive winners get calls their way. Jackie only led the league in stolen bases twice and only topped thirty once; yet there was something electric about him on the basepaths. Lou Brock and Maury Wills, who stole so many more bases, never quite had his dramatic qualities. Joe Morgan, among more recent players, may have come closest.

Though Robinson was hardly a diplomat, I respected his tough outspokenness. He was an eloquent speaker with a distinctive timbre to his voice that stamped it "Jackie Robinson" and no one else. He was unique among all baseball players and ranks among a handful of the game's greatest figures. To borrow a line from Howard Cosell about Jackie: "He was, in a word, unconquerable."

Except for giving him a ride to O'Hare Airport after we both spoke at the American Management Association lunch in Chicago in 1971, I had no contact with Robinson until 1972. He had avoided baseball functions, making it clear that his boycott was a message that baseball was not treating black players fairly. He felt they were not being hired for front-office positions, not being selected for the final spots on rosters and, most importantly to Jackie, not being considered for managerial jobs.

The 1972 season was the twenty-fifth anniversary of his Brooklyn debut. Given the cataclysmic importance of that 1947 event, I thought a suitable baseball recognition was imperative. I asked Joe Reichler, my public relations director, who had covered Jackie for the Associated Press, to contact him about a ceremony at the World Series. I was disappointed but not surprised when the reaction was negative. I asked Joe to go back and suggest to Jackie that we at least talk about it over lunch. Jackie agreed and met Reichler and me on June 20 at the St. Regis Hotel in Manhattan.

Robinson was impressive both in appearance and personality. His strong, handsome visage was mellowed only modestly by his ever-whitening hair. The formidable, challenging personality had not mellowed at all. He gave scant recognition to his seriously failing eyesight, the sad product of his diabetes. If there was any self-pity, this proud man showed none of it. His richly textured voice added a final dimension to a thoroughly extraordinary personality. My mind wandered back to Branch Rickey and 1947 and I thought to myself of Robinson, "God, he was perfect."

If he had come to debate the situation of baseball's blacks, he found no takers. It was readily apparent that we shared the same concerns. As to a black manager, I told him I was working to get that accomplished and was confident I would be successful. Of particular interest to him was my opinion that there was more ownership support than I had imagined. I think he was encouraged by my assessment and by my commitment to the cause that meant so much to him. In any event, he promised to give some thought to participating in a World Series ceremony. I was elated several weeks later when he gave me a positive answer, elated not so much because it meant we could go ahead with the ceremony but rather because his acceptance of the event meant that he had also accepted my commitment.

There was a sidelight to our St. Regis lunch that I will never forget. At one point I looked down and noticed we were wearing identical black shoes. It turned out that we were both wearing size 13 shoes purchased from the same retail shop in New York. What was memorable was not so much the coincidence as the discovery that this most electrifying baserunner had done it all on size 13 feet!

We arranged for Red Barber to be the master of ceremonies and had Jackie and his wife, Rachel, on the field for the second game of the 1972 World Series in Cincinnati. Red, who had been the Brooklyn announcer when Robinson arrived there, was both touching and sensitive in handling the field assignment. Jackie got a superb reception and, true to himself, made a plea for a black manager. He credited me with supporting that cause.

Jackie and Rachel sat with Luisa and me during the game, in which he took a keen interest. Heartbreakingly, his vision problems frequently necessitated his asking us what had happened. I recall his watching Bobby Tolan of the Reds and commenting on the inefficiency of Tolan's high bat posture. That was particularly interesting since Jackie himself had had a very memorable high bat posture. He asked if I could arrange to get him to the Cincinnati clubhouse after the game so he could talk to Tolan. I arranged for several security men to take him there. We said goodbye warmly and he went off, half supported by the security men, to help Tolan. I never saw him again.

Nine days later I was in Scottsdale, Arizona, at a meeting of our general managers. It was there I received a message that Jackie Robinson was dead. When I announced it the room fell respectfully silent. Very appropriate, but somehow I wanted the ground to shake.

Less than two years after Jackie's death, Frank Robinson, baseball's first black manager, was hired to manage the Cleveland Indians. I said publicly that I was delighted but that it had taken too long to happen and baseball should take no bows. At Cleveland owner Ted Bonda's invitation, I attended the press conference in Cleveland at which the announcement was made. I wished Jackie could have been there. He would have been proud of Frank, who gave a poised and adroit performance, reflecting the intelligence and baseball savvy that had earned him the job. The most memorable moment for me came when a reporter asked Bonda, "Did Commissioner Kuhn play a role in Frank's hiring?"

Without hesitation, Ted replied, "No, not at all."

I couldn't believe it. For years I'd been lobbying our most progressive owners, including Bonda, on the matter of a black manager. I'd lobbied some of the less progressive ones, too. At last, the efforts had paid off.

After the press conference, I said to Bonda, "I was a little surprised at your answer."

"Oh, Commissioner, I just didn't want to embarrass you," he replied.

There have been black managers since and there will be more. Blacks have turned down managing jobs. Still, there will be more of them because, like Bonda, who hired Frank Robinson, there are owners in baseball with social consciences. That may come as a surprise to a great many people, but it is true. There have been commissioners of the same stripe.

Opening Day in Cleveland, 1974, was one of the most memorable I ever attended. There were 56,715 fans in vast, old, Depression-built Municipal Stadium. The weather was cold and misty, but the enthusiasm was enormous. We had pregame ceremonies on the field. Rachel Robinson said, "I want to congratulate you all for honoring yourselves by being the first to take this historic step. I've wished since I was asked to do this that Jackie could be here, and I'm sure in many ways he is. I hope this is the beginning of a lot more black managers being moved into front office and managerial positions and not just having their talents exploited on the field."

I went upstairs to join Frank's wife, Barbara, and his two children, Kevin and Nichelle. Rachel threw out the first ball and joined us, too. We had hardly settled into our seats when Frank, who had been signed as a player-manager, came up as designated hitter in the last of the first. On a 2–2 pitch from Yankee George Medich, he lined a long home run into the left-field stands. We celebrated the glorious moment with hugs and kisses. It was one of those isolated but luminous moments in my time as commissioner when I felt tears shimmering in my eyes.

A year later, when fans in each city voted on their team's most memorable moment in history, do you think Lou Boudreau's managing the Indians to the 1948 pennant won? Bill Wambsganss' unassisted triple play in the World Series? Bob Feller's three no-hitters, including one on opening day? The team's record 111 victories in 1954? None of them. It was Frank Robinson's opening-day home run as player-manager.

I first met Rachel Robinson at the 1972 World Series ceremony honoring her husband. I have seen a lot of her in the ensuing years, through travail and joy. I first saw her after the Series at Jackie's funeral at Riverside Church in New York. Luisa and I, following the scriptural injunction, sat at the rear. Rachel, following that same injunction, sent word that we were to move forward. It was there that we heard the Reverend Jesse Jackson preaching a moving, eloquent eulogy for Robinson. It was dramatic as only Jackson can be. It was also very good. Was it my imagination or did the ground finally tremble for Jackie?

Rachel has a lot of qualities, one of which is a sense of humor. It has always given her a somewhat leavened view of the troubled world, more leavened than Jackie's. He always rode a charger and carried a lance. Rachel got to the same places but in her own way. I once introduced her as Rachel Jackson. As she reached the microphone, she put her arm around an embarrassed Kuhn and whispered to me, "It's okay; we all look alike." She has never stopped needling me about that moment, and I doubt that she intends to.

After I left baseball, at Rachel's invitation I joined the board of directors of the Jackie Robinson Foundation, which helps educate underprivileged young people. As commissioner, I had helped in various ways with the funding of the foundation's programs. I still try to help Rachel fulfill Jackie's ideals. That is more a blessing for me than for Rachel because she is a beautiful person, not only literally but spiritually, in a way that makes being in her company a privilege.

Hiring blacks for front-office jobs has proven difficult for baseball, due to the combination of a certain amount of management reluctance, the unwillingness of former black players to accept management salary levels and the reluctance of qualified blacks to take front-office jobs.

Although blacks are measurably strong baseball fans, there has always been a notable failing on the part of the major leagues to turn them into paying customers. Why this is, I have never been quite sure. It obviously is not an economic problem, as blacks attend other entertainment events in great numbers, paying higher ticket prices.

I have had many conversations over the years with black leaders, black players and black fans, but no one has ever given me a satisfactory explanation for this phenomenon. Perhaps one black educator in St. Louis came closest when he told me that "somehow, they don't feel welcome in a ballpark. There's a feeling that it's a white man's place to be."

A greater presence of blacks in the front office would serve the clubs well in relating better to the black community. It would also help in finding answers for the lack of black attendance. Even Bill Veeck, who related as well to the black community as any owner baseball has ever had—he was the man who had the first black player (Larry Doby) and second black manager in the American League (Larry Doby again), as well as the one who brought Satchel Paige to the majors—was unable to solve the riddle of the black fan.

10

While Addressing the Wahoo Club . . .

B eginning in 1974, the year he broke Babe Ruth's career record of 714 home runs, I had two relationships with Henry Aaron: one through the press and one personal.

Aaron had concluded the 1973 season with 713 homers, so it was obvious that he would tie and then break Ruth's record early in the 1974 season. It would be a remarkable achievement, one that even ten years earlier had been considered unattainable by anyone. Think of the magnitude of the accomplishment—if you averaged 35 home runs a season for twenty years, you would still come up short.

Bill Bartholomay, the owner of the Braves, decided in early February that Aaron would *not* make history on the road. The Braves were scheduled to open the season with a three-game series in Cincinnati, and Bartholomay publicly announced that Aaron would not play in those games. He said Aaron would make his season debut in the Braves' home opener on April 8 against the Dodgers. He was perfectly honest about his reasoning: It would be an accommodation to the Atlanta fans and a financial windfall for the Braves. Both reasons were valid from his point of view. It was also a classic case where overriding baseball interests were more important than the club's. In keeping Aaron out of the lineup in Cincinnati, the Braves would not be putting forth their best effort to beat the Reds. It was a matter of the game's integrity.

Baseball has always paid a price for the honor of being known as the "national game." It has traditionally set higher standards of integrity than other sports and been willing to make financial sacrifices to do so. It had recognized its obligations to the public since the days of the Black Sox and Commissioner Landis. Every commissioner since then had sought to enforce those standards and meet that obligation. Sometimes the issue has been fairly clear-cut, such as Landis's lifetime ban of an owner who had been betting on games or my decision in the Parvin-Dohrmann case. Lineup questions, such as those presented by the Aaron case, were not usually so clear-cut. For instance, when a manager juggled his pitching rotation on the road so his premier pitcher opened a home stand, was the manager doing his best to win or was he generating extra dollars at the gate? This was a harder question to call, and commissioners had to live with this sort of thing. If you pressed the manager, you would hear that the pitcher needed an extra day of rest. But Aaron was perfectly capable of playing in Cincinnati just as he had been through most of 1973, when he started two of every three Braves games.

I telephoned Bartholomay and told him I had a major problem with his decision. Asking him to reflect on the matter, I strongly urged him to play Aaron in Cincinnati. I wanted Bill to make the decision for himself. I much preferred to work by persuasion where feasible, and Bill was a reasonable type who would see the light— or so I told myself.

I took my family to Florida for ten days, beginning February 14, while the press continued to speculate on the merits of Aaron's sitting out the opening series. One evening, *New York Times* baseball writer Joe Durso and I talked at length about Aaron. Joe seemed to feel that Aaron should be promptly ordered to play in at least two of the three Cincinnati games, since that had been his pace in 1973. I think Joe felt I was too courteous to the Braves in giving them time to make their own decision. From a public relations point of view he was no doubt right. There is among some in the press an unmistakable, almost romantic yearning for sports leaders who autocratically assert their authority over those "arrogant owners," telling them on a daily basis to march this way and that according to the whim of the leader. That surely makes good headlines and in the short term at least is good for the leader's image, but I am afraid it is also bad government whether in sports or politics. The abuse of power is more dangerous than leadership problems associated with a more restrained style. Ultimately, the latter course is more productive.

Bartholomay visited me in New York on March 4. I told him it would be far better if he made his own decision, making it clear that I would write Aaron into the lineup myself if he left me no alternative. I was confident he would go along. We had been close for nearly a decade, going back to the days of our common cause in moving the Braves to Atlanta. I thought I could read his mind. I was wrong. He stubbornly stood his ground, arguing that lineups had been tuned to the gate on many occasions in baseball history without interference from the commissioner. Ever so politely, he challenged me to write his lineup. I assured him I would. If Bill had not been so open in the way he handled the Aaron matter, he probably could have gotten his way. If Aaron had somehow been "hurt" in Cincinnati, with no advance publicity, there would have been little I could do.

On March 18, I sent the following letter to Bill:

As I advised you on the telephone last week, I will expect you to use Henry Aaron in the opening series in Cincinnati in accordance with the pattern of his use in 1973 when he started approximately two of every three Braves' games. Of course, this would be barring disability.

Notwithstanding our disagreement on this subject, I have confidence that you will carry out the requirements of this letter. The only way to do so is to lean over backward in the event of a question arising about his use. Any doubt should be resolved in favor of starting him and continuing to use him in any game. Obviously, it would appear very much amiss if he did not start the opening game.

I would have to view any failure to comply with the requirements of this letter as not in the best interests of Baseball, necessitating the imposition of penalties. I feel that any such failure would result in a grave injury to Baseball's reputation, including the reputation for integrity on the field. Therefore, the penalties would have to be commensurate with the seriousness of the offense and could include those provided in the Major League Agreement and Major League Rule 21, as well as the suspension of the benefit of Major League rules as provided in Major League Rule 50.

The reputation of the game is in your hands.

Sincerely yours,

Bowie Kuhn

With reluctance, Bartholomay said he would comply. Eddie Mathews, the Atlanta manager, made some rather feisty comments in the newspapers attacking the decision, and Aaron echoed that view.

Cincinnati is always the scene of the National League opener, an honor that goes to the Reds, founded in 1869, for having been the first professional team. I invited Vice President Ford to attend, and Luisa and I flew from Andrews Air Force Base to Cincinnati with him in *Air Force Two.*

Jerry Ford ranks at about the top of my list of favorite politicians. I suspect that a lot of people who know American politics would agree. As I found him, the private Ford was the same man the public saw. Whether he was congressman, vice president or president, he was the same man. No pretensions emerged, no exaltation of himself. I remember his telling me that Reggie Jackson had invited him to attend a baseball chapel service with the Oakland A's when they visited Baltimore. He was impressed with Jackson's interest in the subject and with the whole idea of a baseball team's gathering together for a prayer service. But he said he did not think he would do it. Somehow it would be "inappropriate." It was plain enough that the vice president had no intention of using a religious service to attract attention to himself. While the style was modest, he exhibited a quiet confidence in himself that instilled trust, confidence and affection in others.

Luisa and I were five minutes late for our rendezvous with the vice president at Andrews. He showed not a trace of annoyance as we hustled onto the aircraft. Once aloft, the vice president turned the conversation to baseball's newly adopted salary arbitration system and whether it had any application to other industrial situations. In addition, he covered the great Aaron debate, baseball chapel and the manufacture of a correct martini. With the courtesy of a perfect host, he asked if I had any objection to a brief detour so the plane could fly over the city of Xenia, Ohio, which had been devasted a day earlier by a tornado that had killed thirty people. Coming in low over the city and circling, *Air Force Two* gave us an appalling view of the damage wrought by the tornado. The problems of baseball fell into proper perspective.

Finally arriving at Riverfront Stadium, we were seated behind the Reds' dugout. Dick Wagner, a top executive of the Reds, was seated across the aisle with other club executives and their wives. The vice president threw out the first ball and the game was under way.

Jack Billingham, one of the players used to settle the Clendenon-Staub deal five years earlier, was on the mound for the Reds. Since Aaron was scheduled as the fourth hitter, the fans began to stir when Ralph Garr walked to open the game. After the next two batters were retired Aaron came to bat. The excitement was palpable. When Billingham ran the count to 3–1, I turned to Vice President Ford and said, "This isn't a bad place for it." With that, Aaron took his first swing of 1974 and coolly drilled Number 714 well over Pete Rose's head into the left-field stands. Knowing they had seen one of the very greatest moments in baseball history, the crowd went wild. It was also a tribute to Henry and his remarkable professionalism. With all the pressure, with all the debate, with all the sports world watching, he took one swing in his first at bat and did the job.

Arrangements had been made with the Reds to stop the game so that the vice president and I could walk onto the field for a brief ceremony. Apparently, no one had bothered to inform Dick Wagner, and he ran the stadium. When the ladder to let us on the field did not appear, I turned to Wagner and asked where it was. Dick was an able executive who had helped make the Reds one of our finest organizations, but he could be stubborn. Baseball people called him "the Field Marshal" and pronounced his name, in German, like the opera composer's.

"Nobody's going on the field," he said. "We won't interrupt the game."

This was not a time for gentle persuasion. Gerald Ford was on his feet right behind me.

"Dick," I said, "this is very simple. The vice president is going to participate in a field ceremony right now. You have a ladder brought out, or you're suspended immediately." We glared at one another. Then he called for the ladder and we had the ceremony. The vice president handled it charmingly, giving no sign that he was aware of Wagner's behavior.

The controversy in Cincinnati then took a new turn. Aaron was still required to start one more game. But before Game 2 on Saturday, manager Eddie Mathews called a press conference. "We've been fair enough," said Mathews. "My thinking changed now that he's hit the homer."

He announced that Aaron would not play Saturday or Sunday and would next appear on Monday night in the Braves' home opener.

"Right or wrong, this is Eddie Mathews's decision," he said.

Johnny Johnson, our administrator, was in Cincinnati to keep his eyes on the Braves, whose past performance in the Aaron matter had done little to instill our confidence in them. He called me and told me about the press conference and Mathews's remarks. We agreed that there was no basis for changing my edict and that Aaron was to play one of the two remaining games in Cincinnati. I did not care which. Johnson was to so advise Mathews in the strongest possible terms. To say I was annoyed at the Braves would grossly understate the situation.

Mathews then released a statement that said: "The commissioner has unlimited powers to impose very serious penalties on individuals or the ballclub itself. For the first time I realize that these penalties are not only fines but also suspensions and other threats to the franchise itself. Because of this order and the threatened penalties, I intend to start Hank Aaron tomorrow."

Aaron faced Clay Kirby three times, grounding out and taking two called third strikes. "I couldn't believe he didn't swing on an 0–2 count," said Kirby.

The Braves went home for their opener on Monday night.

My schedule for Monday was a day of work in the office and a long-standing speaking engagement in Cleveland to address the Wahoo Club, a booster organization for the Indians. As a matter of protocol, I asked Monte Irvin to represent me in Atlanta and stay with the Braves until the record fell. Obviously, there was no telling when that might happen. I told Monte I would join him at some point in Atlanta although, given the behavior of the Braves, I had no enthusiasm for such a trip.

Monte and his wife, Dee, packed enough clothes for two weeks. Even Henry Aaron, after all, could have a home-run drought. They found Atlanta Stadium packed with enthusiastic fans. The nation tuned in with NBC on hand for its first Monday-night telecast of the season and a vast press corps as well.

Meanwhile, in snow-covered Cleveland, I was exhorting the Wahoo Club to support the Indians. Was it a wise public relations move? Probably not, although I can assure you I had all the votes in Cleveland that night. Maybe commissioners should worry more about the Clevelands of baseball anyway. Having seen Aaron hit Number 714, I felt no obligation to follow him day by day until Number 715 came along. Who could predict when that would be?-But I have a stubborn notion that media concerns inordinately dominate the thinking of public figures. I put that notion into frequent practice and clearly paid a price for doing so. By hindsight, would I have opted for Cleveland or Atlanta? The answer is Cleveland, but how I wish I could have been two people in two places that night.

For whatever reason, the Braves gave Monte a hard time with his seating. In the process, he and Dee were separated. The game began, and in the last of the first Aaron came to bat with the crowd roaring. Al Downing, pitching for the Dodgers, walked him on a 3–1 pitch. He came up again in the fourth. Downing threw one in the dirt for a ball; then he came in with a low fastball. Aaron swung, and the ball took off toward a BankAmericard billboard that said THINK OF IT AS MONEY in the Braves' bullpen. Number 715.

Poor Monte, still struggling for his seats, barely got to the field in time for the chaotic ceremonies. Dutifully introduced as "here representing Commissioner Bowie Kuhn . . . ," he received a cascade of boos.

If they ever decide to start the Hall of Fame all over and place decency above all else, Monte would be the first man in. This man is one of the sweetest people I have ever known. I doubt that he was ever booed; well, maybe a little at Ebbets Field where he wore the visiting uniform of the hated Giants. There was not a finer man in baseball, nor could I have had a more responsible and dignified representative. And now they were showing Monte their anger, anger meant for me.

At this point, Aaron began periodically criticizing me in the media, usually about my failure to be in Atlanta for Number 715. This, I imagine, reflected Henry's frustration over what he felt was a general lack of recognition and appreciation of his historic achievement in breaking Ruth's record. He somehow saw my absence as an effort to demean this achievement. Nothing could have been further from the fact. I doubt that anyone was more outspoken in praise of his superb career than I. But Henry was undaunted and continued his attacks on me, which seemed to inspire a mimicry in the press. Year after year I would read about my inexcusable absence from Atlanta and what an affront this had been to Henry Aaron. The obvious insinuation was that my absence was a product of my being antiblack. The job of being commissioner was a wonderful way to learn patience.

Whenever Aaron and I met, however, he was the soul of friendship and good humor. Never a bad word, never a criticism. This was the Aaron who reminded me of his parents, whom I had met on various occasions. They were lovely. His mother was robust, outgoing and friendly, with an easy smile like Henry's; his father was a slight, quiet, serious man who engaged easily in conversation. Somehow, even when Aaron would make his most biting attacks on me, I would try to think of his parents and his finer qualities. That helped. Make no mistake about it, attacks from decent people (among whom I number Aaron) hurt. I never adjusted to Aaron's criticism, however unfounded I knew it to be.

In 1980, at a magazine reception in New York, I was to present him with a plaque for producing the 1970s' most memorable moment. Aaron, who had accepted an invitation to attend, sent a representative who read a carping statement recalling my absence from Atlanta six years before: "I understand that Mr. Kuhn requested that he present me with the award for the outstanding moment of the 1970s in honor and recognition of the all-time home-run record set on the eighth of April, 1974. However, looking back on that time, I remember the commissioner did not see the need to attend."

I was embarrassed for Aaron. Such an obvious stunt was beneath his dignity. The press gave this newest attack on me full coverage but privately their reaction was much like mine. Henry was chipping apart the monument that his incomparable career records had created.

In September 1981, I went to Atlanta for a press luncheon given by a committee that was endeavoring to fund a statue of Henry, to be built at the stadium. What I was doing there after all the grief he had given me is hard to explain. I imagine it was partly an exercise in turning the other cheek. It also reflected my stubborn affection for Aaron no matter what. We sat together, shook hands and embraced. It was very genuine and touching. "I think we both understand each other and it's all over with," said Aaron. I said, "History is history, and people will view it as they choose to view it. I'm just here because I think the commissioner of baseball ought to be here. It's better in some cases to forget the past."

11

Charles O. Finley

He had few redeeming virtues as far as I was concerned. Charles Oscar Finley owned the Kansas City and Oakland Athletics from 1961 to 1980. One more like him and I would have gone to work for Marvin Miller.

Before I became commissioner, I was in Joe Cronin's Boston office once during a telephone conversation between Joe, then president of the American League, and Finley. I could hear most of the conversation. It was a long, obscene call. Finley was abusive, disrespectful and coarse, painstakingly and repetitively so. Joe patiently heard him out. I was appalled, not only by Finley's gutter mouth but by his disrespect for Joe. Since my early childhood, Joe Cronin had been one of my idols. I had come to know him personally in the 1960s and developed a special affection for him. What I had heard Finley saying was unforgivable. When Joe put the telephone down, I said, "Joe, you should hang up on that miserable bastard; you should not put up with that." I would have to say that Joe was a better Christian than I. He replied, "Oh, that's just Charlie, you have to let him run on." (This from a man who could be volcanic on those rare instances when he was enraged.)

I first seriously focused on Finley in 1967, when he persuaded the American League to let him move the Athletics from Kansas City to Oakland for the 1968 season. As I watched the baseball scene from my lawyer's vantage point he had always seemed like a gadfly to me. The mules and goats, the preposterous ideas, the petulant release of Hawk Harrelson, all gave Finley's operation a Three

Stooges look. At worst he had been an embarrassment to baseball and Kansas City. Now he suddenly looked more like a dragonfly as he cajoled the American League into the tomfoolery of permitting him to move to Oakland. Knuckling under to despots, petty or grand, guarantees problems to come. That would prove painfully true in Finley's case.

During a 1967 conversation between American League lawyer Sandy Hadden, Washington lawyer Paul Porter and myself, we agreed that Finley was becoming more of a menace and that a good lawyer might give him a little stability. After sorting out a number of names, Porter came up with John Paul Stevens of Chicago, who is now an associate justice of the United States Supreme Court. Stevens had represented the minority Republicans on Chairman Emanuel Celler's House committee, which had evaluated baseball's antitrust status in the early 1950s. He was highly regarded by those in the baseball community who had worked with him. While we doubted that Finley would pay much attention to our suggestion, Sandy discussed it with him. To my considerable surprise, Finley liked the idea and retained Stevens, whose influence proved to be beneficial for Charlie. Unfortunately for baseball, he adroitly argued for the ill-conceived transfer of the A's to Oakland before moving to the federal bench in 1970.

My first battle with Finley after I became commissioner was in May 1970 over Reggie Jackson. In 1969, a twenty-three-year-old Reggie had hit thirty-seven home runs by the All-Star break and forty-seven for the season. Paid $20,000 in 1969, he sought $75,000 for 1970. Finley offered $40,000 and would not budge. Signing only ten days before the season opened, Reggie started slowly. In June, Finley announced he was sending Jackson to the minors. This was ludicrous, exactly the kind of abuse of the reserve system that, if tolerated, would ultimately destroy both the system and public confidence in the game. Most club decisions to farm players out were made for good and sensible reasons, mutually benefiting both club and player. This was not such a decision. I reprimanded Finley.

As I would later testify, Finley's action "was a threat directed at a star ballplayer and it was a clear abuse of our system. It played right into the hands of the critics of the reserve system by suggesting that club owners held complete power over their players and that such power could be exercised arbitrarily or capriciously. In addition, the action was unfair because it was motivated by personal reasons unrelated to Jackson's ability."

It was my feeling that the particular source of Finley's immediate anger was Jackson's refusal to attend a team barbecue at Charlie's LaPorte, Indiana, estate.

Finley, reacting as if I had suspended him for life, requested a hearing. He came to my office with Bill Myers, who had been a partner of John Paul Stevens and had succeeded Stevens as Finley's attorney. Here we were, Bowie and Charlie, face-to-face in controversy for the first time—but not the last.

At first glance, the well-dressed, white-haired fifty-two-year-old man across the table seemed normal enough, hardly the devil or the buffoon his baseball conduct often made him appear to be. He looked very much like what he was, a successful insurance salesman, nothing to create alarm. But then one noticed the voice and the eyes. The eyes were dark, riveting, cold. They fastened on what they saw like talons. Had mirth or kindness ever danced there? I think not. The voice had a rasping, low, nervous quality and was punctuated by little coughs and hesitations.

Finley argued that the commissioner had no right to meddle in individual club-player relationships, that there were subtleties there beyond my fathoming, that there was no precedent for my action and that I had opened a Pandora's box of problems that I would regret. While there were factual flaws in his presentation, it was the right argument to make. Backed up by Myers, Finley made his case well enough and with more decency than would characterize some of his later performances. I told him I would take it under advisement. Soon after, I advised him by letter that I was standing by my decision.

While this was the first of many instances where I would rule against Finley, we were not invariably at odds. From the beginning, we cooperated on the designated hitter and other experimental rules. I supported and applauded him on the adoption of more colorful and stylish uniforms. Indeed, the green and gold Oakland colors came pretty close to being my favorites. I made no secret of my respect for the skill and tenacity he personally showed in developing Oakland championship teams in 1972, 1973 and 1974. Later, we were oddly matched partners in efforts to move the A's out of Oakland. He even once doubled a postgame fireworks display when Luisa and I were in Oakland, having discovered that Luisa liked fireworks. When Luisa thanked him, he was pure Charlie in explaining that it had cost him "an extra hundred bucks."

But more characteristically we were battling, always in situations that started with questionable conduct or public remarks on his part. I never took action against him unless provoked, and at all times, in accordance with my policy, I avoided provocative public statements about him. At times that took Herculean efforts, but I managed it. If I talked about him in speeches, it was usually to repeat something he had said about me: "Charlie said last week he had good news and bad news about Commissioner Kuhn [always pronounced "coon" by Charlie]; the good news is that our good commissioner is going to Japan; the bad news is that he has a round-trip ticket." That was very mild by Finley's standards. After he left baseball, I missed having fresh Finley stories to tell. Still, there were plenty of the old ones.

The Oakland A's of the early 1970s, winners of five straight division titles and three consecutive world championships, were a beautifully constructed team. The architect was Finley. He sensed correctly that he could develop a winner once the amateur free-agent draft was adopted in 1965. It favored the second-division clubs like the A's. If they selected well, they had access to the best talent. A form of baseball socialism, the new draft rule was meant to penalize the strong organizations like the Yankees and Dodgers and benefit their weaker partners. It did just that. Finley was shrewd enough to hire top-quality scouts so as to correctly identify the best talent. After a young high school player had been drafted by the A's, Finley often personally negotiated with the player and his family. If it meant donning an apron and frying chicken in Blue Moon Odom's kitchen to impress his parents, Finley did it. By all reports, he did it well. He also very effectively picked the brains of other clubs on player matters. Because this was like Ford's getting General Motors to help on a new car design, I was always puzzled by the amount of help he got. He called general managers and sought their evaluation of trades or player moves he was considering. And they helped him! This was all the more remarkable when you realize that most of their bosses could not stand Finley. He was getting the best baseball advice in the world absolutely free—and from the very fellows who were competing with him for talent. The only fair deduction is that he was a superb salesman. I say "deduction" because, while I personally never saw any hard evidence to prove the point, it was hard to quarrel with the results. I got a sample of the Finley technique from a general manager who said Finley had just called and left him in stitches. Finley's opening line was, "Finley's meat market . . . players for sale." I guess some people thought that was funny.

Even before the free-agent draft began in 1965, he had managed to sign Bert Campaneris, Dick Green, Rollie Fingers, Joe Rudi, Paul Lindblad, Odom and Jim Hunter, whom he promptly nicknamed "Catfish." He got Rick Monday in the first draft and later traded him to the Cubs for Ken Holtzman. He drafted Sal Bando from Arizona State and a year later drafted his teammate Reggie Jackson, lucking out when the Mets, with first choice, took a catcher named Steve Chilcott. Year by year, he filled in more pieces, drafting Gene Tenace, Phil Garner and, finally, Vida Blue (who declined Finley's nickname "True").

In skillful trades, he picked Mike Epstein, Darold Knowles, Ray Fosse, Deron Johnson and other veteran players to round out his roster. I think it was the best baseball team we have seen in some decades. That was bitter gall for the other owners, who detested Finley, and that, I suspect, was part of his inspiration. In all candor, I myself found it distasteful to hand Finley the world championship trophy for three straight years. Nor was that obvious fact lost on him.

Finley had a knack for stirring up petty problems. One year he invited Mayor Joe Alioto of San Francisco to throw out the first ball at a World Series game in Oakland. This was an obvious insult to Oakland and part of his continuing war with that community and its leaders. Finley always conducted guerrilla warfare against people with whom he did business. I reminded him by telephone that the World Series is played under my jurisdiction. I told him there was no way I would embarrass the city of Oakland. He told me, "Commissioner, I don't give a damn what you think." There were more expletives but that conveys the idea. He refused to cancel Mayor Alioto. I told him I would. I called the mayor, who completely understood, remarking, "I thought it was strange myself."

Finley also had a gift for embarrassing and demeaning people. At World Series games, it was customary to have the home team assign a person to the commissioner's box to handle errands and get refreshments. Usually this was a youngster who worked in some part-time capacity for the club or concessionaire. In 1972, Finley assigned the job to former player Jimmy Piersall, much to our mutual embarrassment. So there was Piersall, throughout the game, prepared to run and serve us hot dogs and peanuts. I must say that poor Jimmy handled it well under the circumstances. At the end of the game I said, "Jimmy, whatever you do, for your own sake and mine, don't come back here tomorrow." He did not.

Finley's penchant for bullying young players came to the fore again in 1972 and involved the game's most exciting young pitcher,

Vida Blue. Blue had come up late in 1970, pitching a no-hitter in September as a warm-up. Then, in 1971, his first full season, he won both the MVP and Cy Young awards, posting a 24–8 record with a league-leading 1.82 ERA and 301 strikeouts. He was a fabulous gate attraction throughout the league. The A's also won their first western-division title. For all of this, Finley had paid him $14,500, although he did throw in such bonuses as a car and automobile insurance. President Nixon accurately called Blue "the most underpaid superstar in sports."

At contract time after the 1971 season, Vida asked for $115,000. Finley offered a nonnegotiable $50,000. There they sat as the months, and ultimately spring training, went by. The game's hottest talent was at home in Louisiana talking about retiring and going into the plumbing business. It was a bad scene for baseball. Not only was the American League losing a stellar gate attraction and getting bad publicity, as Joe Cronin reminded me almost every day, but Finley was exacerbating an already unattractive situation by his pigheaded remarks and style. Actually, his $50,000 offer was not outrageous by 1972 standards, but Finley had a way of making it seem so.

I knew that Paul Derringer, who pitched in the National League in the 1930s and 1940s, had once had a similar holdout problem with the Reds. Judge Landis had intervened because he felt the Reds had not been negotiating in good faith. He told the Reds to get together with Derringer and work something out. A deal was soon concluded. But Finley detested authority with a passion that bordered on paranoia. I knew he would not be enchanted to hear from me when I decided in late April to bring the parties together.

His response was that it was none of my business. Commissioners were not supposed to involve themselves in salary disputes. As far as I was concerned, I was the paterfamilias of the game and I could step in wherever I thought appropriate. A federal judge had so described the commissioner's role in a 1930 lawsuit brought by Phil Ball, owner of the St. Louis Browns, against Commissioner Landis. Landis had told Ball he could not option a player named Fred Bennett to the minors. Outraged, Ball went to court and precipitated a decision upholding the powers of the commissioner in the broadest possible terms. Unlike the Magna Charta, which guaranteed the rights and privileges of English feudal barons over their monarch, this decision affirmed Czar Landis's vast powers over the barons of baseball. Runnymede in reverse.

Finley knew he had no real alternative and was present on April

27 at my suite at the Drake Hotel in Chicago. Blue and his lawyer, Robert Gerst, had no objection to the meeting and were present, too. Finley was alone. Our general counsel, Sandy Hadden, joined me for what proved to be a twenty-two-hour session. Hostility flooded the room. Finley loathed everybody. Sadly, Blue seemed as ill-tempered as Finley. That surprised me, because Blue had charmed the baseball world since his 1970 arrival. He was bitter and suspicious, exactly as I would find him during the rest of his career. I have never felt so much like a Louisiana bayou sheriff. I was also surprised because I had not previously encountered player hostility. Both Blue and Finley viewed me with equal suspicion, each suspecting that I favored the other side.

I explained at the outset that all I cared about was getting Blue signed and back on the mound. I urged both to be flexible in the interest of agreement. But Finley would not increase his $50,000 figure. Attorney Gerst was more reasonable and was prepared to compromise. People excused themselves to take naps. We sent out for food. Finley stuck to the $50,000. He occasionally switched from malice to charm, but malice was winning. Gerst, Sandy and I got along fine. Three lawyers, you know.

Finally, as the sun began to rise, we persuaded Finley to offer bonus payments: a four-year college scholarship worth $8,000 (only for tuition and only if Blue ever attended college), plus a $5,000 signing bonus. The total value of the package was $63,000, which Gerst and Blue were willing to accept. I thought we were done.

But Finley wanted the exact terms announced, the $50,000 salary and the bonuses, while Blue wanted it announced as a $63,000 contract. Incredibly, there was no deal.

At a brief press conference in the Drake, I said that Charlie had made a fair offer. I urged Blue to sign and I ordered Finley to keep the offer open until May 2. I was confident that Blue and Gerst would come around given a few days to reflect.

When Finley heard that I'd "ordered" him to keep the offer on the table, he went off like an Oakland fireworks display. "He's got no business being in this," he said. "It's a two-way street. I'm just very bitter about the way he's handled this. The commissioner forced himself into contract negotiations with Blue and I don't believe he has the authority to do so. I don't like it one damn bit."

Unmoved by Finley's outburst, I said, "I am ruling that the offer has been made and will remain in effect. We will have a deal if Vida is willing to accept it, and I am going to urge him to do so."

I called Gerst and tried my own brand of charm. It is not immodest to say it was better than Finley's. Gerst and Blue agreed. I set a meeting for May 2 in Joe Cronin's American League office in Boston. I called Finley and told him to be there. "You can go to hell," he said. "I'm not going." I replied, "Charlie, either you show in Boston and sign a contract with Blue, or I will make him a free agent. Take your pick." He again suggested I try an excursion in hell and hung up. Finley may be without redeeming virtues but he is not dumb. He came to Boston and signed Blue.

Finley followed this up by attacking me repeatedly in the press. This resulted in an ugly telephone conversation in which he denounced me in the most obscene language at his command. I can assure you, it was a scatological work of art. I listened briefly, advised him I was fining him for unbecoming conduct and hung up. I suspect some of his best stuff went into a dead line.

We scheduled a May 5 hearing in New York to review the situation. His lawyers arranged for six postponements of the hearing, then requested the matter be dismissed because "it is stale and will serve to rekindle old fires." We finally had the hearing on June 27. I fined Finley $500 and issued a reprimand.

I wrote Finley: "I readily acknowledge and indeed defend your right to make comments, criticisms, and suggestions concerning my actions as Commissioner of Baseball. However, whether or not your public remarks were well taken is totally irrelevant, the place to air your grievances was within the confines of Major League Baseball. However valid you might have felt those grievances were, your private judgment as to the jurisdiction of the Commissioner's Office could not serve to excuse a public display of disrespect—or immunize it from redress."

It happens that $500 was the maximum fine the commissioner could impose on an individual at that time. While it seems a small sum in terms of ownership finances, the ego of some of these men was such that there was no real difference between $500 and $50,-000. They could not abide the idea of being fined. Finley wrote me a six-page letter, enclosing a personal check for $500. In part, the letter said: "It is perfectly obvious that this entire matter is one of principle. It seems to me that I can best underscore the error of your ways by allowing you to take full credit and full responsibility for the horrible precedents you have established in the course of your dealings with me. . . . Because of your unauthorized, improper and arbitrary action in the Vida Blue case, I believe that you should be reprimanded and found guilty of conduct contrary to the best interests of Baseball. However, there appears to be no procedure for instituting charges against the Commissioner. And if you were to be the final judge of your own conduct, there is no doubt that you would exonerate yourself. . . ."

Well, he was certainly right in that last sentence. I acknowledged receipt of his payment and wrote him back, noting: "It is my continuing judgment that your conduct undermines Baseball's central administrative system and public respect for that system. Unfortunately, you seem to have little or no appreciation of how critically important that system is to the game. You seem to put first and foremost your own desire to act as you feel serves your own interest. Left unchecked, such conduct would destroy the Major League partnership to which you are a party through the Major League Agreement and Rules."

Vida Blue was never again the superstar of his first full season. He won six and lost ten games in 1972. Although he had 301 strikeouts in 1971, he never subsequently reached even 200. The bitterness I had seen seemed to become part of his character. Eventually, I wound up having to suspend him for the 1984 season for cocaine involvement that had brought him a jail term. It was a sad comedown in a career that had such bright promise. Maybe Vida was always heading for trouble, strictly on his own. But I wonder how he might have fared had he started out with one of our good organizations, like the Brewers or the Dodgers, instead of Charlie Finley. One thing was certain. Finley's abuse of his players was knocking away the props that supported baseball's reserve system. The responsible people in the game understood that. Bob Howsam, the Branch Rickey disciple who built the Big Red Machine in Cincinnati, once said to me, "Commissioner, the biggest mistake you made with Finley was not throwing him out of the game for life." Maybe so.

A shocking example of Finley's cruelty involved Mike Andrews during the 1973 World Series. Andrews, a key member of the pennant-winning 1967 Boston Red Sox, had drifted over to the A's, victim of a chronic sore shoulder. Generally relegated to designated hitter duties, he had played only twenty-nine games in the field in 1973, fifteen of them at second base.

Dick Green started the second World Series game against the Mets, was removed for a pinch hitter and replaced at second base by Ted Kubiak. Andrews later hit for Kubiak and replaced him in the field. In a wild twelfth inning, the Mets' John Milner hit a bases-loaded grounder to Andrews with two out. That should have ended the inning with the Mets ahead 7–6 on Willie Mays's game-winning hit, his last hit in the major leagues. Instead, the ball went through Andrews's legs. Two runs scored and the Mets then led 9–6. Then Jerry Grote also grounded to Andrews. Another run scored when Andrews's throw pulled Tenace off first for his second error. The Mets led 10–6. It was a devastating moment for Andrews and I felt for this popular, likable young man. I hoped there would be better days ahead. As far as Finley was concerned there would be no other days for Mike Andrews. Overnight, as the teams prepared to move from Oakland to New York, he produced a letter from the Oakland club physician, Dr. Harry R. Walker, that read:

October 14, 1973

To whom it may concern:
At the request of the Oakland A's, I examined Mike Andrews, second baseman, today (Sunday). He has a history of cronic [*sic*] shoulder disability. He attempted to play, but was unable physically to play his position because of a bicep groove ten-cosynovitis in the right shoulder. It is my opinion [that] he is disabled for the rest of the year.

Sincerely,
Harry R. Walker, M.D.

At the bottom of the letter, Mike Andrews had signed under a line that read, "I agree to the above." Not only was Finley trying to humiliate and punish Andrews for his errors, but he also had the gall to request on October 15 that Manny Trillo, a rookie second base-man, replace Andrews on the roster.

Trillo was a talented young player who would go on to be an All-Star second baseman in both leagues; however, he had not been on the A's' roster on September 1 and thus was not eligible under the World Series rules. Finley, whose club had actually opened the Series with a shorthanded roster of twenty-four players (he had foolishly sold one of his twenty-five eligible players after September 1), had tried to get me to approve the addition of Trillo before the Series began. Since the rule was clear, I declined. But I advised him through our administrator, Johnny Johnson, that I would have no objection if the Mets would consent. The Mets, however, refused and were fully within their rights in doing so. This annoyed Finley, who told Johnson he wanted a public address announcement before Game One saying that he was playing shorthanded because the Mets forced him to do so. Johnson refused permission for the announcement, which was plainly designed to inflame the Oakland crowd against the Mets. So Finley arrogantly went ahead and had the announcement made anyway. He was immediately advised that I would deal with that performance at the end of the Series. Now, the very next day, he was trying to dump Andrews and replace him with Trillo.

Back in my New York office on Tuesday, I talked on the telephone with Andrews and Dr. Walker. There was no basis or justification for Finley's request. Andrews was no more disabled than he was when the Series began. The maneuver was a clumsy deceit on Finley's part. I delivered privately and released publicly a letter to Finley that said:

To: The Oakland Club

Reference is made (1) to your oral application yesterday to this office that Mike Andrews be replaced on the Oakland World Series squad by reason of disability and (2) to the attached letter from Harry R. Walker, M.D.

Dr. Walker's letter indicates that Andrews has a "chronic shoulder disability." There is no suggestion that this condition has changed or worsened since the Series began or that he has been injured in the Series. The fact that he was used in Game 2 by the Oakland Club would appear to indicate the contrary.

Mr. Scheffing of the New York Club has advised us that he will go along with whatever disposition of this application is made by this office.

I can find no basis to grant the application and it is accordingly denied.

I might add that the handling of this matter by the Oakland Club has had the unfortunate effect of unfairly embarrassing a player who has given many years of able service to professional baseball. It is my determination that Andrews remains a full-fledged member of the Oakland World Series squad.

Bowie K. Kuhn

All the pregame attention that Tuesday night at Shea Stadium was on Andrews, whom Finley had maladroitly made into an overnight folk hero. Manager Dick Williams posed for dugout pictures with Mike, giving him a hug that had been so needed two days before.

The next night, in Game 4, Andrews was used by Williams as an eighth-inning pinch hitter. I have no idea what prompted Williams to use Andrews. I would like to think, as may well have been the case, that it was decency and a sense of fitness. In any event, it was an inspiration. The warming roar of the crowd was at once a compassionate tribute to Andrews and a rejection of the sordid values that guided Finley.

Mike Andrews never came to bat in the major leagues again. I wish he had driven the ball to Coney Island in that last at bat, but perfect drama is a rarity. He grounded out.

I met with Andrews before the game to find out why he had signed Dr. Walker's letter, as I was now evaluating whether Finley should be disciplined. He told me he had at first refused to sign the letter because it lied when it asserted that he was disabled. He said Finley persuaded him to sign it for the best interests of the team, even though it was a lie.

The Series ended with the A's world champions again. I dutifully presented the trophy to Finley on October 21 and five days later fined the Oakland club $7,000. Of that total, $5,000 was for the Andrews matter. I fined the club $1,000 for the public address announcement, and another $1,000 for Finley's having turned on the stadium lights without receiving directions to do so from the umpires. Finley requested a hearing, which was held on November 16. As for the field lights, he claimed they were turned on for public safety. I concluded, "This argument might be more persuasive if the lights had been turned on when the opposing team was at bat, or if Mr. Finley had asked the Umpire-in-Chief to order that the lights be turned on. He did neither."

Regarding the public address announcement, which said that the Mets were "forcing the Oakland club to play with twenty-four men," Finley argued the commissioner had no power to prohibit public address announcements. I responded, "The power of the commissioner to restrain such a public announcement cannot be open to question, especially in light of the possibility that it might incite the fans in the Oakland Coliseum to engage in behavior which could have resulted in delay of game, or worse."

I concluded my decision by stating, "The whole incident [Mike Andrews] is clearly another example of Mr. Finley's knowingly over-reaching in an effort to gain an advantage for his team. Under the circumstances, I can see no basis for changing the penalty I have previously imposed."

One of the problems posed by Finley and some of our other

tiresome owners is that the commissioner will be so affected by their conduct as to deviate from the test of fair-mindedness in dealing with the affairs of their clubs. The temptation was certainly there. I had to be constantly on guard against letting them have the second barrel of the shotgun when that second trigger was so handy. Although the press at times charged me with yielding to that temptation, I am satisfied that I managed to keep the scales of baseball justice fairly balanced. A case in point was the 1972 bat-throwing incident of Bert Campaneris of the A's.

During a brief but heated moment in the second game of the 1972 American League Championship Series, an angry Campaneris fired his bat at Detroit pitcher Lerrin LaGrow, who, Campaneris felt, had intentionally hit him with a pitch. President Cronin decided to suspend Campaneris for the remainder of the League Championship Series.

I then spoke to Cronin and said, "Joe, I frankly don't think that's enough. I think there ought to be a stiffer penalty for that." He responded, "Commish, I agree. I've suspended him for what's left of the American League season. I have no problem at all with your going farther. Be my guest." Every time I mention Cronin I am tempted to reflect again on what a wonderful man he was to work with. A Hall of Famer who had won all the honors and attained all the positions baseball could offer except commissioner, he had none of the egomania that so often afflicted owners—and even league presidents, like his controversial predecessor, Ban Johnson, who had ruled the American League from its inception in 1900 to 1927. Cronin always came down solidly in favor of what was best for the game and worked within the system to that end. By contrast, National League presidents Warren Giles and Chub Feeney after him tended to be more protective of their league, more reluctant to see the commissioner get involved. Though one of my favorite baseball characters, Feeney was easily the most isolationist league president of my thirty-five years in the game. Certainly, the conservative ownership of the National League brought pressure to sustain that policy. While it had historical roots in turn-of-the-century feuding between the two leagues, it has been nurtured in recent decades by the National League's resentment of American League owners like Finley and George Steinbrenner.

So I studied my options in the Campaneris case. I could have suspended him from the World Series, but that would really be hurting the A's and their fans. With all the big guns on the A's, it was in many ways Campaneris who made the lineup work: fielding well, getting on base, stealing bases, igniting the attack.

As I often did in matters like this, I sought a precedent and found one. In 1942, the Yankees' Frank Crosetti was suspended for thirty days by league president Will Harridge for an altercation with umpire Bill Summers. The suspension would have carried into the World Series. Commissioner Landis then decided it would be unfair to the Yankees and their fans to have Crosetti suspended during the Series. So the suspension was imposed for the first thirty days of the 1943 regular season. Following that precedent, I suspended Campaneris for the first seven games of the 1973 season.

In 1974, Catfish Hunter of Oakland and Jim Palmer of Baltimore were the premier pitchers in the American League. Hunter won twenty games for the fourth consecutive season, and the A's won their fourth consecutive western-division championship.

Hunter's 1974 salary of $100,000 was to be paid half during the season and half deferred to a time to be specified by Hunter. In September, Hunter's lawyer J. Carlton Cherry of Ahoskie, North Carolina, asked Finley to use the deferred $50,000 to purchase an insurance annuity for Hunter.

Finley had no problem with paying the $50,000, but he was concerned about the tax consequences of purchasing an annuity. Would he be able to get a tax deduction? Would Hunter be taxed on the payment? These were legitimate questions. Nevertheless, Cherry pressed Finley to purchase the annuity at once.

The Player Relations Committee advised Finley that while he was not obligated to purchase the annuity, he should send the money directly to Hunter, which he did on October 4. Hunter sent it back, saying, "I can't take it. I've been advised by my attorney that the check must be sent directly to the Jefferson Insurance Company."

As a result, Cherry's request was not met, the money was not paid as Hunter wished, and the grace period passed. Dick Moss wrote to me on October 7 and requested that I declare Hunter a free agent, a request I denied. I felt that free agency was too severe a penalty in light of the various tax complications and Finley's offer to pay on October 4.

The Players Association filed a grievance seeking free agency on the basis of Finley's having failed to make the payment. Charlie then offered to pay the money to the arbitrator, who would hold it until the dispute was settled. This was refused as well.

The grievance was heard by arbitrator Peter Seitz on November 26 in New York. The witnesses included Hunter; his attorney, who had negotiated his 1974 contract; Lee MacPhail and Finley.

On December 13, I began my day with a dental appointment, which may have been a portent of things to come in Hunter's case. Then I went to lunch with some of my former Willkie Farr & Gallagher partners who wanted to talk about my leaving baseball and returning to the firm.

It had, in fact, been on my mind. I was forty-eight years old and knew that if I were reelected in 1975 my absence from active law practice would be much longer than I had ever contemplated. I wondered how long I could be away and still effectively return as a lawyer. As exciting and stimulating as baseball was, in many ways I missed the order and thoroughness of the law, the intellectual challenge and the warm friendships at Willkie Farr. As I listened to my former partners over lunch, I was intrigued. They talked about the dramatic growth of the firm. We joked about whether all this was happening in spite or because of my departure. They talked about important clients on whose matters I was needed. Yes, it was intriguing.

I told them I would like to think it over. They knew I was preoccupied because the Player Relations Committee had advised me that the arbitrator's decision to be announced that afternoon would grant free agency to Hunter. There would be shock waves throughout baseball, although the full stunning impact would not at first be realized.

On learning the bottom line of Seitz's decision, my reaction was that he had gone much further than was necessary. To forfeit the contract over a few days' delay in paying the $50,000 was like giving a life sentence to a pickpocket. Hunter's contract was of enormous value to the Oakland club. It should not have been forfeited unless Oakland was guilty of serious wrongdoing. Finley clearly was a pickpocket, trying to hold the $50,000 in his own account for as long as possible, but so far as I knew, that was the worst of it.

So I waited for the full decision, thinking it would resolve the mystery. Perhaps Seitz had found Finley guilty of such egregious bad faith that forfeiture was warranted. Perhaps he had determined that Finley lied during the hearing. I had heard that Finley's testimony was far from persuasive. When I read the decision, the mystery deepened. Seitz found no special circumstances.

Reading between the lines, I could not escape the conclusion that Seitz was punishing Finley on general principles. While I could hardly quarrel with the essential justice of the decision viewed on a much broader stage than the Catfish Hunter case, and though I certainly had no affection for Finley, I was troubled by an outside arbitrator's seizing the right to punish him. It had troublesome implications.

Seitz was a respected veteran arbitrator who had been jointly selected by the Players Association and the Player Relations Committee in 1974. There were some misgivings on the PRC in selecting Seitz because he was thought to favor the labor side of issues. But he had served in the same role in the NBA with no disastrous results.

The use of an outside arbitrator for resolving player-club disputes had been agreed to in 1970. Before that date, such disputes would usually have been resolved by the commissioner. While I thought the change was neither necessary nor beneficial, and though it could not have been made without my consent, I reluctantly went along. There had never been a commissioner whose fairness in disputes between clubs and players could be questioned, and if anything they had probably been more sympathetic to the players' side of disputes. But provisions of this kind were commonplace in American collective bargaining agreements and could not realistically be resisted by sports managements—nor have they been. So the clubs and I concurred.

However, as commissioner, I did not want an outsider resolving disputes that involved baseball's integrity or public confidence in the game. I insisted and the Players Association agreed that disputes involving such questions could be taken over by the commissioner and resolved finally and without appeal. This reservation of power has always troubled the Players Association. As recently as the 1985 negotiations, the Association pressed to have this provision removed. Commissioner Ueberroth wisely stood his ground.

The Players Association also had a qualification. Since the Association was challenging the legality of the reserve system in the then-pending Flood case, it did not want its new collective bargaining agreement to embrace that system. Accordingly, the clubs agreed to the Association's proposal that the new agreement would "not deal with the reserve system," and it also agreed that further bargaining on the reserve system was foreclosed until the Flood case was concluded.

There was ill-concealed resentment of Finley by other club owners. They felt as I did that Seitz would not have granted free agency, but for Finley's checkered past. While they were just about to put on one of America's most memorable displays of rampant free-marketeering, in pursuit of Catfish they understood that Finley had rocked a frail boat. They did not know how watery the consequences might be. In my office we did anticipate that, given Hunter's Cy Young Award quality, the bidding would be vigorous and the money high.

I imposed a moratorium on any dealings with Hunter, notifying the clubs by telex, "I have not yet had an opportunity to review the decision and I am advised that the Oakland club intends immediately to seek a court restraining order to prevent Hunter from contracting with another club. Direct or indirect contact between Hunter and the other clubs is temporarily prohibited."

Finley did go to court, but to no avail. It was determined at two levels of the judiciary that Seitz had acted within his jurisdiction. Finley's effort to upset Seitz was a long shot in light of the presumption of correctness that the law gives to arbitrators' decisions. Absent capricious, arbitrary, or dishonest conduct, they are difficult to overturn. Moreover, the PRC gave Finley lukewarm support, however much it felt Seitz's decision was incorrect. Even so, Marvin Miller howled that the PRC was undermining the collective bargaining agreement by not requiring Finley to accept Seitz's decision. No one was willing to go that far. Finley was entitled to take a shot, given the loss of one of baseball's finest pitchers.

Miller also charged that I had no right to halt contact with Hunter. I was unconcerned about that challenge and had other things on my mind. First, I wanted an orderly and fair bidding process. I did not want the richer clubs to run down to North Carolina the next day with their checkbooks open. And I wanted the less affluent clubs to have a chance to plan their strategies and get their financing established. I also gave some thought to the possibility of giving second-division teams first crack at Hunter, since this could hardly harm Hunter and would be consistent with the way our amateur draft worked and with my philosophy of maintaining competitive balance. Over the years, I would make frequent decisions keyed to that philosophy.

Unfortunately, the legal ice was too thin for the second division approach. So, on December 18, I lifted the embargo and the race was on to Hunter's law firm of Cherry, Cherry & Flythe in Ahoskie, North Carolina.

The rush to Ahoskie occupied the sports pages throughout the

Christmas season of 1974. Club owners Gene Autry, Peter O'Malley, Gabe Paul, John McHale, Ted Bonda, Ruly Carpenter, Brad Corbett, Dan Galbreath, Ewing Kauffman, Ed Fitzgerald, Bud Selig and Bob Short all went. So did high-level club officials like Jim Baumer, Peter Bavasi, Joe Brown, Joe Burke, Al Campanis, Harry Dalton, Jim Fanning, John Harrington, Bob Howsam, Dan O'Brien, Dick O'Connell, Paul Owens, Eddie Robinson, Phil Seghi and Haywood Sullivan. Even managers Walter Alston, Billy Martin, Dick Williams, Gene Mauch and Eddie Kasko appeared. Pitcher Gaylord Perry tried to talk his fellow North Carolinian Hunter into going to Cleveland.

In the end, the reinvigorated New York Yankees landed the Catfish. George Steinbrenner had bought the club from CBS in January 1973 for the amazingly low price of $10 million, which reflected the low estate to which that once-proud organization had plunged since it last won a pennant in 1964. Steinbrenner brought in Gabe Paul from the Indians to be the club president and backed him up with a full pocketbook. Though George was brooding under a two-year suspension, at the time of the great Ahoskie fishing contest, Gabe was working vigorously and was backed up by Clyde Kluttz, the scout who had signed Hunter for Finley in 1964. Kluttz and Hunter had remained close friends.

The Yankees made the announcement on New Year's Eve in their offices across the street from Shea Stadium. Hunter was introduced to the press by Gabe Paul. His contract, which included salary, bonuses, life insurance, attorney's fees and appearance fees, had a total estimated value of $3.5 million.

A franchise that had been purchased for $10 million two years before had just committed 35 percent of that price to one player. It was fiscal insanity. Baseball did not know it yet, but the Hunter deal heralded an era of fiscal irresponsibility by ownership that has not abated to this day. Finley, who treated players like plantation hands, had opened the door for what would soon be the greatest player affluence in the history of sports. At the same time, he had set in motion the collapse and in time the sale of those once-wonderful Oakland A's.

12

Reelection

T he summer of 1975 was the logical time to consider my reelection. My first seven-year term would end in August 1976, and under our rules, a commissioner's reelection was set for a year before his term expired. Another seven-year term would carry me through August 1983 and might commit me to baseball for the rest of my working life. As 1975 began, I was not sure that I wanted to make that commitment.

I was increasingly asked in press interviews what my plans were. I was noncommittal, although I often said that I did not need the baseball job and had other things I could do just as well. That this answer annoyed certain owners did not alter the frequency with which I gave it. And, in fact, I was having difficulty making up my mind. Ownership was overwhelmingly supportive. I had little doubt the votes were there. Walter O'Malley even went so far as to say that if I pulled out, there would almost certainly be unfortunate misinterpretations of my motives, such as the appearance of my being forced out.

I liked the baseball people. By and large, they liked me. One after the other, they—men like John Fetzer, John Galbreath, Dick Meyer and Bud Selig—urged me to continue. Ed Fitzgerald said he could not imagine why I would want to continue, but he hoped I would. It was impressive and I was human enough to be flattered. I was getting the same message from Sandy Hadden, with whom I had the closest daily working relationship. He knew my hopes and frustrations better than anyone except Luisa. He also doubted that I would be happy returning to law practice, especially in contrast to the almost hourly excitement of baseball.

Next to Sandy, I worked more closely with the league presidents than anyone else apart from my immediate staff members. While they always had some reserve about the commissioner's getting too deeply involved in league affairs, my relationships with Chub Feeney and Lee MacPhail were close and fraternal. I respected them and endeavored to carry out my duties with a minimum impact on those areas where I felt they should have autonomy. This approach fostered an effective working relationship among the three of us. I rarely made an important decision without consulting Sandy and the league presidents, three men whose concern for the welfare of the game was genuine and unadulterated. Now that reelection time was approaching, both Chub and Lee urged me to continue. That was important.

The most important consideration was my family's opinion. Luisa clearly preferred that I continue. She got along charmingly with the baseball crowd and firmly believed the job was good for me. We both recognized that some of the more scandalous press attacks on me were difficult for our four children, who then ranged in age from fourteen to twenty-three, yet they never complained. My three sons all favored my continuing. My daughter, Alix, was a lone and mild dissenter. While there were pros and cons, the clear majority of family factors favored staying on.

My discussions with Willkie Farr & Gallagher continued. From time to time, I lunched or had a drink with different members of the firm. They genuinely cared and made my return to the firm look very attractive. They argued that I had certainly fulfilled any duty I had to baseball in six years. That was correct. Also, the financial advantages of the law had a considerable edge on baseball. I finally decided that I would have to discuss the situation very frankly with my Executive Council before I reached any conclusion.

I called a meeting of the Council. In attendance were John Fetzer, Ed Fitzgerald, Walter O'Malley, John McHale, Chub and Lee, along with Sandy Hadden. I told them I was seriously considering not standing for reelection but would be prepared to complete my term through August 1976. However, I told them I felt that before I made any final decision, I should have their views. What ensued surprised me, not so much because they all urged me to continue but because of the intensity of their views. I expected expressions of polite disappointment. After all, these men were friends and supporters. In essence, they said instead that my leaving would be a serious disservice to the game. They stressed that any new commissioner would have to go through a long learning period, which the game could ill afford. They called on my sense of duty to baseball. While I questioned the existence of such a duty, they pressed the argument, knowing full well that I could be susceptible to persuasion. Everyone was certain the votes were available for an easy reelection. Lee MacPhail acknowledged that Baltimore's Jerry Hoffberger and Charlie Finley were opponents but thought even they might go along if I ran. He felt that in no event would there be a problem getting the necessary 75 percent vote (nine clubs). Chub Feeney felt the National League was unanimous. I told them I would talk to Luisa, Sandy Hadden and the firm, and then give them an answer. Lee was asked to survey his league to confirm his assessment of the votes.

As I reflected, I found the appeal of the Council hard to resist. Perhaps I had hoped that this would happen, that they would give me an irresistible reason to continue. Luisa and Sandy both agreed with the Council. Calls from men like John Galbreath further weakened my resistance. Willkie Farr & Gallagher understood; they said the candle would always be burning in the window there. MacPhail reported that his American League survey still revealed no serious problem.

So I told the Council they could put my reelection on the agenda for our summer meetings in Milwaukee, where the All-Star Game would be held.

In June, the *Chicago Sun-Times* reported a "Dump Bowie Club," with George Steinbrenner, Jerry Hoffberger and Charlie Finley as its members. Even if it existed, the "club" was one vote shy. I was, nevertheless, confident of MacPhail's evaluation and did not think Steinbrenner would be negative. To the press, he had said, "I would never vote against the commissioner because of anything he did within the perimeter of his authority. People seem to think the Yankees will vote against him because of my suspension, but that is not true. I will not enter into retaliatory attempts of any sort." At this stage, I was prepared to take Steinbrenner at face value. I even said he was free despite his suspension to cast the vote on my reelection himself.

So, I went to Milwaukee, to see the seventh All-Star Game of my tenure, to welcome Secretary of State Henry Kissinger as my special guest and to see my term extended to 1983. All three events turned out as one might have forecast. The National League won the All-

Star Game 6–3, Henry Kissinger was a beguiling guest and I was reelected in a landslide. Only somebody wrote a bizarre script for the landslide event.

On Wednesday, July 16, the day after the game, the two leagues met informally at the Milwaukee Club, with individual league meetings to be held later on. First to speak at the joint meeting was Gussie Busch. Gussie has an inimitable style of speaking. In his distinct, impatient, harsh tones, he delivered a vigorously supportive speech urging the reelection of "our commissioner by acclamation here and now." I was touched and not really surprised by the suggestion. He was an impetuous man, not given to dawdling over matters once a course seemed clear. We had gotten along well during our years together in baseball despite his irascible personality and imperial style. I liked the old man.

Then, from a dark side of the room came a sound from Dante's *Inferno*. It was the rasping voice of Charlie Finley, saying with characteristic punctuating coughs that there were four American League votes against the reelection of the commissioner and they were not going to change. He identified supporting votes from Oakland, Baltimore, New York and Texas. Had Finley's cabal escaped MacPhail's prying eye after all? None of his three allies disputed his count. I announced that we would postpone the balance of the joint meeting agenda to permit the leagues to meet independently to consider the reelection question, all very measured, routine, low key —and misleading. As the assembly headed into the other meeting rooms, you could feel the excitement. Baseball people love a good fight and Finley had set the stage for a brawl.

I talked briefly with Lee MacPhail, who was embarrassed, that the Finley "club" had eluded him. He assured me he would keep me fully posted on developments in the American League meeting. Luisa and I telephoned our four children, my parents, my brother Lou and sister Alice and my secretary, Mary Sotos, to let them know what they would be reading in Thursday's papers. We told them it was too early to call the result; anything could happen. Alice, who is a very bright lady and had never liked the way baseball treated her little brother, thought this was a great time to tell them where to go.

Luisa, Sandy's wife, Susan, and the Haddens' six-year-old daughter, Kate, were in the suite. The Haddens were treasured friends, as close to us as our own family. They were a special treasure that day with their knack of finding the lighthearted side of the gloomiest scene. When we told them the proceedings of the meetings we had just left, nobody saw any rays of light, let alone humor. Indeed, mutterings from the ladies about Finley will not be printed here.

One of the curses of the commissioner's role in baseball is sitting in suites waiting out league meetings. The invariable luxury of the suite provides no antidote for this curse. Matters of great importance are resolved while the commissioner stares helplessly into parking lots. One prays for a knock on the door or a telephone call, anything to relieve the vacuum of knowledge. Sandy and I frequently passed such times by working, although concentration was not easy. Sometimes we reminisced. This time we ruminated about whether Finley was correct in his view that the Yankees and Rangers would vote no. We conceded him the Orioles but were not so sure about the other two. We had trouble imagining a motive for a new owner like Brad Corbett at Texas to buck the landslide of votes that stood behind me. Steinbrenner may have been getting even for my suspending him. But did he really think a new commissioner would set the prisoners free?

So Sandy did a crossword puzzle, marking the letters in *ink*—a pretension that no doubt developed with his Yale education. For my part, I spread open the *Milwaukee Sentinel* classified section, which I appeared to be studying as visitors arrived. No matter who showed up at the suite during that long day, they found me crouched over the classifieds with my pen. Why let Finley have all the fun?

Late in the morning, the National League came by first with Chub Feeney, Walter O'Malley, John Galbreath, John McHale and my former law partner, Lou Hoynes. They said the National League vote was solid. Ray Kroc had passed on the first straw vote with the eleven others voting yes. Ray said he would like to know their reasons. One by one they extolled my virtues. Here and there a wart was mentioned but nothing serious. Ray was persuaded and the National League had twelve votes. They said their feedback from the American League was not good; apparently the Finley "club" was holding. Still, they said the negatives had to hold all four votes; a one-vote defection ended the game. John Galbreath, who invariably found the bright side, was optimistic about cracking the bloc. O'Malley was more guarded, but beneath the smiles, wisecracks and cigar smoke, I think he felt he would find a way. He always did. The National League would go into its regular agenda in the afternoon, with its operatives steadily working the corridors, baseball's real action center. Executives were in and out of meetings like bees around a hive. Just hang out in the corridors long enough and everybody comes by.

The next delegation was an American League group. In addition to Lee MacPhail and attorney Jim Garner, there were John Fetzer and Ed Fitzgerald. No flashes of optimism brightened this group. Finley and Hoffberger were adamant and difficult. They wanted a joint meeting called promptly and a formal vote taken on the commissioner. Hanging firmly in the no column with them were Pat Cunningham for the Yankees and attorney Mel Snyder for the Rangers. Bronx Democratic leader Cunningham had been designated "acting general partner" during Steinbrenner's suspension. When Brad Corbett left the meetings, his negative vote was turned over to his attorney. With both Cunningham and Snyder apparently voting no on instructions, and the Finley-Hoffberger votes locked in place, there was nothing the other league members could do to reverse the situation. However, they had no intention of being forced into an immediate joint meeting no matter how loudly Finley and Hoffberger screamed. If they bided their time, something might happen.

And thus the afternoon wore on in a virtual filibuster. The emerging strategy was to adjourn the meetings in late afternoon to resume the next morning. The thinking was that overnight New York or Texas could somehow be persuaded to change.

I thought the strategy had a chance to work and I went along with it, although as the day wore on, my patience grew thinner. I would later call this spectacle "obscene." Here was professional baseball being pushed around on a critical issue by four owners whose motives had nothing to do with baseball's general welfare. Over 80 percent of the voters were stopped in their tracks by a petulant minority of four. That Charlie Finley was the public spokesman for this minority was the ultimate degradation. If I had seen this coming a few months earlier, I would surely have refused to stand for reelection. Now the battle was joined and there was no way I would not go along with a strategy to beat them. The meetings were adjourned.

Ed Fitzgerald spirited Luisa and me out of the Pfister Hotel to a small Italian restaurant that was a favorite of his. For the first time in many hours we relaxed. Ed and the fine fare were the right medicine. Ed is one of those people who always manage to be the right medicine.

We talked about Brad Corbett and the developing theory that Bob Short's influence was at work. When Corbett bought the team from Short in 1974, Short retained a 14 percent interest and was in Milwaukee for the meetings. The thinking was that Short, in retaliation for my attempts to keep him from moving to Texas, had convinced Corbett to vote against me.

Interestingly, a decade later, I was dining in Rose's, one of my favorite New York restaurants, which is owned by Bob Short's nephew by marriage, and he said, "You know, Uncle Bob told us he'd cost us a good customer when he tried to stop your election. But you were in here twice the next week and have been coming ever since."

After dinner with Fitzgerald, Luisa and I slipped quietly into the Pfister through the garage and were in bed by ten o'clock. There was nothing I could do at that point but lie back and let events wash over me. There was a lot of washing in the Pfister that night; I slept peacefully through it all.

The anti-Kuhn bloc was looking for another American League vote, reflecting its doubt as to whether it could hold the four votes overnight. The most gratuitous lobbying effort was made by the inebriated duo of Billy Martin and Mickey Mantle. They knocked on doors and cornered people in the lobby, urging them to vote against me. Mantle was in Milwaukee because I had asked him to serve as honorary captain of the American League All-Star team, with Stan Musial captaining the Nationals. Martin was in Corbett's employ as manager of the Rangers and may have been trying to score points with his boss. He apparently failed; Corbett fired him a week later. Comic opera though their effort may have been, when I learned of it the next morning it contributed to my feeling that this process had become an obscenity.

At 6:00 A.M. I was awakened by a call from Walter O'Malley. Sometime during the night he had reached Corbett by telephone at a Florida hotel and applied the extraordinary O'Malley powers of persuasion. Brad agreed to join the forces of light and telephoned his attorney Snyder to tell him to support me.

That left Steinbrenner out in the cold, since I now had the votes for reelection. When Dan Galbreath, a fellow horse breeder, called George, he, too, agreed to support me. George asked Dan if he would use his good offices to persuade the commissioner to lift his suspension. Dan agreed to do so but not until my election was assured. The first I knew of that suggestion was some weeks later when an ill-at-ease Galbreath did make such an appeal, but only in the most dutiful terms. He said he knew I would do what I felt was right. When George's suspension was lifted in 1976 some press sources asserted that a deal had been cut with me. Nothing of the kind had happened.

At 9:00 A.M. on Thursday morning, I convened a joint major-league meeting. The more I had heard about the anti-Kuhn activities of the night before, the more outraged I became. Sandy Hadden called the roll, with Boston absent. The first item of business—the reelection of the commissioner—was put later on the agenda.

Finally a Boston representative arrived, and I left the room with Sandy to return to my suite. Lee MacPhail and Chub Feeney took over the chair. They polled the clubs. MacPhail announced that the American League had voted 10–2 for Kuhn. The National League, announced Feeney, was 12–0.

Lee and Chub graciously came to my suite with the news. They escorted me downstairs to the meeting room, and as I entered I received a standing ovation. For all I know, Finley and Hoffberger, who had cast the two negative votes, were on their feet, too.

"Thank you, gentlemen, especially those who voted for me," I said. "It's too bad it took so long but it's not surprising, considering the quality of the opposition."

Finley bellowed, "What a joke!"

Hoffberger, outraged by my remarks, shouted for an American League meeting as I left the room.

My remark about the "quality of the opposition" was ill-considered and I later regretted making it, not because it was unfair but because it lacked style. A winner can afford more graciousness than I showed. Nor can I excuse myself by saying it was spontaneous. It was nothing of the kind. I had thought about the situation for some hours. More than anything else it reflected my impatience and lack of respect for Finley.

Indeed, even six days later, I was still upset, and sent a testy letter to Lee MacPhail. A letter he sent to me had managed to appear in the press before reaching me. I wrote:

Dear Lee:
I think my remarks in Milwaukee last Thursday were quite restrained under the circumstances. Since your letter was in the press as I received it, I think it is better that any clarification which seems needed be handled directly by me with the people involved. You and I can discuss this at great length when we are next together.

I greatly appreciate the message of good wishes from you and the American League member clubs.

Sincerely yours,
Bowie

In Milwaukee, a press conference immediately followed my ree-lection. As the press assembled, Don Grant of the Mets urged me to forgo the conference. He argued with good practical sense that my mood was wrong and that I might rue what I had to say. While I appreciated Don's avuncular advice, I was in much too stubborn a mood to heed it. As I called the session to order, I noticed that Finley had, in the same room, assembled a group of writers to give his version of what had transpired. It was typical Finley chutzpah, which I was in no mood to tolerate.

"Charlie, you may leave my room," I told him over the micro-phone for all to hear.

"Thank you, Commissioner," he answered. "That just shows more class." And he left, with writers tagging along.

The press conference actually went smoothly enough. My answers were more curt than usual, but adequate. I did call the entire pro-ceeding "obscene," and when a reporter asked what I meant by that I snapped that he could look it up in the dictionary.

I know my ferocity surprised a lot of the press, who had always thought me too aloof for such a show of emotion. Some writers later suggested that, if I had shown more of this over the years, I might have had more friends among the press. My imperturbability gener-ally bothered them.

Six days later I sent the following letter to Finley:

Dear Charlie:
With the events of last week behind us, I think you will agree with me on the importance for the future of closing ranks to deal on their merits with the problems which confront our game.

While you and I have had our differences in the past, I have always attempted to resolve matters involving the Oakland Club without personal rancor and on the basis of the overall good of Baseball. I will certainly continue that course in the future.

For the best interests of the game, it seems obvious that we should both do everything possible to understand each other's point of view. If you would like to meet at any time to discuss matters informally, I hope you will feel free to let me know. So far as I am concerned we can close the door and talk about anything either of us would like.

Sincerely yours,
Bowie Kuhn

Reading this letter many years later, I don't know why I bothered. Pearls before swine. The only explanation is that I was determined, so long as I was commissioner, to turn the other cheek in the interest of harmony. Needless to say, there was no reply.

There remained the matter of Jerry Hoffberger, who sent me a clipping from the Baltimore *Morning Sun.* The story had been written by Lou Hatter and it recounted what had transpired in Milwaukee and reported on Hoffberger's disdain for my remarks.

On July 28, I wrote Jerry:

Dear Jerry:
Lou Hatter's piece you sent me is, as usual with him, quite accurate. However, in the interest of clarity, while I have often disagreed with you and sometimes quite sharply, my expressed dissatisfaction with events in Milwaukee was not directed at you.

Sincerely yours,
Bowie

A final footnote to my reelection was written on April 9, 1984, almost nine years later, when I received the following letter from Brad Corbett.

Dear Bowie:
Bobby Brown has told me that his relationship with you has been quite rewarding, and he felt that I made a mistake in my judgment. It wouldn't be the first one. This is very hard for me to put in writing, but I would like to say I'm sorry that I gave you a negative vote when you stood for reelection and I was involved in baseball. I want to compliment you on the outstanding way you carried on the tradition of the commissioner's office, and may I wish you the very, very best in your future endeavors.

Very truly yours,
Brad

13

The Fox in the Henhouse

As 1975 unfolded, Marvin Miller could look back on nearly ten years of leadership of the Players Association. They had been years of progress for the players, with gains in the benefits plan and modifications of the reserve system. They had also been years of failure. Baseball, alone among the major sports, had no form of free agency. The NHL and NFL had introduced free agency some years before, although in football it seemed more theory than fact. A system for free agency was in the works in the NBA. Miller had made a major assault five years earlier in the Flood case and that defeat had been a galling experience for that proud man. Playing the lion had been a failure; now he was playing the fox.

The strategy was simple enough: have a player go through an entire season without signing a contract and then use the grievance procedure, not the courts, to claim free agency. The obstacles were forbidding. Miller and the Players Association had always claimed that the reserve system was peonage that bound a player from first signing to the grave. How now did this miracle of free agency suddenly emerge so far from the cemetery? It had been agreed in 1970 that the collective bargaining agreement did not cover the reserve system. How could that contract commitment be circumvented?

The owners had already agreed that Peter Seitz could be the

arbiter of grievances. That looked like a good omen for Miller. With the decision in the Catfish Hunter case, Seitz seemed more like a sympathetic ally all the time. Wonder of wonders, he had made that crucial decision so contrary to the owners' interests and had not been fired.

Nine players declined to sign 1975 contracts, thereby forcing their clubs to exercise the renewal option in their 1974 contracts. Seven of the nine signed 1975 contracts during the course of the season. The remaining two, Andy Messersmith and Dave McNally, did not. McNally, the former Orioles star then with Montreal, retired on June 8. Messersmith played the entire season for the Dodgers; then it was a fox who took him in tow. Though McNally's case was of doubtful value since he was no longer active, he and Messersmith were made grievants in a free agency grievance that was filed by the Players Association in October.

The PRC promptly filed a lawsuit seeking to restrain the Association from proceeding with its grievance on the ground that the arbitrator had no jurisdiction over such claims. The lawsuit was filed in Kansas City, although the PRC lawyers had recommended filing it in Cincinnati because they felt the law of that federal circuit was more favorable. The plans for Cincinnati were dropped when the Reds unaccountably objected. The fox was getting help he had not counted on. After a hearing, Kansas City Judge John W. Oliver ruled that the grievance should proceed with the understanding that the clubs, if dissatisfied with the arbitrator's decision, could subsequently contest his jurisdiction before Judge Oliver. Since the PRC felt Judge Oliver should have enjoined the grievance there and then, it was not happy with this decision. The fox was digging under the henhouse fence.

On November 12, a PRC meeting was held in John Gaherin's office in New York. Attendance was good; on the agenda was whether or not to fire Peter Seitz. The question would not have arisen except for one clear and powerful reason: the pending Messersmith-McNally arbitration. Either side was free to fire an arbitrator at any time. I was there because I thought the question was vital to baseball.

The PRC lawyers had been asked to analyze the pros and cons of Seitz as the man to decide the survival of the reserve system. They recounted in great detail Seitz's decisions as NBA arbitrator and reviewed his Catfish Hunter decision. They had also studied his writings and whatever else might give the PRC clues as to the inner mental workings of Seitz. National League attorney Hoynes felt that Seitz was capable of letting his personal convictions affect his decisions as an arbitrator. Feeling that Seitz's personal convictions were inimical to a system as restraining as baseball's reserve system and that he was by nature uncomfortable with baseball's conservative ownership group, Hoynes concluded that Seitz was a dangerous man to decide the Messersmith-McNally arbitration.

The ensuing lengthy debate clearly revealed the conservatism that characterized ownership thinking. The PRC members were concerned about what would happen to their relations with the Players Association and baseball's public image if they were to fire the grandfatherly Seitz, a man with a good reputation who was well regarded in arbitration circles. He was also the man who had risen in public esteem by freeing Hunter from Finley's shackles. Their thinking was reinforced by the lawyers' evaluation of baseball's side of the arbitration. Both on jurisdiction and on the merits, counsel had correctly advised that baseball's case was strong. The PRC members said you could argue that a competent arbitrator like Seitz should inevitably see the legal light. John McHale was the one owner who argued the other side of the issue. He was impressed by Hoynes's argument that Seitz was dangerous. With so much at stake, he favored firing Seitz and taking the chance on another arbitrator.

I often attended PRC meetings, usually as an information-gathering exercise. Only infrequently would I try to govern or shape their views, and then only if I thought some major baseball issue was involved. I respected the PRC and their able chairman, Ed Fitzgerald. Ed's sense was as good as anybody's in the game. But now I addressed the Seitz issue.

"Gentlemen," I said, "you had better listen very closely to Lou's evaluation of Seitz. There's a great deal at stake here. Don't worry about public sentiment. Look at Seitz's record carefully. Remember that an arbitrator has enough leeway to virtually ignore your strong legal arguments. Think very carefully before you vote on this issue." My remarks were brief and moderate. If you pushed these fellows too hard, they were apt to head in the opposite direction. I thought I knew how to herd them in the right direction, which I was sure was too clear to be missed. But miss it they did. I left the room at that point to take a long telephone call. When I returned, I found they had broken for lunch at a club upstairs. Joining them, I found to my astonishment that they had voted to retain Seitz by a 6–1 vote, with only McHale voting no. These men, who routinely and unflinchingly fired managers, were more concerned with public relations and some theoretical rocking of their relationship with the union than they were with the clear and present danger of Seitz.

With lunch completed, we returned to Gaherin's conference room. No longer concerned with diplomacy, I told them their decision to retain Seitz was a fundamental mistake. What crept out of the lawyers' careful analysis of Seitz's history was a barely concealed, antimanagement bias. Kindly and well-intentioned, he was a prisoner of his own philosophy and would rationalize his way to the destruction of the reserve system. As commissioner, I explained that that was a source of profound concern to me. We were faced with potential anarchy with no guarantee that the Players Association with its short-range vision would cooperate in reconstructing a system that would protect the interests of the clubs and fans. Without a reserve system, our vast array of minor leagues would hardly survive. The major leagues would have no incentive or ability to continue to subsidize them. In the helter-skelter of all our players' becoming free agents, the Hunter madness could be magnified many times over. It was not hard to imagine that we could even lose a major league. My strong advice to the group was to fire Seitz and take their chances on another arbitrator. By all means, negotiate further changes in the reserve system but do it from a position of strength. I asked them to vote again on Seitz. The result was the identical 6–1 vote to retain him. The fox was past the fence and heading for the henhouse.

I had one more option open to me. It was spelled out in the grievance portion of the basic agreement. Article 10, item A.1. (b), reads, "Notwithstanding the definition of 'Grievance' set forth in subparagraph (a) above, 'grievance' shall not mean a complaint which involves action taken with respect to a Player or Players by the Commissioner involving the preservation of the integrity of, or the maintenance of public confidence in, the game of baseball." Article 10 meant that I could take the Messersmith-McNally grievance myself, removing it from Seitz, under the "integrity–public confidence" clause.

There was no doubt in my mind that the game's integrity and public confidence were at stake in the potential destruction of the reserve system. I asked Gaherin what would happen if I took the grievance and, following the law, held against the Players Association's paper-thin contention that players could achieve free agency by "playing out their options." John said the effect would be twofold.

First, an emerging spirit of cooperation and good feelings that was developing under the Fitzgerald PRC chairmanship would be destroyed, as the Players Association's reaction would be bitter and acrimonious.

Second, he thought the players would strike. I was persuaded he was right on both counts. I had learned to respect John's judgment, which was practical and dispassionate. He thought my taking the grievance was not the path of prudence. My most trusted counselors Fitzgerald and Hadden agreed.

With the worst misgivings, but with the conviction that I had to give the system a chance to work, I backed off. Given the results, I am sorry I did. Our repeated attempts to create a good relationship with the Association never really worked and never would so long as Miller was there. It served Miller's purpose to scuttle every effort that ever was or would be made in that direction. And was there any real danger that Miller could mount a major strike to achieve free agency? Up to that time the Players Association had never struck to achieve changes in the reserve system. I am confident that had I resolved the Messersmith-McNally grievance, a free-agency system would have been negotiated that would have worked far better from the point of view of the fans than the one we have today courtesy of Seitz. The very fact that I would have been seen as "high-handedly" deciding Messersmith-McNally would have created enormous pressure for a negotiated free agency. In hindsight, my greatest regret about my sixteen years as commissioner is that I did not take that grievance and head off Seitz.

Before the arbitration was slated to begin, the Dodgers actually could have signed Messersmith and avoided the grievance. It would have required their giving him a no-trade clause, which they were prepared to do. As a matter of policy, the PRC asked them not to do so and the Dodgers, being good organizational soldiers, complied. Subsequently, the PRC relented and no-trade clauses became commonplace in player contracts in later years.

The arbitration that would try baseball's soul began on November 21 at Manhattan's Barbizon Plaza. The fox was sitting in the henhouse, for the arbitration panel consisted of Miller and Gaherin and Seitz, who of course had the controlling vote. Witnesses poured out their views for three days. I was one. There I sat in a solitary little chair in a large empty space facing the panelists: Seitz, benign and gracious with visions of the Emancipation Proclamation dancing in his eyes; Miller, full of mock judicial gravity and anticipation of a succulent chicken dinner; and Gaherin, looking worried. I gave a sermon on the history and importance of the reserve system and the grave consequences of its elimination. Somehow I had a feeling no one was listening. When I had wound down, Seitz had the rapt attention of everyone when he said: "You have also said that you believe that matters of this sort not only should but can be resolved by collective bargaining. This particular train is right on the tracks. The arbitration panel, unless something else happens, must proceed to its destination. . . .

"It is a little late in the game, I realize, to ask whether collective bargaining can determine this issue rather than the panel, however more desirable it would be for that process to be followed rather than the quasi-judicial process on a matter as large as the one before us.

"But I don't know where your statement leaves us. I don't know whether I am to take your statement as encouraging me to persuade the parties to try some more, or whether you are merely deploring the fact that both of them, or one of them, has not done all that it might have done in collective bargaining to avoid this conflict."

Whatever else this meant, and there was considerable debate about it in the days that followed, Seitz was saying he was prepared to hold up a decision while the parties negotiated suitable changes in the reserve system. In effect, he would supervise the negotiations and the suitability of the changes.

The PRC met to evaluate the situation. They wondered if Seitz was saying he would decide against baseball. I thought it a clear possibility that Seitz's train was on that track. Or was he just threatening an adverse decision so as to bring about a solution through supervised bargaining? The lawyers felt they had presented an overwhelming case. After all, no one had ever seriously imagined that the reserve system had a large, heretofore undiscovered ocean of free agency floating in its midst. That was nothing more than one of those myths Miller spent so much time inventing. The PRC certainly wanted no part of Seitz's supervising their negotiations with the Players Association. There was no telling where that might lead. If Seitz went against the law and bought the myth, there was always judicial review. On balance, the PRC concluded, it was best to let Seitz go ahead and rule.

Rule he did.

The news began to filter back to me from Gaherin. After the hearings, the three panelists had three meetings in executive session. It was becoming clear that Seitz was hell-bent for free agency. His decision upholding the grievance was publicly announced on December 23. The PRC now made two inevitable decisions of its own. It fired Seitz and elected to pursue its challenge in the federal court before Judge Oliver in Kansas City.

The firing of Seitz seemed mean-spirited to the public, but baseball was preparing to do battle in court. Since baseball had the power to fire, how would it look in court if it did not register its displeasure by dismissing the arbitrator? It was done more as a legal point than in anger. But make no mistake, there was anger, too. Had there been no lawsuit to pursue, Seitz would still have been fired, in part because in American arbitration practice, it is commonplace to dismiss an arbitrator who has slain one of the party's sacred cows. Seitz had done just that.

In 1982, less than a year before his death and at a time when I myself was beset by a group of militant owners, Seitz wrote me a letter reflecting his dismay at the manner of his discharge, saying, "Normally, a hapless pitcher, being removed from the mound in the course of an inning will get a few kind words from the manager for his efforts, perhaps a reassuring pat on the back and even an opportunity to doff his cap in deference to the applause of the more sensitive and appreciative audience. This is part of what makes baseball a sport rather than a cockfight. I am afraid that too many of the franchise owners, your clients, are unaware of this."

I replied, "Baseball people like their brethren in other businesses often act in a graceless way. Perhaps this is the product of the time-honored convention of screaming at umpires. Of course, that does not excuse it. I am a firm believer that there is no excuse for bad manners and I am truly sorry that you were subjected to that, at least on the part of some of our people.

"For the record, I myself was very critical of your decision and publicly so. However, I believe that my criticism was within the bounds of good taste."

In Judge Oliver's court, baseball pressed its argument that under the arbitration agreement Seitz had no jurisdiction over a reserve-system question and also argued that he was wrong on the merits. On both arguments, legal presumptions of correctness heavily favored the arbitrator. Oliver upheld Seitz. The PRC appealed to the Eighth U.S. Circuit Court of Appeals, which on March 9 upheld the district court by a 2–1 margin in a decision that plainly could have gone either way. Baseball had come within an eyelash of reversing Seitz and failed. The fox was having supper.

Thus, after successfully defending the reserve system in court proceedings over half a century, three times before the United States Supreme Court, baseball had seen a single arbitrator knock the whole thing over and plunge the game into chaos. For nearly a decade the Players Association had cast about for some way to upend the system. Now they had played a long shot and pulled it off; better to be blessed with luck than logic.

What ensued was baseball's most important labor negotiation ever. The entire basic agreement had to be bargained, and free agency with it. Taken literally, Seitz's decision would make every player a free agent after a one-year option renewal of his existing major-league contract. Somehow a new reserve system was going to have to be patched together through collective bargaining if chaos was to be averted and the long-term interests of the public and the clubs were to be protected. Obviously, what Seitz had done served nothing except the financial interests of the players. At this stage the average major-league player was making about $50,000, not bad by professional sports standards of the time but not good either measured by the short supply of quality players and the vast popularity of professional baseball. No one could reasonably argue that some increase was not warranted. The reserve system had surely placed an artificial restraint on salaries. But unless the system decreed by Seitz was substantially modified, the potential for financial madness as exemplified in the Catfish Hunter case was very great indeed. What if hundreds of players became free agents? I shuddered to think of the effect on the stability of the game, let alone the effect on baseball's ticket prices, which were widely regarded as the best buy in the world of entertainment. If there was ever a time to be concerned about the best interests of baseball, this was it.

By March 9, when the Eighth Circuit Court affirmed the Seitz decision, the PRC knew it was in hand-to-hand combat with the Players Association alone. In an effort to generate some momentum, the PRC had announced on February 23 that it was closing all spring training camps until an agreement was reached with the players. The wisest owners saw this as a calculated bluff designed to stampede the players into some kind of rational solution and focus public attention on the seriousness of the problem. For other owners this was a macho reassertion of owner prerogatives; there would be no baseball until they got their way.

A step worth taking, it had a chance to help if the owners recognized they could not carry it into the regular season. At that point it became a lockout, with the clubs possibly liable to pay the players under their individual contracts. That was a risk the clubs were not going to be happy to take. Some might, but predictably there would be a weak-kneed core, always the Achilles heel of the owners' bargaining unit, that would hopelessly undermine the others. With that prospect, the best course would be to open the camps in time to play the regular season on schedule. The Players Association was not threatening a strike. Far from it, they were still ecstatic over Seitz's ruling. Their game was to figure out just how much they should give back in order to keep the owners sullenly placated. Therefore, it was not surprising that Miller entered the negotiations in a constructive mood. I think he realized that a reserve system of some type was necessary. I found this encouraging, although it still left us the highly complex problem of trying to put together a workable system.

Would players be reserved for ten years? Five? Two? How would they become free agents and who could negotiate for them? Would there be any form of compensation for clubs losing players? All of these were vital, difficult questions.

The negotiations inched along in March. Progress was being made but not enough to bring about a prompt settlement. The closed camps clearly put some pressure on the players, who would have been inhuman not to want to get on with the game and take advantage of free agency. For his part, Miller plainly doubted that the owners were prepared to take the risk of locking out the players in the regular season. So he could wait and hope for better offers than those he was hearing across the table from Gaherin.

At a March 16 meeting of the PRC in Florida, I said that the closed camps were no longer serving any purpose. I urged them to open the camps and get on with spring training before delay caused a late opening of the regular season. I told them I would not rule out opening them myself, if they would not. On March 14, I had told the Associated Press that I expected the camps to open shortly.

I rarely disagreed with PRC chairman Fitzgerald but we were at odds here. That made me uncomfortable, as Ed was as consistently right on major issues as anyone in baseball. He felt the pressure was building on the players for important concessions. As I was sure Miller was reading the PRC mind, I questioned Ed's evaluation. The owners by and large are a garrulous group, too proud and self-confident to keep secrets or strategy under wraps. It took no genius to read their minds. Oftentimes, the whole story could be read in the newspapers.

The conservative majority of clubs opposed opening the camps.

Vociferously on the other side of the ledger was newly unsuspended George Steinbrenner, who may have been the least unhappy owner over Seitz's emancipation of the players. He saw it as an opportunity. Gussie Busch, who best exemplified the conservative owners, felt that the Players Association was just days away from caving in. This was a dream world.

Jim Kaat, the veteran pitching star of the Philadelphia Phillies, called me a number of times, urging me to consider opening the camps. He argued that the shutdown simply was not accomplishing anything.

As I flew back to New York alone on March 16, I sorted out each member of the PRC: Ted Bonda unequivocally wanted the camps opened; Dan Galbreath, John McHale and Lee MacPhail all were leaning that way; Ed Fitzgerald was leaning against an opening but was uncomfortable; Chub Feeney, Bob Howsam and Frank Cashen were negative.

The next day I called Gaherin in Florida and said, "John, I really want to know how you read this situation. I want your best judgment."

"Commissioner," he said, "I work for the PRC. If you quote me on this, I'll deny it. But if I were you, I would open the camps. We're not getting anywhere. Miller is laughing up his sleeve because he knows the clubs have got to open the camps. He told me so. That's my advice, but you've got to protect me on this." I told him not to worry.

At the farewell luncheon we gave John when he retired from baseball, he gave a short, touching and at times hilarious talk. He looked at me and said, "You can always turn your back on the commissioner and not worry."

I struggled through the day with the problem. As usual I talked to Sandy Hadden. On all tough questions over the fifteen years we were together, I always turned to Sandy, one of the few people I have ever known who truly has an open mind. Not that he has no biases, but he could push them aside on the big issues. Deterred only by our mutual regard for Fitzgerald, we agreed to open the camps immediately. Before giving the information to the press, I attempted to call everyone on the PRC to inform them of my decision. I either spoke to them or left word. Unfortunately, Fitzgerald, who had left his office in Milwaukee, and Bob Howsam, who had gone out to dinner in Tampa, were in the latter category. Both were embarrassed and upset with me for not reaching them before I went public. I cared a great deal for their friendship, and their concern troubled me deeply. Still there are times when things simply will not wait. In two days, all twenty-four camps were operating.

On March 20, three days after my order, we had a major-league meeting at New York's Plaza Hotel. The opposition went after me. They said I had destroyed their chances of a good agreement with the players. Busch was the most outspoken. An upset Jerry Hoffberger said that there was no opportunity to bring the negotiations to a conclusion as long as the players thought that they had another alternative available—the commissioner. Time would show that it was all bitter humbug, but they were entitled to a forum and they made the most of it. John Fetzer eloquently defended me, noting that opening the camps had an adverse effect on the clubs' interests but not on the fans' interests, and he congratulated me. Count on John.

Walter O'Malley delivered the dramatic message that the Dodgers would sign no free agents. He obviously hoped the others would follow suit. Given a preview of the message before the meeting, I told O'Malley that he was free to adopt any policy and say anything he wanted short of seeking agreement with the other clubs. I watched his message fall on a puzzled, silent audience. They were not sure what to make of it. There was one pointed exception: Steinbrenner countered O'Malley by suggesting that there be "no discussion between the clubs at all regarding the bidding for free agents." He was showing his desire to take advantage of the opportunity Seitz had provided. Hardly understood at the time, that desire would affect the game more emphatically than anything that had happened since the arrival of Jackie Robinson. A bit player until then, Steinbrenner was moving toward center stage.

Finley criticized the PRC and urged that salary arbitration be eliminated, an understandable but impractical suggestion. He also suggested that the PRC hold back on any improvement of the benefits plan until an acceptable reserve system was in place.

After our March 9 setback before the Court of Appeals, I imposed a week's waiting time, as I had with Catfish Hunter, before the clubs could contact Andy Messersmith. The bidding proceeded much more slowly than it had for Hunter the year before, perhaps not surprising in light of the difference in their abilities. Finally, on March 31, the Yankees announced that they had signed him.

Overnight, Messersmith seemed to have a change of heart. He claimed that agent Herb Osmond, who had negotiated with the

Yankees, did not have authority to make a deal on his behalf. I called a hearing in my office to resolve the dispute and drew an all-star cast, including Miller and Dick Moss from the Players Association, Gaherin and Barry Rona from the Player Relations Committee, Steinbrenner, Gabe Paul, the Yankee lawyers, Osmond and Sandy Hadden. Messersmith was missing. Since he was vital, I insisted he be there the next day and he was.

It became apparent that although the Yankees had acted in good faith, there was a serious flaw in Osmond's authority. Privately I told Steinbrenner that Messersmith had a valid point.

On April 3, the Yankees decided to drop their claim to Messersmith. They issued a press release that was a two-page quote from George. We had not yet learned his style, but this release was a good example of things to come. The general form on display here was to become classic George, the "let's make a virtue of necessity" department, brevity not being a requirement:

I have stated publicly many times how I feel about the great tradition of the New York Yankees and how I expect my players to feel about the privilege of being a Yankee and wearing the pinstripes. I have stated that there really can be no place in the Yankee organization for any player who cannot find it in himself to understand and feel this. I bear them no malice, but I feel that it is essential to what I am trying to build here—to borrow the title of a great movie, *The Pride of the Yankees.*

For the Yankees to pursue Andy Messersmith at this time, in view of Andy's stated feelings about not wanting to play for the Yankees, would be totally inconsistent with what I am striving for—it would not be fair to the other men on the Yankee team —past and present.

This is in no way a criticism of Andy, whom I found in these proceedings to be a very fine young man—which is still more important than being a very fine young pitcher. My only issue with Andy would be his statement that the Yankees did not deal in good faith, and the testimony offered clearly shows that we did. It was in my opinion an unfortunate statement for Andy to make.

Someday, Andy may feel entirely different about representing the New York Yankees and if that day should come we would certainly be willing to meet with Andy and pursue that possibility, but for now I consider the Messersmith matter closed as far as the Yankees are concerned and I so advised the Commissioner this afternoon. The wearing of the Yankee uniform is not something anyone will be allowed to take lightly so long as I am the principal owner.

By the time the season began, Messersmith found his way into an Atlanta Braves uniform. In two years with Atlanta he was 16–15. Then the Braves sold him, on December 12, 1977, to—the Yankees! Apparently, he was ready to wear the pinstripes with "pride."

Andy finally got his big contract from George, pitched six games, went 0–3 and then spent most of the year on the disabled list. The Yankees released him in November 1978. He finished his career in 1979 with his old friends on the Dodgers, before being released on August 28. In the four years after gaining his free agency, he was 18–22.

While there were many issues on the table, the main goal of the PRC was to bargain for control of players for the maximum achievable number of years. Ten years, for example, would have been excellent from the PRC viewpoint but not from Miller's. Both sides worked vigorously throughout the spring trying to nail an agreement together. Considering all that was at stake, the negotiations proceeded with a remarkable lack of bitterness once the camps opened. Public statements by everyone involved were uncharacteristically moderate.

Finally, the negotiators reached agreement in early July. The agreement gave the clubs six-year major-league control of players before they could opt for free agency. It also protected the right of all players on major-league rosters to play out their options as Messersmith had done. This meant the clubs would be negotiating new contracts with most of their players. The costs to the clubs would be considerable. Nonetheless, it was, in the words of Lee MacPhail, "a deal which gave us the best reserve system in sports."

It was true. Clubs could now spend money on player development, knowing that they would retain the player for at least six seasons in the major leagues, a reasonable time to recoup their investment. I viewed it as an excellent deal.

A meeting was scheduled to consider the agreement at All-Star Game time in Philadelphia. We had scheduled the game in that cradle of our liberty because of the nation's bicentennial celebration. The night before the game Bill Giles of the Phillies staged the most splendid All-Star party baseball had ever seen.

President Ford, on hand for the game, gave the event special cachet. We received word that he wanted to walk alone onto the field from behind home plate. It being a campaign year, I could understand it, but I worried about security and cautioned his people, "In Philadelphia, they'd boo the Pope. I wouldn't want to have the president embarrassed."

He arrived well before the game, in time to greet the players in both clubhouses. When game time arrived, he walked alone onto the field to greet the crowd. I have a good ear for boos, but if there were any that evening they were disguised as applause. It was a touching moment.

Mark Fidrych, the most talked-about athlete in the land, was the starting pitcher for the American League. His histrionics, including animated chats with the baseball, pleased the crowd. But the National League pleased it more, beating the American League as usual, this time 7–1.

The clubs had their meeting the next day at the Bellevue-Stratford Hotel, their headquarters in downtown Philadelphia. (Just seven days later, an American Legion convention moved into the hotel and twenty-nine people died from a mysterious virus that came to be known as Legionnaire's disease.) Ed Fitzgerald as chairman of the PRC made a detailed presentation of the new basic agreement. He thought it was a decent deal that gave the clubs a chance to avoid irrational salary escalations, although obviously salaries were going to increase. He congratulated the bargaining team. There was a perfectly reasonable assumption in Ed's remarks that the clubs would behave rationally in their own self-interests. Time proved they would not.

As always, there were critics. Lou Susman, the attorney who had become counselor and confidant of Gussie Busch, read a statement on behalf of his employer describing the deal as "surrender terms," and a "mortgaging of the future." He said more time was needed to study it. Finley said that a bad agreement was better than no agreement at all, but thought this was a "bad agreement."

I cautioned that delay could result in a deterioration of the clubs' bargaining position and urged approval. I gave the clubs until July 19 to register their votes by teletype.

The approval was overwhelming (seventeen out of twenty-four). We had gone from almost nothing to a sound agreement that in practice should have worked adequately. True, we were going to have to generate additional revenues to meet the cost of negotiating new contracts with the players, but baseball had been on a roll of popularity during my years in office that, if it continued, would help provide more revenue through attendance and broadcasting. I told the press I thought Marvin Miller had played a constructive role in shaping the new reserve system. Sadly, it was the last time I felt I could say that about Miller, but I said it then because he deserved it.

What we had not counted on was how ridiculously the owners would behave once the free-agency bugle blew.

Over the years, George Steinbrenner has not ranked high on the players' list of popular owners. He may well challenge Finley for the bottom rung. Still, no one did more to set the players off on a wild sleigh ride to riches.

I would certainly rank George ahead of Miller in terms of their respective contributions to player prosperity. Finley set the stage with his guerrilla tactics. Miller opened the coffers with a lucky assist from Seitz. Steinbrenner then took charge by inaugurating the reign of fiscal insanity that ensued, impoverishing club operations—including his own—pushing up ticket prices and enriching the players beyond their imaginations.

In the first three years free agents were available, Steinbrenner firmly established himself as the most formidable figure on the scene. He signed Catfish Hunter for $3.5 million. He thought he had signed Andy Messersmith for four years for another $1 million. Then, in the first year of the reentry draft, he signed Reggie Jackson for five years for $3 million and Don Gullett for six years for $2 million. In 1977, he gave Goose Gossage $2.8 million for six years and Rawley Eastwick $1.1 million for five years. In 1978, he doled out $1.4 million over four years to Tommy John and $740,000 for two years to Luis Tiant. Eventually, those figures would come to look like bargains, although they certainly were not at the time. In each succeeding winter, George escalated the stakes.

Would people like Gene Autry, Ray Kroc and Ted Turner have gone as high as they did in signing talent had George not set the pace? I doubt it. Once George started signing star after star, public opinion forced the hands of the others, the pressure being even greater when the Yankees won successive American League pennants in 1976, 1977 and 1978. Year after year we were faced with enormous salary increases, far beyond the inflation rate. The following table amply demonstrates the problem.

Year	Average Salary	Total Player Payroll*	Percent Increase in Total Player Payroll from Previous Year
1976	$52,300	$31,380,000	—
1977	74,000	48,100,000	53
1978	97,800	63,570,000	32
1979	121,900	79,235,000	25
1980	146,500	95,225,000	20
1981	196,500	127,725,000	34
1982	245,000	159,250,000	25
1983	289,000	187,850,000	18
1984	325,900	211,835,000	13
1985	364,000	236,600,000	12
1986	431,000	268,944,000	14

SOURCE: Player Relations Committee.
*Total player payroll based on 600 players (1976), 650 players (1977–85), 624 players (1986), excluding disabled players in the interest of uniformity. Total increase by percentage for the eleven years, 757%.

Salary arbitration, which had worked well in the years before free agency, became a disaster and contributed to the salary spiral. Young players going to arbitration were having their salaries determined by comparison with the artificially high salaries of the free agents, men usually with longer experience who had worked their way up through the system.

Cubs relief pitcher Bruce Sutter, no doubt a quality performer, went to arbitration in 1980 when he was, at twenty-seven, only a five-year veteran. The Cubs proposed $350,000; Sutter asked for $700,000. The arbitrator, required to select either one or the other, weighed the salaries of great veteran relievers like Goose Gossage, a nine-year veteran who had gone through free agency, and went for the $700,000. Dick Wagner of the Reds said the award was "like an atom bomb to our industry. It will have a rippling effect throughout the leagues."

By 1983, two-year veteran Fernando Valenzuela was able to command a one-year salary of $1 million from an arbitrator who turned down the Dodgers' offer of $750,000. The players could no longer "lose" in arbitration—the clubs' offers, in desperation, had to be higher than sanity dictated.

One of my immediate concerns was that free agency would eliminate or diminish the incentive of the clubs to maintain effective player-development programs. If so, there would be a destructive effect on our minor leagues, which contribute significantly to the great strength and popularity of baseball, and on our competitive balance. A strong player-development program can permit a small market like Cincinnati or Milwaukee to compete with the larger markets. Although the Yankees flirted with the idea of curtailing player development, almost all clubs perceived that cultivating the young players through an effective farm system was more necessary than ever as an antidote for free agency. Since a club would normally be able to control a player for about a decade of major–minor league play, there was enough incentive to develop young players. As a result, strengthened player-development programs became the mode, offsetting the threat to competitive balance presented by the free-agency system. Even the Yankees joined in.

The minor leagues, terminating a decline that had begun in the early postwar years, began to grow in popularity and attendance. Once a drug on the market, minor-league franchises became increasingly valuable, sought after and profitable.

Ticket prices rose because of the increased cost of free agency, but not enough to hurt baseball's standing as the family game; the increase was not inordinate, owing to admirable club restraint in setting ticket prices and to attendance and broadcasting revenue gains, which were paying the ever-increasing salary costs.

Still, the threat to the family-priced ticket remained clear enough. The only beneficiaries of the increased revenues were the players. As red ink engulfed the game in the 1980s, one had to wonder if the ticket price could be maintained. The danger was starkly revealed in the 1985 labor negotiations when Commissioner Ueberroth ordered the clubs' financial statements to be furnished to the Players Association. The overall losses were staggering.

I was thankful that our clubs had been skillfully expanding their marketing expertise in response to competition within the entertainment industry. It was a vital competence, as baseball sought increased revenue sources, and was a principal explanation for our attendance and broadcasting gains.

Not only were baseball's marketing skills growing, even more important, so were its overall executive skills. The game's lurching course of the 1950s and 1960s had ignited increasing concern for our future. Provident ownership reacted by fortifying the executive level. A lot of ample girths disappeared in the process. Messersmith's good fortune further expedited the trend.

An immediate product of free agency was multiyear contracts. Contracts for three, four or five years became commonplace. By 1980, 42 percent of our players had long-term contracts. Since free agency had given the players and their increasingly adroit agents the upper hand in bargaining, these contracts guaranteed the players would be paid almost without regard to what a player might do. By 1985, players no longer active were still on the payrolls to the tune of $40 million. So fierce was the competition for talent that clubs would often accede contractually to perfectly foolish guarantees to assure acquiring players.

As the number of these contracts and the dollars they guaranteed increased, concern grew as to the effect on player performance. I am afraid that performance on the field has suffered. While there would always be many players like Pete Rose, Dave Winfield, and Gary Carter who would never give less than their best, too many others have not measured up. This goes to the very heart of baseball's integrity. Very few baseball executives would disagree with this conclusion, though it is hardly a subject they like to discuss for attribution. Who can blame them when the quality of play is the basic attraction of the game, not to mention the genuine honesty of the players' efforts. I have heard all the arguments about the players' pride guaranteeing best-efforts performance. I am perfectly prepared to accept that argument in many, perhaps most, cases, but that still leaves a shortfall of substantial proportions.

Players themselves must see this shortfall as clearly and surely as anyone, and yet only occasionally will you read of a quality player grumbling about his teammates' efforts. The unwritten rules of the Player Association "club" would preclude any admission that multiyear contracts are the cause.

Multiyear contracts also undermine the leadership of the executives, managers and coaches. To perform at its best, a sports team must have leadership and athletes who respect that leadership. There must be discipline and adherence to rules as one would find in an efficient military organization. If these elements are not present, inferior performance will be the result, and that is what is happening in baseball. We see shoddy, halfhearted efforts on the field, lack of respect for managers, indifference to fans, increasing player days on the disabled list and abuse of drugs—to mention only some of the symptoms of this illness. In 1974, the total of games missed on the disabled list for all players was 489. In 1985, it exceeded 8,000. To make matters worse, the Players Association has militantly defended the players by grievances against disciplinary action and has often succeeded, fostering even greater disorder as players become convinced they are immune to any discipline: "The Players Association will always protect us" syndrome.

If player compensation were negotiated annually or even biennially I am convinced that most of the abuses I have described would either stop or be significantly reduced. Is annual or biennial negotiation achievable? I think it is, but only if there is a sufficient sense of outrage at all interested levels: baseball administration, clubs, public, press and, hopefully, even the players. That outrage does not exist today. It should.

Can we still sell fans on baseball? Absolutely. Is it as good a game as it can be? No, not today, not with what free agency has brought.

14

A Liquidation Sale in Oakland

On June 15, 1976, I flew to Chicago with Lee MacPhail and Sandy Hadden for a meeting of the PRC at Chicago's O'Hare Hilton. Their discussion of the impending basic-agreement deal seemed routine enough. The negotiating cadences were such that I could pretty well see the shape the deal was going to take. Late in the meeting Cincinnati's Bob Howsam asked if I had heard anything about Finley's selling some players. When I said I had not, Bob said, "I've heard it from several sources, just a rumor, but I wanted you to know." Since the Reds were on their way to a second straight world championship, Bob would take a natural interest in player moves that might change the balance of power.

I asked league presidents Feeney and MacPhail if they had heard about Finley's selling any players. They had not.

June 15 had long been an action date in baseball because it was our trading deadline. Always an exciting time in the baseball year, it was about to lose much of its significance as free-agent moves would more and more supplant the carefully structured player trades that had generated so much baseball excitement in the past; a major loss for the game. I wondered if Finley was up to something. If anything was really afoot, I would know it soon enough from my administrator, Johnny Johnson, who was carefully monitoring the trade deadline.

After the PRC meeting ended, Sandy, Lee and I taxied over to Comiskey Park to see the White Sox and the Orioles with Jim Palmer against Goose Gossage, who was a starter that year. I loved Comiskey. Poetry and nostalgia reveled there together. If you loved baseball, you could see them. They were as plain as the rusting old girders. A lot of our new guys could not see them at all.

Before the game, Sandy and I had dinner with Bill Veeck. Veeck and I were never close. He was too much a "hustler," self-confessed at that, for my ethics-oriented style. He worked me over in the press, always behind my back. I knew it and ignored it. Socially, he was invariably gracious, as he was that night. He was a rogue all right, but at least he was an interesting one. "Commissioner, you had better watch Finley," he said, over a beer. "He's trying to peddle his best players for big bucks." There was the rumor again. I told Sandy we had better check with Johnson immediately after dinner.

To Nancy Faust's superior baseball organ playing, Sandy and I settled into a mezzanine box. Shortly thereafter, the telephone in the box rang. White Sox general manager Roland Hemond said it was Johnson.

"Commissioner, I'm sorry to pull you away from the game," Johnson said, "but I had to tell you this right away—Finley's made deals to sell Rollie Fingers and Joe Rudi to the Red Sox for two million dollars, and Vida Blue to the Yankees for a million five." I asked him where he got the information and he said, "Finley."

I had learned to expect almost any kind of aggressive move from Finley the winner, but not this. Sandy and I talked. We agreed he was liquidating the A's, disenchanted as he was known to be with free agency. A bully and cheapskate by nature, he could hardly face up to a world where the hired hands had the better of him, or to the bleak financial prospects.

I picked up the telephone in front of me and asked the Comiskey operator to get me Dick O'Connell, the Red Sox general manager. She reached him immediately. He sounded as if he was expecting my call.

Dick was one of baseball's true characters; irreverent and hilarious, he was dedicated to the game and to Tom Yawkey, the super-rich Red Sox owner who had spent his way through the 1930s, unsuccessfully seeking a championship by buying future Hall of Famers like Joe Cronin, Jimmie Foxx and Lefty Grove. Dick never took anything seriously, which may be why I liked him in this game grown rapidly too somber.

"Dick, I've just gotten word from Johnny Johnson that you bought Fingers and Rudi for a million each. Is this true?"

He chuckled on the other end of the line. "Yeah," he said, matter-of-factly, "it's true."

"Would you mind explaining to me what you think you're doing?"

Dick was sharp, needing no explanation of that question. We both knew the laissez-faire days of baseball were gone. No more were the titans going to sell stars like peaches. Connie Mack had done it twice with two A's championship teams. Yawkey had been a principal buyer the second time as Judge Landis benignly watched. When baseball adopted the free-agent draft in 1965, we made a basic policy decision: We wanted no more dynasties like the Yankees; they would be sacrificed in the interest of competitive balance among our clubs. Said another way, the game would be a lot more attractive to North American fans if we sent to the gallows the old-time patricians of rule by the rich and the few. About thirty years late, baseball was adopting the spirit of the New Deal. Dick well understood that the sack of peaches he had just bought was going to create "commissarial" dyspepsia.

"Well, you know, Commissioner, we're having a pretty good year. Mr. Yawkey's got the money to spend. Charlie's offering, so what the hell, we took it! It'd be nice to win one for Mr. Yawkey." The Red Sox had lost a gripping World Series the prior October to the Reds. More poignantly, Tom Yawkey was dying, and O'Connell knew it.

"Dick, I've got a real problem with this."

"Commissioner, that's what you're there for! If you don't like it, you can kill it, and that's it! There'll be no complaint from the Red Sox. I was just thinking of Mr. Yawkey."

I called Johnson and told him to try and reach the players and make certain they did not report to their new clubs. I also asked him to alert the Yankees to my concerns. As I did so, I thought we had yet another telltale sign that Steinbrenner was going to be trouble.

The Red Sox happened to be in Oakland, so Rudi and Fingers only had to walk across the field to change teams. They even briefly donned Boston uniforms, but Johnson moved to keep them off the Red Sox roster and out of action. Blue would have to go to Minnesota to join the Yankees. Johnson held him up in Oakland. Next I called Finley. The operator told him who was calling. There were no pleasantries.

"Charlie, I'm at Comiskey and just heard from Johnny about your sales. I don't like the look of these sales at all. I'm putting everything on hold until I can decide whether or not to stop them. I want you to know that. I've also advised the Red Sox and Yankees." Unemotional and businesslike.

"Commissioner, it's none of your damn business. You can't stop me from selling players. Guys have been selling players forever and no commissioner has ever stopped them." The characteristic, hoarse voice revealed anger.

I had personally put Finley on notice of my concern. Nothing more was necessary. Our telephone conversation was headed toward an explosion. Then I thought, why not in all fairness give him the forum of a personal meeting if he wanted one; we were both in Chicago. So, with no great enthusiasm, I suggested a meeting with Sandy and me. His brief hesitation was pregnant. Finley, who trusted no one, was swiftly trying to scent my game. I could picture the distrust in the darting, dark eyes.

Then I heard the voice, now softened, suggest with more than passable courtesy that we meet in the coffee shop of the Pick-Congress Hotel near his insurance office on Michigan Avenue.

Sandy and I were given a ride by a White Sox staffer to the hotel. Finley was there with his son Paul, a pleasant young man in his twenties who was brought along to witness the proceedings. It was about 10:00 P.M.

Finley suggested we drink Black Russians, a horrid concoction made of vodka and Kahlúa. Oddly enough, Sandy and I agreed, impelled I imagine by an instinctive urge for conciliation, if only at the cocktail level. Good ol' Charlie the insurance salesman now drew the curtain back and for over two hours gave a soliloquy on his views of the player marts. A bemused audience of three listened with little interruption. By my personal measure of Finley's shows, this was above average, full of intense, almost pleading sincerity.

"Commissioner, I can't sign these guys. They don't want to play for ol' Charlie. They want to chase those big bucks in New York. If I sell them now, I can at least get something back. If I can't, they walk out on me at the end of the season and I've got nothing, nothing, nothing at all. Now, if I get the money for them, I can sign amateurs and build the team again, just the way I did to create three straight World Series winners. I know how to do it. You know I do. You've seen me do it. And you shouldn't be thinking about getting into this. Hell, owners have been selling players forever and no commissioner ever said they couldn't, not Landis, not anybody. This free agency thing is terrible. The only way to beat it is with young players. That's where I'll put the money."

These were not irrational arguments. Still, I had to wonder if he could not have signed these players. He *had* signed Blue in preparation for the sale to the Yankees. I learned later he had boasted to John Fetzer that he could have signed them any time he wanted. More basically, I wondered if you could believe anything Finley said, and even if you did believe him, did it make any difference. Could I let these sales stand?

We went on until past midnight. Sometimes he slipped back into bluster and profanity at the thought of my intervention. But he would appeal to me again and again to leave him alone.

I wound things up by saying, "Charlie, you've made your points, you've given me something to think about and I'm going to have to do just that. I can't tell you anything tonight. But I'm freezing those players right now until I decide how to handle this."

He was not happy but was civil as we said goodnight.

I set up an Executive Council telephone conference for one o'-clock the next afternoon in New York. We had noticed in both the Chicago and New York airports that all the newspapers were treating the sales as headline news and speculating on whether I would stop Finley. Sandy and I talked about the Finley problem as we flew back. Neither of us could see any answer to a major difficulty: If we let Finley's deals go through, how were we going to stop the weaker clubs from selling off players to the stronger ones and what would become of competitive balance? Also, a night's sleep had not persuaded either of us that Finley was doing anything but liquidating.

During the telephone conference I told the Executive Council I was giving serious thought to stopping the sales. The league presidents, MacPhail and Feeney, along with Fetzer, leaned toward letting the deals stand. They were concerned that otherwise there would be an ugly court battle with Finley and wondered if there was enough precedent to support a veto. Walter O'Malley, John McHale and Ed Fitzgerald went the other way. They did not at all like what Finley was doing. I decided to have a hearing the next day.

Those in attendance at the hearing were Finley, Steinbrenner and his lawyer, Bill Shea, Marvin Miller, Sandy Hadden and David Kentoff (of the law firm of Arnold & Porter). David's presence there was a sure sign we were anticipating trouble. The Red Sox sent no one.

Before the hearing began, Finley privately objected to Miller's presence and criticized me for inviting him. I brushed off the objection; the players were entitled to a spokesman, though I doubted I would like what he had to say.

With the hearing under way, Finley made pretty much the same arguments he had made two nights before over Black Russians. Shea, whose use over the years by Steinbrenner has always dignified the Yankees' cause, urged that the sale go through, essentially following Finley's logic and expressing his own perplexity as to why the commissioner would want to interfere. Following Players Association dogma as proclaimed by none other than himself, Miller mildly questioned the power of the commissioner to deprive players of their rights. He always professed to be puzzled over how the commissioner could do almost anything that affected players without the consent of the Players Association. He and I both understood that was necessary union posturing. I closed the hearing by saying I expected to make a decision the next day. Finley, uneasy but playing the good soldier, marched out.

On June 18, I called a press conference and announced I was "disallowing the assignments." My written decision said: "Shorn of much of its finest talent in exchange for cash, the Oakland club, which has been divisional champion for the last five years, has little chance to compete effectively in its division. Whether other players will be available to restore the club by using the cash involved is altogether speculative although Mr. Finley vigorously argues his ability to do so.

"Public confidence in the integrity of club operations and in baseball would be greatly undermined should such assignments not be restrained. While I am of course aware that there have been sales of player contracts in the past, there has been no instance in my judgment which had the potential for harm to our game as do these assignments, particularly in the present unsettled circumstances of baseball's reserve system and in the highly competitive circumstances we find in today's sports and entertainment world.

"Nor can I persuade myself that the spectacle of the Yankees and Red Sox buying contracts of star players in the prime of their careers for cash sums totaling $3,500,000 is anything but devastating to baseball's reputation for integrity and to public confidence in the game, even though I can well understand that their motive is a good faith effort to strengthen their clubs. If such transactions now and in the future were permitted, the door would be opened wide to the buying of success by the more affluent clubs, public suspicion would be aroused, traditional and sound methods of player development and acquisition would be undermined and our efforts to preserve the competitive balance would be greatly impaired. . . ." I would not change a word of that statement today.

"He's the village idiot," roared Finley, in one of his less profane moments.

"Baseball in Chaos: Bowie Kuhn Jolts the System," *Sports Illustrated* plastered on its cover.

The Sporting News ran a poll that showed that only 12.7 percent of its readers approved of my action.

Ewing Kauffman's secretary called from Kansas City to read a wire Kauffman was sending. "The Royals are completely opposed to Commissioner Kuhn's decision."

Tom Yawkey, the Boston owner who died only twenty-two days later, said, "I don't know what the hell he's basing his decision on, but I'll sue nobody. There've been too many lawsuits in baseball already!"

Finley was otherwise inclined. His announcement of a $10 million lawsuit surprised no one. It was filed in the Chicago federal court in the Northern District of Illinois seven days after my decision.

After working with baseball law for twenty-five years, no one knew that law better than I did. I knew the case law and the historical developments in the ebb and flow of the powers of the commissioner. And I was confident that Finley would lose. Beyond the law and history, my confidence was based on a philosophy I have about the American legal system: Whatever its imperfections, it is guided by a sense of basic morality that transcends the letter of the law. By that test, Finley was in for trouble.

I called Chuck Tanner, the Oakland manager, and reminded him that the three players had been restored to his roster and I expected them to be used properly, just as if there'd been no sale. Tanner, a fine and decent gentleman whom I respected, was fully understanding and cooperative on this point.

I called Cubs owner Phil Wrigley and asked him if there was any objection to our using his Chicago law firm as local counsel. During the conversation, Wrigley told me he did not think I should have stopped the sales. I asked if he was questioning my authority to do it. He said he was not. He further explained his feelings in an interview with Joe Goddard of the *Chicago Sun-Times.*

"In the days of Colonel Ruppert's Yankees," he said, "there were so many poor teams, they had to sell players just to keep going." He did not mention but had to be thinking about Ruppert's purchase of Babe Ruth from the financially troubled Red Sox. Wrigley then switched to the reserve system, long a source of concern to him. "You know," he continued, "Larry MacPhail and I worked out basic modifications of the reserve system—that was many years ago, back in the 1930s, but nobody paid any attention. Baseball never did anything until the roof fell in—it looks like it's falling in again." I thought he was taking an unnecessarily gloomy view of the situation.

On the cheerier side, he was delighted to have us use his firm of Sidley & Austin as local counsel. So I renewed an old alliance with their first-class litigation partner, Jim Baker, with whom I had worked as co-counsel on broadcast antitrust litigation in the early 1950s. We had helped baseball fend off a rather special character named Gordon McLendon, whose self-given sobriquet was "The Old Scotchman." Gordon, having learned to re-create baseball games on radio station WELI as an undergraduate at Yale, put the idea to work with a national radio network called the Liberty Broadcasting System. The backbone of Liberty's programming was baseball, much of it re-created. Ultimately the network failed, but the ensuing litigation that charged baseball with antitrust violations kept Baker and me busy for years.

As my mail came in and the press reaction continued, it appeared I had done the impossible: I had turned Charlie Finley, however briefly, into a sympathetic character. Editorials supported him, some owners supported him, and the fans felt sorry for him. The general feeling was that I had no legal basis for keeping the $3.5 million out of his pockets. Finley began to feel cocky.

On July 7, he sent a wire to all the clubs, with our office included on the list, saying:

CHARLES O. FINLEY WISHES EVERYONE IN BASEBALL TO KNOW THAT HE WILL BE THE GUEST STAR ON JOHNNY CARSON'S SHOW TONIGHT. MR. FINLEY SAYS PLEASE TUBE [*sic*] HIM IN FOR THE FACTS OF LIFE AND BASEBALL.

Secretary of State Henry Kissinger was among the intrigued observers of the newest "Bowie and Charlie Show." Luisa and I were with him aboard the U.S.S. *Forrestal* on July 4, 1976, to watch the tall ships in New York's harbor on the nation's two-hundredth birthday. I took the occasion to invite him to join me at Yankee Stadium the following evening.

As we sat in George Steinbrenner's mezzanine box, Kissinger brought up my veto of the Finley sales. "Do you really have the authority to sustain that?" he asked, noting that the press obviously thought I did not.

I gave him my short course on baseball legal history and the powers of the commissioner. I said I had no doubt I would win. As to the press, I told him most of them had faithfully gobbled up all of Finley's uninformed propaganda about the law. Finley was trying his lawsuit in the press—a big mistake and one I was not going to make.

The secretary listened intently. Like most men of affairs, I think he enjoyed power struggles. He said, "I hope you make it work. A leader needs power to get things done, whether it's the commissioner of baseball or someone else. But power unused is valueless. If you have the authority to use power, you must use it from time to time. You must show that it's there. Then you will have the respect that permits you to get things done."

In an effort to goad me into intemperate replies, Finley launched a campaign of villification in the press. He called me "the village idiot," "the nation's idiot" and "his honor, the idiot in charge." He hoped that a mutual name-calling contest would convince the court that I was biased against him and was motivated by bias in blocking his sales. I am sure he also hoped that I would fine him as I had for his abusive remarks during the Vida Blue imbroglio. He got a lot of ink; the press faithfully printed and reprinted his garbage. I bit my tongue and said nothing. I knew the real test would come in the federal courthouse, not in the newspapers. I quietly watched Finley digging his own grave.

It reminded me of Judge Harold Medina's stoic fortitude in a 1949 Smith Act antisedition trial in New York's federal courthouse. The lawyers for the Communist defendants had contemptuously attacked the judge throughout the trial, but he patiently let them roar until the jury returned guilty verdicts. Then he put the lawyers in jail for criminal contempt.

Finley kept after me throughout the summer, the fall and on into 1977. The trial itself did not begin until February 10, and he was still attacking me even as it progressed. One morning during the trial, we found ourselves walking toward each other down a long courthouse corridor. As we drew abreast of one another, I said, "Good morning, Charlie."

"Blank you, you SOB," he answered, using a common if ungraceful four-letter word. A man of ineffable charm.

The fifteen-day trial played to full houses. There were 2,059 pages of transcript, over a hundred exhibits and twenty witnesses. I was on the stand for two days, during which time Finley, sitting straight ahead of me in the well of the courtroom, stared malevolently at me as if transfixed, unblinking, ferretlike. He moved only to shake his head vigorously when he disagreed with my testimony. I imagine he hoped the judge was taking note. It was such an odd performance, I hoped the judge was watching, too.

The judge in question was Frank McGarr. He was a highly respected, efficient, no-nonsense jurist whose selection to hear this case we applauded. We were hopeful he would have little use for the antics of a man like Finley.

Judge McGarr's brief six-page decision was issued on March 17, on the feast of St. Patrick, one year to the day after I had opened the spring training camps in 1976. My affection for that venerable saint only increased as I read Judge McGarr's decision. It stated: "The fact that this case has commanded a great deal of attention in the vociferous world of baseball fans, and has provoked widespread and not always unemotional discussion, tends to obscure the relative simplicity of the legal issues involved. This case is not a Finley-Kuhn contest —though many fans so view it. Neither is it an appellate judicial review on the wisdom of Bowie Kuhn's actions. The question before the court is not whether Bowie Kuhn was wise to do what he did, but rather whether he had the authority."

Judge McGarr held that the Major League Agreement gave me all the necessary authority. He quoted the pertinent passage, which says the commissioner may: "(a) . . . investigate, either upon complaint, or upon his own initiative, any act, transaction or practice, charged, alleged or suspected to be detrimental to the best interests of the national game of baseball; and (b) To determine, after investigation, what preventive, remedial or punitive action is appropriate in the premises, and to take such action either against Major Leagues, Major League Clubs or individuals, as the case may be."

Sweet indeed to me was Judge McGarr's rejection of Finley's contentions that my actions were motivated by malice or ill will. He could not find "anything other than the commissioner's good faith judgment that these attempted assignments were not in the best interests of baseball. . . ."

Finley cited the decision as ". . . eighteen years of blood, sweat and sacrifice down the drain" and immediately appealed. The U.S. Court of Appeals affirmed Judge McGarr on April 7, 1978.

Nothing so strengthened my hand during my sixteen years as commissioner as this decision. Henry Kissinger's judgment was borne out. Power had been used, challenged and stood the test.

. . .

During the trial I again got wind of a player sale in the offing. On February 18, 1977, I sent the following directive to all clubs:

> This office is in receipt of information indicating that certain Clubs may be considering a transaction involving the assignment of a star player's contract for a very large sum of money. If any club seriously contemplates such a transaction, please advise this office concerning the details prior to making any commitment.

The next day, without notice to me, Finley sold his veteran relief pitcher Paul Lindblad to the Texas Rangers for $400,000. Finley was behaving like a general in a battle: Tie your opponent up with a major attack on his front and then, when you have him preoccupied, as he had me in court in Chicago, slide a corps around his flank and hit him there. Maybe Finley knew something about how Robert E. Lee had slipped Stonewall Jackson through the Wilderness and around Hooker's Union army at Chancellorsville and won the day.

Naturally, reporters rushed right to Finley and asked how the commissioner would view this latest transaction. Naturally, he answered, "Kuhn can read about it in the papers."

Lindblad, although an Athletic all the way back to their Kansas City days, was not really one of their stars, certainly not the equal of Fingers or Knowles. Still, I wanted to be sure that the Lindblad sale was not part of a liquidation plan.

We had another hearing. It was held on March 2 in Texas. On hand were Finley and his son Paul; Finley's attorney, Neil Papiano; Eddie Robinson and his lawyer from the Texas Rangers; Lindblad; Dick Moss from the Players Association and Sandy, Johnny Johnson and our attorneys.

Finley made an effective presentation, citing the fact that Texas had initiated the deal and had been after Lindblad for some time. Since Lindblad's home was in Texas, the Rangers felt he could be a popular addition. Moreover, Finley urged that the deal was a coup for Oakland as players of greater merit had moved for a lot less. He also noted that, at thirty-six, Lindblad was past his prime. All of this, he argued, was inconsistent with my concerns about a liquidation scheme.

Papiano presented the same arguments we had all heard in court the month before: (1) that I lacked the authority to intervene; and (2) that I was harassing Finley for personal reasons. Neither I nor Judge McGarr was persuaded.

After reflecting on Finley's arguments, I made a decision on March 3 approving the Lindblad sale, concluding that it was not part of an overall liquidation plan. Approval did not mean I had abandoned my concerns about liquidation. We had learned that Finley had offered for sale Gene Tenace, Sal Bando, Don Baylor, Bert Campaneris, Phil Garner and Mike Torrez, in addition to Lindblad, Fingers, Rudi and Blue. He had failed to re-sign Rudi, Fingers, Campaneris, Bando, Baylor and Tenace, and likely would not have signed Blue except for the attempt to sell his contract to the Yankees. Other clubs, faced with the new world according to Messersmith, were re-signing their players. Finley was not really trying.

In the first reentry draft for players who had become free agents, Oakland drafted negotiation rights to twenty-two, signed none, negotiated with only three, and had draft rights taken away for three others by the Player Relations Committee because of Oakland's lack of interest. So I noted in my decision that I intended "to scrutinize with great care any player assignments of the Oakland club which involve substantial payments of cash to the Oakland club, and will not hesitate to disapprove such assignments if I find that they are not in the best interests of baseball and to take such other action either remedial or punitive as the circumstances may warrant."

More significantly, and this is the point that gave the Lindblad case continuing significance and notoriety, I decided to make the $400,000 sale price a ceiling for all major-league player sales. I did it by edict rather than by seeking the votes to adopt a new rule. I usually preferred the democratic voting process but sometimes an edict was the only way to get the job done. I knew I could not have gotten the votes to adopt the $400,000 limit, because too many clubs would put their own self-interest ahead of what was best for the game.

When I so notified the major-league clubs, some were upset. Cincinnati's Bob Howsam was the most outspoken and critical. Gabe Paul of the Yankees strongly voiced his objections, which were consistent with the laissez-faire attitude of both Gabe and Steinbrenner. Many general managers thought I had deprived them of a needed flexibility in running their clubs. They argued, for example, that the sale of a fading star might provide vital funds for a player-development program or might just balance the books in a bad year. They felt that they, not the commissioner, should make these judgments.

Of course, there was something to their arguments, and, of course, I was playing "big daddy" by superimposing my judgment on theirs, but after years in baseball, I knew instinctively when restraints were necessary. I could evaluate the big picture better than individual general managers, whose views were understandably parochial. Free agency had opened up a new era in baseball. The free spenders were prepared to make colossal offers for talent, whether on the free-agent market or from other clubs. This threatened our competitive balance. I could not control the free-agent market because that was a matter for collective bargaining, but I could control the deals with other clubs. Judge McGarr had established that and I intended to do so. I was protecting the clubs from themselves. Our 1965 rule that prevented clubs from selling amateur draft rights had exactly the same purpose and philosophy.

Howsam continued to argue this point for years, bringing it up regularly at general managers' meetings and league meetings and in the Executive Council after he joined that body. He had plenty of support but I was never persuaded. Even with the passage of time, I declined to accommodate critics who said, "At least adjust it for inflation." My answer, which was only half facetious, was that I had probably set the limit too high in the first place.

Why $400,000? It just happened to be the handy number in the Lindblad sale at the time I decided to set a dollar-limit policy. It was as good a benchmark as any. Besides, I rather liked the idea of Finley's very own number being the limit.

In applying the limit, we tried to avoid being obstructionists. For example, when Steinbrenner sent Oscar Gamble to Veeck's White Sox for Bucky Dent in April 1977, the cash involved exceeded the limit. Veeck was exactly the kind of operator who prompted me to set a limit. Hard up for money, he would always be tempted to put immediate financial considerations ahead of team development.

Rather than void the deal, I called George and suggested he try to restructure it. He did, adding two minor-league pitchers and reducing the cash to $250,000 in order to get Dent. That turned out, fortuitously, to be beneficial to the White Sox. One of the minor-league pitchers was LaMarr Hoyt, who won the Cy Young Award for the White Sox in 1983: one of Bill Veeck's best trades.

Finley not only knew General Lee's strategy at Chancellorsville,

I think he had also studied Ulysses Grant's patient pounding of Lee from Cold Harbor to Appomattox Court House. Like Grant, Finley kept pounding me, looking for a breakthrough. He would make one last effort to beat the system.

Near the close of our 1977 Honolulu meetings, I had the occasion to sit next to Howsam at a banquet. Truth serum had been flowing freely. He leaned over to me and said, "Commissioner, just think about what I'm going to tell you. Don't give me a fast answer. Don't even answer at all. Just think about this. I want you to think about whether you would have a problem if I bought Vida Blue."

I rolled my eyes in dismay.

He held up his hand. "I just want you to think about it, Commissioner. The rules ought to be flexible sometimes. Just think about it. This is not the time to talk. We'll talk later."

Less than two days later, on December 9, as the meetings were breaking up, Oakland and Cincinnati jointly announced a trade that would send Blue to the Reds for a minor leaguer named Dave Revering and $1.75 million.

I saw what Bob was trying to do. He was a winner, as he had shown with the Reds throughout the 1970s. They had been world champions in 1975 and 1976, but had lost out in their division to the Dodgers in 1977. Now, he saw a chance to get back on top with Blue. So he took him. I could read Bob's mind: He knew he carried great weight with me; somehow he would persuade me that this deal was different.

Finley no doubt loved this. Not only had he sold Blue for more than four times my $400,000 ceiling, but he had made the deal with one of the "solid" figures of the game. By throwing in Revering, they no doubt hoped that they had found a loophole in the $400,000 rule, since this was a trade and not a sale; the money was just incidental.

Needless to say, I told them this transaction was in serious trouble and scheduled a hearing. The baseball world was dumbfounded: What did Howsam think he was doing? There was also resentment that he had given Finley respectability in one more effort to pound the commissioner.

We held the hearing in New York on January 24 and 25. Howsam, in a battling mood, insisted that the rule should have its exceptions. He argued that I was asking him, in order to make the trade, to give up players who in his opinion would weaken the Reds to the extent Blue would strengthen them. "The purpose of every trade," he insisted, "is to strengthen your club. Every trade I make or that which any other baseball man makes, is with that in mind."

Finley said he would use the money for player development, although I knew he had not been making any attempt to sign his amateur-draft choices. They tried to convince me that Revering was more than just a throw-in.

Marvin Miller argued that my disapproval would somehow constitute an interference with the collective bargaining agreement. That was just plain wrong.

On January 30, I announced that I would not approve the transaction. In my decision, I dealt with the commissioner's power to act in the best interest of baseball and the parties' insistence on a precise definition: "This term is of constitutional generality, and necessarily so. It cannot be defined comprehensively in three or four words or three or four pages, or in any rigid fashion. It was intended by the framers of the Major League Agreement to be broad and all-inclusive, to be flexible and adaptable to the new and different, and unforeseeable, problems which the framers knew would inevitably arise with the passage of time."

I dealt with competitive balance and my concerns that the less affluent clubs would sell their star players to the rich clubs, contrary to the fans' interests. I noted how strong the Reds were at the time, and how Oakland had declined.

Then I covered the matter of fairness. Why should I bend the rule for the Reds and the A's when I had already forced other clubs to adhere to the rule? Besides, I knew for a fact that the Yankees, Angels, White Sox, Rangers and Royals had all been deterred from pursuing large cash deals for Blue and other players.

Finally, I told them they could renegotiate the deal at the next interleague trading period or alternatively trade Blue or Revering elsewhere. I imposed no penalty on them, despite their clear effort to circumvent my dollar-limit directive.

The Reds reacted bitterly in the press. On March 15, Finley traded Blue to the Giants for seven players and $390,000. That was more like it.

15

The Battle for Toronto

I n March 1976 the American League voted to expand to Toronto
for the 1977 season. No provision was made for Washington,
notwithstanding my 1971 assurance that major-league baseball
would not expand or transfer a franchise without making provision
for Washington. The toughest defeat I suffered while commissioner,
it led me to submit my resignation less than a year after I had been
reelected for a second term.

San Francisco–Oakland was the root of the difficulty. By the spring
of 1975, I had placed a high priority on resolving what had become
our Bay Area problem. Attendance figures were emphatically telling us that the Bay Area could not support two clubs. The Giants had
averaged 1.5 million in attendance during the years they were sole
occupants, from 1958 to 1967. Since the coming of the A's in 1968,
the two franchises together were totaling only that much. We hit
bottom in 1974, when the Giants' attendance barely topped 500,000
and the A's, winners of a third consecutive world championship,
failed to reach a million.

I began having conversations with all the principals in the area—
Mayor Joe Alioto in San Francisco; Mayor John Reading in Oakland;
Bob Nahas, head of the Oakland–Alameda County Coliseum com-
plex; Horace Stoneham, owner of the Giants, and Finley. Brooding

over the loss of Catfish Hunter and no doubt already plotting my early demise as commissioner, Finley was the least accessible.

In a series of meetings, Alioto came across as open-minded, willing to search for solutions. Urbane, sociable and bright, he was an ideal man to work with, and I appreciated his quick lawyer's grasp of our problems. Because he was serving his last year as mayor, there was a question how much he could do in the months before he left office.

Nahas, an extremely successful real estate man, was the key man across the Bay. Nahas was one of those people I liked from the start. We became friends and remain so today. He doubted that any real cooperation could be expected from the San Francisco politicians, doubted that the East Bay politicians would want to give up any part of the A's and distrusted Finley. He had to be careful lest any move he made be treated by Finley as a breach of lease. However, he was willing to talk about solutions because, like Alioto, he knew there were problems. Unlike Alioto, he was inclined to attribute those problems more to baseball's shortcomings than to a basic overpopulation of the area by two major-league clubs. He detested Finley and had a low regard for his marketing skills.

I sent a letter to Alioto and Nahas on May 13 outlining the problem and telling them that our Major League Franchise Committee "feels that there must be a solution which fair-minded men should be able to develop."

To my delight, but not surprise, Alioto's response expressed his belief that a solution could be achieved. He suggested we sit down and find the answers. To that end, he appointed a group of distinguished San Franciscans to negotiate details of a reasonable agreement.

Nahas's lengthy reply detailed all of the problems involved in working out a solution. He was as discouraging as Alioto was optimistic.

On May 15, Mayor Alioto told a press conference that "you can't argue with the attendance figures—maybe one team is the answer." Alioto came to see me in New York on May 19. He told me that Cyril Magnin would chair his committee on the baseball problem. I was beginning to feel that a solution was within reach.

My idea at that time was to move one of the clubs out of the Bay Area and split the other one between the two cities, half the games to be played in Candlestick Park, and half in the Oakland-Alameda Coliseum. Because Finley was so difficult and Alioto so cooperative, the best solution seemed to be selling the Giants to Toronto, which was assiduously seeking a major-league club. I had an understanding with the key Washington interests that such a move would not be viewed as a breach of faith with them.

By May 23, Nahas told me he had been unable to work anything out with Finley. He speculated that perhaps Finley was trying to lay the groundwork to move the franchise himself. He also cast a pall over my idea of playing half the A's' games in San Francisco. "San Francisco never gives us anything but problems," he said, "why should we give up half our games?" Without cooperation from the Oakland side of the Bay, no solution was possible. As the months went by, it became clear we were not going to solve the riddle by the end of 1975. Significantly, 1975 also marked the departure of Alioto and the arrival of George Moscone as San Francisco's new mayor. Alioto may have left the baseball scene but hardly the Oakland scene. As attorney for Al Davis's Oakland Raiders, he later masterfully steered them through the legal shoals on their way to becoming the Los Angeles Raiders. That would have a major impact on baseball, Finley and me, as we shall see.

In January, I flew to San Francisco to meet Moscone at his home. Nahas was there, as was Corey Busch, Moscone's press secretary (he later became a vice president of the Giants).

Not surprisingly, Moscone had none of Alioto's enthusiasm. Having been mayor for only a few weeks, how could he back the politically explosive departure of the Giants? The meeting broke up without progress or prospect of a solution.

The Giants, meanwhile, had been meeting with Toronto interests. On January 9, 1976, Labatt's Breweries had reached agreement in principle to purchase the team for $13.5 million and to move them to Toronto in time for the 1976 season. On February 13, San Francisco got a preliminary injunction to stop the Giants from moving in violation of their lease.

I was in regular communication with Toronto's metro chairman Paul Godfrey and Labatt's president Don McDougall. Obtaining the Giants was their preference, but now that looked hopeless. Expansion would do and they were not going to stand on ceremony as to whether it was the American League or the National League. They did not want to get caught in the politics between the leagues or in baseball's political problems in Washington. They just wanted major-league baseball, and the sooner the better.

The American League, having voted on February 6 to expand to Seattle to settle the antitrust litigation that followed the 1970 transfer of the Pilots to Milwaukee, needed to find another city. On

March 21, they approved a resolution to put a club in Toronto, and five days later, granted the franchise to Labatt's. The American League fully understood my concerns about any expansion that did not include Washington, but was politely and clearly motivated in ignoring my concerns by three things: a desire to settle the Seattle litigation; a high regard for Toronto; and Jerry Hoffberger's driving determination to keep baseball out of Washington. Hoffberger was smoldering over my continuing support of Washington, my reelection the prior summer and my opening of the spring training camps a few days before the American League voted to expand to Toronto. American League owners who would normally have bucked Hoffberger in any confrontation with me were quietly siding with him because of the lure of Toronto. How had Toronto suddenly become so attractive when round after round of expansion in the 1960s had totally ignored it? More than anything else, the success of Montreal was the answer, taken together with the strong leadership of Chairman Godfrey and Don McDougall. Montreal had emphatically put Canada on the major-league baseball map.

I was caught squarely in a three-way crossfire between the two major leagues, both of whom coveted Toronto, and Washington, whose officials were reminding me of baseball's commitment to that city. I now antagonized my friends and enemies alike in the American League by encouraging the National League to expand.

On March 29, the National League voted on whether to expand to Toronto and Washington. If the proposal passed, I would support it as the better plan, in effect vetoing the American League plan. At that time, a unanimous vote was required for expansion of the National League; ten clubs voted for expansion with only two opposed —not unanimous but overwhelming.

I now had two alternatives: to persuade the American League to revise its plan to include Washington or overrule the National League's unanimous-vote rule. I discussed the latter course with Chub Feeney, who argued that I was being misled by the 10–2 vote. He said, "A lot of those ten were political. They wanted to support you. They knew the two votes to kill it were there, so they had nothing to lose." I told him we might have to take another vote to test his theory.

During the week I heard from a number of people in Washington who urged me to take whatever steps were necessary to return baseball to Washington. They included President Ford; senators Mike Mansfield, Robert Griffin, Thomas Eagleton, Hubert Humphrey and Edmund Muskie; House Speaker Carl Albert; congressmen Tip O'Neill, John Rhodes and Al Ullman; and the congressmen who headed the D.C. Baseball Committee—Bernie Sisk, Frank Horton and Mel Price. I also heard from Mayor Walter Washington and Sterling Tucker, chairman of the D.C. City Council.

This was a trying, tense time for baseball. The Messersmith decision was brand new; we were negotiating a new basic agreement; I had just ordered the spring training camps opened, angering a lot of owners; the two leagues were scrapping over Toronto; and Congress was on our back.

I had to respond to the American League expansion plan; I was not prepared to watch them blithely ignore Washington and baseball's commitment there. After a lot of mental anguish I issued a directive on April 1 that I knew had little prospect of resolving the dilemma. I said: "It is difficult for me to see how I can ignore [the American League's] failure to provide for Washington. . . . Under the circumstances, it is my decision that the American League should be permitted to carry out its plan provided that it first make suitable provision for Washington. While Lee MacPhail is generally familiar with my views as to what would be sufficient, I am ready to sit down with him immediately in an endeavor to work this matter out and am willing to give the League every reasonable assistance. I believe that 7 days would be sufficient time to conclude this matter. In the meantime I am directing that the League and its members take no steps of any kind designed to further its Toronto plan. . . . If at the conclusion of 7 days time it should appear that the American League was unable or unwilling to make suitable provision for Washington, then I will consider [the National League's expansion plan of Washington and Toronto] which I described at the outset. While that application presents both legal and practical problems which need careful attention, I am not prepared to say at this time that those problems are insuperable."

Tensions were building on all sides. I took pains to reassure Metro Chairman Godfrey and Labatt's McDougall that Toronto would have a club, American or National, in 1977. They were nervous about the situation, not wanting to offend any of the baseball parties, but willing to bide their time.

On April 7, I notified the leagues that only two days remained before I would "proceed to impose a solution which I feel does essential justice all around."

But by April 9, Lee MacPhail bought some time by informing me that Baltimore's Hoffberger was traveling out of the country and was needed to help work out the problem. Hoffberger was a key player. He plainly had Lee's ear and was battling to keep baseball out of Washington to avoid competition with the Orioles.

On April 14, I met with the American League Planning Committee in Chicago. Despite a long and thorough discussion, we could not come up with an acceptable solution for Washington. The discussion had an interesting twist.

With the White Sox doing poorly under Veeck's stewardship and old Comiskey Park crumbling into multimillion-dollar repair bills he could not afford, Veeck was discussing with Denver's fabulously wealthy Marvin Davis the possibility of Denver's acquiring the Sox. If a sale to Denver was possible, then so was one to Seattle. Veeck was not bound by any lease since the club owned Comiskey.

So the committee pondered selling the club to Seattle and expanding into Toronto and Washington. The American League would find a way to return to Chicago if a new stadium were built. MacPhail was firmly opposed to the entire scheme and became more stubborn as he perceived that it was getting some support. Finally, he turned to me and said, "Commissioner, do you really want to see the American League abandon Chicago, one of the finest baseball cities on the continent?" He knew how much I detested franchise moves. My answer was no.

We even toyed with a one-club expansion of each major league to thirteen clubs, with interleague play to make the schedule work, but the National League would not accept that concept.

So I issued another directive: "The National League plan [expansion to Toronto and Washington] should now be given preference in light of the (1) inability of the American League to make suitable provision for Washington and (2) the inclusion of an expansion club for Washington in the National League plan. Therefore, I will give the National League two weeks to put its plan into effect for both Washington and Toronto, this being the same period of time previously given the American League with extensions. . . . At the conclusion of the two-week period . . . I will consider ending any restraints upon the American League if it appears that the National League will be unable to put its plan into effect."

When this reached the American League office, my temperate friend Lee MacPhail, my ally before and since on innumerable issues, went straight into orbit. He was furious: There was no obligation to Washington; the American League was not going to pass up

Toronto; they would battle the commissioner. From a strictly American League point of view, he was right—a franchise in Washington could hurt Baltimore, and Toronto was a plum. From an overall baseball point of view, he was wrong. As commissioner, I had made a commitment to Washington in 1971 that the American League was prepared to breach. Neither major-league baseball nor the American League had ever repudiated that promise nor had they repudiated the commissioner who made it. Hoffberger had tried at my reelection in 1975 and had failed. Not only was baseball's honor at stake, so was its relationship with the Washington establishment. By taking the low road of self-interest, the American League was jeopardizing that relationship. We would quite promptly pay a costly price when an unhappy Congress got around to tax reform and deleted the tax shelter advantages of owning a professional sports club in the Tax Reform Act of 1976.

I could forgive Lee who, after all, was putting the interests of his league first. Arguably at least, that was his job. What I found hard to forgive was the opportunism of the quality American League owners. Where were the good guys? Where were the guys I thought I could count on when decency and the general good of the game were at stake?

To add to my disenchantment, there were the usual insinuations that Walter O'Malley was maneuvering me to protect the National League's aspirations for Toronto. I had no idea what O'Malley's thinking was regarding Toronto and I cared less. I cared a lot about baseball's commitments.

On April 26, the National League met again to vote on expansion. This time, only seven clubs voted for expansion, five votes short of the unanimous vote required. Feeney's judgment of the earlier 10–2 vote was proven correct. Had they voted 10–2 again, I was prepared to declare that adequate, since the unanimous vote provision was unreasonable. But there was little I could do when only a bare majority supported expansion.

So I was beaten. I could not sensibly veto the American League plan. To do so would produce a war, ugly and bad for the game. As a practical matter, it is difficult for a commissioner to challenge an entire league. Having no alternative, I told MacPhail the American League could proceed to implement their plan. I have a lot of spirit and not much has ever kept it from soaring. This time, something had.

On April 30, I sat at my desk, pulled out a white lined pad and penciled out a message of resignation: "After long consideration I have decided to submit my resignation as Commissioner. In making this decision I am substantially motivated by the Washington baseball situation. As you all know, we have failed to keep a commitment regarding Washington. While many in baseball honestly differ with this assessment, I ultimately have to live with my own view of it and my own conscience. I would appreciate your advice as to an effective date. I would be prepared to stay on for a reasonable period of time if you feel it is useful for purposes of transition. I thank each of you for the help you have given me over the past eight years."

I gave Sandy Hadden the courtesy of commenting. He very quietly said he had no comment; he could not blame me. If he was troubled by what this could do to his career in baseball or by the end of the partnership he and I had enjoyed since 1970, he was not going to bother me about it. He simply asked, "How do you want me to send it?" I replied, "Just call all the Executive Council members as fast as possible and read it to them individually; then do whatever they suggest. Also be sure to let Jim and Lou know." Jim Garner and Lou Hoynes were the league lawyers.

Luisa and I had talked the night before. For once there was little discussion. She understood.

Luisa and I took off for Millerton, New York, to visit my in-laws for the weekend. Their home was always a place of rejuvenation for me. I loved the Degeners, their old colonial farmhouse and the beautiful farmlands of Dutchess County. It was a wonderfully relaxed weekend. I had lost the battle, but I had held the high ground, and now I was doing the right and only thing to do.

Sandy had set up a conference call with the Executive Council for Monday morning, as they had requested. They asked if I would meet with them and arrangements were made for May 6 at the Arizona Biltmore in Phoenix. The telephone conference was very subdued, exquisitely polite, curiously procedural. Nobody talked about the main show.

Sandy and I had plenty of time before Phoenix to talk about the shape of things to come. I wanted him to come to Willkie Farr & Gallagher with me. That was a possibility. We speculated on who the new commissioner might be and whether Sandy might want to continue with a new administration. Obviously, he would be invaluable. We both liked Ed Fitzgerald for the job. Sandy certainly would want to continue with someone like Ed. We doubted baseball would be lucky enough to talk him into it. I had no telephone calls about the Phoenix meeting. The Council was sitting tight on my news. Somehow I was not at all sure I liked that.

The Biltmore meeting began at 9:00 A.M. with a full house consisting of John Fetzer, Walter O'Malley, John McHale and Ed Fitzgerald, in addition to league presidents MacPhail and Feeney. Hoynes and Garner were there, too, as was Sandy. Nine solid friends. I thought, "Oh, oh, now I'm in trouble. My friends get me in more trouble than anybody. Watch out."

I watched Lee at the meeting. I could feel the tension between us. He said not a word during the course of the morning, uncharacteristically quiet.

I heard all the arguments I expected: baseball needs you, you have just been reelected, we have free agency hanging over us, the clubs like and trust you. It was all beautifully and feelingly said. As always, Fetzer was eloquent, concluding, "If you leave, I'm going to sell the Tigers and get out."

Finally, Lee spoke: "You know how I feel; you know I agree with everyone else in the room. I want you to stay as commissioner."

Only a year earlier I sat with this same group and heard the same arguments genuinely advanced, only then it was about whether I would accept reelection. This time was different. The subject was whether I should continue despite the fact that most of them had not backed me up on a critical issue. Now I pressed that point. "What support will I get on Washington?"

Walter O'Malley expressed his own view that I had gotten myself "out on a limb," that I had never had the support on Washington that I asserted. I sharply disagreed. "All right," he said, "it doesn't make any difference; however you got out there, you're the commissioner and you're entitled to go out on limbs. If we don't like where you go we can change commissioners or we can back you up; so, gentlemen, obviously we're going to have to find a way to back up the commissioner. Tell us what you want."

There were two things I really did not want to hear that day: what Walter said about backing me up and Lee's words of support. If either had been absent I would have been on my way. Walter had me cornered. Of course, he had quarreled a little with my Washington position, but his tell-us-what-you-want conclusion, by giving me virtual carte blanche to name my terms, closed off my escape routes. To make it more binding, nobody in the room was disputing Walter.

In a way, I hated to answer. Almost any answer I gave was going to be accepted. They also knew the American League expansion to

Toronto and Seattle was water over the dam. I would not and could not now ask for a reversal of that decision. I felt like reading the *Encyclopaedia Britannica* aloud to them, or the complete works of James Fenimore Cooper. I looked at Sandy Hadden for inspiration. He looked back as if he were already on page 1 of *The Deerslayer.* I was trapped. Maybe somewhere in the secret vaults of my mind that was what I really wanted. Even now, I am unable to psychoanalyze myself clearly enough to answer the question. I am sure that I did not arrive at the Arizona Biltmore intending to be seduced. The only subject I had any serious intention of discussing was the transition to a new commissioner.

But I was responding to Walter's question and the seduction was under way. I said, "I must have your absolute assurance of support on returning baseball to Washington even though I know perfectly well that some of you don't believe in Washington. This could be through National League expansion or a new stadium for the Orioles between Washington and Baltimore or by dividing Orioles games between the two cities or whatever provides a reasonable solution." O'Malley said that was agreeable. That was it.

There is a disappointing postscript to this story so far as Washington is concerned. Ten years later there is still no ballclub there, only the Redskins. During my final years as commissioner I supported a phased expansion plan of six new clubs. Washington was certainly a significant factor in my support. The clubs supported the *concept* and asked for a careful study. Sadly, this support has dissipated since I left, a victim of baseball's worsening finances. Washington deserves a happier fate.

16

A Man Called George

I welcomed the arrival of George Steinbrenner when his group purchased the Yankees in January 1973. In hindsight that seems an incredible statement.

CBS had struggled for a decade to rebuild the team but failed. The sure executive skills that made the network a model in the broadcasting industry did not translate into sports. The Yankees had settled into a period of mediocrity unprecedented since their pre-Ruthian days. I believed that a strong, competitive team in the Bronx would help stimulate baseball's recovery from its doldrums. Mind you, I wanted no return to dynasties; just a nicely balanced, competitive recovery would be fine. Steinbrenner's dynamo vitality seemed to be the right answer.

Gabe Paul was brought in, first as director of special projects but later as president, and Lee MacPhail departed the Yankees to succeed Joe Cronin, who was retiring after 1973, as American League president. Mike Burke, who had run the Yankees for CBS, also left, he and George being ill suited as partners. When popular manager Ralph Houk retired, it was clear that change was becoming a way of life at Yankee Stadium.

Bittersweet though their relationship was, George and Gabe were a good team. Gabe, a veteran baseball executive I had always liked, had never before had strong financial support. He did now. He made trades that buttressed the Yankees, acquiring Lou Piniella, Mickey Rivers, Willie Randolph, Chris Chambliss, Ed Figueroa and Dock Ellis, all major contributors, along with free agent Catfish Hunter, to a 1976 pennant, the first for the Yankees in a dozen years.

On September 5, 1973, as Steinbrenner's first season was coming to a disappointing close, a story broke that would have momentous consequences for him and for his relationship with me. It was reported that Watergate special prosecutor Archibald Cox was investigating possibly illegal 1972 campaign contributions by the American Shipbuilding Company to the committee to reelect President Nixon. Steinbrenner was the CEO of AmShip. At first blush, it was hardly a matter of great concern. A number of corporations had been fined for making illegal contributions, hardly a traffic violation but not murder, either. Unfortunately for George, the AmShip story had a nasty twist. Cox was looking into allegations that AmShip employees had been induced to make the contributions, had been illegally reimbursed by AmShip and then were persuaded to participate in an elaborate scheme designed to frustrate and obstruct the federal investigation. Illegal contributions may be one thing but obstruction of justice is quite another. To make matters worse, the mastermind of the scheme was alleged to be Steinbrenner.

This was not exactly a promising situation. People get put in jail for obstruction of justice. The last owner to be sentenced to jail was told by Commissioner Ford Frick to sell his baseball interest. That was Fred Saigh, owner of the St. Louis Cardinals, who in 1953 was sentenced to fifteen months in jail for tax evasion. He sold the Cardinals to Anheuser-Busch.

As I pondered the problem, I found it hard to avoid the conclusion that Steinbrenner was headed for the same fate as Saigh if indicted and similarly sentenced. The gravity of the matter was not lost on George, who hired leading criminal attorney Edward Bennett Williams to represent him. I myself hoped that George could exonerate himself. I had no reason to wish him other than well and saw him as the man to resuscitate the Yankees. George was chipper enough, exuding a certain brash confidence that all would be well, a confidence that I suspect masked a sleep-stealing concern. I did little to reassure him. He pointed out to me one day that the events under investigation went back to 1972—before he bought the Yankees— and had nothing to do with baseball. I replied that those facts would not keep me from taking a serious look at disciplinary action if all this resulted in a conviction. George purported to be very perplexed by my attitude but said, "Commish, we'll give you every cooperation on this and I'm sure we'll persuade you that there is no reason for you to do anything."

Things went from bad to worse when, on April 5, 1974, Steinbrenner was indicted by a federal grand jury in Cleveland on fourteen felony counts, the essence of which was that AmShip had violated federal law by covering up corporate contributions to the Nixon reelection committee and that Steinbrenner had been guilty of obstruction of justice.

Faced with these charges, George made a smart move. After talking to me, he decided of his own volition to remove himself from the daily affairs of the Yankees. Correctly anticipating the likelihood of a suspension, he had beaten me to the punch; in the process he earned some credit with me and probably achieved a more flexible set of restraints. To his credit, George never tried to hide from the seriousness of the matter. Another type of owner would have kept his distance from me, but not George. He kept in touch with me and openly discussed all developments, reflecting a confidence in his own ability to overcome the toughest problems and in his powers of persuasion.

George and Williams had a dilemma. They could fight the indictment and by prevailing end any problem with me. Or they could try to work out a deal with the prosecutor, which could leave them vulnerable with me. I thought they were going to have trouble working out a suitable deal, since I had heard that Special Prosecutor Leon Jaworski, who had succeeded Cox, viewed the Steinbrenner case as very serious.

I was surprised when George was permitted to plead guilty in August to a single felony count of the indictment which charged him with conspiracy and to an information charging him with being an accessory after the fact to an illegal campaign contribution. Sentencing was set for August 30 before Federal Judge Leroy Contie, Jr. It was a difficult time for George. Judge Contie had the power to impose a jail sentence. Such a sentence would almost surely have ended George's baseball career as Fred Saigh's had ended in 1953. At the hearing, Steinbrenner admitted causing his employees to give false information to the FBI and attempting to influence those employees to give false testimony to a federal grand jury. At the conclusion Judge Contie fined George $15,000 and AmShip $20,000.

Six days later George and Ed Williams arrived in my office. Only two owners had been seriously disciplined in the history of the commissioner's office: Saigh of the Cardinals and William D. Cox of the Phillies, who was permanently suspended in 1943 by Commissioner Landis for betting on Phillies games. I told them that a suspension was a real possibility in light of the obstruction of justice charges to which George had pleaded guilty. Ed argued with some fervor that there was no basis for a suspension since Judge Contie had settled for a fine, and a modest one at that. I said I was not persuaded but would have to complete my investigation before making a decision. Ed and George were unhappy enough with that news but their dismay was doubled when I said that I wanted George to continue his separation from the daily affairs of the Yankees until I made a final decision. Ed argued that an interim suspension was inconsistent with my handling of the Cesar Cedeño case in 1973.* He said I had not suspended Cedeño while murder charges were pending against him. I replied that there was nothing to suspend Cedeño from during the off-season while we completed that investigation. Players, unlike owners, have no off-season duties. Reluctantly, they went along with the interim suspension, but Ed pounded home the argument that there was no basis for any suspension beyond the interim period. He was politely threatening. If I disagreed, there would be a fight. Throughout our discussion, George played the role of an incredulous friend who simply could not understand what the commissioner was talking about.

After returning from my travels with the New York Mets on their tour of Japan after the World Series, I had Williams and Steinbrenner in my office again on November 13. I told them I was close to a decision. They renewed their arguments against a suspension and also stressed George's good citizenship as demonstrated by his many acts of philanthropy.

As I pondered the decision, I could not escape a basic fact: George

---

*Cedeño, the twenty-two-year-old Houston star of four seasons, was arrested on December 11, 1973, in his native Dominican Republic and charged with voluntary manslaughter after a nineteen-year-old woman was found shot to death in his motel room. Cedeño had been the only other person in the room, and the gun belonged to him. After some legal maneuvering, the charge was reduced to involuntary manslaughter and he was fined the equivalent of one hundred dollars plus court costs. We made our best efforts to determine if a cover-up had taken place, and whether there were any facts beyond those brought out in trial, but our efforts produced nothing further. Under the circumstances, I took no disciplinary action.

had pleaded guilty to a serious felony. Had he been sentenced to jail, it would have warranted permanent suspension. By merely imposing a fine, the court had pretty well precluded a permanent suspension by me, perplexed though I was by the court's leniency. So I concluded that a substantial suspension was necessary.

On November 27, I announced a two-year suspension. My decision explained my concern: "Attempting to influence employees to behave dishonestly is the kind of misconduct which, if ignored by baseball, would undermine the public's confidence in our game. Ignoring this conduct could easily lead to suspicion that such conduct may occur within the game itself and affect play on the field. . . . I have decided to place Mr. Steinbrenner on the Ineligible List for a period of two years. In accordance with this decision, Mr. Steinbrenner is hereby declared ineligible and incompetent, for the specified period, to manage or advise in the management of, the affairs of the New York Yankees."

Sports Illustrated said "The Commissioner Homers" and the media reaction was generally good, although some thought the suspension fell short.

Red Smith, writing in *The New York Times,* said, "Giving him a two-year 'suspension' that costs him nothing is like sending a naughty boy home from school for the Christmas holidays."

United Press International's Milton Richman questioned whether the punishment was enforceable. "To me, it is like a manager being thrown out by an umpire," he wrote. "One way or another, he finds some covert way of relaying his instructions to his surrogate, and I'm sure George will too."

George used irony in calling it a "fine Thanksgiving present," and said, ". . . we are shocked beyond belief by Mr. Kuhn's decision." But to his credit, he never followed through on a threat to sue, never questioned my authority to impose the suspension and prepared to face his punishment.

The terms of the suspension needed to be clearly defined, for the obvious question was, How do you suspend an owner?

So I spelled the terms out for him in a letter from my office:

Within 20 days of the issuance of this order, Mr. Steinbrenner shall delegate to a person or persons satisfactory to this office, and for as long as he remains on the Ineligible List, all of his powers, duties and authority to manage, control, and make all decisions affecting the business and assets of the New York

Yankees, including, without limitation, all powers, duties and authority granted to the General Partner. . . . Except, as otherwise provided in this order, Mr. Steinbrenner shall not, while he remains on the Ineligible List, (a) exercise any of such delegated powers, duties and authority, (b) visit or be physically present in the Yankee clubhouse or offices, (c) confer, consult, instruct, advise or otherwise communicate, either directly or indirectly, with the person or persons to whom such powers, duties and authority are delegated with respect to their exercise of (d) associate or communicate with any Major League Club (including the New York Yankees) or its personnel or any person having business or financial dealings with the New York Yankees in connection with any matter involving the New York Yankees or Baseball. These prohibitions shall not be interpreted as prohibiting Mr. Steinbrenner from associating with such persons on a purely social basis during which there shall be no discussion of the affairs, financial or otherwise, of the New York Yankees or Baseball.

Ostensibly, at least, Steinbrenner complied with the terms of the suspension. When his bankers insisted he be involved in certain discussions, he came to me and sought permission. One would have to be naive to think that the telephone did not provide the means for some circumvention of my order but even that had its obvious limits. If he went too far, word was apt to filter back to me one way or another, my grapevine being quite effective. The risk of being caught violating his suspension was too great to permit cavalier behavior on his part. The suspension also shut him off from all public communications regarding baseball and the Yankees as well as from baseball meetings. For a man of George's ego and love of public forums, this was a significant deprivation. As Phil Pepe wrote in The New York *Daily News,* "When you take these things away from a George Steinbrenner, you hurt him where he lives."

With Gabe Paul and his staff in charge, the Yankees' operation was in good professional hands. They were putting together the pieces that would bring the Yankees a pennant in 1976 when they returned from a two-year sojourn in Shea Stadium, where they had played in exile while Yankee Stadium was being rebuilt.

During George's time in Coventry, there was no clamor from any constituency for his return. The owners were content to see him serve out his time except for Danny Galbreath, who made a perfunctory plea in his behalf. I received little mail from the public on the subject, although I do recall various letters from nuns asserting that I was being unduly harsh with George. The players were silent with one exception. One day during the 1975 season, I bumped into Thurman Munson in the runway of Shea Stadium that led from the Yankees clubhouse to the first-base dugout. I admired Munson and his tough, gutsy style of play and saw him as another Hall of Fame catcher in the Yankees tradition. I had seen a lot of him during the 1973 All-Star days in Kansas City, when he developed a friendship with my son Paul and spent time in our suite at the Alameda Plaza.

"Commissioner," he said, "I just wanted to say that I hope you might do something about George. We really need him back!" Such an endorsement of an owner was unusual, but Thurman and George were both compulsive winners. I think Thurman felt George would be a positive force in resuscitating the Yankees ballclub, a goal with which I was not unsympathetic. I tucked his appeal away in my mind for future reference.

In October 1975, Pat Cunningham, who had been serving as acting general partner (the very thought of anyone "acting" for George even now seems anomalous), submitted an application for reinstatement that I considered over the winter. Finally, on March 1, 1976, while the spring training camps were shut, I decided to lift the suspension.

In a written decision, I cited three reasons for doing so:

1. My November 1974 decision was designed to assure public confidence in the integrity of professional baseball. I think that purpose has been achieved.
2. Nearly two years have elapsed since April 1974 when Mr. Steinbrenner voluntarily removed himself from the daily affairs of the Yankees.
3. The management and financial problems of the Yankees asserted in support of Mr. Steinbrenner's reinstatement would be significantly alleviated by his reinstatement and attendant benefits to the team and Yankee fans.

I also sent George a handwritten note, welcoming him back and urging him to get on with making the Yankees a competitive team. He took me quite seriously. The Yankees won the next three American League pennants.

In 1976, George roared back with a particular vengeance, as if to make up for two years of lost time. He tried to sign Messersmith and failed, tried to buy Vida Blue and failed, pulled off a ten-player trade with the Orioles (sending them Scott McGregor, Tippy Martinez, Rudy May, Rick Dempsey and Dave Pagan for Ken Holtzman, Doyle Alexander, Elrod Hendricks, Grant Jackson and Jimmy Freeman); blasted the umpires, ripped Lee MacPhail for refusing to admit to umpire failings, blasted Bob Holbrook (the man who ably designed the American League schedule), named Munson the Yankees' captain, won the League Championship Series in five games on Chris Chambliss's homer against the Royals, got beaten in four straight in the World Series by the Reds, used a controversial technique of walkie-talkies in the Series to position fielders from the press box, signed Reggie Jackson and Don Gullett as free agents, halted a program that brought underprivileged kids to the stadium, claiming acts of juvenile delinquency were occurring (he relented the next day), and stole the New York headlines away from the Mets after a dozen years of Mets domination.

George was back.

He was also embarrassed. I visited with him briefly after the World Series debacle. Gloom had spread like tar over the room in which he joined his top staff and a few friends. He apologized to me for the Yankees' poor showing. He said that would never happen again. When the Yankees lost four straight Series games in 1981 after winning the first two games against the Dodgers, Steinbrenner, like Pavlov's dog, dutifully issued a public apology, though certainly none was called for.

He loved feuds. Over the years he developed a generous number. The commissioner, Lee MacPhail, other owners (his lawyer Edward Bennett Williams and Eddie Einhorn were good examples), umpires, anybody who looked like a schedule maker, Joe Podesta and the Major League Baseball Promotion Corporation, Tony Kubek, and selected writers were his most common targets. He was like a *Titanic* in search of an iceberg; only in George's case it was never wise to bet on the iceberg. His penchant for feuding made the Yankees a constant source of news media attention. A star-studded roster, a volcanic owner and a base in the media capital of the nation combined to make the Yankees a continuous storm center.

George's father had been a hurdler on the track team at MIT. Having learned the skill from his father at twelve, George competed in the hurdles at Culver Military Academy and at Williams College. Not surprisingly, George saw life not as a smooth sprint, but as a succession of hurdles to be conquered in the pursuit of victory. Challenges, everywhere he saw challenges.

He was a man in perpetual motion, whether physical or intellectual. In his Yankee Stadium box, where he invariably was a generous host to my family, he was capable of suddenly screaming at the umpires, the players, the manager, his secretary, his organist, his publicist, his security people—anyone. He would bound regularly to the telephone for an onslaught on some poor victim or to his adjoining office to pace in thought or worry.

He behaved as if he were guided by a compass that pointed unerringly to trouble. In 1979 Lee MacPhail and I agreed that putting George on the Executive Council might have salubrious effects on his general conduct—an essentially insane piece of wishful thinking. So the American League appointed him to fill a vacancy.

Before the Council at that time were the pending negotiations with the umpires, on which the league presidents were making periodic reports. It soon came to our attention from a reliable source that these reports were being leaked by George to Richie Phillips, the union head. This was hardly a surprise as it was well known that George was trying to ingratiate himself with Phillips, perhaps as an antidote for his constant criticism of the umpires.

In advance of a Council meeting at the time, members arrived early and filtered into my office to discuss the leaks with me. Presently I had everybody: both league presidents, Bill DeWitt, Ed Fitzgerald, John Fetzer, Bob Howsam, Ruly Carpenter, John McHale and Walter O'Malley. The more they heard about the leaks the more disturbed they became. In the midst of the hubbub, I learned over the intercom that George, having gone to the empty conference room, was now in my outer office and wanted to come in. I walked to the door and let him in. One look at the faces in that room told George something was afoot.

I confronted him with our suspicions about the leaks to Phillips. He flatly denied it. Not a soul in the room believed him and he knew it.

A few days later, I received a letter of resignation from George. He was not going to serve if the members did not trust him. So ended George's short, unhappy, little-lamented term as a member of the baseball establishment. His resentment against the Council members, whom he called "Bowie's bobos," never abated, although the owner membership changed completely over the years after the Phillips incident.

Whatever his relationship with umpire leader Phillips, his war with the umpires never ceased. He was eternally making tapes of what he viewed as their bad calls. Often when I was at Yankee Stadium, George would take me to the scoreboard booth and cue up tapes of "lousy umpire calls." More often he would rush tapes to the American League office for MacPhail to witness, and demand better umpires for the next "crucial series." Everything, of course, was crucial to George. He was forever trying to position me as his ally against Lee, who had control of the American League umpires. It never worked because I respected Lee and the job our umpires performed. This is not to say that club executives should not complain to league offices about umpiring. They should, but there is a right way and a wrong way.

In the spring of 1983, George went into a rage over calls by National League umpires in an exhibition game against the Expos. Although he claimed his remarks were private, he audibly asserted that the National League umpires always gave the close plays "to their own." The press ran the story. Now George was in my ballpark. As a general custom, regular season games are subject to the disciplinary control of the league presidents, but interleague games from the World Series to exhibition games belong to the commissioner. I called George and told him his assertions had gone to the very heart of our integrity by questioning the honesty of the umpires. To his credit, he made no denial, arguing only that what he said was meant to be private. Brushing past that tenuous position, I told him the maximum club fine of $5,000 permitted by the Major League Agreement was not enough and asked if he had any suggestions. George and I both knew that under our clumsy disciplinary structure, the commissioner could fine $5,000 or suspend. Rumors flew that I was thinking about the latter course. Well, he knew $5,000 was insufficient and he certainly did not want another suspension. So I heard a long, rambling answer that dwelt on all the times I had fined the Yankees, and along the way he said, "You know, Commish, if you come up with fifty-thousand dollars for this, I guess I'd just have to understand. I've never challenged your authority at any time." I fined him $50,000 the next day; it was paid without complaint.

This large fine reflected my serious concern about any kind of attack on our umpires. They were a rugged group whose work on the field had brought great credit to our game. Criticized unmercifully on all sides, they rarely responded in kind, content to let the excellent quality of their work speak for them. They were well-trained professionals with a long history of tough minor-league experience behind them. They knew their job and did it better than any officiating group in sports. No television replays were needed to review their work. As commissioner I could sympathize with them over the abuse they took in protecting the integrity of our game on the field. There was a lot of similarity between my job and theirs. Our mutual sympathy came out in the conviviality of innumerable visits I paid to umpire rooms, where I spent many of my happiest baseball moments.

During spring training of 1978, NBC's Tony Kubek, a former Yankees player, told sportswriters that George "has one of the most expensive toys in the world, and what he does is manipulate people. He's not the only one, either. The same is true of most of the owners in baseball. Steinbrenner won't let anybody relax. It's what I call his 'corporate mentality.' He throws a fear into everybody. . . . He makes the players fear for their jobs. That's his theory and it works. But it's not a pleasant way to have to play."

This led to a long-running feud between George and NBC, which began with the opening series that season in Texas. Kubek was assigned to interview Yankees players; Steinbrenner told his public relations director, Mickey Morabito, that if any players spoke to Kubek, Mickey would be fired. Tony of course protected Morabito's job and Joe Garagiola handled the interviews. But the battle lines were drawn.

In a way you could forgive George some of his aggressiveness. It reflected an earnest desire to win. What most baseball people found unforgivable was his being a bully. He bullied his staff and his players. He said rookie pitcher Jim Beattie "looked scared stiff" and ordered him sent to the minors. After rookie pitcher Mike Griffin had a bad spring training outing against the Mets that was shown on New York TV, George said, "We found out about Mike Griffin today. You say you can't tell from one outing? The hell you can't. This spells it for Mike Griffin." He was shipped to Columbus.

He tried bullying my staff on more than one occasion. In 1981, for example, we halted a trade that would have sent Jason Thompson to New York from Pittsburgh for three players and $850,000. As the money far exceeded my $400,000 limit, we would not approve the deal. Bill Murray, the former New York Mets controller, had by now become my administrator, replacing Frank Cashen, who had moved to the Mets as executive vice president. It fell to Bill to telephone

George to say the deal would not pass muster. This assignment reminds me of the old joke about the Spanish cabinet voting on which cabinet minister would have to tell Francisco Franco he was dead. There is not a finer gentleman in baseball than Bill Murray. Rage turned Steinbrenner into another of his endless character types: George the hoodlum. He told Murray he had made an enemy for life, warning him to keep looking over his shoulder because he would be after him, no matter how long it took.

When Steinbrenner went public with his criticism of Murray, implying that Murray had killed the deal in order to open the way for the Mets to acquire Jason Thompson, I fined him $5,000.

A 1979 incident reveals a lot about George. He called the office on a June Friday looking for my top broadcasting executive, Tom Villante, and found he was playing golf, prompting George to write me a letter complaining about Tom's Friday recreation "when we're all working our asses off."

There was a natural tension between George and Villante, since George made a policy of promoting his local broadcasting to the disadvantage of our national network operations of which Villante was the able guardian. So George was undermining Villante, whose unwillingness to be subservient did not sit very well with George. He was also trying to undermine me by attacking the "slack" work habits of my staff. He increasingly criticized me to others in baseball about the expense and quality of my operation. I knew that because much of his criticism came straight back to me. I was learning that George would bear a lot of watching.

17

The Old Guard Passes

As the Civil War doomed the Old South, the Messersmith-McNally decision and the coming of free agency doomed the old, tradition-bound ownerships of baseball. While some were to hold on longer than others, they soon began to vanish. The new game was high-stakes poker, a game most were not prepared to play.

Whereas ownership had been remarkably stable over the first three quarters of the twentieth century, no fewer than eighteen clubs have either changed hands or sold significantly large minority interests since free agency. In the exodus, which was to have profound effects on baseball and on me, we lost many of the owners who could be characterized as "sportsmen." Definitions of that term may vary but I think of those men as persons who loved and cared about the game and who would support what was best for the game overall, even if that was adverse to their club's interests. Tom Yawkey would be an ideal example. So would Phil Wrigley and Horace Stoneham. They would grumble and fight with city hall, they were highly opinionated, but the thought of bucking central administration on a matter critical to the game was anathema to them. They loved the game. Finley was not a sportsman by my reckoning; he may well have loved the game but he was too much the practicing maverick to have any concern about its overall interests. Charlie came before the game. Joan Payson of the Mets may have been the quintessential sportsman—I apply the masculine term to her with apologies, but the word works best in the masculine form. Joan never grumbled or fought with city hall, certainly not my city hall. John Fetzer was a sportsman; his conduct almost defined the term. Bill Veeck was not, because he was indifferent to the game's general welfare, too much the self-centered hustler. All of these people are gone.

The new order quickly counted veteran San Francisco owner Horace Stoneham among its victims. He sold the club in March 1976 to Bob Lurie and Bud Herseth after first making an unsuccessful effort to sell to Toronto interests. In terms of quality this was a trade-off for baseball. Lurie, who soon bought out Herseth, was himself fashioned from the sportsman mold. Horace and his father had controlled the Giants since 1919. They had known the glory years from McGraw and Mathewson to Mays and Marichal. Baseball was his preoccupation. Unlike his fellow traveler from New York, Walter O'Malley, Horace had never found gold in the California hills. Still, he left behind one of the most colorful legends in baseball history.

No one knows the Stoneham legend better than his nephew Chub Feeney (Chub's mother is Horace's sister), who has the greatest known collection of Horace anecdotes, mostly featuring Horace's affection for Scotch whiskey. But any baseball man of standing has Horace stories. I remember the National League meetings in 1968 during which Montreal and San Diego were granted expansion franchises. Horace arrived at the morning meeting still well supplied with Scotch and determined to support Buffalo after Montreal was easily selected as the first choice. The sentiment of the meeting favored Dallas, but it became clear that Judge Hofheinz of Houston had no charity for that idea, thus blocking it under the league's unanimous-vote requirement. O'Malley then began to maneuver for San Diego and the mood began to swing in that direction. Set on Buffalo, Horace would hear of nothing else. If a supporter of San Diego so much as said, "I move . . ." Horace shouted, "San Francisco votes no!" It certainly saved calling the roll. It finally got so bad that if a San Diego man dared look at Horace he voted no. At a lunch break, Horace mercifully went off and never returned. Chub Feeney, as vice president of the Giants, voted for San Diego and the Padres were born.

Lurie had no comparable affection for Scotch, which is a blessing. It is also a blessing that he had a deep financial pocket (*Forbes* magazine listed his wealth as $200 million), as the Bay Area has been a near-disaster for baseball since the foolish move of the A's to Oakland in 1968. Bob has inherited the affection of the baseball community in much the same way that Horace did. Could the remorseless winds of Candlestick Park breed sympathy? His emergence as owner of the Giants rewarded a personal effort of mine and Feeney's to persuade him to acquire the club.

Tom Yawkey of the Red Sox would not have been driven out of baseball by free agency. He could afford it. But he lost a battle with leukemia in July 1976. Two years later, after entertaining offers from a variety of would-be purchasers, his estate sold this most special of all franchises to a partnership of which the general partners were his widow Jean, Haywood Sullivan and Buddy LeRoux. Another triumph for sportsmanship and Horatio Alger, too. Sully had once been a catcher for the Red Sox, while Buddy had been the club trainer. With the disappearance of the Washington Senators, no franchise was so close to my heart as Boston. You could feel the magic there—in the enduring simplicity of the old ballpark and its plain, avocado green left-field wall; in the memories of Speaker, Hooper, Cronin, Williams, Foxx and so many more, memories somehow more vivid there than elsewhere; in the distinctive New Englanders who filled Fenway's narrow seats; in the quaint streets of Boston, where the Red Sox were as much an article of faith as the Catholic church; and throughout six maple-clad New England states, where the pastoral qualities of the game survived best "yet as pure as the unsullied lily," as Shakespeare wrote in *Love's Labors Lost.* Sadly, there was no magic in the new Boston partnership, which divided sharply between Jean Yawkey and Sully on the one hand and Buddy LeRoux on the other.

John Allyn sold the White Sox thirteen days before the Messersmith decision. He had bought the club from his brother Arthur. Both Arthur and John cared about the game but had little success with the struggling White Sox, who seemed overshadowed by the Peter Pan popularity of the Northside's Cubs. Nor was either brother comfortable with the raucous world of baseball. It was no surprise when John decided to sell, but he stunned the American League when he elected to sell to Bill Veeck, whom the owners would rather have left dozing on the sandy shores of Eastern Maryland than prowling Comiskey's precincts with his bag of mischief and faded marketing skills. I saw Veeck as equal parts charlatan and rebel. At a time when the White Sox needed an ownership that knew how to build for the long-term in this key baseball city, we had drawn an owner whose marketing and management skills were of another time.

"If the timing of our purchase . . . had been reversed," Veeck later said, in reference to the Messersmith decision, "I never would have bought the team." Although he had long advocated modification of the reserve system, he had not expected Peter Seitz to rule as he did. That decision caught him with perilously limited finances and little ability to compete.

There had been talk of moving the financially troubled White Sox before Veeck came into the picture. The problem was complicated by the condition of Comiskey Park. Built in 1910, Comiskey Park was baseball's oldest. Bill stepped into this setting as the man of the hour, backed by a syndicate of more than forty people. The fans saw him as the savior of the franchise.

The American League voted him in at our 1975 annual meetings in Hollywood, Florida, although some last-minute statesmanship was needed by Fetzer to persuade his fellow owners. "Gentlemen," Fetzer told his brethren, "we have given this man conditions, and he's met them. We now have an obligation to honor our word." Unfortunately, the conditions were not tough enough and Veeck had contrived a financially leaky ship to meet them. With no great enthusiasm, the American League lived up to its word.

Veeck was always a critic of commissioners, practically making a career out of ridiculing Ford Frick. I had crossed swords with him a decade earlier, during the trial over the move of the Braves to Atlanta. Appearing as an expert witness for the Milwaukee interests, Veeck gave a performance that left us lawyers on the other side virtually tumbling over one another to cross-examine him. I cannot recall ever seeing such a lust to examine a witness. Veeck conveniently left town. To the dismay of our side, the judge let his direct testimony stand. To this day I needle Bud Selig, who was deeply involved in the Milwaukee side, about the quality of their "expert" witness. Nor was I thrilled when Veeck showed up as a witness for Curt Flood in Flood's antitrust suit against the reserve system. Now he had bought the White Sox and inherited free agency. That was a kind of justice.

More as a matter of duty than anything else, I invited Bill to my suite at the Diplomat Hotel after the American League's favorable vote. "After all," as I told him, "I've just been reelected for seven years. You're going to have me around for a long time." I certainly imagined I would be around a lot longer than he would, Bill having a reputation for moving in and out fast as any self-respecting hustler should. Free agency made that all the more certain. As it turned out, his five seasons were longer than I expected.

We spent an uncomfortable hour together. We talked perfunctorily about the tough problems faced by the White Sox. I offered to help in any way I could. I did suggest that he might lead the way in showing how we could increase our black attendance, given his excellent reputation with the black community. He said he would try. I felt a little wistful as I watched him heave himself with difficulty out of his chair and limp from the room on his artificial leg. He was a world apart from me, but he had guts.

The next morning he set up a table in the hotel lobby, prepared to wheel and deal players just like the old days. It was embarrassing. Bill was back. At his side was Roland Hemond, whom Veeck retained as general manager. That was a good decision.

By July 1980, convinced that he was not going to be permitted to sell the Sox out of town, Veeck began talking about selling the club to Edward J. DeBartolo. This was an arresting twist. DeBartolo was one of America's wealthiest men, having amassed a huge fortune in shopping center development. His son Edward Jr. operated the National Football League's San Francisco 49ers. Having flirted with both Marvin Davis and DeBartolo, Veeck certainly knew a rich man when he saw one.

I had some real problems about DeBartolo's buying the White Sox. His ownership of racetracks in Ohio, Illinois and Louisiana was a major stumbling block. I had gone along uncomfortably with the small interest the Galbreath family had in Churchill Downs and George Steinbrenner's 50 percent interest in Tampa Bay Downs. My discomfort had become unbearable by the spring of 1980, so I issued a directive to all clubs saying thereafter I would not permit ownership of racetrack interests by baseball people. I said I would "grandfather" the existing Galbreath and Steinbrenner interests, which had been innocently acquired. In issuing the directive I was motivated by two perils. First was the growth of illegal betting on sports. There was no accurate count, but the figures were thought by knowledgeable experts to be stupendous and growing. Second, I was concerned about the increasing efforts to legalize gambling on team sports. I was death on that concept because I thought it was

My parents, Louis and Alice.

On my right, my brother, Lou; on my left, my sister, Alice.

The Griffith Stadium scoreboard in Washington as it appeared during the 1940s when I served as scoreboard boy. My window to the field was near the Washington, seventh-inning area.

On my first full day as commissioner, I visited Marvin Miller (above) at the Players Association office, and then experienced my first Howard Cosell interview (below). Photos courtesy Herb Scharfman/Sports Illustrated.

Three sports commissioners gather at a USO luncheon. On my immediate right is Walter Kennedy of the National Basketball Association, and to his right, Pete Rozelle of the National Football League.

Visiting with a young Reggie Jackson during his Oakland days. I had to intercede on his behalf when Charlie Finley attempted to farm him out.

Determined to call them as I saw them. On assignment as umpire at the 1969 congressional baseball game between the Democrats and the Republicans. Photo courtesy Roy Hoopes.

Presenting a season's pass to President Reagan in the Oval Office, 1981.

Marvin Davis. Photo courtesy
UPI/Bettmann Newsphotos.

Jerry Hoffberger.

The only time four baseball commissioners were ever together—the gala 1969 Centennial Dinner in Washington. Joining me are (left to right) *William Eckert, Ford Frick, and Happy Chandler.* Photo courtesy Wide World Photos.

Jackie Robinson throws out the first ball at the second game of the 1972 World Series in Cincinnati. Nine days later, he was dead. Photo courtesy Wide World Photos.

A bitter Charlie Finley and a disillusioned Vida Blue face the press with Joe Cronin and me following an all-night session to end Blue's 1970 holdout. Photo courtesy UPI/Bettmann Newsphotos.

The Yankees' Mike Burke (right) was an early advocate of promotion, but in a minority when I became commissioner. This was Opening Day at Yankee Stadium, 1969, with Simon and Garfunkel handling the ceremonial first-pitch honors.

A stern John Gaherin (right) *joins me in announcing the settlement of the thirteen-day player strike in 1972.* Photo courtesy Wide World Photos.

San Juan, Puerto Rico, January 4, 1973, following a memorial mass for Roberto Clemente, victim of an air crash. Rodrigo Otero Suro, president of the Puerto Rico Winter League, is beside me, with the great Spanish broadcaster Buck Canel just behind. Photo courtesy Wide World Photos.

On the steps of the Baseball Library at the Hall of Fame ceremonies in Cooperstown, New York, 1974, after the induction of Mickey Mantle.

An unsuccessful attempt at fence-mending with Bill Veeck after he bought the White Sox at the 1975 annual meeting in Hollywood, Florida. Photo courtesy UPI/Bettmann Newsphotos.

Peter Seitz. Photo courtesy
UPI/Bettmann Newsphotos.

Eddie Chiles.

Ray Kroc.

Edward Bennett Williams.

Walter O'Malley.

John Fetzer.

Ed Fitzgerald.

John McMullen.

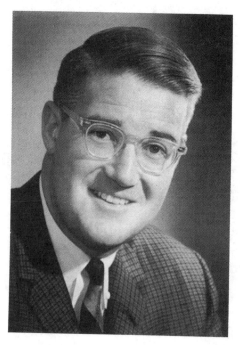

Louis Susman. Photo courtesy Jim
Balmer.

Peter O'Malley.

Edward J. DeBartolo, Sr.

Nelson Doubleday.

April 8, 1975, and baseball has its first black manager. I was on hand to congratulate Cleveland's Frank Robinson on his debut. Photo courtesy UPI/Bettmann Newsphotos.

A congressional hearing room in Washington, December 9, 1981. Ted Turner (right) leans forward to deliver an odd message that marked the beginning of the long effort to change commissioners. Photo courtesy Wide World Photos.

The best seat in the house during a trip to Japan. The great Sadaharu Oh wears uniform number one.

Baseball's Executive Council, 1982. Seated left to right: Bob Howsam (Cincinnati), Ewing Kauffman (Kansas City), Bob Lurie (San Francisco), Ballard Smith (San Diego). Center: Haywood Sullivan (Boston), Dan Galbreath (Pittsburgh), Bowie Kuhn, Chub Feeney (National League president), Bud Selig (Milwaukee), Sandy Hadden (secretary-treasurer and general counsel). Top: Jim Garner (American League attorney), Lee MacPhail (American League president), Lou Hoynes (National League attorney).

In Cooperstown, New York, following the 1982 Hall of Fame induction of Henry Aaron.

A warm meeting with Willie Mays at my 1984 retirement dinner. Photo courtesy Wide World Photos.

George M. Steinbrenner.

Peter Ueberroth and I meet the press after his election as baseball's sixth commissioner, March 3, 1984, in Tampa, Florida. Photo courtesy UPI/Bettmann Newsphotos.

A family gathering in Cooperstown, July 1983, with my decision to withdraw from re-election consideration in place. Top left to right, my sons George, Paul and Stephen; *bottom,* George's wife Carole, Luisa, me, and my daughter Alix.

a deadly threat to us. I was determined to keep baseball on the highest possible ground to avoid these perils. The further we were removed from gambling of all kinds, whether legal or illegal, the better positioned we would be to resist gambling on our game.

Another problem was that DeBartolo was not a Chicagoan. We much preferred local ownership where we could get it. It gave us a better promise of franchise stability as opposed, for example, to a Bob Short who, caring nothing about Washington and having no roots there, was perfectly prepared to move to Texas rather than do the kind of long-term building job Washington needed. We could not always get local ownership. The CBS-owned Yankees had been on the market for some time without local buyers coming forward when Cleveland's George Steinbrenner emerged. There had even been talk that the Yankees would have to be moved. Fortunately, Jerry Reinsdorf, a successful real estate syndicator, was putting together a group to bid for the Sox, and Jerry was solidly based in Chicago. DeBartolo's fabulous success had also spread him too thinly across the country. It was hard to see how he could give Chicago the attention its problems demanded.

MacPhail had fully conveyed to Veeck our concerns about DeBartolo and I hoped Veeck would read our signals and drop the flirtation. Unfortunately, Veeck moved swiftly to close a deal with DeBartolo, a deal that on August 22 was approved by a special committee formed by the Sox ownership to study bids for the club. Always the maverick, Veeck would let no commissioner tell him how to run his club. I was determined that the days were over when individual owners were going to make franchise decisions that went against the best interests of the game. Veeck was prepared to make a bitter fight against that principle. And a bitter fight he got.

MacPhail and I decided to go directly to DeBartolo in an effort to head off a confrontation. We met him and Paul Martha at an airport hotel in Pittsburgh. Andy McKenna was there representing the White Sox ownership. Andy later became president of the Cubs under the Tribune Company ownership. Martha, a lawyer and key executive in DeBartolo's organization, had once been an all-American tailback at the University of Pittsburgh and later starred for the Steelers. He would prove to be a balance wheel on the DeBartolo side of this debate.

DeBartolo was a man in his early seventies, severe, unsmiling, lean, conservatively clad in a dark suit. Every move was businesslike, his manners proper. As I set out to explain baseball's concerns about his proposed purchase of the White Sox, his stern, lined visage revealed no trace of sympathy, let alone understanding. MacPhail briefly expressed his support of my remarks. Put in tandem, Lee and I are a fairly persuasive team. We were not persuasive with DeBartolo. He was outraged, brushing our reasons aside as frivolous. If we blocked his acquisition, he said, he was prepared to spend "millions of dollars" to defeat us in court. The meeting grew tense. I was equally tough with him: "We will fight you every inch of the way; we're not going to be bluffed by threats of lawsuits; and just to make it clear if by some unlikely chance you got by the American League, I will veto your application so long as you are not in compliance with our standards." Two proud men had made things exquisitely clear to one another and neither liked it.

I suspected his outrage was grounded in a belief that we had a hidden agenda of objections we were not revealing and I told him so. I told him there was no such agenda; there were no dire facts in his background that prompted us to oppose him.

The meeting took on a friendlier tone. He began to talk about various solutions to our objections: Perhaps another member of his family could buy the club; perhaps plans could be developed for selling the racetracks. Lee and I suggested that his talking to some of the American League owners might help. On a much more cordial note, we adjourned to an adjacent room where his people had arranged for an excellent cold buffet. The meeting broke up with assurances that we would all reflect on possible solutions.

DeBartolo tried some personal diplomacy. He had a meeting five days later with John Fetzer and Bud Selig. A week later he saw Ewing Kauffman. He also appeared informally before an American League meeting in Chicago on September 17. Nonetheless, when the American League met on October 24, the DeBartolo application fell two votes short of the required three-quarters vote. He had eight affirmative votes and six negative. I was surprised he fared as well as he did, given the fact that no solutions had been found regarding the racetracks or the lack of local ownership. I suspected that some of those eight votes were being polite.

The American League then made an unusual move. It decided to give DeBartolo another chance. They would put the matter on the agenda again at our Dallas annual meetings on December 11.

Two things ensued that sealed DeBartolo's fate. In November, the White Sox signed free agent Ron LeFlore at a salary figure that was viewed as ludicrously high by the American League clubs. There was little doubt that DeBartolo had played a role in the decision to pay such a sum for LeFlore. Six days before the American League meeting, Vince Bartimo, who operated the Louisiana Downs racetrack for DeBartolo, accused me publicly of opposing DeBartolo because of his Italian heritage. Specifically he said, "Every successful Italo-American is always suspected of having ties to the underworld. The reason that Bowie Kuhn will never approve Mr. DeBartolo happens to be that Mr. DeBartolo is of Italian descent. It's that simple."

The DeBartolo cause hit bottom. Peter Bavasi of the Blue Jays and Selig called Martha and urged him to persuade DeBartolo to withdraw his application to avoid the embarrassment of another rejection. DeBartolo would not hear of it. The American League voted against DeBartolo 11–3.

Over the years I had suffered through some despicable attacks, but I recall none that embittered me more than Bartimo's. Nonetheless, in my postmeeting press conference, I continued to defend DeBartolo against insinuations that he had underworld ties and certainly gave him the benefit of the doubt in evaluating his decency. "There is no basis for questioning the decency or ethics of this man," I said. "There is no background matter that haunts any of us. There were things that did disturb me. I've taken pains not to put Mr. DeBartolo in a bad light. But his pressure tactics were an underlying force. In our first meeting, he mentioned the possibility of litigation, and I told him not to approach it that way. He then put pressure on various people in baseball and that set badly with certain owners. I think that hurt him."

I did not lack for defenders on Bartimo's anti-Italian calumny. None touched me more than Nick Mileti, who had owned the Cleveland Indians from 1972 to 1975. When the Bartimo story broke, Nick called me and said, "Your honor, please tell any of those guys in the press who want the truth to talk to me." A UPI syndicated story by Milton Richman resulted that in part said:

Mileti believes any such accusations are utterly groundless. Strictly on his own, he picked up the phone the other day, called Kuhn and told him so.

"From personal experience, all I can say is that if he had any prejudices against Italians, I certainly was an easy target," Mileti says. "He never showed me any prejudice at all.

"On the contrary, he went far out of his way for me. I remember the first meeting in his office before I became involved in buying the Indians. He said, 'Anything I can do to help, Nick, I will.' And he did."

Nick was long out of baseball and certainly had nothing to gain by defending me, nothing, that is, except freely, warmheartedly and generously fulfilling his own sense of decency. Milton certainly had better stories to write, I suspect, but do not know, that he wrote this story out of the same freely manifested sense of decency that inspired Mileti. No one knew better than Milton that the Bartimo type of defamation is hard to answer by the victim, who can deny but is hard-pressed to prove the false quality of the assertion. Milton was the kind of writer who would be embarrassed by the fact that his profession was guilty of giving currency to Bartimo's charge. He saw a way to help straighten the record. That was decency.

Milton Richman died as I wrote this book. It hardly seemed possible. He could still outrun anybody in sight. Dick Young and Johnny Bench spoke at Richman's funeral service, which was attended by more notables by far than most of us are apt to get. They were eloquent, but in Milton's case that was easy. He was such a sweetheart. He had called only a week before to ask some questions about a column he was doing on Peter Ueberroth. In passing, he asked how my book was coming, a subject on which he gave me endless encouragement. Then he asked why they did not see me at the ballpark more often. When I said something about its being "awkward" in New York, he replied, "Bowie, come out and sit with us; the fellows miss you more than you know." The one missed is Milton.

Once the sports pages carry that kind of story across the country, the truth cannot be fully retrieved. What Nick and Milton and others did was gallant but had no prospect of success. Bartimo alone shouting lies is of no consequence until the press becomes his accomplice. Then his words ring out nationally. The rebuttal, however truthful, rarely wins the day. While we hear a great deal about First Amendment rights, we often see in practice too little of the responsibility that should accompany the exercise of those rights. In this case, the Bartimo story was not fit to print and should not have been run.

Insidiously enough, the problem is apt to be complicated by subsequent press restatements of the original rubbish, even at some remove in time. I was annoyed when Dave Anderson in a January 1982 *New York Times* column, quoted DeBartolo as saying, "Bowie Kuhn was prejudiced and I think that's what kept us out of baseball."

When I expressed my views in a letter to Anderson, concluding with the question "Where is any sense of fitness or responsibility?" he replied, "I can appreciate your annoyance at the quote by Mr. DeBartolo, but I thought his opinion was important." Where indeed is any sense of fitness or responsibility?

On January 29, 1981, the American League unanimously approved the sale of the White Sox to the Jerry Reinsdorf group. Reinsdorf was a lawyer who had become an extremely successful real estate syndicator as the head of Balcor Corporation. That success had made it possible for him to move into the even more speculative business of professional baseball. My lawyer friends gave Jerry high marks. He brought into the White Sox ownership one of sport's most flamboyant and colorful figures—Eddie Einhorn, the best packager of televised sports specials in the land. I knew Eddie by reputation to be an intense baseball fan. I also knew he was close to my friend Joel Segal, senior vice president of Ted Bates Advertising in New York. I asked Joel if Eddie was a man I could trust. Joel said you could trust him but his style of doing business was strictly homemade. That was good enough for me. I was used to odd styles; being able to trust someone was paramount.

They did not endear themselves to their fellow owners when they signed free agent Carlton Fisk, who had achieved that status through another arbitrator's decision that was unpopular with the clubs. Fisk was seen as "Mr. Red Sox," the clutch-hitting catcher and leader who had electrified the baseball world in 1975 with his sixth-game-winning World Series home run, hit into the night above Fenway. We all hoped that the splendid New Englander would work things out and sign with the Red Sox. His signing with the White Sox pointed up one of the significant drawbacks of the free-agency system: the loss of identity of great players with their franchises. The Fisk signing was resented by some clubs even more than by the Red Sox, who feared that in any event they would lose Fisk after the 1981 season.

In 1982 I was drawn into a verbal barrage between the Yankees and the White Sox. I had warned clubs repeatedly about the unacceptability of derogatory public comments concerning baseball personnel. Now Reinsdorf, annoyed about George Steinbrenner's signing of free agent Steve Kemp, who had driven in ninety-eight runs for the White Sox in 1982, fired first.

"We should consider putting another franchise in New York," he said. "The man [Steinbrenner] is totally irresponsible."

Regarding the White Sox's signing of Floyd Bannister, in whom

George was interested, Reinsdorf said, "We beat fat George out of that one!"

Never one to stand back from a good fight, George replied, "One of the bigger mistakes we've made in baseball was to allow our commissioner to reject Ed DeBartolo as White Sox owner. Instead, we got Jerry Reinsdorf and Eddie Einhorn, who come to our meetings and can't agree on anything. They're the Katzenjammer Kids of baseball. They've got a great act. They're Abbott and Costello."

I fined George $5,000 and the White Sox $2,500, the lesser fine being attributable to the fact that the White Sox were first offenders. They soon moved up in grade. In 1983, I fined the White Sox $5,000 for Reinsdorf's and Einhorn's saying, "Do you know how to tell when George Steinbrenner is lying? It's when his lips move." They had actually delivered those lines on stage during the entertainment portion of a baseball party preceding the 1983 All-Star Game. No investigation was necessary. I was right there in the room, listening.

The press reported fines of this kind as somber acts of anger on my part. George was inclined to see them the same way. In fact, they were simple acts of routine duty designed to keep the acrimony between our clubs from getting out of hand. Nobody laughed harder at some of this stuff than we did around my office. To this day, I like to ask Reinsdorf and Einhorn which one is Abbott and which Costello.

Bill Veeck died as I was writing this book. That gave me pause as to what I should say about this curious man. When Senator Joe McCarthy died, former secretary of state Dean Acheson, who had been brutalized by McCarthy, said only, *"Nihil de mortuis nisi bonum."* Speak only good of the dead. That was a graceful way of saying nothing. Wherever the shade of William Veeck resides, and I have several clear theories as to where that may be, the last thing it would want said of Bill is nothing.

Though we crossed paths intermittently for two decades, I was never as close to Veeck as I was to most of the other prominent baseball figures of his time. Nor should that be any surprise. I can hardly imagine two people more unalike than Kuhn and Veeck, sharing so far as I could see little more than a passionate and sentimental affection for the old ballparks. Bill was the original flimflam man, who could profess his undying dedication to the fans of Southside Chicago while quietly negotiating to sell the franchise to Denver. He defined himself in his own books: a man with a swindler's heart and a conniving spirit.

In an earlier age he would have been the "Music Man," shamelessly selling elixirs to the unwary. For all his self-confessed faults, Veeck was more rogue than scoundrel, though at given times the distinction was hard to detect. His fumbling, self-effacing charm and his iconoclasm toward the baseball establishment endeared him to millions of fans, if not to baseball management or commissioners. Fortune eluded him, though one wonders if he would not have kicked fortune away had it been otherwise. At heart he was a beer-drinking, fun-loving populist, ill at ease with his baronial peers and ill at ease too with every commissioner he ever knew. He viewed constables of any sort as an abomination and commissioners as the archetype of this species. I never knew a self-respecting commissioner who failed to return the compliment. He brought a bright humor to the game, whose contours and alleyways he understood as few ever had. It almost redeemed him. He reminds me for all the world of what Bugs Baer wrote about Ping Bodie as a base stealer: "He had larceny in his heart, but his feet were honest."

We lost a truly great sportsman when Phil Wrigley died on April 12, 1977. Shy as a partridge, Phil was rarely seen at baseball events or even at the old ballpark that bore his name. His dour facade belied the highly civilized man hidden behind; belied the corporate leader who had guided the William Wrigley, Jr., Company to success as the world's leading producer of chewing gum; belied the visionary baseball executive whose soaring otherworldly perceptions about the game were often anathema to his fellow owners anchored to their more earthly views. He was a legend to me when as a young lawyer I first met him at the Arizona Biltmore Hotel in Phoenix. That was 1955. I was there on a brief sojourn with Phil's lawyer, Jim Baker, Jim and I having just come from San Francisco, where we had gotten a court order enjoining radio station KYA from its unauthorized carriage of major-league games through skillful recreations by Les Keiter. Like many business executives I have known, Phil tolerated lawyers but was hardly enthralled by them. Still, he was gracious to me and made an impression as we lunched together that remains vivid three decades later. Surely, on that day neither of us pictured me as apt to be commissioner of his beloved baseball fourteen years later.

In many ways he was a purist about baseball, wanting no part of lights at Wrigley Field, or artificial turf. In the interest of aesthetics, he was the first to seed the area between the pitcher's mound and home plate, bringing to a close the era of the dirt path between the batterymates. He loved the ivy on the outfield wall and the severe, old-fashioned lines of the ballpark. But even on the subject of lights he showed some flexibility. In 1971, when the Cubs were playing well in the early part of the season, I discussed with him our commitment to night games in postseason play. I anticipated adamant opposition from him should the Cubs be involved. Trying to predict Phil was risky business. He surprised me by saying, "We would just have to figure something out." "Something" might include installing permanent or temporary lights at Wrigley Field, or even playing at Comiskey.

In November 1970, he sent me a long letter explaining why he would not attend the December annual meetings. There are several paragraphs I particularly like:

> In the first place, I have reached an age where I can figure I have put in a good long stint of traveling around the country to the point where I am now entitled to stay home and enjoy my creature comforts.
>
> In the second place, the annual meetings are always held during my birthday. For many years, this did not make much difference, but more recently the family likes to have me available on my birthday which I do not particularly appreciate because it sort of gives me the feeling that they do not know how many more birthdays they will be able to celebrate. . . .
>
> I am writing you this rather long explanation as we have not known each other for the long periods of time that I was associated with the other Commissioners and former League Presidents who, over the years, became accustomed to my peculiarities.

My favorite exchange with Phil came early in my commissionership, arising from a quote by him in the Chicago press to the effect that the commissioner was spending too much money. I advised him by letter that criticism of that type should be made directly to me, not through the newspapers. His response was to say most respectfully that he had been doing business that way a long time and reserved the right to continue. I closed the subject by saying that I respected his decision, but reserved my right to do what was necessary if he did continue. It was a good, old-fashioned example of therapeutic masculine strutting and posturing. Of course, nothing ever came of it.

When Phil died, controlling ownership of the Cubs passed to his son, Bill. Though Bill and his brother-in-law, Bill Haganah, operated the club for four years, various circumstances made a sale seem inevitable. That was too bad, for both Bills represented the kind of sportsman ownership I thought was good for the game.

The sale to the Tribune Company, which owned the *Chicago Tribune* and WGN-TV, came in 1981. WGN owned the rights to televise Cubs games and was carrying about 150 of them annually. In 1978, WGN had become a superstation, which meant that 150 Cubs games annually were available to cable systems around the United States. To complicate matters, the Tribune Company also owned WPIX-TV in New York City, which owned the rights to televise the New York Yankees.

While the Tribune Company was a respected and successful company, well led by its CEO, Stan Cook, I drew a deep breath over its compatibility with baseball. The Cubs were an attractive acquisition for the Tribune Company, not so much because the baseball business was attractive but because the Cubs provided vital programming for WGN and for its superstation network. Where would the Tribune Company stand when conflicts developed between baseball interests and broadcast interests? It seemed quite clear to me the latter would prevail.

I told Chub Feeney to let the National League know the matter required careful study and was not a candidate for automatic approval by me and should not be by the league. I reminded him that an incautious approval of Ted Turner's acquisition of the Braves in 1976 had led to the Braves' becoming a property of superstation WTBS-Atlanta. Chub did not share my concern, arguing that the Tribune Company had an outstanding reputation and would be a responsible owner. The Tribune Company was approved.

I want briefly to mention some other activity before moving on to describe the fascinating goings-on in Baltimore.

- In 1980, Brad Corbett sold the Texas Rangers to Eddie Chiles, known in the state for his wide-ranging, conservative radio broadcasts that began with the warning "I'm mad." It made him a colorful and controversial character, well qualified for our ranks.

- The Seattle franchise had had problems since its start in 1977, but the bright spot there was Danny Kaye. He was part of a loosely structured Mariner partnership that did not work very well. But for a "brief, shining moment"—four years—we had Danny as a baseball owner. Sadly, if he belonged in baseball at all, he belonged with the Dodgers, his first-and-only true baseball love from his days as a lad in the streets of Brooklyn. Tommy Lasorda could tell you what color Danny's blood truly ran: Dodger blue. His quicksilver skills with word and song, his ballet feet, his twinkling wit were lost in the leaden affairs of owners. His forum stretched shimmeringly across the wide world of children, young and old, where make-believe and sweetness prevailed. He was the eternal prince of joy who could understand Roy Campanella, Stan Musial and Orel Hershiser but never the industrial types who were picking their way into our game. He was the prototype of what I had always wanted baseball to be but knew it could not be.

  The Mariners floundered competitively, financially and structurally. In January 1981, Danny and his partners sold control of the club to George Argyros, an Orange County, California, man grown wealthy in real estate deals. Long on opinions but short on baseball knowledge or appreciation, Argyros was a painful contrast to Kaye. His heavy-handed style did little to endear him to the Seattle community, to me or to his fellow owners. I still believe that Seattle and the Northwest will prove to be a strong baseball area. Whether George can lead it there remains to be seen.

- In Philadelphia, the Carpenters, father and son, reigned from 1943, when Judge Landis deposed William Cox, to 1981. Bob Carpenter was a true sportsman who gave the franchise stability but did not have much success with the Phillies aside from the pennant-winning Whiz Kids of 1950.

  He turned the club over to his son, Ruly, in 1973. Ruly, a powerfully built former Yale football and baseball player and a ranked handball player, related well to the players, whose contemporary he was. He loved the game with a sportsman's heart that had to have cracked a little with the family decision to sell out in the face of the new baseball economics. Although the Phillies had contributed to the salary madness with the costly signing of Pete Rose in 1978, the Carpenters felt that the free agent era made no sense for private individuals. Ruly and I had a long talk in March, before the decision was announced. I was disappointed and tried to persuade him to hang on. I talked about the resurgence of the Phillies under his leadership, their having won their first World Series the prior October. I told him he was the kind of quality owner we needed, a man who deeply cared for the game. But it was in vain; he was not to be persuaded. The Phillies were put on the market a few days later.

I was encouraged when Bill Giles said he would put together a group to purchase the club. Bill had been with the Phillies since 1969, when he was hired as vice president, business operations, prior to the opening of Veterans Stadium. He and Ruly had turned the Phillies into an exciting and successful ballclub. No one was prouder of Bill's success than his father, Warren, who was National League president through 1969. Because of my association with Warren I had known Bill since he was a kid. I had an odd collision with Bill shortly after I had angered the Houston club in 1969 with my ruling in the Rusty Staub deal. Bill, then the Houston public relations vice president, had had some fun at my expense by putting a message on the Astrodome scoreboard asking who was more unpopular, the umpire (shown as XXXX XXXXXX, but apparently John Kibler, who had made a contested call against the Astros), Pete Rozelle, Frankenstein's monster, or Bowie Kuhn. When I heard about this, I ordered Giles onto my New York carpet. I gave him a lecture about bad taste, which he received with grace. In ten minutes it was over and Bill was on his way back to Houston. I can say with the advantage of time and perspective that it was one of the most inexplicably stupid things I ever did. I had more important things to deal with than what the Houston public relations man was putting on the Astrodome scoreboard.

By the end of October 1981, the Giles group had bought the Phillies for $30 million. The key investor was Taft Broadcasting Company of Cincinnati. There was also a solid group of Philadelphia people to round out the partnership. Bill was the general partner, as he deserved to be.

• The 1983 sale of 49 percent of the Kansas City Royals by

Ewing Kauffman to Avron Fogelman was dismaying in that it seemed to foreshadow the ultimate sale of Ewing's retained interest. There was hardly a soul in baseball who did not regret that fact. This had nothing to do with Fogelman, whom baseball people did not know. It had everything to do with the remarkable popularity of Ewing. I am not aware of anyone who was his enemy or even his detractor, with the possible but only occasional exception of George Steinbrenner. Whatever Ewing's shortcomings, and he managed a few, they were forgiven. And this was not a function of his compelling humility. His wife, Muriel, called him "Mr. Wonderful" and there is not the slightest reason to think he demurred at that evaluation. Happy Chandler when in his eighties liked to say that he had "grown too old for humility." Ewing had grown too old for humility when he was a young man. Nevertheless, he had a combination of personal qualities that endeared him to baseball people and most specially to me. He was fun, gregarious, cocky, sporting, compulsive, and, though a master salesman, he was honest. Grown used to a sport of David Harums, I was often surprised by his total honesty in dealing with me. Taken together with his other qualities, that honesty made for one remarkable man.

So there was sackcloth and ashes when Ewing sold an interest in the Royals, because we knew it meant he was preparing for his ultimate exit. We would all look back to 1969, when he set in motion the resurrection of Kansas City baseball from the ruins Charlie Finley had left behind. We would remember how he assembled a quality executive staff with Cedric Tallis, Joe Burke, John Schuerholz, Herk Robinson, Lou Gorman, Bryan Burns, Bob Wirz and Dean Vogelaar; how they soon built the expansion Royals into contenders; how they brilliantly marketed baseball, with attendance consistently over two million in one of our smallest franchise areas. And we would never forget Muriel, Ewing's wife, bright as a fox, sweeping through the baseball scene, all ermine and sable, magnificently clad in Royals blue and white, and Ewing decked out to match. They were unique.

We talked a lot as he progressed toward the Fogelman sale. There were different bidders along the way but it came down to Fogelman. The conversations became more personal, more sentimental. We were both basically sentimentalists.

He did not like the changes in baseball or some of the newer characters. He resented their attacks on me. For my part, I hung on to him because he was an endangered class act. He summed it up one day, "Partner, I'm not sure they deserve either one of us; let's go out together. Hell, we'll both have more fun doing something else."

During 1977 the Hoffberger family, which controlled the Orioles, decided to sell the club. I have no idea what prompted them to sell but I doubted Jerry Hoffberger would have made this decision were it only his to make. He loved the baseball operation and was dedicated to it and the contribution it made to Baltimore. Although my dealings with Jerry often were acrimonious, I still believe that beneath his humorless exterior and behind the abrasive style was a better guy than we normally saw.

I spent a lot of time with Jerry and his wife, Alice, when Luisa and I accompanied the Orioles on an autumn trip to Japan in 1971. We were able to put aside our debate over a team in Washington and concentrate on the excitement of visiting Japan and rooting for the Orioles. The Orioles themselves were the most engaging group of young men I have discovered in baseball. No other team has ever come close: Brooks and Frank Robinson, Boog Powell, Elrod Hendricks, Jim Palmer, Davey Johnson, Dick Hall, Don Buford and on and on, a special group.

It was on that trip that Jerry told me, "I'm fifty-two years old, and what you see is the way I am. I know I don't always please people, but that's my style, my manner. I've grown up with it. Maybe I'd be smart to change, but at this point, I can't. I know I get on people's nerves, but there's not a darn thing I can do about it. They'll have to take me as I am."

It was a startingly candid self-analysis that I thought of often as we battled over just about everything during the 1970s. No matter how bitter the encounters, the poignant memories of that tour of Japan played back on me and helped me across the uneven ground.

The 1977 news that the Hoffbergers were willing to sell was not the first time I had heard such news. For several years, there had been recurrent rumors that the family was willing to sell. Convinced they now meant business, I was hardly distraught. Under new ownership, I saw the opportunity to have the Orioles play some games in Washington or perhaps to get a stadium between the two cities and a shared franchise. Maybe I can find a buyer for the club, I thought to myself, not let Jerry know I'm behind it, and come up with a solution.

Avoiding my involvement was not a formula I had come up with on my own. It was Jerry's idea. In January 1978, he came to see me in New York. With obvious reluctance he told me the Orioles were indeed for sale, although he was still flirting with a notion he had pushed in 1977 that the Orioles join the National League, an arrangement that would have given each league thirteen clubs and brought about interleague play. I knew this was hopeless because the National League was not interested. They did not like Jerry. He even suggested that Congressmen Bernie Sisk and Frank Horton might persuade the National League. Knowing there was not a chance, I politely discouraged him. Now he was throwing in the towel. The Kuhn-Hoffberger debates were coming to an end—well, almost.

I listened to his conditions. Mind you, Jerry would never do anything simply. Even when folding his tent, Jerry would impose conditions. First and foremost, the buyer should not come from me. Any buyer so professing would be rejected. In addition, the buyer must not talk about moving the club or any split of games between Washington and Baltimore. In another moment of candor that took my mind back to our 1971 tour of Japan, he said one reason he was willing to sell was that he really did not get along with the "senior people" in the game. He cautioned me that he would not become involved in the "rape of Baltimore." He had a reputation he was determined to protect. He mentioned but showed no interest in the fact that Denver's wealthy Marvin Davis had called about acquiring the Orioles. Davis's only interest would be moving the club to Denver. Jerry wanted no part of that. Finally, he said the price was $13 million and he would consider staying in for a $2.5-million share. That was it. I knew it had been a difficult session for Jerry. Having said as little as possible, I told him I fully understood his conditions.

At this point, I considered various possible buyers for the Orioles. I had a number of conversations with Bob Linowes, who was the chairman of the Washington Board of Trade, and with Dick O'Connell, former Red Sox general manager, who represented the interest of Ken Pollock, who owned eastern Pennsylvania coal-mining properties. Both were intrigued with the idea of an area franchise with games equally divided between Baltimore and Washington. There was also some talk of pooling their resources. The names of prominent Washington real estate men Bob Smith and Jim Clark also came up. There was an obvious difficulty: Anybody who had too much of a Washington look was going to be a problem for Hoff-berger. As the months went by, I began to focus on another possible buyer who might impress Hoffberger and escape his negative scrutiny. That was William Simon, secretary of the treasury in the Nixon and Ford administrations, writer *(A Time for Truth)* and conservative political philosopher, who was now in the investment business in New York. I had first met Simon when he was energy czar (federal energy administrator) under President Nixon, and we had jointly announced a voluntary energy conservation program for professional baseball. Because of the high visibility of baseball, Simon considered our program important in setting a pattern for other industries. Naturally attracted to "czars," I also liked his spirited, direct, engaging style. I had discovered that he was a real fan, which rather surprised me for his public reputation focused on his financial skills and political philosophy.

I called Simon and asked if he might be interested in Baltimore. He said, "Let's talk." We met that evening at the New York supper club "21," where I spelled out the story as I understood it. He said he was definitely interested and would think about it. We followed up with a dinner meeting in May 1978 with Dan Galbreath. John and Dan Galbreath had always taken a strong interest in returning baseball to Washington. We urged Bill to at least talk to Hoffberger and see what was possible. He agreed to do it. I cautioned him to leave my name out of the conversation. Bill had a friendly, half-hour telephone conversation with Hoffberger the next day. Hoffberger advised him that the club was not for sale, contrary to Kuhn's reports, but that the family would consider offers. He also said they were not interested in selling to anyone planning to move the club forthwith to Washington. They discussed alternative possibilities of selling stock or assets and Jerry said he might like to stay in for a "couple of million." It was left that Bill would look at the financials.

In August, Luisa and I had lunch with Bill and his wife, Carol, in East Hampton, New York. The serious conversation began after lunch on the beach at Simon's home. It was a perfect, sunny day on the Atlantic. Baseball seemed remote until Bill said, "If I'm going to seriously pursue Baltimore, I'd really like to have a partner. Do you have any ideas?"

"I certainly do," I told him. "Edward Bennett Williams has told me for years his first love was baseball. What do you think of Ed?"

"Oh, that's a super idea; I like Ed," he responded. "I'll call him tomorrow!" Not a man to let a good idea waste away, Bill called me the next day and said Williams was very much interested. I cautioned him about overplaying Ed's name because of his connection with Washington. The advice was sound but proved unnecessary.

Simon continued his discussions with Hoffberger. Things progressed to a point where lawyers went to work drafting a contract. Then problems began to develop such as leaks in the press about the negotiations and roadblocks of various kinds with which Jerry began to clutter the path. By December, Simon was still optimistic and determined but beginning to wonder about some of the things Jerry was doing. Sources close to the Hoffberger family were urging Simon to stay firm and not let Jerry "pick the deal to death."

By the end of December, Simon advised me that he, Williams and Ed's partner, Bob Schulman, had met with Jerry and his cousin Roy Hoffberger and had made a deal. Moreover, the Orioles would be free to play thirteen games in Washington in 1979 and there was no restriction with regard to the number of games in 1980. I talked to our Washington representative, Bill Timmons, about trying to arrange a presidential opener for RFK Stadium in 1979.

I was beginning at long last to see a solution for Washington that I honestly thought would also be the best in the long run for Baltimore—a shared franchise. I should have known better. The contract that had been fully negotiated by the end of December had not been signed. In mid-January 1979, Hoffberger was still talking to a local Baltimore group. It appeared that Hoffberger wanted to give the group more time to put together its financing.

By late January Bill Simon, who had been a model of patience, persistence, diplomacy and charm, was beginning to develop serious doubts about Hoffberger. I was amazed that Bill had been so patient and long-suffering. Williams saw Roy Hoffberger and told him that Bill was extremely upset and found that Roy, too, was upset with the delay. Roy was afraid they would lose Simon and the local group would then dissipate. Bill told me he might pull out and in any event would be in Palm Springs and Hawaii the next two weeks. My euphoria of only a month before was evaporating.

On January 31, Hoffberger and Simon talked and agreed on a February 2 deadline. When that date passed with no word from Hoffberger, Simon threw in the towel in disgust. He had Williams call Hoffberger to say the deal was dead. He then went public with the story, telling the Baltimore *Sun:* "I've never seen such duplicity in a deal in my life. It's like dealing with the Scarlet Pimpernel. As far as I'm concerned my offer is withdrawn. Mr. Hoffberger wants to play both ends against the middle. Well, he can forget this end. I think at this point and at this time, the game is over. . . . He has damaged the merchandise and acted in bad faith. I think I've been played dirty pool every way to Sunday. . . . This is pure insanity."

Hoffberger purred to the same newspaper: "I regret that this turn of events has taken place because Mr. Simon is a gentleman. He would have been an asset to baseball as would his partner."

I called Williams and asked him if he would pursue the Orioles on his own, Simon having made it painfully clear to me that he wanted no further part of Hoffberger. The answer was that his interest indeed was continuing; he would talk to Hoffberger at the right time.

While Simon had left the door ever-so-slightly ajar in his public comments, he told me privately he was too disgusted with Hoffberger to try to pick up the pieces. Bill was not a man to linger or brood over a failure. His imagination and energy were so vast that the world seemed like an endless sea of new opportunities.

A sidelight to this Baltimore story was my hiring in February 1979 of Frank Cashen as administrator. Frank would succeed Johnny Johnson, who had handled the job with great efficiency since 1970. Johnny had moved up to become president of the National Association of Professional Baseball Leagues—the minor leagues. Frank, who had been executive vice president of the Orioles for a decade through 1975, had been languishing in the Hoffbergers' fading beer business and was now considering an offer to go with Labatt's in Canada. Given my high regard for Cashen and my desire to preserve him for baseball operations somewhere, I hired him for the administrator's job pending the development of a suitable club-level position.

By the end of March, Williams told me the Hoffbergers were looking for an angel. There was nothing but a lot of "small bettors." Ed said he was back at the table in Baltimore, having resurrected the Simon-Hoffberger contract. While the press continued to speculate on the fate of the club and I talked publicly about a regional team for Baltimore and Washington, Ed was watching for his opportunity. By June, Baltimore's Mayor Donald Schaefer was saying the city needed a "heavy hitter" to save the Orioles. Several days later, in the wake of press reports that Williams and NFL commissioner Rozelle had had a bitter debate over the NFL policy prohibiting its ownership to buy clubs in other sports, ABC's Barbara Walters announced a rumor that Williams was trying to buy the Orioles. By early August, Ed had closed the deal with Hoffberger. Jerry had done what he always said he would not do: sell to a Washingtonian. No one was more prominently a Washingtonian than Williams, the Redskins' president. Jerry emerged as president of the Orioles under the Williams ownership. Since the sale was not effective until November 1, 1979, Jerry was still the boss during the Pittsburgh-Baltimore World Series, during which he drew a fine from me for inviting Governor Harry Hughes of Maryland to throw out the first ceremonial ball. This was contrary to our sound World Series rule against using local politicians. It was a typical owners' trick designed to give the commissioner fits: invite a popular local governor to do the honors and then say how churlish the commissioner is for standing in the way. I let the governor go ahead and collected my fine with help from Williams.

It was also at the 1979 World Series that I had a rare visit with President Jimmy Carter, who told me that he was more interested in participatory sports than in observing team sports. Since one of those participatory sports was softball, I could be forgiving. He also demonstrated his skill as a broken field runner when the game ended and together we dodged fans in dashing toward the pandemonium of the Pittsburgh clubhouse for a harried trophy presentation.

Williams, keenly aware that his Washington anchor gave the Orioles the look of a club packaged for RFK Stadium, reassured the Maryland fans by saying he had not bought the club to move it. He assured me that he would give careful consideration to playing part of the schedule in Washington. He also would evaluate the possibility of building a new stadium in an area that would accommodate both Washington and Baltimore fans. I was satisfied with those assurances.

Two years later, I would wonder not so much about those assurances as about the whole process I had set in motion to bring Ed into baseball.

Another major change in ownership was set in motion by the death of Joan Payson of the Mets in 1975.

Joan was the first woman to hold a club presidency aside from two widows who succeeded their husbands.* She loved baseball. For a

---

*Grace Comiskey was the White Sox owner from 1941 to 1956, and Mrs. Schuyler P. (Helene) Britton ("Lady Bee") ran the Cardinals in 1916. Mrs. Britton

time she had been a minority owner of the New York Giants. When the paper-structure Continental League was organized in 1959 under the leadership of Branch Rickey, she became a 30 percent partner in its New York club. As with all her involvements, she lent class to that embryonic league. When in time and under the pressure of Rickey's efforts both leagues decided to expand (predictably one year apart), she became the controlling owner of the New York Mets.

Joan Payson felt that owning a baseball team should be a "fun experience." She left the handling of business and player matters to her trusted friend and financial adviser, Donald Grant. She preferred the game itself and the social events that were a part of baseball life. Shea Stadium, under her ownership and Don Grant's guiding hand, became one of the most hospitable places on the baseball circuit.

With her death, the club's presidency passed to her daughter, Lorinda de Roulet, and along with it the problems of free agency in 1976. Bad times befell the Mets. The club made a brave effort to stand firm against free agency, which placed the Mets in sharp contrast to the rival Yankees, who under Steinbrenner's leadership were vaulting into the new market. Abstractly, the Mets' philosophy was sound, but precious little works abstractly in baseball. The other clubs, some enthusiastically, most reluctantly, were following in Steinbrenner's path. The Mets were left behind. Their 1977 trade of Tom Seaver to the Reds further complicated their problems. Not a bad trade when analyzed unemotionally, it nevertheless sat badly with Mets fans, who were very emotional about Tom, the most popular player in the history of the franchise.

In 1979, Linda de Roulet decided to sell. Immediately buyers lined up. The Mets had already proven that in good times they could be very successful. The Mets enlisted National League attorney Lou Hoynes to sort through the prospective owners. I met some of them, including Robert Abplanalp, President Nixon's friend, and Nelson Doubleday.

I met with Doubleday over lunch at "21." I had never met him before. A ruddy-complexioned, hearty man, Nelson was, like me, a Princeton graduate. His great-great uncle, Civil War general Abner Doubleday, is credited with inventing baseball—at least that is the

---

hired Miller Huggins as manager to replace Roger Bresnahan, who was, in her mind, "foul-mouthed," according to historical accounts of the time.

popular story. He was best known as the head of Doubleday & Company, the prominent publishing concern. Fred Wilpon, an outstanding young real estate executive in New York, was included in Nelson's group.

Doubleday and his associates prevailed, buying the club in January 1980 for the price of $21 million. Although at the time some thought the price was high, there was no question in my mind that Doubleday had acquired a bargain. Properly operated, the Mets could challenge the Dodgers as the game's best-drawing club. I felt comfortable in promoting the attractiveness of the Mets to Nelson as I felt his group would be good for the franchise. They got a fast green light from my office when they came up for National League approval.

Not long after Nelson purchased the Mets, I talked to my administrator, Frank Cashen, about his interest in going with them. He was interested, although his first love was his native Baltimore where his family still lived. I was convinced that Frank had the talent to resurrect the Mets. As a result, I encouraged Doubleday in the strongest terms to make Frank the chief operating officer of his club. A month later Frank was hired as executive vice president of the Mets. A careful builder, painstakingly thorough, Frank would cause some dismay in the press during the years of rebuilding the Mets. The media in its impatience would become more preoccupied with his bow ties and taciturn style than with the basic progress the organization was making. All was forgiven by 1984 when the fruits of Frank's work became obvious and the Mets were once again contenders. To his credit, Doubleday never wavered in support of him.

It was not long before Cashen was caught in cross fire between the Mets and my office. At a January 27, 1980, press conference, Doubleday said, "Do you want to go past the Bronx House of Detention? I don't want to knock George's operation, but . . ." Nelson no doubt thought he was being funny, but I did not like the tone of what he said. I thought I could sense what might be coming: a public slugging match between the Yankees and Mets over the safety of their respective ballparks. That was not going to serve any useful purpose. So I told Sandy Hadden, "Get ahold of Cashen and tell him to get these things stopped. We can't have one club sniping at another like this." Sandy talked to Frank and was assured the warning would be brought to the attention of the responsible Mets executives.

In March the Mets hired Jerry Della Femina's advertising agency to prepare a campaign for the club. In public interviews he said Shea Stadium was far cleaner and safer than Yankee Stadium, of which he said, "I feel threatened when I go there; it's not a very positive experience."

Not surprisingly, Steinbrenner reacted, saying, "Since they've chosen to snipe at the Yankees with that old inaccurate ploy that it is safer to attend a ball game at Shea Stadium than at Yankee Stadium, perhaps it is finally time to set things straight once and for all. We haven't chosen to bring this out publicly before because we didn't want to hurt the Mets' attendance any more. However, since they have seen fit to try to mislead the public with innuendos, here is the accurate, long—and I stress accurate—long story!" He went on to cite crime and arrest statistics that put Yankee Stadium in a more favorable light than Shea Stadium.

I directed both clubs to discontinue public attacks on one another and in April, after a brief investigation, imposed a $5,000 fine on the Mets for having failed to control Della Femina, noting that they had been warned in January that I was not going to tolerate that sort of thing. Doubleday later denied that this incident had any effect on his attitude toward me. Maybe so, but I had to wonder.

John McMullen had been a limited partner in the New York Yankees when he and a Houston group purchased the Houston Astros in 1979. "There's nothing so limited as being a limited partner of George Steinbrenner," he said. I asked my security chief, Henry Fitzgibbon, to do the usual background check on McMullen. Fitzgibbon reported that the National League was about to get a stormy character who had left a trail of corporate battles throughout his business career. Apart from that background, we found no reason to recommend against him. I so advised the National League, which routinely approved the sale. I told John at the time of the approval that the worst we had found out about him was that he was a controversial character. His reply was, "If that's the best Fitzgibbon could do, you oughta fire him."

I thought it was a pretty funny line at the time. As a matter of fact, I still do. It also catches the character of McMullen. In the years ahead I would have major problems with this difficult, pugnacious man, but his self-effacing sense of humor leavened my view of him.

McMullen's arrival marked the end of Judge Roy Hofheinz's role in baseball. Actually, the creditors had taken control of the franchise some years earlier, but now even his limited involvement had ended. He had been one of our most extraordinary characters. It was incongruous that he left us so quietly: no explosions, not even a stampede or a small tornado.

McMullen went out of his way to be cordial to me. When he discovered my son Stephen had applied to Boston College, John, who was a trustee, expedited his acceptance. (Stephen decided to go to Middlebury College instead.) John generally went out of his way to be supportive and friendly. I was a frequent recipient of long telephone calls in which I was lathered with advice on every conceivable subject. He was also both opinionated and garrulous. An hour on the telephone was nothing for John. I began to take his calls less and less.

Tal Smith was the able and popular general manager of the Astros when John took over. Tal was a bright, strong-minded man. I had learned to respect and listen to him. When Luisa and I attended the 1980 League Championship Series in Houston, Tal asked us to sit with him and his father in his press-level box, which happened to be adjacent to the ABC broadcasting area where Howard Cosell and Don Drysdale were handling the telecast. Luisa and I stayed in Houston for the final three games of the Phillies-Astros LCS, which was the best postseason series I have ever seen. For sustained action and drama, it was incomparable. I rarely indulged myself by staying long in any one place. Normally, I would not have stayed three days in Houston, but the quality of the series plus the good company of Tal and his father along with Cosell and Drysdale kept us there. I could feel the tension between Tal and McMullen, who kept his distance, sitting in his field box with player agent Dick Moss. It was noteworthy that McMullen made no effort to socialize with Luisa and me.

In a move that most baseball people and I viewed as insane, McMullen fired Smith not long after. He hired Al Rosen to replace him. Rosen had returned to an executive role in Bally's Atlantic City casino after voluntarily resigning as president of the Yankees, weary as he was from dealing with Steinbrenner. There now arose an investigation by the New Jersey attorney general of certain irregularities at Bally's. Since Rosen, by reason of his executive position there, was potentially involved, I, too, instituted an investigation. McMullen called and insisted that I clear Al's name at once. McMullen was in a spot of his own making. The firing of Smith was extremely unpopular in Houston. Now Smith's successor was under investigation.

"I can't do that, John," I told him. "We're looking into it, and we've got to find out what the story is."

"But Al hasn't done anything wrong and this New Jersey investigation is putting an unfair cloud over his name," he replied.

"John, you are probably right, but I am not going to clear him until we're satisfied that our homework is complete. It would be wrong for us to do otherwise. We're in touch with the attorney general and are pressing him for a prompt resolution on Al. I think we'll get it. You know Brendan [Byrne, governor of New Jersey]. Why don't you get him to put some heat on the attorney general?" As much as I personally respected Rosen, then and now, I was not going to be hustled by McMullen into a premature clearance. Happily, Rosen was in time fully cleared, but McMullen was furious over the delay and remembered.

I imagine that were Al Rosen a different kind of man, he too might have been unhappy over the delay and held it against me. But Rosen is a decent man, and what's more, a man of courage. Later when it became public that his boss John McMullen was vigorously seeking my elimination, Al told the press that he disagreed with McMullen and was supporting me.

It was during the 1983 American League Championship Series in Chicago that Jim Campbell of the Tigers called me with the news that his club was about to be sold. In his trenchant way, he said, "We've got a young fellow ready to pay fifty million!"

I listened to Campbell. I remembered hearing the same tone more than ten years before, when he told me he was making the McLain deal with the Senators. The tone was "Please don't get in our way, Commissioner."

The buyer was Tom Monaghan. Campbell said Monaghan was in Chicago as was John Fetzer, and they would like to visit me in my rooms at the Ritz. Campbell told me I would find Monaghan "refreshingly different."

It was a bad time for me to see anybody. For once in my long career as commissioner, I was not well. I had been on the road for almost a week in Los Angeles and Chicago, attending the LCS while running a temperature of 102 degrees. An infection in the lining of my mouth had left me unable to eat solid food. Having lost twelve pounds since I left home, I was drawn, suffering and miserable. I had spent the morning in a Chicago hospital. But this was my postseason swan song as commissioner and I was going to stick it out through the World Series if my life depended on it. To make matters worse, Luisa told me that people, noting my haggard appearance, were taking pity on me, feeling my imminent departure from baseball was causing my misery. That was the last reaction I wanted. So, injured in both body and pride, I awaited the arrival of the Detroit contingent with stoic determination. When they arrived, I could see right away that Monaghan was different. A young forty-six years old, he was almost a choir boy.

He had been brought up in a Catholic orphanage and had made a fortune building Domino's Pizza. The chain had grown to some 1,500 stores nationwide and was second only to Pizza Hut in the United States in revenue among pizza operations. As we talked, I learned that Tom was a genuine Tiger fan. I noted approvingly that he treated Fetzer with deep respect. Tom told me that John would continue as chief executive officer of the Tigers while Tom learned the ropes. He was also going to retain Campbell, whom he correctly considered to be one of the best operators in our business. This was all too good to believe. I kept asking questions to find some missing and ghastly piece of the story. I found none. I knew Fetzer had wanted to sell, having wearied of the new owners and their attacks on me. Yet there was no way he would sell to anyone not dedicated to Detroit or not measuring up to his high standards of ethics and decency. In seraphic Monaghan he had found precisely what he wanted. It pleased me that Fetzer would continue to lead the club. So Monaghan won the ownership of the Tigers with hardly a ripple on the baseball waters, just a lot of baseball folk wondering if this man could be true, and sailed into a world championship in his first year. Charles Dickens would have blushed to write such a tale.

I called Walter O'Malley on April 23, 1979, on Executive Council business. He was unable to take the call. A few days later, I received the following letter:

My dear Commissioner:
When I was unable to take your phone call the other morning I realized that it was about time to change the guard. Over the years I have enjoyed being on the Executive Council and my work with you as Commissioner and with the other members of the Executive Council has been most rewarding.

Be good enough, Commissioner, to send me out to pasture at your convenience.

All the best,
Walter

He died on August 9, not quite four months later, at the Mayo Clinic in Rochester, Minnesota, where he was revered by the medical staff as he was in baseball. Six years later, Peter O'Malley and I went to the Mayo Clinic together to submit our anatomies to their skillful and reassuring perusal and found Walter everywhere from the boardroom to the restaurants, clinics and Kahler Hotel; everyone talked about him.

He was seventy-five years old at his death, defying medical logic to have gone so long, given his history of cancer. I had seen him only sparingly in the last year of his life as he found it harder and harder to maintain his usual baseball schedule. He had missed the 1978 World Series between the Dodgers and Yankees, having been admitted to Our Lady Queen of Angels Hospital in Los Angeles. After the Yankees won the sixth and deciding game at Dodger Stadium, I went by myself to visit Walter.

The room was simple, almost spartan. That was fitting; Walter was never a physically pretentious man. His world was intellectual, as were his achievements. His illness had changed him very little. He was affable, with his humor fully intact. He appreciated my visit and wanted to talk. First he passed off my sympathy over the Dodger defeat. I had observed over the years that Walter took baseball victory or defeat in stride. He always had excellent player-development executives and counted on them to give him a good product. They usually did. Even so, he understood that victory could be elusive. After chatting lightly about some of our current difficulties, he moved to the subject of baseball's future.

"We have come a long way in this game," he said. "There was a time when we were down, when frankly I wouldn't have bet much on our future. But not anymore. I think our future is unlimited nationally and internationally. Under your leadership I think we can do things we would never have imagined possible. I didn't think a club could ever draw three million people, and we've done that. Others can do it, too. The trick is to think on a big scale. You can do that. Let your imagination go and follow it. You're going to do great things. Anything is possible. Remember we just elected a Polish Pope."

Except for the last line, it had all been serious. None of the usual O'Malley twinkle. He meant to tell me something. I remembered those remarks when in December 1981 I decided to challenge those who opposed the values I held.

I saw Walter once more before he died. I went to see him at his house in Los Angeles during the spring. When I rang, he surprised me by coming to the door himself wearing pajamas and a bathrobe. We talked easily but about nothing of consequence. The twinkle and spirit were there but physically he was losing ground. He insisted on walking me to the door as I left.

When he died, I issued a statement. It was short but said what I felt about Walter:

> He was as great an executive talent as I ever saw, or think that I am apt to see.
>
> While baseball was his medium, his skills would have flourished in any walk of life. He was unfailing in his support of the Commissioner's Office and a powerful ally for the good of the game. His unique ability, his charm and wit are not replaceable. He was my personal friend.

Six years later, I would add a thought. "Friend" he was. I cared about him and I think he cared about me above and beyond the normal business relationship that might exist between a commissioner and an owner. Still, we had disagreed on many issues; some went his way, some mine. Nor was I happy with his periodic efforts to maneuver things that were in my domain, and I resisted them. He was not too happy about what I believe he saw as my sometimes romantic view (he might have said impractical) of the game and the commissioner's role. So it is fair to say that our friendship was not without friction, but it is also fair to say that it was real and warm.

A by-product of Walter's death was a strengthening of my relationship with the American League. Though I felt I had been impeccably dispassionate in dealing with the affairs of the two major leagues, there was a sense among some American Leaguers that I had a bias for the Nationals. After all, my law firm had represented the National League. But it was really not so much that as O'Malley himself who caused that sense to exist because he was seen by many as the power behind the throne. It was not altogether chance that the four votes that sought to derail me in 1975 came from the American League or that my most difficult struggle as commissioner through 1976 was with the American League over bypassing Washington in expansion. The air was now cleared. By the time my final showdown came along, the American League was my strong ally.

I made a spontaneous visit to Walter's gravesite in 1980. I had been met at the Los Angeles airport by Ike Ikuhara, the able executive who had long served as special assistant to Walter and Peter O'Malley and who had been an invaluable informal consultant to me on matters relating to Japan and the Orient. He was dedicated to the Dodgers and the O'Malleys. As we left the airport, he asked if I would like to see the gravesite, which was not far away. I said I would. Bathed by a gentle breeze that swept up the rise where we stood, Ike and I remained for perhaps five minutes looking at the two simple gravestones that marked Walter and Kay O'Malley. My Japanese friend and I stood together in silent tribute to these two remarkable people who had meant so much to us. They were our ancestors, too.

By 1984, it was Calvin Griffith's time to sell. I had known Calvin longer than any other baseball executive. Almost forty-five years earlier, he had been my paymaster when I was a dollar-a-day scoreboard boy at Griffith Stadium. My brother, Lou, had gone to Roosevelt High School in Washington with Cal's brother Sherry Robertson, who later played for the Senators and had a pretty good left-handed power bat. Cal was born a Robertson but became a Griffith when he was adopted by the Senators' owner, Clark Griffith. Clark's wife was a Robertson and Calvin's aunt. More than anybody in baseball, Cal was like family to me. His "good ol' boy" North Carolina style forever reminded me of the overgrown southern town that was the Washington of my youth.

Cal was cut from a different cloth than the other owners. Guileless, homespun, uncomplicated, Cal knew more about baseball than any major-league owner in the game and he cared passionately about it. Baseball dominated his whole life. Though some like Steinbrenner mocked him for it, I loved his fidelity to his family, best evidenced by the jobs he gave them with the Senators and Twins. The family had a shrewd understanding of the baseball business and gave as good an account of themselves per dollar spent as any organization in baseball. Of course, that was their problem: dollars. By baseball standards, they were church mice. Outstanding players like Rod Carew, Larry Hisle, Lyman Bostock, Bill Campbell, Dave

Goltz, Geoff Zahn, Dan Ford, Butch Wynegar and Ken Landreaux slipped through their grasp either through free agency or free agency–related trades, because they lacked the funds to compete in the post-Messersmith era. Still, no one developed better young talent.

If Cal struggled with finances, he also struggled with public relations. The press, understandably upset by his blunt remarks and threats to move the Twins from Minnesota, pummeled him regularly and mercilessly. He hit bottom in 1978 with tasteless remarks denigrating black sports fans. It was national news. I found myself in the fence-mending business, calling the Reverend Jesse Jackson and NAACP head Benjamin Hooks to express the embarrassment of baseball. I publicly reprimanded Cal and disowned his remarks.

Cal was always blunt. I recall the time he voted one way in my Executive Council meeting and the other way in the following major-league meeting. Since it was an issue I particularly cared about, I called him on it. His answer was pure Cal. "Commissioner, you should never believe owners; they'll always lie to you."

When he began talking about selling to Tampa interests, I called him up. "I can understand your wanting to use the Tampa group to help you negotiate a better deal in Minnesota," I said, "but if you get any respectable offer from Minnesota, take it. Don't make any mistake about it—we're not going to move that franchise!"

To his credit, Cal made no complaint. He might have argued that the NFL's Al Davis had created new freedom for franchise owners with his successful, if appalling, abandonment of Oakland for Los Angeles. He did not, arguing only that he was entitled to a fair price. He well understood that baseball had not moved a franchise in fourteen years and was determined to maintain that record. Lee MacPhail and new American League president Bobby Brown were as determined as I that Minnesota would remain major-league territory. Whatever may have been the merits of Davis's challenge to the National Football League and however he may have brought off his inexcusable departure from Oakland, I was satisfied that any such legal assault on major-league baseball by a footloose owner would fail. Moreover, we had a qualified potential buyer in Minnesota in the person of Carl Pohlad, with a net worth of $375 million according to *Forbes* magazine. Pohlad was definitely interested.

There was a troublesome complication when the Tampa group, headed by Bill Mack and Frank Morsani, made an agreement to purchase the 42 percent interest in the Twins held by Gabe Murphy of Washington. Without that 42 percent, Pohlad was going to lose interest in buying the Twins. Bobby Brown and I met Morsani and Mack and persuaded them that the future interests of Tampa were not going to be served by obstructing Pohlad's efforts. When they graciously stepped aside, Pohlad closed the purchase of the Twins for a hefty price, around $45 million.

Hall of Famer Clark Griffith came to baseball in 1888 as a pitcher. Thus, the Griffith dynasty stretched back almost one hundred years. Now it was over. It was a sad time for a baseball romantic like me.

18

Good Night, Sweet Charlie

Predictably, the process of sweeping Charlie Finley out of the game was one of my most complex challenges.

There has never been a doubt in my mind that baseball's blunder of putting two clubs in the San Francisco–Oakland area would sooner or later have to be corrected. Oakland's three successive world championship clubs in 1972, 1973 and 1974 did nothing to change my conviction. They drew poorly. Finley's poor marketing was no doubt a factor. Still, a winner on the field is the best possible form of marketing, as Finley correctly argued, and winning had been received with apathy.

This perception led to my 1975 lobbying efforts with Mayor Alioto of San Francisco and Bob Nahas of Oakland. After the abortive effort to move the Giants to Toronto, and the sale of the Giants to Bob Lurie, whose $200-million net worth gave some hope of stability to the San Francisco side of the equation, we turned our hopes for a solution to the East Bay.

Unfortunately, 1976 was a lost cause because of the Messersmith decision and its ramifications, including my veto of Finley's sales of Blue, Fingers and Rudi. Any solution of the Oakland problem should have involved communication and cooperation between the commissioner and the Oakland club, but Finley's lawsuit against me guaranteed that communication between us for the time being would be via four-letter words.

With the loss of his lawsuit in 1977, Finley, ever accommodative to circumstances, was prepared to do business again with the commissioner. What ensued was a three-year joint effort on the part of Finley and me to sell the A's. Since it no longer served Finley's purpose to provoke me, the vitriol that had characterized our relationship for the past eight years vanished. But first, he had to deal with a serious and worsening health problem.

On September 15 Finley had major heart bypass surgery in Chicago. There was some black humor that destiny was at long last solving our Finley problem. I could not share the humor, but did wonder how my tough old antagonist would handle this challenge. Some days later I had my answer when Mary told me that Finley was on the telephone. Sure enough; he was on the line sounding as if he had just returned from a Caribbean cruise. Not only did he tell me in detail about his operation but he showed even livelier interest in describing his "beautiful nurse" who, he said, was sitting on his bed. Indeed, Finley, who reveled in his Lotharian reputation, insisted on having her talk to me. She was charming.

While he may have called to regale me about his nurse, selling the A's was the principal reason for his call, and that was the subject to which he then turned. There had been overtures from New Orleans and Washington. And also from Marvin Davis in Denver. I knew that Finley was not going to be able to sell the club to anybody away from Oakland without the consent of his landlord, the Oakland-Alameda Coliseum, and the cooperation of the San Francisco municipal government and the Giants. To get that consent and cooperation he needed my help, a miserable spot for a proud man. And now he was asking for it, explaining that his doctors had told him he could no longer safely operate a club. The key player was Bob Nahas, head of the coliseum. I told Finley I would discuss the situation with Lee MacPhail. I preferred not dealing with Finley. I also liked to work with and through the league president on matters of such importance to a league.

I did talk to Lee, who encouraged me to contact Nahas. Bob had no more enthusiasm for helping Finley than he had had when we first discussed the subject two years earlier. He said Finley had made a mess of the Oakland operation and could not in any event be trusted.

I could not blame Nahas. Finley threw a blanket of suspicion over everything he touched. I was also busy trying to find some answer for Washington and talking to various possible buyers of the Baltimore club. And I was watching Finley's player operation, far from satisfied that his liquidation efforts were over.

I was curious about Denver's Marvin Davis, who had been talking to Finley. Since he had a net worth said to be in the billion-dollar zone, one had to suspect he could play in our financial league. Finley was quoted as saying, "Hell, he could buy the other twenty-five clubs." I wanted to know more about Davis. Finley was reporting him to be a great guy. That made me suspicious.

Luisa and I flew to Honolulu on December 2 for baseball's annual meetings. It was a memorable nine days. Early risers, Luisa and I would walk at daybreak to the beautiful old Royal Hawaiian Hotel for breakfast overlooking the ocean. Each morning we would find Walter O'Malley there, full of scandalous suggestions about what we were doing abroad at such an hour. It was funnier and more outrageous each day. This sort of thing was part of the O'Malley mystique and people loved it. But the crowning event came on December 9 when Cincinnati announced it had traded Dave Revering to Oakland for Vida Blue and sweetened the deal with $1,750,000 on the side.

As I described earlier, this news ratcheted my relations with Finley down a few more notches. Several days later Finley closed a deal to sell the A's to Marvin Davis. For a man who had gone through major heart surgery only three months before, Finley was showing remarkable recuperative powers. He would need them. Nahas's coliseum board promptly went to court and obtained a temporary restraining order to prevent the sale.

MacPhail urged me to get Nahas to sit down and talk. I reached Nahas on the telephone. He asked, "Could we control Finley?" Bob and I did not talk like opponents but rather like partners trying to solve a mutual problem. I told him I fully understood all his reservations but thought we should try having a meeting of the principals. He was willing to think about that. One thing was certain; he was not going to return any calls from Finley. He said he would be in Palm Desert for a week wrapped around Christmas. The next day Bob told me his lawyers wanted no meetings until there had been a court hearing on the coliseum's request for a temporary injunction. He was "sorry this thing has taken this turn." Bob wanted to help but his distrust of Finley made that difficult.

Two days later I got what I wanted. At a hearing before Federal

Judge William Orrick, all parties agreed there would be no sale to Davis without the coliseum's consent. It was also agreed that Finley and coliseum officials would talk about a possible solution. After a three-day pause for Christmas, Finley called me himself. Now he was really pushing hard with no extraneous pretensions of either anger or cordiality. "I have talked to Lee," he said. "He says you want to help if possible and that you have good relations with Nahas. This is our chance to pass the club to Davis." He reported that Jerry Gray, Davis's top man, wanted a meeting on December 30; time was important. I doubted that, but why take any chances? By the end of the day, Finley and I were working like a pair of carriage horses and had set up separate meetings with Davis and Nahas in Palm Springs for December 30. Finley closed the day by telling me, "Davis is an excellent man." I replied, "So I hear."

There were wisps of uncertainty in Nahas's telephone remarks to me. He had heard that Giants co-owner Bud Herseth was talking about selling to Washington interests. He wondered if San Francisco Mayor Moscone had not agreed in 1976 to let the Giants leave after three years of poor attendance. The implication was, Why not let the Giants leave and keep the A's?

On December 30, American League attorney Jim Garner and I flew from New York's LaGuardia to Chicago's O'Hare, where Finley came on board, and headed on to Palm Springs. Finley drank champagne and behaved. Diverted by bad weather into Los Angeles' Ontario Airport, we had to devise alternative travel plans to Palm Springs. While Garner and I rented one car, Finley chartered two airplanes. I never found out why. Probably in a fit of activity like a ravenous fish. In any event, we cancelled the car and one airplane and took off in the other, which I later learned Finley had charged to my account. Airborne and with time to kill, Finley in an expansive mood asked if I would like to see his bypass scar. Actually, I was interested, knowing next to nothing about such an operation. With that, Finley proceeded to fling most of his clothes either open or off, revealing a majestic scar that ran virtually from groin to Adam's apple. I have often wondered what the sports world would have made of this scene: Kuhn doing a clinical study of a nearly nude Finley torso in a tiny airplane high above the California desert. I have Jim Garner to swear it all happened.

We proceeded to a meeting at the Palm Springs Canyon Hotel with Nahas, Neil Papiano, Finley's lawyer, and MacPhail. Nahas was constructive, observing that 162 home games were too much in the

Bay Area and that perhaps the playing of 50 percent of the Giants home games in Oakland might open the way for the A's departure. However, he noted, there were various interests that would have to be consulted and more time was needed. Finley said time was critical and that without a solution he would be forced into Chapter 11 bankruptcy. Stressing his flexibility, he said he would sell to an Oakland buyer if Nahas could find one. Nahas promised to evaluate all possibilities and get back to us the following week.

Nahas limped out of the meeting with a painful back. Big and rangy, Bob was prone to low-back problems of the type that have plagued me most of my life. It was one of various points of sympathy we had for each other. In fact, our gathering had commenced with me on the floor giving Bob a demonstration of the back exercises I had recently been given by Dr. Peter LaMotte, the former New York Mets team physician. I tend to become a crusader for health improvement methods I have tried, whether exercises, running, low-cholesterol–high-carbohydrate diets, vitamin supplements or regular physical examinations. A lot of people have had to suffer through my bursts of enthusiasm on such subjects. The stress of a three-hour meeting with Finley added to Nahas's pain. I knew enough about stress and backs to be sure of that.

Finley, Papiano, MacPhail, Garner and I went to the Pamarisk Country Club for a meeting with Davis. It was my first encounter with Davis, a grizzly bear–proportioned captain of the oil industry. It was immediately apparent that he was more than a match for Finley. If Finley was awed by money he was immeasurably more awed by a tough giant-sized businessman with a billion dollars. Our joint report to Davis on the Nahas meetings was encouraging, a little too much so I thought, as I listened to Charlie's version. I tried to keep a moderate damper on the enthusiasm. Noting my reservations, Davis pressed me on how soon we could announce the deal. Taking him aside, I told him there were problems that would take time to solve, if they could be solved at all. He said he did not like dealing with Finley and urged me to clear the situation up as soon as possible.

We all drove to Davis's handsome, well-guarded house in Palm Springs. As he showed me the grounds I told him my concerns about excessive spending in baseball. He read the implication that I was concerned about him and dispelled it. "Bowie," he said, "I'm not a damned fool; I know how to run a business; you won't have to worry about me." Some weeks later over lunch at his club, I raised the same question. This time he bristled, "Bowie, I've already answered that question; you don't have to ask me twice." He was a refreshingly direct man, his directness being an endowment I appreciated, perhaps because I found so little of it in the everyday circumlocutions of the baseball world.

When I heard from Nahas a few days later, the news was bad. The East Bay politicians were determined to keep the A's and wanted no part of the Giants. Nahas thought they were "inflexible." Tapping his sources, Finley told me Nahas was being "defensive" about the East Bay position. His information was that they still hoped Bud Herseth could force a sale of the Giants to Washington buyers.

We knew that was nonsense; so Finley, Lurie and I continued to push for an East Bay solution. We got some encouragement. On January 19 I made a one-day visit to Oakland and talked to key politicians: more encouragement. MacPhail and I had lunch in New York with Davis and his father in early February. He was getting impatient. When big Marvin got impatient he was a formidable force. We could only tell him we were working miracles as it was. What leverage did we have on the politicians on either side of the Bay? Yet they were listening. Marvin agreed to keep the "door ajar" and said so publicly after the lunch.

Actually, the best part of the lunch was the senior Davis, a one-time English light heavyweight fighter who had succeeded nicely in the New York garment trade and staked Marvin to a small oil business in Colorado. Marvin had a deep and loving affection for his father and one could see why: He was a charmingly good-humored man. He and I got along well. As lunch broke up, he turned to his son and said, "Marvin, I like this commissioner; why don't we put him into an oil well?" Unfortunately for the Kuhn family fortunes, Marvin never took that paternal advice.

The same day I had a call from Louisiana senator Russell Long. He was concerned that I was "pushing Denver" as the new home for the A's. He said New Orleans wanted the A's and would make a "substantially better offer." He assured me that because this was very important for Louisiana the governor would make this a "good deal for baseball." He also assured me that he could help baseball in Washington. No one took Russell Long lightly. He was one of the ablest and most powerful legislators in Washington. He had engineered the legislation that made possible the NFL-AFL merger, a merger that produced the New Orleans Saints as part of the NFL. While I liked and respected Long, I was not happy to hear from him for two reasons: I thought Denver was preferable to New Orleans; and, after years of working with New Orleans, I had never found the kind of solid, well-financed owner I felt we needed there. Nor had the senator suggested that such an owner had now materialized. I told Long I would talk to Lee MacPhail and give the matter some thought. Realistically I knew there was not much I could do for New Orleans.

During the next two weeks, as we talked incessantly to all the key politicians, the basic problem emerged: Oakland's insistence on sharing Giants home games equally with San Francisco (forty-one in one city, forty in the other) and the latter's unwillingness to give up more than thirty games. We worked out the problem of what to call the shared club and how much to pay Oakland to release the A's from their lease. Both mayors, Oakland's Lionel Wilson and San Francisco's Moscone, were trying, but when we could not bridge the difference on shared games, the deal looked dead.

By mid-February a desperate Finley was talking to me about selling to a New Orleans buyer he called a "backwoodsman," about selling to Davis without consent from Oakland and letting Davis take whatever litigation might ensue, about his fear that Davis might buy the Giants and about embarrassing Moscone into acquiescing on 41–40 parity on games. The pressure on Moscone would come when the *San Francisco Examiner* reprinted a letter Moscone had written in 1976 to the National League expressing the possibility that the Giants could leave after the 1978 season if certain attendance levels were not achieved.

I suspect Finley leaked the letter to the *Examiner.* He told me they were "goofy and thrilled over the letter." He even rehearsed for me the comment he would make on the letter, "I am surprised to learn of this letter; Moscone is taking an awful gamble." It was a nifty insight into Finley's method of operation.

The publication of the letter did not stampede Moscone, although it did embarrass him politically. Seeing no immediate hope for the situation, I took off with Luisa and my son Stephen for eight days in two of my favorite winter areas, Vermont and Maine. I was deep in the snows of Belfast, Maine, when Mary called. She said there was an article in the papers about Finley's attacking me. I was hardly surprised. My veto of the Revering-Blue trade several weeks earlier, taken together with the difficulties of the Davis-Finley sale, had the effect of a full moon on Finley. He was no doubt in his werewolf phase. The article said he was ready to climb to the top of the Sears Tower and hold up a sign saying FIRE BOWIE. Though that was tepid stuff by his standards, it looked as if we were back in one of the "we ain't talking" stages, which was when I enjoyed the old reprobate most.

On March 7, Finley called and was all conspiratorial charm. "Commissioner," he said, "we've got a chance to make a deal in San Francisco yet. If you'll just help me, we can do it. The finance committee of the San Francisco Board of Supervisors is meeting tomorrow afternoon. If you'll go testify in favor of a parity solution, they may go along. That means splitting Giants games equally between Oakland and San Francisco. Will you do it?"

I asked him what made him think there was any chance now for that long-rejected solution. He hissed that "his sources" told him so. I never scoffed at "his sources." They were apt to be quite reliable. I told him I would check it out myself. He urged me to get back to him.

"Where can I reach you, Charlie?" I asked.

"Well, right here in my Chicago office, of course," he answered.

"Oh, I thought maybe you'd be on the top of the Sears Tower," I said.

There was a long pause on the other end of the telephone, then a rumbling laugh and Finley saying, "Commissioner, you really know how to hurt a guy!"

So I flew to San Francisco and appeared before Quentin Kopp's finance committee the next afternoon. I urged parity and a sensible accommodative name solution. I assured them that San Francisco would be held harmless against any financial losses. I warned that the survival of baseball in the Bay Area could ultimately be at stake.

For the next three weeks, the politicians, the baseball administration and the lawyers struggled to find solutions. At last, amazingly, parity was agreed to. The team name would be the San Francisco Giants except in Oakland, where it would be the Giants. Financial payments to the Oakland Coliseum were set at $3.25 million. The internal fight within baseball was difficult when Finley would put up no more than $1 million as his share of the coliseum payment. Even that we were finally able to persuade the clubs to accept. But when we asked him to waive claims of any kind against baseball, he balked.

He admitted he and his lawyers were preparing a lawsuit against me for vetoing the Vida Blue sale to Cincinnati. The Associated Press quoted him as saying: "I want to sell but I won't give up my Constitutional rights. There is no way any red-blooded American would agree to sign such an idiot agreement that they are trying to force down my throat."

There it was: Finley's paranoid determination to have another shot at me in court. There was no way we were going to pay the major cost of bailing him out of Oakland and leave him free to harass us with whatever lawsuits he wanted thereafter. I announced we were terminating our efforts to work out a solution. I was convinced that Finley had gone completely around the bend.

In fact, he never pursued a lawsuit regarding my Blue decision, probably discouraged by an April 7 decision of the Seventh Circuit Court of Appeals upholding my handling of the Rudi-Fingers-Blue sales. He took that defeat to the United States Supreme Court. In October the Supreme Court declined to review the Seventh Circuit.

By June 1978, I was back at work trying to persuade Nahas there was still some solution. Bob and his wife, Eva, had a place on Lake Tahoe to which they invited Luisa and me for three days that June. We had a lot of things in common: love of the water and late-evening conversation, tennis, peanut butter for breakfast and a low regard for Charles Oscar Finley.

During our three days in Tahoe, we solved most of the world's problems—to our own satisfaction at least—but did nothing about Finley. Bob was disenchanted with the whole process. He really hoped Finley was, too; if so, he might be ready to sell to an Oakland buyer. I told Bob that Oakland needed an extremely well-financed owner of a type we had not seen and had little prospect of seeing. We agreed it was too early to judge the situation and Bob suggested we get together again at his place in Idaho. As he drove us out of the mountains to the Reno airport, we were all discouraged.

Bob's hopes for an Oakland buyer sunk lower when a respected professional marketing study concluded that turning around baseball in the East Bay was like "trying to bring back Ipana Toothpaste." In early 1979, Nahas told me he had asked for a firm local offer and gotten nothing. MacPhail and I thought it was time to crank up our best vehicle: Marvin Davis. I began talking to Davis's Washington lawyer, Bob Schulman, and putting some numbers together. Schulman, who had been talking on and off with Finley for the previous four months, told me that Finley was seeing the Edward J. DeBartolo, Sr., people in Chicago in several days. We both recognized that Finley was looking for leverage in dealing with Davis.

I asked Bob Lurie if he was interested in resurrecting the scenario that Finley had destroyed nine months ago. Lurie said he could try, but he also pointed out that the Oakland Raiders' lease ended after the next football season. Their owner, Al Davis, could be looking to either of two courses, enlarging the Oakland Coliseum or moving to Los Angeles. He also told me that Finley was offering players to the Giants for $400,000 apiece. The old liquidator was still plying his trade.

While the East Bay was losing interest in the A's, there was a great enthusiasm for the Raiders. The last thing the Oakland people wanted was Al Davis's taking off for Southern California. It was clear to me that if baseball could put enough money on the table to help expand the coliseum to meet Davis's demands, we had a chance to get Finley out of his lease. Schulman strongly supported that view. He told me that politically it was impossible for the coliseum to let both the Raiders and A's go. He urged me to give Nahas some help; Nahas was interested and agreed to meet me at the Los Angeles airport with MacPhail. At the meeting, Bob talked about "something over $4 million" and we talked about "as much as $3.6 million." We all knew that kind of difference could be resolved. Bob said he would talk to Al Davis on January 23. He said, "It all hinges on Davis."

When I heard nothing from Nahas, I asked Schulman what he knew. It was not an idle pursuit. Schulman had wires running in many directions, including a reliable number in the NFL. He told me what I feared, that Davis had made no deal with the coliseum. He said Davis might want to fight to get the Raiders to Los Angeles. He assured me that the NFL was very much against a move and was prepared to be tough. I did not like Davis's chances of fighting his way through both the NFL and the East Bay authorities, particularly given the outstanding record of support the Raiders had received in the coliseum. That would help us in getting the A's out. It was also going to be difficult to enlarge the coliseum for Davis without interrupting the baseball schedule there and breaching Finley's lease. That would be another reason why Nahas should negotiate Finley's exit.

This roller coaster had no end. Nahas now advised that a new local group featuring executives of Combined Communications, Kaiser Aluminum and Clorox was prepared to save the A's. James Nederlander would be the principal owner. With the concurrence of such a group, Nahas hoped to refurbish the coliseum and save both the A's and Raiders. Still, I heard the usual uncertainty. He said, "Whether this flies, I don't know." The next day he announced that under no circumstances would the A's be freed from their lease.

While all this was transpiring, Finley glumly advised Sandy Hadden that he had talked to "about a hundred corporations," including SONY, Royal Crown Cola, Westinghouse Broadcasting and Wendy's. None was interested in buying the A's. "I don't know where to turn," he told Sandy. He reported that Marvin Davis had dropped his offer to "ten mil." Now the chutzpah: he wondered if I could revive Davis's interest in the $12 million offered earlier. "I'll be home all evening," he said. "If the commissioner wants to call me, I would appreciate it." If I had been in the office that day, I would have been tempted to call and ask Finley something about whether "home" was on top of the Sears Tower. It so happened I was in Pittsburgh, meeting with that city's mayor and John and Dan Galbreath about the Pirates' operating problems. The next day I was pursuing baseball's legislative interests in Washington meetings with Senator Ted Kennedy and others. Finley drifted out of my mind.

But Bob Lurie could always get my attention and did so emphatically with a call to me in St. Petersburg in early March advising me that San Francisco supervisor Quentin Kopp was ready to consider parity scheduling of the Giants between San Francisco and Oakland. Even more significantly, Nahas had called him the day before to say he was willing to take another look at the parity-name-change concept of 1978. Characteristically, he had linked that observation with the view that the Oakland buyers of the A's were serious. When I checked Nahas several days later, the 1978 concept vanished and he pressed the Oakland buyers as "the cream of the East Bay." "Besides," he told me, "Al Davis only wants sixty-four super boxes, not stadium expansion." (The super boxes could be built without disrupting the baseball schedule.)

It was becoming clear that East Bay baseball was merely a pawn in a larger game to accommodate Al Davis and the enormously more popular Raiders. Moreover, in the prior year the Raiders had generated $941,000 in revenues for the coliseum complex as against a paltry $395,000 by the A's.

With the opening of the 1979 season, the A's' situation was "pathetic" (that was the word Finley used when he called looking for my help in April). The A's were drawing about 3,000 people per game. Finley said the Nederlander group was offering mostly "Chinese dollars." On a plaintive note, he said his health was not good and his doctors had advised him to get out of baseball. I said I would talk to Nahas. Somehow, Finley could always find a way to play my sympathetic strings.

I tried Nahas one more time and discovered that the city and county people wanted to sue Finley for inadequately promoting his club. As to letting the A's go, he called it a "political impossibility."

Finley now publicly condemned the coliseum management for making him the villain of the abortive 1978 attempt to move the A's to Denver. He told the *Los Angeles Times*, "They made it look like I was the one who asked to move. . . . Naturally, the fans said to hell with Finley; if he doesn't want to stay, we won't support him." The defense was a typical Finley fabrication. Of course he wanted to move and had gotten me to help him. The coliseum management so answered when asked by the *Times;* I confirmed their version.

In late April, the coliseum management filed a lawsuit against Finley for breach of lease by failing to promote the A's. Valid though that assertion was, it could hardly advance a solution to the Oakland problem. Yet I could well understand the frustration of the East Bay authorities. Finley had that effect on people.

The litigation chugged along, worsening feelings on all sides, while Al Davis escalated his threats to take off for Southern California. I continued to talk to Marvin Davis and Bob Schulman about Marvin's patient pursuit of the A's.

As the dissatisfaction grew all around, so did our imaginations. Bill Veeck, who wanted to sell the White Sox, would have been happy to sell to Davis. Lee MacPhail wanted no part of that unless another club was simultaneously moved into Chicago. Finley would be happy to sell the A's to any Chicago buyer who would be willing to battle the coliseum people. That general scenario got a lot of attention. By late September, Davis told me he was ready to sign a contract with Veeck subject to American League approval. The possibility was serious enough for him to again assure me that he was "a bottom line guy, not a George Steinbrenner." He was also sure he could find a buyer for the A's in Chicago. Failing a Chicago buyer, we saw Marvin operating the White Sox in Chicago until a replacement club could be made available. Meanwhile, Veeck was denying that the Sox might leave Chicago as he negotiated to do just that. However, the Chicago press was beginning to question Veeck's fidelity to the Windy City.

At the end of September, Davis sent his plane to New York to fly Lee MacPhail and me to Denver for a long session on possible solutions. The more we talked, the more we became convinced that we should make one final effort to negotiate our way out of Oakland.

Flying back to LaGuardia that night in Davis's plane, contemplating the peaceful sweep of the Great Plains below, I wondered if we would ever see an end to this dilemma.

However, my outlook was brightened by the prospect of a telephone conference the next morning with Peter O'Malley, Bob Smith, president of the International Baseball Association, and Rod Dedeaux, USC baseball coach, regarding international amateur baseball. The four of us were an informal kitchen cabinet endlessly searching for the formula that would put baseball into the Olympics as a gold-medal sport. Smith was president of the organization, under whose banner were gathered all the diverse interests of the amateur game worldwide—interests as varied as those of Americans, Cubans, Nicaraguans, Italians, Japanese, Taiwanese, Mainland Chinese and Indians. Bonded together by a common love of baseball, this international fellowship worked with an affection and efficiency that put to shame their national counterparts. The kitchen group was a tonic for me. They always took my mind away from the Finleys and the endless problems of the professional game. To this day, we maintain that partnership.

As the World Series approached, MacPhail and I continued our efforts to persuade the East Bay sachems to let the A's go. We even utilized the off-day between the fifth and sixth games to fly to Oakland, where we met with coliseum officials, including Nahas and Oakland's Mayor Lionel Wilson. Very reluctantly, they decided to go along with our plan to pay the coliseum $4 million to release the A's. Finley had worn them down, leaving them bitterly resentful but resigned. We were euphoric to see at long last a solution to the Oakland puzzle.

Two days after the Pirates became the fourth team to overcome a three-games-to-one deficit and win the World Series (a Pirates team had also been the first in 1925), I advised all major-league clubs that I would no longer approve any Oakland player transactions involving more than $50,000 cash. I concluded that Finley's continuing player sales (e.g., Bruce Robinson, Greg Cochran, John Henry Johnson), though within my $400,000 limit, were causing a cumulative and unacceptable deterioration of the club's competitive ability. I also noted that the A's' efforts to sign amateur players had "noticeably slackened." In other words, Finley was still liquidating piecemeal. One club executive objected, Dick Wagner of the Reds. Dick, who had succeeded Bob Howsam as chief executive officer, was now a harsh and constant critic. An excellent number two man to Howsam, the stress and demands of the club presidency taken together with succeeding a man of Howsam's stature seemed to take their toll.

The same day I curbed Finley's liquidation process, I spoke at a Fellowship of Christian Athletes lunch in Dallas. I was there at the invitation of Coach Tom Landry of the Dallas Cowboys. The coach and I were both trustees of the fellowship. I could not help but reflect on the paradox of dealing with Landry and Finley on the same day.

Communication between Finley and me dropped to zero. Fortunately, MacPhail remained an effective and continuing go-between, as all of us sought to implement the accord we had achieved in Oakland during the World Series.

Then came the development I had most feared. Before we could complete our settlement with the coliseum, Al Davis announced, on January 18, 1980, his plans to move the Raiders to Los Angeles. Our deal was dead, irretrievably dead after all those years of effort and walking on nails with Finley. There was no way the coliseum could voluntarily give up the A's once Al Davis headed south, down the Pacific shore.

In February 1980, Marvin Davis, not one to fret over failure, turned around and bought Twentieth-Century Fox. Maybe movie moguls were easier to deal with than sports moguls like Finley and Al Davis—well, at least at the start.

I regretted that we had lost Marvin Davis, whom I liked, and, as importantly, I regretted that we had not parlayed a solution of the Bay Area problem into the inclusion of an attractive city like Denver in the American League. Sooner or later, Denver's time will come, but it should have been 1980.

In the summer of 1980, MacPhail told me something was brewing again in the East Bay. Visions of more bootless maneuverings sprang into my head. Lee said there could be a buyer to keep the club in Oakland. Since there were no relations, diplomatic or otherwise, between Finley and me at this stage, I had to rely on Lee for information. In due time he told me that the possible buyer was the Haas family, which owned Levi Strauss & Co. The Haases would not present any problem of league or commissioner approval, a consideration of which I was keenly aware since we were then moving into the DeBartolo-Reinsdorf contest to buy the White Sox. Lee cautioned me that the information was confidential since Finley did not want me apprised. Dear Charlie had not forgotten me. He knew perfectly well Lee would tell me about a matter of that importance.

Mirabile dictu, it was announced in August that Finley had agreed to sell the A's to the Haases. Naturally, Finley said I had driven him out of the game. In a more straightforward moment, he gave his real reason for selling: "It is no longer a battle of wits, but how much you have on the hip. I can no longer compete." Succinct, honest and accurate.

The Haas family included Walter Haas, Jr., chairman of Levi Strauss, his son Wally, and Roy Eisenhardt, his son-in-law. They were sportsmen and bright, attractive people. I had lunch with Roy in New York and found him an articulate, serious-minded young executive. He had been a law school professor, a role for which I could see he was well suited. I discovered that he was not afraid to dream and had a strong social conscience. These were qualities I liked. I gave him my appraisal of the Bay, that it could not support two teams. He believed that skillful marketing could change that. I hoped he was right.

The old guard was passing not only from baseball but from my personal life. Between October 1980 and May 1981, my father and Mary and George Degener died, three people who had been vital parts of my family life. The Degeners died suddenly, several months apart. My father had lingered for over a decade after a stroke had formidably impaired his ability to function, leaving him to survive on courage and a powerful heart, which gave out when he was eighty-eight. These personal losses affected my life and in a way my view of baseball. Nothing could ever make baseball unimportant to me, but its importance had diminished. Happy Chandler put it in his own way upon offering his sympathy on my father's death when we were together at the 1980 World Series in Philadelphia: "A man never recovers from the loss of his daddy, no matter how old or how ill."

My father's death left my mother alone in their house in St. Augustine, Florida. Now eighty-eight herself, she carries on there amidst her fertile gardens and friends. She faithfully reads *The Sporting News,* roots for the New York Yankees and Peter Ueberroth, and corresponds with Happy Chandler, who is ten days her junior. Next to flying north for her Christmas visit with us, I think she would rate her annual spring visit to Dodgertown at Vero Beach, Florida, as her favorite. The reason is her abiding affection for Peter O'Malley. As we shall see, that is an affection for which she has good reason.

19

Banning Ted Turner

When Ted Turner bought control of the Braves from Bill Bartholomay in 1976, he was pretty much an unknown, notwithstanding his ownership of television station WTCG (later WTBS) in Atlanta and his skills as a yachtsman. The Braves were his first "high-profile" acquisition. But before long, he turned WTBS into the nation's first superstation, created the innovative Cable News Network, followed that with CNN Headline News, acquired the NBA's Atlanta Hawks, won yachting trophies (including the 1977 America's Cup), made headlines by attacking the major networks and generally stirred things up wherever he went.

He had not been in baseball long when his general manager, John Alevizos tampered with San Francisco outfielder Gary Matthews by asking Matthews about the possibility of his playing for Atlanta in 1977, once his free agency was achieved. For this, I fined the Braves $10,000 (two separate $5,000 violations) and took away their first-round draft pick in the January 1977 free-agent draft of amateur players. That should have foreclosed any further problems as to Matthews. I was amazed to learn that Turner, while attending a 1976 World Series cocktail party in New York, confronted Bob Lurie of the Giants and said he would pay whatever was necessary to sign Matthews. Overheard by a host of writers, Ted's comments not only were a clear violation of our tampering rule but also made it virtually impossible for Lurie to sign Matthews. Five days later, Lurie filed a formal complaint with my office. With the approach of the reentry draft on November 4, I hoped that Turner would now use good sense and not draft Matthews. I was not in a position to forbid the drafting of Matthews since our investigation had shown no misconduct by the ballplayer.

Turner drafted Matthews and signed him thirteen days later.

I held a formal hearing in my office on the day of the draft, at which time Ted made light of the World Series cocktail episode, pointing out that because he had consumed "a few drinks" he should be excused. I was not impressed by his logic but had to struggle to keep a straight face as he hammed his way through his defense.

Ted asked to see me again before I made a decision. So we made a date for 7:00 A.M. in my Los Angeles Hilton suite on December 7. This was during the week of our annual meetings. As befitted the Pearl Harbor date, he came at me in waves. I was still wiping the sleep from my eyes as it all began, with Ted addressing me as "Principal." As I sat there bemused for forty-five minutes, he roared from room to room—dining room, bedroom, bathroom, atrium—never breaking his delivery—appearing, vanishing, reappearing. "C'mon, Principal," he said, "you can't take me seriously when I've had a few drinks. But no matter what, you can't take Gary away from me." There was no humor this time; he was dead serious.

His greatest concern was that I might nullify the Matthews signing. "Take it out on me," he pleaded. "Fine me, suspend me, do anything but don't take away Gary!" To drive home the suspension point, he said he would be away most of the 1977 season anyway, sailing for the America's Cup.

I struggled throughout the remainder of December over the right decision in Turner's case. Ted had challenged the system, directly, substantially, openly and destructively.

Two days later, I completed my struggle with the Ted Turner problem. I said it was "painful"; it was, as with a parent punishing a wayward child. On December 30, citing the gravity of the double tampering violation, I suspended him for a year and deprived the Braves of their number one draft pick in the June 1977 amateur draft.

He asked for a hearing, which was held on January 18 in the law offices of Arnold & Porter in Washington. First I met with a group of Atlanta civic leaders, including Mayor Maynard Jackson, who argued that Ted's enthusiasm was contagious and its removal would dampen the baseball spirit of the city. He also stressed Ted's importance to Atlanta and argued that the punishment did not fit the crime. Sensing he was getting nowhere, he tried a "mercy of the court" approach. Jackson later said he found me as "cold as ice, jaws set tight, cordial but businesslike, and lacking a graceful way to tell us our mission was doomed to failure."

I was impressed by the sincerity of the group and their dedication to Ted. For all his eccentricities, or perhaps because of them, Ted generated loyalty in people, a loyalty that may have been rooted more in emotion than reason. There was after all something unreal about Ted, as if he were not so much flesh and blood as a kaleidoscopic galaxy of swirling emotions.

To an outsider Turner is incomprehensible. With paper and pencil I can scarcely do more than scratch the surface of his personality. But listen to his own words when he appeared before me that day in Washington: "Give us a way out of this thing if you can as the guy who is supposed to be the Big Chief of baseball. The little Indians. I am like the little Indians out in the West. You hear about the Big Chief back in Washington, the Great White Father, who says 'You've got to move off your reservation.'

"We kept moving the Indians back and back and back until they had to fight. A few of them had to fight. I do not want to fight.

"Great White Father, please tell me how to avoid fighting for what little we have left. The buffalo are gone. The white man came and killed off all the buffalo.

"They drove the trains through what we were told we would have —this land, you know? The Black Hills. Now this gold you want— the yellow metal—you want us to leave and go to the dust bowl of Oklahoma and these are our homes.

"Please go back to the Great White Father, Soldier Man, and tell him to please help us.

"I am very contrite. I am very humble. I am sorry. I would get down on the floor and let you jump up and down on me if it would help. I would let you hit me three times in the face without lifting a hand to protect myself. I would bend over and let you paddle my behind, hit me over the head with a Fresca bottle, something like that. Physical pain I can stand."

I really think this type of performance came right off the top of his head without calculation or premeditation—spontaneous emotional combustion. Ted's remarks were memorable. I had a feeling he thought he was Sitting Bull and I was Custer. Missing was any explanation of how I was to ignore successive tamperings by the same club with the same player, especially when I had warned after the first tampering that the Braves were running the risk of suspension if there was a repeat violation. Baseball's rules meant nothing if clubs could do that with impunity.

I confirmed the suspension. Ted sued.

The thought of Turner's sitting still in a courtroom was hard to imagine, but he showed up in U.S. District Court in Atlanta for the two-day trial on April 28 and 29. His suspension was on hold until we had a decision from the court. Fortunately, I had the benefit of the McGarr decision the month before in the Finley case upholding the broad authority of the commissioner.

When I was asked on the stand about Turner's having made his tampering remarks while drinking, I replied, "A good deal of base-ball business, wisely or unwisely, is carried on by people who have been drinking. If we had two sets of rules, the result would be a shambles."

Turner, on the stand, insisted that "the punishment doesn't fit the crime." He did not like the tough grilling he got from my attorney, Richard Wertheimer, and at one point responded to a question by saying, "Keep that up and when this is over you'll get a knuckle sandwich." For all his undeniable charm, Ted knew how to play hardball when he thought the occasion required it. As to the "knuckle sandwich," he would save a symbolic version of that for me.

On May 19, Judge Newell Edenfield announced his decision, which we called "a 95 percent victory." He upheld my power to suspend Turner but overruled my forfeiture of the June draft pick. I thought he was on thin judicial ice in returning the draft pick to the Braves. Still, we had won the main show and had established beyond any doubt the commissioner's power to discipline the own-ership. With the help of Finley and Turner, the dominance of the commissioner was firmly in place as it had not been since the days of Judge Landis.

A week before the decision, Ted created a bizarre diversion. Hav-ing sent his manager, Dave Bristol, off on a scouting mission, he hopped into an Atlanta uniform and announced he would manage the Braves, then mired in a sixteen-game losing streak. National League president Feeney and I conferred and decided we would not allow such a farce. Chub ordered him out of the dugout the next day.

So Ted, suspended from both owning and managing, departed for the azure waters of Newport Sound off the coast of Rhode Island. There he won not only the right to represent the United States in the America's Cup aboard *Courageous* but also overcame the challenger *Australia* in the final matchup. *Sports Illustrated* put a handsome picture of him on its cover at the helm of *Courageous* and headlined "Terrible Ted Takes Command." He sent me a laminated copy inscribed, "To my good friend Bowie Kuhn, Best Regards, Ted Turner." He was irrepressible.

Two years later, competing in the 600-mile Fastnet Race off the coast of southern England, he survived seventy-mile-an-hour wind gusts and torrential rains to win a race in which fifteen people lost their lives.

With typical bravado, he announced "It's no use crying. The King is dead. Long live the King. It had to happen sooner or later. You ought to be thankful there are storms like that, or you'd all be speaking Spanish."

At the 1977 World Series in Dodger Stadium while Ted was suspended, I spotted the president's mother, Miss Lillian Carter, sitting nearby with Shirley MacLaine. I walked over and introduced myself to them. Miss Lillian said, "I know perfectly well who you are and I don't know that I really want to talk to you!" When I wondered how I had managed to include her among those I had offended, she fired back, "I'm a great admirer of Ted Turner, and you suspended him!" It was said with a nice mixture of outrage and fun. I suggested we might talk after the game, not because I thought I was going to persuade the strong-minded woman of anything, but because I liked her. Subsequently we had a long talk about baseball in general and about Ted Turner. We got along famously on everything but Ted. As to Ted, she never gave an inch. Ted has some great loyalists.

Ted's behavior was exemplary during his suspension. As the 1978 spring training season approached, I was inclined to lift the suspension several months early. He asked to see me in New York to discuss the status of his suspension. I really did not need to see him but the opportunity to attend yet another Turner performance was too good to pass up.

He arrived at my Rockefeller Center office where, to the disappointment of my secretaries, I suggested we walk the streets of Manhattan while we talked. "You talk, I'll lead the way," I told him as we headed west on Fifty-second Street to Sixth Avenue, then north past his deadly enemies at CBS and ABC. All the while, Ted rattled on about Steinbrenner's suspension having been lifted early, about how much the Braves needed him, and about what a "good boy" he had been.

I led him into Central Park. He was tagging along, making his arguments. I wandered to one of my favorite spots in the park, the zoo. He never seemed to notice. I sat down on a bench facing the polar bear cage. Ted stood between me and the cage, the polar bears visible behind him. He began pacing back and forth. So did the bears.

I sat there watching the two polar bears and the one Ted Turner pacing back and forth as though part of an act. I doubt that anything about it struck Ted as odd. As we walked back to the office I told him I would lift the suspension.

In the autumn of 1978 the Yankees played the Dodgers again in the World Series. Peter O'Malley told me Miss Lillian Carter was in the ballpark again, seated in a mezzanine box. I found my way to where she was and asked about my status. "You're forgiven," she pronounced. "I like you a lot better now!"

20

Speaking of Sportscasters— Howard Cosell

W hen I think about the sports media in my time, no figure dominates it like Howard Cosell. His domination is multidimensional: intelligence, recognition, influence, courage, breadth, long-term effect. It has nothing to do with whether he is liked or disliked. A great many people dislike Howard.

I am not one of them, though I once was. I am a convert to Howard's cause. Like most converts, I am more passionate about my subject than those to whom faith comes naturally and originally. I had to struggle to get there but it was worth the effort.

Howard and I are an odd couple. No one who knew much about us would suspect we were friends. I confess it: we are friends, very good friends indeed. Having said that, I must also say that Howard is frequently a pain in the neck. That is directly attributable to the fact that, to borrow from F. Scott Fitzgerald, he has an ego as big as the Ritz. Not all of it is real. You must remember in evaluating Howard that he has a thorough appreciation of the theatrical aspects of television. He has crafted a distinct character that he presents to the public, and that particular character is strongly egotistical. So part of his egocentricity is cosmetic. But it is only a small part. Most of it is real. It is a product of his clear understanding of those elements that have made him the dominant sports media figure that he is. The Coach, as his ABC staff called him, fully recognizes his own intelligence and skills and does not question them. Actually, I know few people who have worked closely with Howard, or know him well, who would question that intelligence and those skills, however much they may resent him for other reasons.

Cosell's high self-esteem also stems from the adulation given him by the public. That may surprise many observers who equate the public view of him with what they read in the newspapers. After all, many of his fellow journalists (he would resent the application of that word to most writers) hold him in low regard, at least in print. Howard has generated a feud with sportswriters and they have, not surprisingly, responded with a full measure of rage. But that does not measure the public attitude. The public's reaction to him, whether it is love or hate, is based more on his performance on radio and television and to a lesser extent on his books, syndicated columns, and public appearances. While a significant segment of the public does not like Howard, a larger segment does. And many who say they do not like him are in truth entertained by him.

I have spent a great deal of time with the Coach—on the baseball beat, on the lecture platform, in hotel lobbies, in restaurants, at universities and simply walking along the street. The adulation he receives in most of those settings is comparable to that given superstars of the sports and entertainment worlds. I have certainly seen exceptions, such as the reaction by the fans against him in Baltimore during the 1979 World Series and the occasional ugly epithet hurled at him from a crowd, but these are truly exceptions.

Why the adulation? My own case may shed some light on the subject.

I first met Cosell in 1968. I was walking along West Fifty-second Street with the Yankees' Mike Burke, who knew Howard well. I found Cosell cold and self-important. That impression stayed intact during the next eight years and, if anything, worsened; his work on ABC's highly successful "Monday Night Football" gave him a heightened popularity that he repeatedly used to criticize baseball. I reluctantly gave him credit for the popularity of "Monday Night Football," which was dominated by his powerful personality, but resented his increased dedication to football, which seemed to foment ever more vigorous attacks on baseball.

Nonetheless, I was in the "Monday Night Football" audience. The more I watched the more I was determined to find a way to duplicate the Monday concept in baseball.

It would surprise most people to know that baseball and NBC invented the Monday concept. Under the guidance of Detroit's John Fetzer, we had gone to a three-game Monday format in 1966, but it had not been a ratings success. I thought it deserved a better test than three games but saw little chance of persuading NBC to expand the format. Thus, the man I targeted when network negotiations began in 1975 was ABC's Roone Arledge. He was an innovator, as he had shown with "Monday Night Football" and in a variety of other ways that had underscored ABC's growing popularity in sports. He also had guts and vision, as he had shown by installing Howard on "Monday Night Football." We put together a deal with ABC that called for up to sixteen Monday-night games in 1976. While I saw this as a major breakthrough for baseball, one ingredient of "Monday Night Football" I did not want was Cosell.

Not only had he been identified as one of the chief critics of baseball, it was also ABC's style to let him loose on the air to voice his criticisms. As we worked to better market the game, we did not need Cosell dissecting baseball for the benefit of our ABC audience. During our talks with ABC our negotiators, John Lazarus and Sandy Hadden, had assured me there would be no problem about Cosell, even though ABC quite understandably insisted that they would make all final decisions on announcers.

Still, as the date of the first broadcast approached, I was disturbed to hear rumors that Cosell might do some games. I put my fears in writing, telling Arledge that "whatever contract rights you might have, any such move would be most destructive to our relationship, and would violate the spirit of our understanding." A series of telephone conversations confirmed my fears. Arledge in his velvety way was diplomatic but firm about ABC's prerogatives and faintly puzzled about my concerns. He suggested that we get together over lunch with Cosell.

Eight years had gone by since I first met Howard on Fifty-second Street, but I had not in any sense gotten to know him. At lunch, Arledge cited Cosell's success on "Monday Night Football" and tried to persuade me that Cosell would attract a more diverse audience for baseball and also had the ability to hold an audience in an 11–0 game. Underplaying his own contractual right to make the decision regardless of my objections, he urged me to consider what he had said.

As Howard listened attentively, I expressed my concerns that it made no sense to put such a dedicated baseball critic on our telecasts, that there would be deep resentment by fans and our clubs, that the club resentment would sour the relationship with ABC that I was trying to develop and that Cosell would do us a lot more harm than good. When I had wound down, Arledge turned to Cosell and said, "Howard, what do you think?"

Cosell, in his most theatrical style, said, "I agree with much of what Bowie has said. I do not agree with any implication that my criticism of baseball has been unfair." He then launched into a defense of his criticism, making the point that it had not been directed at the game itself but rather at baseball people and their mismanagement of the professional game.

He described his love of the game going back to his Brooklyn childhood. He concluded by saying superfluously that it was Roone's, not baseball's, decision to make. I was painfully aware of that fact. Had it been otherwise, there would have been no necessity for a lunch. I would have already carved Howard out of the baseball picture. Nor was I buying most of what Howard had said. It was left to Roone, who was not going to omit his hottest sportscaster from this new and unproven package. Cosell did some Monday-night games in 1976 and baseball sulked.

Luckily, it was also the year Mark Fidrych brought his endearing ways to the scene with all his elfin appeal. Indeed, Cosell, too, was captivated by Mark's inimitable style, and I began to hear things from Cosell that sounded like a lifelong baseball fan.

When I learned that Cosell would "probably" be working the League Championship Series, I again complained to Roone. The result was a long, three-hour lunch (without Howard), covering not only Howard but other problems that had troubled our relationship and had led me to threaten to terminate our ABC contract. Roone was patient and persuasive, arguing that time was needed for our partnership to mature. He was determined to find a way to secure his ties to baseball. On the Cosell issue, it was still Roone's decision and he made it in favor of Howard in the LCS. I had to admire his fidelity to "the humble one."

I watched the ABC telecasts of the Kansas City–New York LCS with Cosell as commentator. He was comfortable with the Yankees and had a commanding grasp of the team and the Steinbrenner organization. I picked the brains of other knowledgeable viewers. Our consensus was that Howard strengthened the telecasts. I began to ease off on Howard, not all at once, but surely and irreversibly the conversion was under way, not as to the man so much as to the television personality. I had great faith in my staff. They were people who cared deeply about baseball. They not only liked Howard on baseball, they suspected that his doing baseball television would bring back the old-time baseball religion of his Brooklyn youth. He was a powerful opinion maker. It would be nice to have him on our side.

Emmy and Howard Cosell have a summer house in Westhampton Beach on Long Island's south shore. Several miles farther east, along the Quogue canal in the tiny village of the same name, Luisa and I have a house. I invited the Cosells to have dinner with us at a Westhampton restaurant and they accepted. I suspect that all four of us approached the evening as one of those business necessities you have to endure. Emmy actually worked that thought into the cocktail conversation. I had shark for dinner, which may or may not have been significant. Somehow we all endured. Howard was neither as talkative nor as truculent as I had anticipated and actually made polite, sociable inquiries about the Kuhn family. It began to dawn on me that Howard was not some monstrous invention of Arledge's wilder moments and even had the potential with a little more probing to prove to be a nice Jewish boy from Brooklyn. We all went home with our guard not completely dropped but Luisa and I were surprised that the evening had gone as well as it had. Remarkably, it was repeated some weeks later at Howard's invitation. And was repeated again. In time it became a fixture in our lives and remains so to this day.

An incident during the World Series of 1977 helped to greatly warm our relationship. During a flight from Los Angeles to New York, Cosell was accused by the *Philadelphia Daily News'* Stan Hochman of striking him with four or five hard slaps around his ear and temple. Hochman went to the crew and demanded that Cosell be arrested for battery when the plane landed in New York City. The matter had Emmy in tears and Howard very upset.

Had such a scene occurred, it would have taken place just in front of where Luisa and I were seated, but we saw no such thing. Later on, I filed an affidavit with the Los Angeles Prosecutor's Office in which I said I saw no such incident, and the authorities decided not to proceed with any prosecution. Howard was greatly relieved, and openly and warmly appreciative.

No one can really understand Howard unless there is first an understanding of the relationship between Howard and Emmy. It is a real partnership in which all the admonitions of the wedding vows are remembered and kept. It is an old-fashioned, romantic marriage. The fidelity of one to the other is remarkable. They are partners against the world. If you plan to take on Howard, also be prepared to take on Emmy. I would sooner tackle Howard.

He is also utterly dedicated to his daughters Jill and Hilary and to Jill's four children, Justin, Jared, Caitlen and Colin. I use the adverb "utterly" because it is right and also because it is one of Howard's favorite words. There are certain workhorses in his broad vocabulary, and "utterly" gallops through his prose. Until you have seen the touchingly affectionate father and grandfather, you cannot put the familiar, aggressive television personality of Howard Cosell into proper focus.

I have been fortunate to have seen the domestic side of Howard. How many hours have I spent on the deck of his Westhampton Beach house watching the pleasure-boat traffic through the Quogue canal and the distant steeple of St. Mark's Church across Quantuck Bay? How many hours have I spent there debating every conceivable sports and public issue with Howard, or just talking to his family or warding off the family dogs, from Great Dane to terrier? Just below that deck is the Cosell tennis court where I have been pounded mercilessly by Patrick Turner, Hilary's husband, who must have misspent his English childhood to play tennis so well. Indeed, it was on that court during one of my humiliations at Patrick's hands that I heard Howard intone from the deck above, "Kuhn, you don't belong at Forest Hills; you belong at Forest Lawn." It was there, too, that a passing yachtsman once hailed me as "Howard." I am still trying, but obviously failing, to forget that episode.

The domestic Howard is my friend. There is another and different Howard who is stiff-necked and unforgiving. He neither forgives nor forgets a wrong done to him. A writer who puts on paper a critical line about Howard can become "lousy" overnight though he might have been "passable" the day before, or even (rarely) "good." You can say, "Howard, what difference does it make?" or "We all make mistakes" or "For God's sake have a little charity" and hit granite, deaf and unyielding. The best sports commentator in America should have a little charity. He does not. Oh, if Emmy, or the kids, or even Luisa or his pals Sig Heiman or Ed Silverman did something wrong, he would forgive it, but he won't forgive those ink-stained wretches or a lot of other people he does not want to think about.

I am probably in a better position than most people to talk about the pros and cons of being charitable to the press. They may have pounded Howard more than me but it would be a close call.

As to charity toward the press, I have argued to Howard that notwithstanding my often unfair press treatment, there are good people and fine writers there. He will have no part of it. At any given time, he might admit there was a handful of decent writers around. Jim Murray and Robert Lipsyte are always in the handful. The balance varies. It may include Peter Gammons, Tom Boswell, Mike Lupica and a precious few others. By mentioning their names here, I have no doubt doomed them to eternal obloquy among their peers. Howard sees the "print media" categorically as a pack of incompetent, spiteful drudges, worse even than the "jockocracy" (former players who do play-by-play sports) and only slightly less villainous than television critics, particularly those specializing in sports.

Among writers, I have discovered a schizophrenia about Howard. Publicly, most criticize him, although he has defenders. Privately, many writers admire him for his best qualities, including his formidable intellect and his courageous willingness to criticize anything that moves in the sports world, not to mention much of it that is inert. But they would not give him the time of day publicly because of their resentment of his broadside attacks on the sportswriting profession and because they see him as arrogant and pretentious.

There is another and smaller group of writers (Dick Young would be an example) who concede Cosell nothing, who would tell you he has no admirable qualities. The feud between Howard and Dick is genuine.

I know something about Cosell's critical skills, since I have often been their object. In his 1985 book *I Never Played the Game,* he details matters on which we differed such as Mays-Mantle, female reporters in clubhouses, and remaining too long as commissioner, upon all of which we still disagree. He knows how to ask the right question; that skill is very obvious and fundamental, but remarkably few reporters do it well. He also asks the incisive follow-up question that prevents his quarry from hiding in the underbrush of some evasive answer. Moreover, he is the very best at producing the quarry in the first place. Unawed by big names, he will go after anyone who relates to a news story and more often than not gets the person he wants. The phrase "Howard Cosell is calling" has impact.

Knowing a news story when he sees one and being willing to work hard at developing and presenting the facts are other Cosell assets of importance. How many times have I heard him say, "We'll have a crew there in twenty minutes; please sit tight." If you told him you were on your way to Timbuktu, the answer would be, "We'll have our Timbuktu affiliate get a crew to meet you at the airport." And likely as not, the Timbuktu boys would have Howard on a split screen when you arrived.

As to the flaws, there is a tendency to say more when less would do and to belabor ideas. His affection for polysyllabic words can seem pretentious. Stories are sometimes stirred up where none really exist. The line between sympathy and bathos is not always well perceived. There is also the Brooklyn boy's perception of union positions as invariably closer to godliness than management's side and to imagine civil rights issues in the most pedestrian sports debates. To me these flaws are greatly outweighed by his strengths; in some measure they are also part of the television personality he has carefully created. Hyperbole, skillfully used, is part of his art.

Various other Howards are variations on the essential Cosell. For instance, there is the self-assured or truculent Howard. A story reveals him. We had lunch the day a sportscaster popularity poll came out showing that some 40 percent of the voters called him most popular and an equal number most unpopular. When I needled him about winning the negative side, he said, "Don't be silly. I got eighty percent of the vote; nobody else was close."

At another time, Emmy, Howard, former Treasury Secretary Bill Simon and I were having dinner at the Flushing Tennis Center before watching John McEnroe annihilate Joachim Nystrom in the 1985 U.S. Nationals. Out of the blue Simon chuckled and said he had been thinking about us three men at dinner and decided it was a table of "has beens." To which Cosell replied, "You're two-thirds right, Bill."

Then there is the Howard who is incapable of avoiding the clutches of charitable institutions. They draw him like drugs draw an addict. He is Damon Runyon's original soft-touch, only Howard is not handing out "fins"; he easily commands $25,000 per night on the commercial banquet circuit. But let a worthwhile charity crook its finger for an MC appearance thousands of miles away and there is Howard, more often than not bone-tired, playing to a full house drawn by his love-hate magnetism. By the time he has done his alternately outrageous and touching sequence, there is a lot more love than anything else.

As unrelenting as Howard is to his enemies, he is faithful to his friends. It is a demanding sort of friendship in that it requires the friend to bear with Howard's caprices. Some good people simply cannot do that. There is a happy number left over who can. Walter Kennedy, NBA commissioner for twelve years, was one. Howard cared deeply for Walter, a man worth caring for. When Walter died in 1977, Howard gave the eulogy in St. John's Roman Catholic Church in Stamford, Connecticut. Extemporaneous, it was as fine a eulogy as I had heard. But beyond its excellence, it opened my eyes regarding Howard. Used to his public style, I found a compassionate, caring man, struggling to comfort Walter's family and friends.

His fidelity to me over many years has been nothing I have earned. I think he suffered more during the final chapters of my commissionership than my family or I did. I will never forget his daughter Hillary, then with NBC, interviewing me about my problems with tears in her eyes. I am not at all sure I can explain why his fidelity exists. What I do know is that our friendship is strong and unshakeable, tested as it has been by the myriad disputes between us that might have broken it. Emmy told me some years ago she thought we would get along while the ABC-baseball relationship lasted. Neither Emmy nor anyone who knows us would think that was the test today.

21

Red Smith

I f Howard Cosell was the dominant sports-media figure of my
time, Red Smith was his closest challenger. In an era when television increasingly dominated the North American sports scene,
it was quite an accomplishment for a shy, mild-mannered little guy
armed with a pen to be in the race at all. He did have one considerable asset in addition to his pen. It was called *The New York Times,*
a newspaper for which he wrote during the last eleven years of his
life.

Cosell and Smith were as different as two people could be. One
thundered and one squeaked. One was an extrovert, the other an
introvert. One was tall, the other short. One was a Jew, the other an
Irish Catholic. One loved television, the other hated it. One used
words like a piston machine, the other like a scalpel. One came from
North Carolina (Howard was born in Winston-Salem), the other
from Wisconsin (Red was born in Green Bay).

Still, you cannot study them without noting the similarities. They
were both skilled communicators (however contrasting their styles);
loved sports; were left of center in political and social philosophy,
although Red hadn't always been that way; sympathized with union
positions; were dedicated, hardworking craftsmen and both could
be ruthless. Is it possible that great journalists, like great linebackers,
have a ruthless strain?

As regards me, they were as different as their personalities. The
tall extrovert liked me, the little shy one was not so sure. Red fancied
himself a deflator of pomposity, and in me he felt he had stumbled

upon the ultimate stuffed shirt. However, there was a period of years before 1976 when they were both members of the "Kuhn is a pompous stuffed shirt" school.

Oh, yes, they did not like each other at all.

There are several other things that should be said about Red. Behind the mild manner lurked a natural polemicist, a man skilled at literary controversy, and a master of satire and caricature. He was also a prose poet. Ernest Hemingway said he was "the most important force in American sports writing." He could have been a great writer beyond the field of sports had he so elected, given the extraordinarily high quality of his prose and the imagination that sparked his efforts. To be honest, there were days when no one wished more than I that Red had turned his talents elsewhere.

As things turned out between Red and me, it is curious that my admiration of Red had always been so great. I can honestly say that no writer stood ahead of him in my esteem, unless it was Shirley Povich, at whose figurative knee I sat as a lad and through whose felicitous writing I had learned sports and the love of sports.

I was a villain in Red's eyes before I became commissioner. A transplanted Wisconsin boy who once worked in the newsroom of the *Milwaukee Sentinel,* he was angered by the National League's decision to move the Braves to Atlanta for the 1966 season. He knew the dramatis personae of that event all too well, including National League attorney Bowie Kuhn, who had successfully argued the related litigation in the Supreme Court of Wisconsin where Milwaukee's cause was lost. Behind the scenes, Red had coordinated his anti–baseball establishment writing efforts with Ben Barkin, the highly skilled Milwaukee public relations executive who guided the efforts of the Milwaukee leaders to awaken the country to what Red called the "rape of Milwaukee." The background coordination of Red's polemic attack on baseball's establishment was revealed in Barkin's files, which we subpoenaed and studied as part of our trial preparation. Those "leaders" included Ed Fitzgerald and Bud Selig, who emerged as chief executives of the Brewers when baseball returned to Milwaukee in 1970. Fitzgerald, Selig and Barkin, by an interesting turn of fate, all became and remain staunch friends of mine.

I was also a villain for Red because I was a key figure in the Major League Player Relations Committee dealings with Marvin Miller's Players Association. Miller was a vital source of information for Red's columns on baseball's labor matters and I felt that Red reciprocated by almost unremitting support of Miller's positions, to which he was philosophically well disposed. Red therefore became the most powerful drumbeater against my election as commissioner on the grounds that I was biased against the Players Association. His first column regarding my election appeared on February 10, 1969. I set the highlights of it out here because I think it explains Red's anti-Kuhn feelings so effectively: his thought that I was the owner's house man.

If the men who own baseball had set out on a calculated campaign to reinforce, buttress, harden, and invigorate the players' resolve to fight for their rights, they could not have found a better way than the method they chose unanimously in Miami Beach this week.

By hiring as commissioner pro tem a man who is totally committed to the side of management, they served notice on the players that all avenues of appeal are now closed to them and any player seeking redress of grievances had better go to his own union.

Then they declared unanimous and uncompromising opposition to the central demand of the players' union for the right to share in the loot from national television and radio.

It is because of their bosses' insistent denial of this right that players are refusing to sign contracts and making no plans to report for spring training. If there was any prospect of players defecting from this position in significant numbers, it has been virtually eliminated by the election of Bowie Kuhn and the "won't budge" declaration of the owners.

Throughout the 24-year administration of Kenesaw M. Landis as baseball's first commissioner, the players not only had a friend at court, the court itself was their friend. They knew they could always get a hearing from Judge Landis, who would see that they got a square shake if he had to beat it out of the owners with a gavel.

None of the judge's three successors had the same reputation, but at least they could put up some pretense of impartiality when they came to the job. Bowie Kuhn can't.

Where his law practice has brought him into contact with baseball affairs, it has always been on the side of management. He was one of the lawyers who defended the National League in the Rape of Milwaukee and he told Circuit Judge Elmer W. Roller that the reason for moving the Braves to Atlanta was to make the national pastime truly national in scope.

Baseball lost the case in Judge Roller's court and won on appeal, not on account of that particular contribution to the argument.

More recently, Kuhn has been a member of the owners' Player Relations Committee negotiating with the players' representatives over division of the television swag.

The "rape of Milwaukee" and my alleged bias against the players obviously disqualified me as commissioner in Red's thinking. I was not to be allowed any time to show how I would perform. The fact is that shortly after this column appeared, I brought about a solution of the February 1969 labor impasse that Red describes. He had believed a solution was "virtually eliminated" by my election. Perhaps most significant are the quotes in Red's column. They came from one person only—Marvin Miller. My opinions were never sought. This would be the pattern of Red's writing on labor matters for as long as he wrote.

The same week Red's column appeared, I gave a party for the press at Toots Shor's restaurant in New York. Red was there and stayed late. At the end, he and I went through the revolving door together onto Fifty-second Street. Standing there in the cold February night, he said in that squeaky voice that for me was part of his trademark, "Commissioner, name two catchers on the 1944 St. Louis Browns." Surprised though I was, I answered directly, "Mancuso and Hayworth." "My God," he replied, "you do know something about baseball."

The exchange was revealing. I think Red wanted to see me as some Wall Street imposter who knew and cared nothing for baseball, unlike men like Chub Feeney and Lee MacPhail whom he liked. He once wrote, "You could set a bear trap in a cathedral and not catch two finer men than Feeney and MacPhail." Red cared a great deal for the game and wanted his commissioner to do so too.

When he received the J. G. Taylor Spink Award in 1977 at Cooperstown, he talked of his love for the game: ". . . for some of us, baseball has meant the pleasantest way of making a living that man has discovered. I loved it so, especially in the days before air travel and before night games when baseball was such a leisurely entertainment and covering it such a leisurely occupation. I loved every moment of it, even the weeks of hit and run barnstorming tours home from training camp when for two weeks or so home was an open Pullman berth. I'm happy to have had a chance to be a baseball writer and right now . . . I'd rather be a moose or a salmon because when they're stuffed and mounted they're dead and it doesn't make them so nervous."

Because he cared for baseball, he was a romantic about the game, as is Roger Angell, who writes so lovingly of the game for *The New Yorker.* Red dreaded the thought of change in baseball. Football, basketball and hockey could modernize to meet the changing needs of the times, but not baseball. I believed that baseball had to change the way it marketed itself to the North American public. We were losing our share of the audience to other sports and other competing entertainment. As much as I yearned to preserve the sacred writ of the game, I knew we had to change, so I was determined to experiment and innovate whether it was with the designated hitter, postseason night games, All-Star fan voting, nationally sponsored promotions, national licensing or whatever made reasonable sense. And I will stand on the record of what we accomplished.

Television was at the seat of another problem between Red and me. I was determined to use television as a marketing and promotional vehicle. Red saw my efforts to harness television as a debauching of the game. Nothing so offended him as night games in the World Series, which I introduced in 1971. Red wanted day games only for the Series. He was undaunted by the fact that night games permitted tens of millions of fans to see the Series, fans whose viewing would otherwise be precluded by work, school or other daytime obligations. He could see it only as a sell-out to television. His unhappiness only increased as I stepped up the number of night games per Series from one to five.

At the 1977 Cooperstown ceremony, he launched his short remarks with a dig at television: "I'd like to reflect for just a moment on the love-hate relationship between baseball and the press that has existed since the time of Mr. Spalding and Father Chadwick. Today, when radio and television produce a substantial part of the baseball income, many people, many baseball people, tend to forget, if indeed they ever really realized it, that were it not for a century of coverage around the year, twelve months a year in the daily press, there would be no television contracts for baseball."

A lot of writers shared Red's feeling about television, though none argued the issue as adroitly as he. It was a life-and-death issue for the newspaper business. The postwar growth of television had caused the demise of countless newspapers. New York in particular was a graveyard of great newspapers: the *Herald Tribune,* the *Journal-American,* the *Mirror,* the *World-Telegram & Sun,* and the Brooklyn *Eagle.* The demise of the *Herald Tribune* in 1965 had destroyed Red's own forum and sent this superb writer into near oblivion as a syndicated writer, his only New York outlet being *Women's Wear Daily* until he was rescued by *The New York Times* in 1971. In addition to fearing adverse consequences to the game itself, Red and others feared that the instant journalism of television's carrying live sports events would minimize print journalism. Moreover, one need only read his columns over the years to see his almost morbid fear of television's effect on baseball. Though television's role in professional football was significantly greater than in baseball, his concern about television always emphasized baseball. And I was seen as the high priest of the insidious cult that was stripping baseball of its traditions. Two events especially galled him.

Because of rainouts, the 1975 Red Sox–Cincinnati World Series included five night games, all nationally telecast. That particular Series had originally been scheduled to have only three night games, but weekend day games 6 and 7 were rained out and I rescheduled them as weekday night games. As a result, this glorious Series had a tremendous North American audience and I think unquestionably contributed to the resulting surge in the game's popularity. Indeed, had Carlton Fisk's dramatic home run to win Game 6 come in a day game, it could have taken place at about 1:30 P.M. on the West Coast, 4:30 P.M. in the East, and lost much of its audience. But in Red's eyes I had betrayed the game to television. He wrote it and also said it in an unpleasant exchange he and I had in a Boston press conference.

A year later he was on my trail again. So smashing was the night telecast–induced success of the 1975 Series that NBC came to me with a proposal to schedule four instead of three night games in the 1976 World Series. The idea was that Game 2, which would normally be played on a Sunday afternoon, would be played at night. After some debate on the subject within my Executive Council, where the conservatives were as opposed as Red would prove to be, I elected to go with the extra night game on an experimental basis. While we had enjoyed decent weather for most of our earlier Series' night games (the exceptions being 1973 games in Shea Stadium), I ran out of luck in Cincinnati for Game 2. It was cold (43 degrees) when the game started and got steadily worse. I sat there coatless, watching an excellent game that the Reds won 4–3 with a run off Catfish Hunter in the bottom of the ninth. From that time on, Red lampooned me mercilessly for not wearing a coat. For him, it was the ultimate manifestation of my surrender to television. So skillfully did he develop this caricature (ignoring the fact that I frequently wore coats at Series games) that sportswriters in large numbers borrowed the lampoon, which they used as a throw-in whenever they were assaulting me on some unrelated issue.

The following winter, Red called me at home one cold, snowy day. I was outside chopping wood. After we discussed his inquiry, I asked if he planned to ask what I was wearing. He seemed puzzled at first and then, sensing the gag, said, "Commissioner, what have you been wearing out there in the cold?" I said, "Oh, just a good heavy shirt and pants and, of course, my ever-faithful thermal underwear." He laughed and said, "You and your thermal underwear!" I wish it had ended there.

Apart from the 1975 press conference incident in Boston, I never had an unpleasant exchange with Red. We talked on the telephone and ran into one another occasionally at social events and press conferences. He was always affable and warm. He normally worked me into his annual Christmas poem with such lines as "Ring out, wild bells, for Bowie Kuhn, that tall and stately czar." This all seemed curiously at odds with the flagellation I received when he got down to the business of writing baseball. I once commented on this to his son Terry at a cocktail party in Washington. Terry, then a political writer for *The New York Times,* said his father normally spoke well of me in family conversations.

Fred Russell of the Nashville *Banner,* one of the senior statesmen of the sportswriting fraternity, was a close friend of both Red's and mine. He told me he had tried to debate the Kuhn issue with Red but drew only the most benign replies. "I've never been around a fairer man than Red," Russell told me recently. "But I could never find out why Red wrote what he did. Maybe it was because he was close to Miller, but I don't know. He never cited any incident."

Gabe Paul, who knew us both well, was as puzzled as Fred. Gabe once suggested that Red and I try having lunch. I was never comfortable with the idea, though I often socialized with the press over meals and drinks. In any event, neither of us ever invited the other. With me, I think it was because of pride.

I was not completely shut out by Red on the positive side. In addition to Christmas poems, he backed me on my handling of the Henry Aaron dispute in 1974 (he called it my "finest hour") and on the concept of suspending Steinbrenner, although he would have preferred a lifetime suspension to my two years. When Red died, his obituary in *The New York Times* linked Steinbrenner and me as Red's favorite targets.

I last saw Red on a side street east of Riverside Church in New York after the funeral of Elston Howard. The date was December 16, 1980. The conversation was pleasant enough. I thought he looked tired. He died in January 1982.

22

Tales of Broadcasting

I inherited baseball's young relationship with the television networks. At the national level, we were doing business only with NBC, while the National Football League had contracts with NBC and CBS, and was poised to add ABC in 1970. Our TV revenue was moderate, the regular season exposure was limited to Saturday afternoons (except for three Monday-night games) and the marketing impact was minimal. There was not even a broadcasting executive on-staff in the commissioner's office. So I asked for and received authority to negotiate network contracts, and I hired Tom Dawson, former head of CBS Television, as our director of broadcasting.

In 1971, in our first negotiation with the networks after I became commissioner, Dawson found no interest outside of NBC, which told us something about the state of baseball's popularity at that time, particularly as compared to football's. So we made a new four-year agreement (1972 to 1975) with NBC, an agreement that increased our revenues but left the broadcasting emphasis at the local level, where the clubs had their own regional radio and television arrangements.

I was convinced we had to use national television as a means of rejuvenating baseball's popularity. The question was how. Dawson and I liked the nighttime national telecasting of the All-Star Game, first tried in 1967. Night telecasts showcased the game better for the viewers at home. So we began talking about night games in the World Series. It is hard to believe from the vantage point of the 1980s that this was revolutionary thinking. Baseball was dominated by conservatives. According to them, World Series games were always to be played during the day. I thought day games made some sense on weekends but none at all for games during the week. Our greatest event was being broadcast when most of North America was working or going to school.

Since our NBC contract provided only for World Series day games, we talked to Carl Lindemann, who was head of sports at NBC, about doing night games in the 1971 Series. Carl liked the idea but the network was reluctant to interfere with established prime-time programming. We finally persuaded them to try one night game on an experimental basis.

Both the morning newspapers and the baseball conservatives were unhappy. Night games interfered with the deadlines of the morning press and reduced interest in their coverage.

While I had some sympathy for the press arguments, they were greatly outweighed by the opportunity to reach vast new audiences. If baseball was going to come out of its doldrums we had to market more aggressively, and using television was one way to do it. The single night game in the 1971 World Series was such a success that we had no trouble persuading NBC to agree to three night games in 1972. We were now harnessing television to our own needs.

In 1975, with our exclusive NBC contract expiring, I had visions of dividing our network package between NBC and ABC. Under the leadership of Roone Arledge, ABC Sports had developed a cachet that I wanted as part of baseball. Having two major networks aligned with baseball had significant promotional, marketing, financial and prestige potential. By this time I had hired John Lazarus away from ABC as our director of broadcasting. It was no coincidence. Our target was ABC; in my judgment CBS could not yet be persuaded to make a major commitment to baseball.

During the negotiating period, I talked to Arledge extensively about the prestige baseball would bring to his network. It became increasingly clear to me that he wanted to be persuaded.

Meanwhile, our discussions with NBC lagged. We were not able to convince them that there should be very significant increases in our rights fees if NBC exclusivity were to be preserved. We finally closed a deal with Arledge for the elements ABC wanted to carry:

the World Series, the League Championship Series and the All-Star Game were to be rotated, and ABC would carry a Monday prime-time series. There was a 33 percent increase in baseball's network revenue.

NBC was distraught. While they did agree to take the other half of the package, they were angry that we had first closed a deal with ABC, feeling their long, exclusive relationship with baseball had not been sufficiently respected. I was satisfied that we had handled the negotiation properly, but distressed by the anger at NBC. Herb Schlosser, president of NBC, and Lindemann, vice president of NBC Sports, were old friends of mine. It was a difficult time.

In a recent conversation, Schlosser told me that he fully understood the necessity of dividing the package, as he doubted that any one network could handle the entire commitment. He felt we had made the right move for baseball.

Lazarus, who along with Sandy Hadden comprised our negotiating team, was seen by NBC as an ABC plant in baseball's management. When he returned to ABC in 1976, my NBC friends were more convinced than ever about their "plant" theory. Whatever Lazarus's origins, he had done an outstanding job for us.

Still unsold were the national radio rights to the World Series, LCS and All-Star Game that NBC had held. When Lazarus suggested to NBC that they renew the radio rights, he was unceremoniously told where he could go. Nor, to our surprise, did ABC want them. Lazarus ended up selling them to the CBS Radio Network for a small sum. Sam Cook Digges, who was the chief executive officer of CBS Radio, knew a bargain when he saw one. Today that package, a tribute to Digges's vision and one of the most valuable in radio broadcasting, is still firmly in place at CBS under a long-term contract we negotiated in 1983 with CBS's Dick Brescia. The $5-million-plus annual price is no longer a bargain.

Our four-year contracts with NBC and ABC ran smoothly as we adjusted to Howard Cosell and the ABC style, which contrasted noticeably with the NBC approach. NBC was less flamboyant, counting on the brilliant work of Harry Coyle as coordinating producer and the professionalism of the men in the booth like Curt Gowdy, Joe Garagiola, Jim Simpson and Tony Kubek. ABC was more issue-oriented, reflecting the style of Cosell. While ABC found it difficult to match the quality of Coyle's pictures, their telecasts had a greater sense of theater due to ABC's probing, journalistic style.

In 1978 I brought in Tom Villante as director of broadcasting and marketing. Tom was a story in himself, with a career that ran from

Yankee batboy to senior vice president of BBDO Advertising. I was attracted to his successes in marketing, a skill I gave him free rein to apply to baseball. Among his marketing accomplishments was the development of our centennial celebrations of 1969 and the "Baseball Fever—Catch It!" theme, which was used and imitated widely in and out of baseball.

Sandy Hadden and Tom negotiated new four-year contracts with ABC and NBC in 1979, contracts that provided for a nearly 100 percent gain in rights fees for baseball. This time there were no *sotto voce* hints to ABC that Howard Cosell was not expected on our telecasts.

As the clubs' local broadcasting activities became increasingly complicated by the development of cable and pay television, Tom's role as counselor to the clubs expanded. The breadth of his knowledge and energy made him invaluable, so much so that I became increasingly concerned that he might leave us due to his interest in starting his own sports marketing firm. This decision was hastened in 1982 by Nelson Doubleday's persistent criticism of Tom's style of operation. Basically, these were attacks on me. Tom was a loyal lieutenant who reflected my philosophy that we should support revenue-sharing in baseball. Television revenues were ideal for that purpose. Doubleday and his New York counterpart George Steinbrenner both resented Tom's efforts to enhance national TV revenue (which was shared), if necessary, at the expense of local TV revenue. In addition, Tom had a bouncy, assertive style that offended their sense of self-importance. I had always told my people that they were not required to pull their forelocks to the clubs any more than I was. That was the only way to establish respect for our office and to avoid the bullying tactics that came naturally to some of our club executives. No one bullied Tom.

Villante and Doubleday had a sharp exchange at a major-league meeting in Scottsdale, Arizona, at which Tom said the Mets were not interested in a strong national TV package because of their overriding concern for their local market. Subsequently, Doubleday rarely lost an opportunity to criticize Tom. By 1982, Villante decided to set up his own business. I could hardly blame him, but it was a substantial loss to baseball. When hints surfaced in the press that I had tossed Tom to the wolves in order to placate Doubleday, I was furious. I said publicly that Tom was welcome to stay as long as he wished "whether Nelson Doubleday liked it or not." All the forelocks were still unpulled.

As the final year of our 1980-to-1983 contracts with the networks approached, it became increasingly clear that the next negotiations would be the most important in our history. Carl Lindemann had moved from NBC to CBS in a special consulting capacity and was working for CBS's Neal Pilson. Carl was telling us that CBS wanted to be part of the baseball picture. This was good news for us, as both NBC and ABC were clearly determined to continue baseball; the more competition the better. Also in the hunt was Ted Turner and his WTBS superstation cable network, which had grown so large that Ted could realistically compete for major sports properties. We were further encouraged by some of the surprisingly high prices the networks were paying for individual properties like the Rose Bowl and by the size of the networks' 1982 National Football League packages.

With Villante gone (though fortunately still available as a consultant), I discussed with my television committee the possibility of using several of our more knowledgeable owners in the negotiations. Both Einhorn of the White Sox and Giles of the Phillies were available and even eager to participate. That suited me well, since neither I nor my Executive Council felt that a commissioner in my ambiguous position (having just failed to gain reelection) should bear the full responsibility for the negotiations. And I had great respect for Einhorn and Giles. Eddie may have known more about network sports than anyone in or out of the graveyard and had a reputation as an expert and determined "hondler." Bill had put together local radio, over-the-air television and pay-television packages in Philadelphia that were models in the industry. Since I probably knew the principal network players and the history of baseball network television better than anyone else, we had the requisite skills among the three of us.

I also hired Bryan Burns of the Kansas City club to succeed Tom Villante. He was an exceedingly able young executive who I knew would do a superior job in our complex administrative world. He was a boon to our operation and specifically to our network negotiations.

We held preliminary discussions with ABC and NBC in December 1982; then moved into high-gear negotiations in January 1983. For three months, the negotiations wore on with little surcease. Art Watson, president of NBC Sports, and his vice president, Ken Schanzer, represented NBC while Jim Spence, senior vice president of ABC Sports, handled the responsibilities for ABC. These men were all friends with whom I had worked closely over the years.

These negotiations were going to require the kind of understanding and patience that would test friendship. From the outset, we made it clear that we were looking for a substantial deal that we felt we could justify on the basis of recent network arrangements for college and professional football and on the advertising dollars we projected could be generated by the baseball package. We were talking about yearly rights fees to baseball that were more than four times greater than we had been receiving.

The reactions of the two networks were totally different. Watson and Schanzer for NBC were at all stages unflappable. Spence for ABC thought we had lost our minds and ever so politely told us so.

Watson was a deceptively relaxed executive with a Will Rogers quality, full of good humor, unpretentious, but canny and perceptive. He was backed up by one of the great network chief executives of our time in Grant Tinker, who was rescuing NBC from the rubble of third place. Watson made it clear in our first meeting that Tinker had given him authority to make a "megadollar" deal with baseball. Everything that Watson and Schanzer did during our negotiations confirmed that Watson was not boasting. His flexible, engaging style nicely augmented the substance of what he was bringing to the table. Night or day, he was ready to talk in any setting—over a table, a drink, a meal or a sandwich. And somehow, he never let things get too serious. So the process was fun.

In the early rounds with Spence, Watson and Schanzer, we did not actually come right out and say we wanted so much per year. Instead, we turned over study papers from which our sophisticated network friends could readily read our minds, and we unleashed the loquacious Einhorn, whose speeches cascaded over our friends, providing both information and obfuscation as the circumstances required.

I vividly recall a long dissertation Eddie gave Watson and Schanzer, who listened as unflappably as ever. When the lesson ended, they asked for a caucus and withdrew. While they were gone, Giles and I told Eddie that we had had no idea what he was talking about but were loath to ask him to explain for fear he would and at length. With that, Schanzer asked if he and Art could see me. When I joined them, they dissolved in laughter, saying they had no idea what Eddie had been talking about. When I told them Bill and I were in the same boat, I thought we would all collapse we were laughing so hard. When we all went back and explained the situation to Eddie, he looked at us pityingly, as any unappreciated genius would. Eddie was a piece of work—endlessly imagining, conceiving, conjuring up or inventing angles for bargaining purposes.

The complexities of the rapidly developing NBC-ABC deals were so great that someone had to be assigned the task of mastering and recording the infinite details. That assignment fell to Ed Durso, our assistant general counsel, who had once played baseball for Harvard. Ed miraculously marshaled all the daily negotiating decisions. The negotiators were moving so swiftly that without Ed's considerable skill, we would hardly have known where we were.

The key development in the negotiations came when NBC in essence offered us $500 million for their half of the package for five years and the same amount for ABC's half. Under the expiring contract, ABC could keep their half by matching NBC's offer. From that point forward, a deal with the two networks was inevitable, although there were still times when we and ABC were not so sure. ABC continued to be extremely unhappy with the price levels NBC had set and with the concept of a five-year arrangement, which gave NBC one more World Series than ABC. As a result, we ultimately added a sixth year and modified the price level, bringing in the total six-year package at something over $1.1 billion. By April 1983 it was all wrapped up. We were tired but elated. Considering the conflicting interests imposed on us by the presence of twenty-six local club broadcasting contracts that we had had to work around, it might have been the best sports deal ever made.

We held a major-league meeting to ratify the new contracts and got virtually unanimous approval. Most important, these contracts gave every club an enormous increase in annual revenue. For those of us who had preached the merits of increased revenue-sharing, this was our greatest triumph. My friends saw it as a great personal triumph for me, given the challenge to my business acumen that had been so persistently raised by Nelson Doubleday and others among my opponents.

We were disappointed, however, that we had not found a way to fit CBS in. We wanted all three television networks. CBS had maintained a strong interest to the end but was discouraged by the high price, which they felt did not make business sense for them. ABC felt pretty much the same way, but as an incumbent rights holder did not want to give up baseball notwithstanding the cost.

Watson and Schanzer for NBC were as unflappable at the end as they had been at the beginning, even if they didn't know what Einhorn was talking about a lot of the time.

. . .

One of the toughest and most persistent problems I faced was that of superstations. A superstation is an independent TV station whose signal has been put on satellite by a separate entity (common carrier) making the signal available to cable systems around the country. The first and greatest of the superstations was Ted Turner's WTBS (previously WTCG) in Atlanta. When Turner bought the Braves in early 1976, there were rumors that WTBS would become a superstation. Thus, before the National League would approve him it required his assurance that WTBS programming would be limited to the Braves' local area. Ted gave it. He would later argue that he "had no idea of the potential extent of cable carriage of the WTBS signal." That is like arguing that Harry Truman had no idea of the damage an atom bomb might do to a Japanese city. Ted understood the potential of superstation WTBS, particularly with its vast schedule of Braves games, although he might not have foreseen the possibility that it would reach the 33 million homes it does today.

Once Turner was approved by the National League, WTBS was made a superstation and cable systems began to carry it nationally. At first, it was not a major practical problem, as the number of subscribing cable systems was small and the Braves were a poor attraction. O'Malley, who had a keen sense of danger, was alarmed. We were both suspicious of Turner's argument that his superstation status was involuntary, beyond his control. I retained experts to study the situation.

Our concern was that if Braves games began going into other professional baseball markets in large numbers, clubs were going to lose fans at the gate and local broadcasting revenues. This could prompt franchise moves and otherwise destabilize an industry that was entering its first year of free agency with foreboding. Then there was the additional fear that one successful superstation might beget imitators, with even more baseball games flooding the local markets. Such fears were not unfounded.

The judgment of the experts was that the superstation problem could be best solved in Congress, even though we had already lost one major battle there when the 1976 Copyright Act granted cable television a "compulsory license" to carry over-the-air telecasts of sports events. In other words, once our games (or hockey or basketball games) were telecast locally, cable systems around the country had the right to carry those games by paying a nominal copyright royalty. This was an obvious subsidy of the cable business at the expense of sports operators, who could no longer control the dissemination of their product. A dreadful congressional judgment, it was so inequitable that we thought there was a reasonable chance that Congress, seeing the unfairness of the compulsory license, would modify it and return control to the sports operators. What ensued was a battle between cable and sports in the Congress. No two individuals so personified the respective sides of that battle as Kuhn for sports and Turner for cable. We lobbied, we testified, we debated in public and argued together privately.

The sports side managed to get favorable bills introduced but they never got out of committee. Congressmen whose names I'm not free to mention would tell me behind the scenes that we were right "but the political issues were tough." What that meant was that the cable industry led by Turner was flooding the Congress with letters and messages from cable subscribers saying, "Please don't take away our sports." Never mind that the telecast rights by any fair and ethical judgment belonged to the sports operators. But the Congress read its mail and sports lost out.

The situation worsened. Year by year WTBS expanded its cable network operations until the number of subscribing homes reached 31 million by 1984. Along the way, WGN in Chicago, which carried virtually all Cubs games, also became a superstation—as did WOR in New York, which carried Mets games, and WPIX in New York, which carried Yankees games. The country was being indiscriminately flooded with baseball. To make it more injurious to the other clubs, all the superstation teams were attractive and competitive or were becoming so. So the cable industry and Turner Broadcasting grew and prospered, subsidized and insatiably fed by baseball telecasts, while the baseball industry sank deeper and deeper into red ink, from real losses.

We decided late in 1983 to explore the concept of creating or acquiring our own cable network or superstation and feeding it the best available games. If it worked, we would generate revenue for all of baseball. Einhorn, Giles and I went to a cable convention in Las Vegas and met with most of the big, multiple-system cable operators. The consensus was that we had a great product except for the fact that the marketplace was already saturated with superstation baseball. We estimated that the superstations cost us well in excess of $100 million a year, perhaps closer to $200 million.

In the last year of my administration, I recommended to the clubs that they substantially reduce the number of games any club could telecast. This would have reduced the injury caused by the superstations, more or less, depending on how deep the game reduction cut. Unfortunately, by this time the anti-Kuhn forces in the National League, which included Turner, could block any broadcasting initiative because of the three-quarters vote requirement, and I realized my efforts were futile.

So great was the scope of the problem that I asked Commissioner-elect Ueberroth to join with me in a notice to all clubs regarding our joint determination to solve the matter. We sent the notice only weeks before I left office. This unprecedented message from two commissioners was window dressing as far as I was concerned, but it did make it clear that Peter was committed to finding a solution. That was all the legacy I could leave to a difficulty that had plagued baseball and me for almost a decade. I hated to leave it unresolved. But while Turner had outmaneuvered us in Congress, he lost badly on two other superstation issues.

As the 1982 race unfolded, the Braves were serious contenders for the National League West championship. I warned Turner that if the Braves did win, they could not carry the League Championship Series on the WTBS cable network, which spread across the country. We had sold a network exclusive to ABC. Ted defied me, making the fallacious argument that he had no control over where the WTBS signal went. Since he had thrown down the gauntlet, I certainly was not going to let it lie. ABC and baseball jointly sued him in federal court in New York, seeking to enjoin his cable network coverage of the LCS. We came before Judge Mary Johnson Lowe. Ted and I were again pitted against each other as the key witnesses for the two sides. Ted's charms failed to impress Judge Lowe when it became apparent that WTBS "operated" the cable network in much the same way that ABC or NBC operated their networks. The sham argument that WTBS was an innocent bystander was stripped away. Judge Lowe granted the injunction we sought.

In the courthouse corridor afterward, an angry Turner, encountering one of my staff members, said, "What are you going to do for a job after we get rid of Bowie?" Ted was not all charm.

The 1976 Copyright Act provided that copyright owners (e.g., sports operators and motion picture studios) whose property was carried by cable systems under the statutory compulsory license were to be compensated by receiving a royalty. The amount of the royalty was initially specified in the act; however, the Copyright

Royalty Tribunal was given authority to make certain changes in those rates. The copyright owners argued that they should receive fair market value while the cable industry argued for what were essentially nominal payments. In the early years, the cable industry prevailed. It began to seem that fate was against us on all cable issues no matter how valid our arguments. But we persisted. In 1982 the tribunal stunned the cable industry with a decision that increased key royalty payments by as much as 1,500 percent. It was far from fair market value, but it was notable progress. The cable industry sued to set aside the tribunal's order and also sought congressional relief, but failed.

Certainly one of the sweetest relationships I had in baseball was with the guys in the baseball broadcast booths. I don't have an altogether satisfactory explanation for the warmth of this relationship. Perhaps the fact that I was always willing to go on the air with them had something to do with it. I even occasionally did play by play. Perhaps it was because one of my childhood heroes was Arch McDonald, who handled Washington Senators' radio. McDonald did more to educate me about baseball and to develop my youthful enthusiasm than anyone else, just as other play-by-play men were doing for kids, housewives and other fans throughout the baseball world. More likely it was because the broadcasters, with some notable exceptions, were more affable and easier companions than their press box counterparts. Since broadcasters were instant communicators, it was hardly a surprise that charm and gregariousness were found in their arsenal of skills.

The Pirates' Bob Prince was a perfect example. I doubt that I was ever in Forbes Field or Three Rivers Stadium without going on the air with Bob and being drawn out about my Kuhn relatives in Pittsburgh. The exception would have been those glorious childhood visits to Forbes Field from my uncle Martin Hayton's house when I first discovered National League baseball and a DiMaggio named Vince. The Pirates' broadcaster in those days was Prince's homespun predecessor Rosey Rowswell, who in his own time charmed a generation in western Pennsylvania.

Prince and Rowswell had their counterparts in scores of broadcast booths across North American professional baseball—major league and minor league. Many of the major league broadcasters learned their trade in the "bushes," men such as Frick Award winner Russ

Hodges, whom I first knew of as the voice of the Charlotte Hornets and who subsequently became McDonald's partner on Washington games. Years later in 1951, Hodges, by then handling the New York Giants, called Bobby Thomson's home run "heard around the world."

We created the Frick Award after Frick's death to honor great broadcasters with recognition at Cooperstown. The roster of men who have received that award nicely demonstrates the quality and sweet-humored nature of this breed: Mel Allen, Red Barber, Bob Elson, Hodges, Ernie Harwell, Vin Scully, Jack Brickhouse, Curt Gowdy, Buck Canel and Prince.

23

The Writers

This is the hardest subject for me to write about. The tapestry is so large, the detail so intricate, the coloring so brilliant here and subtle there. How do I deal with it? How do I do justice to my complex relationship with the press? Space does not permit me to take every writer I knew and talk about how we got along or did not get along as I have done with Cosell and Smith. The result is more generalization than I would like, with all the dangers of generalizations—unfairness and oversimplification. I hope what I've said is not unfair to any members of the profession. It is not intended to be.

Cosell and others see the press as a whole, all the parts of which are interchangeable. They are not. Writers are as varied as, well, people. While some see themselves as wrapped in the spiritual folds of the First Amendment, most do not, being content periodically to put on paper their thoughts on the sports world in reward for which they receive a paycheck. Mostly they like sports, some rather fiercely and partisanly. They seem to like the fellowship of the profession and of baseball. Though they grumble about the size of their paychecks, they generally like what they do. And yes, sooner or later, they criticize the poor soul who happens to be the commissioner of baseball, some with more frequency and vehemence than others. But it is a game in which they all indulge. Various characteristics make baseball the national pastime; one of them is the idea, which fans and sportswriters have, that they know more about baseball than any other sport and certainly more about baseball than the commissioner.

The problems I had with Red Smith, with the exception of his resenting my involvement in the Braves' move from Milwaukee, were pretty much the problems I had with my other critics in the press. I might have been better off had I known the father of Lane Kirkland, president of the AFL-CIO, at least judging by a remark Kirkland recently made to reporters: "You know, my pappy told me never to bet my bladder against a brewery or get into an argument with people who buy ink by the barrel." Perhaps it was my litigation training as a lawyer, but I never hesitated to get into an argument with anyone and that certainly included the press. My philosophy was very simple: I was going to do what I thought was right for baseball. If that meant I was going to be flung on a sacrificial pyre by the press or anyone else, so be it. For years I have carried with me a quotation from Abraham Lincoln that I believe in and that expresses my view concerning critics I have encountered: "I do the very best I know how—the very best I can; and I mean to keep doing so until the end. . . . If the end brings me out all right, what is said against me won't amount to anything. . . . If the end brings me out wrong, ten thousand angels swearing I was right would make no difference. . . ." After sixteen years as commissioner, I thought the "end brought me out all right."

No doubt a major barrier between me and my press critics was their belief that I was a remote, humorless, patrician stuffed shirt. Though an entertainer such as Johnny Carson runs no risks from me, I felt it was a fallacious evaluation. Joe Reichler, who achieved fame as the top sportswriter for the Associated Press and was my first director of public relations, used to say, "Commissioner, I know you'll win them over; if they'll only take the trouble to get to know you, you can't miss." I took Joe's advice seriously. It was unusual for me not to hold press conferences wherever I traveled and any writer who really wanted to sit down with me could sooner or later manage it. I was generally accessible by telephone to the press, although the endless duties of the office did not make that easy.

Some of my most severe critics never asked for a personal interview. I wondered how they honestly felt they could write about what kind of a human being I was. Of course, they could disagree about night games in the World Series or my handling of the DH. Fair enough. But how could they diagnose my personality? Red Smith, for example, who made a career of analyzing my personality, never once asked for an hour or so to get some notion of how I ticked. He was not alone in this. It is hard to avoid the conclusion that these writers either took somebody else's opinion as good enough or else based their own opinion on irrelevant facts such as my Wall Street, ancestral or Ivy League background.

In a sense, I could respect Jerry Holtzman, who regularly worked me over in the *Chicago Tribune.* At least Jerry took the trouble to spend time with me—quite a lot. Forgive me for thinking he made lousy judgments, but he tried. On the other hand, I did not respect Jerry for a fault he shared with a good many journalists. His opinions in print invariably favored his best sources, men like Bill Veeck, Charlie Finley and Marvin Miller. It was a reward, I suspect, for their providing him with story material he needed.

Fortunately, there were a lot of writers who were responsible enough to delve into the old stuffed shirt and get an idea of what the stuffing was like. This group did not write the kind of bad-tempered material that marred the efforts of others. I drew a lot of criticism from these writers on the merits of things I did and failed to do but not vicious attacks on Bowie Kuhn the person. Legitimate criticism of my performance as commissioner did not bother me (at least not much), was a proper journalistic exercise and not infrequently educated me.

Dick Young was an influential writer with the New York *Daily News* during most of my years in office. He was a special case, hard-headed, stubborn and opinionated. He loved and knew baseball. In my early years, we got along abominably. I thought he was arrogant. He thought I was, too. We were probably both right. Unfortunately for me, he worked for a company that bought ink by the barrel. He used a lot on me. For some reason, probably his love of baseball, I refused to give up on him and over the years we made common cause on getting Negro League players into the Hall of Fame. That seemed to thaw the ice on both sides. He also was one of the few writers who correctly analyzed Marvin Miller as *not* more sinned against than sinning. He also had the courage to support Don Grant's leadership of the Mets when the fashion was to denounce him, forgetting the great Mets years of 1969 and 1973. Young was one of the few who saw that Grant was trying with more wisdom than his Yankees rivals to bring sanity to baseball's financial affairs after free agency in 1976. Over the years, Young gave up the personal attacks and tended to support me more often than not on basic issues, such as the need to protect sports from gambling influences and other matters affecting our integrity. He was a unique man whose New York chauvinism left sportswriters around the country fuming.

Another source of friction between the press and me was my disciplining of owners. On the face of it that seems rather curious, since the press in general supported the idea of a commissioner's controlling the "lords of baseball," as Young called them. That was all well and good until the owner disciplined was in the writer's own town. Then many writers, not all, would swing to the defense of the owner. There were several reasons. Owners tended to have powerful influence with local writers, both by reason of familiarity and by their ability to provide service and news. If an owner like Steinbrenner, Finley or Veeck decided to dispute the commissioner, he was assured of some friendly support in the press. No sport has as much clout with local writers as baseball. Since no commissioner of any sport ever battled with owners as much as I did, it was guaranteed that there would be owner-generated press hostility against me.

Another reason for press opposition to owner discipline is that the writers are frequently fans. If my disciplinary action deprived the local club of a desirable player, as when I stopped the Yankees from acquiring Jason Thompson in 1981, writers were apt to behave like disappointed fans and criticize the commissioner.

No shortcoming of the press bothered me as much as the borrowed but unresearched story. If Smith wrote that some disciplining of Finley was vindictive, fellows across the country were apt to write that with no more basis or research than Smith's article. Or, if Young wrote that the decision to reschedule a World Series game at night was made by NBC, many writers would take that as gospel. Never mind that I disciplined Finley for some flagrant rules violation or that NBC had no idea what the rescheduling decision would be until I told them, the first unresearched and inaccurate story is too often accepted and passed on by others. This is bad journalism. I saw a lot of it.

In order to help the press do the necessary research, I developed under the very capable and well-organized Bob Wirz an efficient information department that stood ready to give the press the facts on almost any issue. While there occasionally were matters on which information could not be given (e.g., court proceedings and pending disciplinary matters), 90 percent of the time we were ready to answer and answer accurately. At no time would I give inaccurate answers to the press, nor was my staff permitted to do so. Under these circumstances, I was distressed to see how often the unresearched and inaccurate story was written by the press.

The two wire services, AP and UPI, were models of persistence in trying to get their stories straight. Invariably they would check facts with our information department, with the result that they had a commendable record for accurate reporting. There were certainly writers who worked hard to get their information correct. Murray Chass would be an example.

From the time Chass started writing baseball for *The New York Times* in 1970, I doubt that any writer rang our telephones more in search of facts. Murray was a digger. While I often disagreed with his conclusions, I wished that all writers could have emulated his passion for research. Because of that passion, and because he wrote for the respected *Times,* Murray developed many sources of information. The Players Association was his strongest source, but he also had a string of owners who would give him off-the-record information. Although these sources used him at times to plant what they wanted in the *Times,* a lot of his revelations were accurate and exclusive. I was shocked on more than a few occasions to find confidential information, usually based on an unrevealed source, printed in Murray's column. His suppliers trusted him not to reveal their names. An effective writer has to build that kind of confidence.

I was often quick to defend the writers' right of access and their right to be treated with dignity. The Writers' Association knew they would find a sympathetic ear in my office when writers were intimidated by club personnel. Such an example came in 1983 when I was approached about verbal abuse heaped on the *New York Post*'s Henry Hecht by Yankees manager Billy Martin. Responding to a letter of protest by Joe Vecchione of *The New York Times,* I said, "It was an embarrassment which should never have happened and which cannot and will not be allowed to continue. Any recurrence will be dealt with accordingly. While I cannot assure you there will never be unkind things said and while I do not believe you are looking for any such assurance, I have every belief the media can continue to cover baseball without fear or intimidation."

While I normally tried to reach conclusions in a thoughtful way, occasionally I followed hunches. I did so in 1973 when Waddy Spoelstra of the *Detroit News,* a recovering alcoholic, called and asked if I would fund a program of Baseball Chapel services for each major-league club, a born-again Christian talking to a Catholic commissioner. Spoelstra, broadcasters Ernie Harwell and Red Barber, plus players like Jim Kaat, Al Worthington, Randy Hundley, Don Kessinger, Don Sutton and Bobby Richardson had already been conducting such services on a sporadic basis. Spoelstra wanted to organize it for everyone. My answer was yes, and today, there are weekly Chapel services across the major and minor leagues.

My favorite group of writers had to be the Boston contingent, as quaint and special as Fenway Park. They ripped me, but it was very dispassionate because they ripped everybody. They loved baseball and cared deeply about the game. I cherished sitting in the Fenway press room, perched on top of the stadium and drinking a beer dispensed affectionately by Tommy McCarthy with the likes of Larry Claflin, Clif Keane, Jake Liston, Larry Whiteside, Peter Gammons, Ray Fitzgerald, Leo Cloutier and Hugh McGovern. In fact, I got my only standing ovation from the press in that room. It happened in February 1969 when I fought my way to Boston in a blizzard to meet the Red Sox press corps. Maybe I needed more blizzards.

During the 1977 World Series, *Sports Illustrated* came to us with a problem concerning their reporter Melissa Ludtke. She had not been able to gain access to the Yankees' clubhouse after games at the stadium. SI made the valid point that banning her from the clubhouse denied her equal opportunity with the male reporters. They did not feel that providing interviews away from the clubhouse was an adequate substitute. Nor was the problem confined to Ludtke. A number of other female sportswriters appeared in the 1970s. None of their employers, however, seemed quite as determined as *Sports Illustrated* to force the issue—by litigation if necessary.

The other side of the problem was that many players did not feel it was proper for female reporters to enter the clubhouse at a time when players were undressing and showering. This was also a valid point. They were entitled to their privacy. I had accordingly advised the clubs several years earlier that female reporters should not be given access to clubhouses.

Sports Illustrated argued that the players' problem could be handled by the discreet use of bathrobes and towels. Anyone who knew the mechanics of a clubhouse would doubt the workability of that suggestion. The players were great athletes, not magicians or fan dancers.

I discussed the situation with my Executive Council. I told them my information was that a clear majority of players preferred their privacy, but were willing to go outside the clubhouse to accommodate the female reporters. I said no pattern had emerged in professional sports; the NFL had uniformly resisted, while in hockey and basketball some access had been given female reporters. I knew of no instance where women had been admitted in amateur sports or where male reporters had sought access to dressing areas in women's sports. Trying to balance out the equities on both sides, I concluded that in fairness to our players and to the family-sport image of baseball, we should resist *Sports Illustrated* on the issue. The Council agreed, although O'Malley felt that we were bucking the clear trend of women's rights. We all recognized that was so but felt that because this was a question of principle, we should take a stand even if we lost. The Yankees had recently taken a similar position with regard to female "batboys" and had prevailed.

When we would not admit Ludtke for the 1977 Series, Time Inc. (which owned *Sports Illustrated*) filed a lawsuit in New York federal court on December 30. The case was assigned to a woman, Judge Constance Baker Motley.

At the discovery stage, it became obvious to our lawyers that the Players Association was not going to give us any support, even though this involved an issue on which we should have agreed, namely, protecting the interests of the players. Without player support, our chances of prevailing were pretty well doomed.

In September 1978, Judge Motley decided the case in favor of Time Inc. In essence, she held that since Yankee Stadium was a municipally owned facility, women reporters were entitled to access with their male counterparts. Judge Motley concluded that the athlete's right of privacy was not as significant as the female reporter's right of equal access. Ludtke was given access to the stadium clubhouses in the 1978 Dodgers-Yankees Series.

While our lawyers felt we could reverse the decision, I felt that if we fought the issue across the country, the bottom line one way or another was going to be the same. We had fought on an issue of principle and lost. Like it or not, we now had to accommodate to the new realities. I polled the clubs during the winter to ask what they would do if they were permitted to set their own policy. A substantial majority responded that they would provide equal access, either by simply opening clubhouses to all, by having open-time clubhouse periods or by using separate interview rooms. I told *Sports Illustrated* that most clubs would give equal access and that I was prepared to urge all of them to do so. That ended the litigation. I continued to hear complaints from players from time to time about our policy but I had nothing left to give them but sympathy.

The Ludtke issue was one on which I drew substantial criticism from the media. Quite understandably members of the press saw this as a freedom-of-the-press issue. Cosell was a leading critic. Privately, I was getting quite a different picture from some of my friends in the working press. They were unsympathetic with the institutional media position. They saw it as playing into the hands of those sports organizations that were happy to seize excuses to exclude the press from clubhouses and other player contacts. And they sympathized with the athletes who they knew would inescapably be placed in embarrassing situations by the presence of female reporters.

I struggled for sixteen years to achieve a decent personal relationship with the writers and largely failed. That is so even though in my last years many writers who had been severe critics wrote sympathetically and even supported my reelection. That is so even though many writers became my friends and remained so after I left baseball. I think of such men as Shirley Povich, Fred Russell, Milt Richman, Will Grimsley, Hal Bock, Joe Durso, Peter Gammons, Bill Madden, Bob Hunter, John Steadman and others too numerous to name here. The failure was at a personal level, not at the level of the game itself, which increasingly flourished in public and press perception during my years and shed its once-faltering image. But the perception of the commissioner himself was too mixed, too full of denigration to be called a success. That hurt me and the game because it inevitably impaired my ability to function at maximum effectiveness. It also gave my enemies in the game ammunition to use in attacking me.

Inescapably the question arises, Was the press fair to Bowie Kuhn? I have been asked that question many times during my baseball tenure and since. I think the answer on balance is no. I say that with a realization of my own shortcomings. I can be as stiff-necked on some issues as Howard Cosell is on all. I am often starchy in public appearances and in personal relations, not exactly Herbert Hoover but not Eddie Murphy either. I am rather disposed to pick up gauntlets thrown anywhere near me when the course of discretion might be to ignore them. I am an incurable romantic, sometimes seeing visionary avenues as better routes than more practical ones. And I am confident that this litany of my faults could be quite accurately enlarged.

In my summing up of things, I cannot conclude that my faults warranted the kind of treatment which *generally speaking* I received from the writers. I think too many of them fell prey to their own built-in bias against someone of my background, made me the scapegoat for their rage against the growing domination of television and took offense at my unvarnished willingness to stand for moral issues at a time in our culture when such a posture was unpopular. I suspect that Kenesaw Mountain Landis would have come a cropper too in the press climate of my time in office. I draw some, but not much, solace from that conclusion.

24

Drugs

The two great nightmares of my time as commissioner were the strike of 1981 and drug abuse. The battles between me and owners like Steinbrenner and Finley were part of the landscape. They were the rough places in the road you were bound to rattle across in the normal course of baseball administration. But the strike and drug abuse were nightmarish because they were abnormal problems that had tremendous impact on our fans and threatened the foundations of our relationship with the public.

When I took office in 1969, I never dreamed I would see drug abuse achieve the dimensions it did in the 1980s. I knew we had some minor problems in the early years of my tenure. I initially became aware through press reports, and then through club physicians, that some players were routinely using amphetamine-barbiturate combinations called "greenies." The pills created a high believed by some players to give them added energy or strength. If a player was tired, he felt greenies gave him a lift. A player who had a "long night" and not much rest would be a typical candidate for a greenie.

More important, greenies were illegal without a prescription and were dangerous to a player's health if abused. I was not very happy to learn that they were being distributed in some baseball clubhouses. Nor was I very happy about the example being set for the public by the use of greenies. I retained a drug expert, Dr. Garrett O'Connor of Johns Hopkins University. After consulting with Dr. O'Connor and our club physicians, I established in February 1971 a Drug Education and Prevention Program for professional baseball, the first of its kind in sports.

I encountered some internal opposition, most prominently from Bob Short of the Washington Senators, who argued that we were making ourselves look worse than other sports that had more serious problems than ours. Short was also concerned that if I took command of the situation, there could be player suspensions. He was not enthusiastic about the commissioner's having too much power, especially in 1971, the year he planned to challenge me on moving the Senators to Texas. There may have been something to his public relations argument, but I thought it was imperative to deal directly and publicly with our problem without regard to what I saw as a marginal public relations concern. We had set a bad example for the public and needed to deal with that. As Warren Giles, then president emeritus of the National league, liked to tell me, "If you find out you're wrong, get right."

Seminars were held during spring training camps for both major- and minor-league players and administrative personnel. We produced an educational booklet, "Baseball vs. Drugs," that was distributed not only to players but also to public and school libraries.

In 1978, we added alcohol as a special abused drug and instituted an educational program involving former Brooklyn Dodgers pitcher Don Newcombe, a recovering alcoholic himself.

I felt our drug program and the vigilance of our security personnel had alleviated the drug problem in baseball during the 1970s. By contrast with other sports, we looked pretty good, perhaps better than we deserved. During the 1970s, the National Football League had extensive problems, with thirteen arrests of its players. However, nobody in major-league baseball was laughing. I personally had developed a built-in case of uneasiness. Free agency had sent player salaries winging upward, meaning players had much more disposable income. That presented a clear potential for drug abuse. To make matters worse, the Players Association made a policy of fighting all discipline imposed by my office. This gave players a sense of immunity from control. Occasionally an owner like John McHale of the Expos would tell me he was hearing stories about drug use. I spent a lot of time with our security people looking for information, and enlarging our investigative activity.

Then things began to change. Early in 1980, Bob Welch, the young Dodgers pitcher who had engaged in a memorable duel with Reggie Jackson in the 1978 World Series, revealed that he had spent five weeks the previous winter at The Meadows, an alcohol treatment center in Wickenberg, Arizona. Then Darrell Porter, the Kansas City Royals' catcher, left their Florida training camp and also entered The Meadows in a drug and alcohol rehabilitation program.

On August 25, Texas pitcher Ferguson Jenkins was arrested by Ontario police at the Toronto airport in possession of two ounces of marijuana, four grams of cocaine and two grams of hashish. Five days after his arrest, I had him come to New York for an investigatory interview. I wanted to know the source of the drugs, whether other players were involved and anything else that might be pertinent to the welfare of the game. On the advice of his Canadian lawyer, Ed Greenspan, Jenkins declined to answer questions relating to the possession charges on the ground that to do so might prejudice the pending case in Canada.

What Jenkins was rejecting was the commissioner's well-understood preogative to conduct investigations and to ask pertinent questions. Indeed, when a player signs a contract he agrees to accept the jurisdiction of the commissioner and recognizes the commissioner's right to conduct investigations. There were no lofty questions of constitutional rights in my proceedings against players and executives, as the press so often asserted; none was more vocal than Cosell, who fancied he could find a constitutional right behind every stitch on a baseball. This was not state action as to which such rights might apply, but the conduct of a private organization pursuing rights given it by the players and clubs.

Given Jenkins's excellent reputation, I was both surprised and disappointed by his refusal to cooperate. Since he had failed to cooperate as required by his contract and baseball law, I decided that he should not be permitted to play until he was willing to answer my questions. To make it clear that my action was not intended to be punitive, I did not stop his salary or benefits.

A grievance was immediately filed on Jenkins's behalf. This dashed any hope I might have harbored that the Players Association would take a supportive view of my efforts to deal with the drug problem. It was a signal that the Association would put what they saw as individual player rights ahead of the general welfare of the game and public regarding drugs. Never mind that player careers might well be destroyed by drug abuse; they were not going to cooperate with the commissioner or management on the subject.

A hearing was held on September 18 and four days later arbitrator Raymond Goetz overruled me and reinstated Jenkins. He determined that had Jenkins answered my questions the answers *might* have jeopardized his defense in court. He brushed aside my concern about the drug problem as "mere surmise." I was furious. I did not blame the arbitrator so much as I blamed the system that gave outside technicians authority to determine matters of fundamental concern to sports and the public, matters that they did not or could not understand.

I called the decision a "grave disservice, not only to those of us in sports administration, but to concerned parents and citizens everywhere. Athletes have a tremendous influence on our youth and on society in general. Baseball's policy for decades has been to establish the game as a wholesome family sport. In his contract, a player pledges himself to the public and to his club to conform to high standards of personal conduct, fair play and good sportsmanship.

"The arbitrator argues that the Canadian authorities did not view Mr. Jenkins's alleged possession of cocaine, hashish and marijuana as serious, nor is he persuaded that 'present day attitudes' condemn such possession. I totally disagree. I believe vast segments of society are outraged that some athletes do not show a greater sense of responsibility to a public that idolizes and imitates them, particularly the youngsters who make heroes of athletes."

On December 18, Jenkins went to trial and was found guilty of cocaine possession. Because of his reputation and previously clean record, the judge erased the verdict and gave him an absolute discharge.

I considered suspending Jenkins at that point but I had no illusions about the result of another grievance. So I took the lesser, surer course, and settled with Jenkins. He agreed to contribute $10,000 to a drug education and prevention program in Texas, make public appearances on the program's behalf and appear in public-service announcements produced by major-league baseball. He issued a statement asking the fans' forgiveness.

The worst aspect of the Jenkins decision was the terrible signal it gave our players. That signal was clear enough: the Players Association would protect individual players against any effort of the commissioner to enforce a sane drug program and the outside arbitrator would back up the Association. I am afraid it knocked the last latches off the floodgates.

In November 1980, Ray and Joan Kroc held an alcoholism seminar at their ranch in the Santa Ynez Mountains in California, not far from the ranch of Ronald Reagan. They invited the entire Executive

Council and Marvin Miller of the Players Association. Miller declined but the Council attended. The Krocs had created Operation CORK to deal with the problem of alcoholism and they wanted baseball and other sports more involved.

If Ray Kroc had walked a unique road on his path of success, he was matched stride for stride in unique qualities by his wife Joan. There were no mountains or rivers she could not climb or bridge. Granted she had uncommon financial resources at her command, still Joan left the impression that even if she were penniless, she would somehow bring down the Bastilles in her way. While she could be as implacable as Ray, there was more velvet in her style—less roaring, more cajoling—but in the end both brought down Bastilles. She gave me her support more wholeheartedly than Ray did, and I cherished her for that.

The alcoholism seminar was an eye- and mind-opening two days. The highlight was the appearance of the Dodgers' Bob Welch and his candid recitation of his experiences as an alcoholic. As he concluded, the audience was in tears, as was he. I was never prouder of a player than I was of that commendable young man.

The assembled CORK professionals urged the creation of employee-assistance programs (or EAPs) by each major-league club to deal with alcoholic and nonalcoholic drug problems. The EAPs would provide expert professional help for our employees and would follow the successful pattern of such programs in other industries. At our annual meeting in Dallas the next month, I asked the clubs to give consideration to establishing EAPs. In the ensuing months some did, but many did not. It was a common problem in baseball. Unless direct orders were issued, there were always clubs that would behave irresponsibly. It was the simple reality of living with these complex personalities. Whenever possible I tried to use persuasion to bring about my goals at the club level. When it worked it was a better approach than issuing orders. However, my concerns about the drug situation were such that I was not going much further without having EAPs in place throughout baseball.

During the first half of 1981, we were grappling with the labor dispute that would lead to a strike in June. At the same time, I was watching the small progress the clubs were making on EAPs. With the strike under way, I decided it was as good a time as any to update, unify and toughen our drug program. The league presidents and I issued a new program in July that provided for severe discipline for involvement with dangerous drugs or trafficking in any kind of illegal drugs; the program further provided that a player such as Darrell Porter, who came forward voluntarily for treatment, would not be subject to disciplinary action. While clubs were urged to impose discipline for drug violations, I reserved the right to do so myself if I felt that was necessary. What that really meant was that I had little confidence in the willingness of individual clubs to discipline their own personnel.

I further *directed* each club to establish its own EAP, which would be open to players and front office personnel. Over the years, these Employee Assistance Programs induced a number of players to voluntarily seek help for drug problems.

San Diego player Alan Wiggins was arrested on July 21, 1982, for possession of cocaine. Coincidentally, his arrest came in the same week during which NFL commissioner Pete Rozelle and I had testified before Congressman Leo Zeferetti's Select Committee on Narcotics Abuse and Control. I had told the committee of our continuing vigilance in the area of drug abuse.

Wiggins immediately entered a treatment program at the Care-Unit of the Orange County Medical Center. It was there that Harry Gibbs, who had succeeded the retired Henry Fitzgibbon as my security chief, interviewed him. The Players Association sought to stifle the interview process by insisting that all the questions be submitted in advance. I was not about to comply with that request and was pleased to find that Wiggins and his agent, Tony Antanasio, were fully cooperative, as were Joan Kroc and Ballard Smith of the Padres. After receiving Gibbs's report, I suspended Wiggins without pay for thirty days.

Two years later, I learned from Don Fehr of the Players Association that Wiggins had been paid by the Padres during his suspension. I was appalled. I called Ballard Smith and asked if this was so. He said he would check it out. Embarrassed, he advised me later that Fehr was correct. He said it had slipped through at the pay-office level without the knowledge of club management. One of my last acts as commissioner was to fine the Padres $50,000.

The Wiggins case was covered routinely by the press. I was surprised that there was not more press criticism or alarm. Nor did my mail reveal any special public concern. A decade earlier, the Wiggins case would have caused a furor. I speculated that the press and the public had been lulled into indifference by recurrent problems in other sports and in the American public at large. At that time, according to data released by the White House, 22 million Americans used marijuana regularly and 4 million more were using cocaine. Also, something of the old watchdog attitude of the press was disappearing as a new generation of writers emerged, one more attuned to drug use and less concerned about the public's old-time faith in sports.

Several months later I ran into my most persistent and difficult drug problem: the case of Dodgers' reliever Steve Howe. Howe had been the 1980 National League Rookie of the Year and a star of the Dodgers' 1981 World Series victory over the Yankees. Peter O'Malley called to say that Howe was having drug problems and had volunteered for a five-week rehabilitation program at The Meadows in November and December of 1982. Peter's reliability kept me from being more concerned initially about Howe than I would otherwise have been. The Dodgers were a club that could be counted on to handle something like this correctly. That was a relief to me as I had just gone through a reelection meeting in which my 70 percent support was just short of the 75 percent requirement. Where all that was going quite naturally was engaging my attention.

Howe was released on December 29 from The Meadows, opened the season with the Dodgers, and had two wins, seven saves and had not allowed an earned run when he resumed treatment on May 29, this time at the CareUnit Hospital. His first child was a week old.

I had long talks with O'Malley on an almost daily basis. He was at pains to give me every available fact about Howe. He made it clear that the Dodgers would handle the situation however I thought was proper. "We reserve the right to argue with you," he said, "but in the end, we'll back you up all the way." It was the typical O'Malley position. It was little wonder that I respected the Dodgers organization. If anything, Peter was even more oriented in this way than his father had been. There was no doubt that Peter was doing his best for both the player and the game. His concern for Howe's health was as genuine and touching as it had been for Bob Welch's.

Howe rejoined the Dodgers on June 29, five days after his release from CareUnit. When he rejoined the team, the Dodgers announced that they were docking him a month's salary ($54,000) and placing him on three years' probation. This was a joint decision by Peter and me. I felt that Howe's second round of drug abuse had to cost him something, however cooperative he had been. A month's salary seemed a fair measure. I said publicly that any violation of the probation would result in "the most severe discipline." Privately, I told Peter, I was losing hope that Howe had the determination or ability to overcome his problem.

Notwithstanding the fact that the Dodgers had treated Howe with concern and patience, the Players Association as usual filed a grievance, in this instance challenging Howe's loss of salary. Two days later, on July 15, he arrived three hours late for a game at Dodger Stadium and refused to undergo a test to "determine his condition to play baseball." The Dodgers suspended him indefinitely without pay but reinstated him the next day when he passed a drug test.

For the next two months, things went well for Howe and he continued to pitch well. But on September 22, he missed the team's charter flight to Atlanta. When he caught up with the team there, he refused to take a drug test. The Dodgers suspended him yet again, and he reentered CareUnit.

On December 15, I suspended Howe for the entire 1984 season. He himself would later say, "It was the best thing that ever happened to me; I turned all my weaknesses into strengths; without that year off, I couldn't have done it." I was not so sure whether he would ever overcome his problems but I felt a year away from baseball was the best thing for him personally, and it certainly was necessary in order to set an example for our industry. The Dodgers organization was fully supportive.

On May 31, 1984, the Players Association grievance regarding Howe's suspension was disposed of when I agreed to transfer him from the suspended list to the inactive list, which meant he would receive service time for the benefits plan. It was a modest concession to the Players Association in the interest of clearing away the grievance. Their willingness to close the books on Howe was the first, slight sign that they might take a reasonable position in an individual drug case. I also gave the Dodgers permission to advance him funds for family necessities.

I required him to submit to twice-weekly testing during his suspension, which included testing for alcohol and nonalcoholic drugs. And I placed him on probation for the remainder of his baseball career.

My year and a half with Steve Howe was a difficult time. Because he obviously had medical problems that went beyond recreational drug use, his situation required care and compassion. O'Malley and I both understood that and tried very hard to react accordingly, spending a lot of time consulting our medical experts and one another. In the final analysis, it fell my lot to take tough action against him if our drug program was to have any credibility at all.

In the summer of 1983, with my tenure as commissioner increasingly uncertain, I learned of a grand jury investigation that would seriously affect four members of the Kansas City Royals—Willie Wilson, Willie Aikens, Jerry Martin and Vida Blue. I called Don Fehr of the Players Association saying the situation looked serious to me and suggesting he see that the players had proper legal representation. It seemed all wrong. Kansas City was a model franchise with a wholesome environment, beautiful ballpark, enthusiastic crowds and Ewing and Muriel Kauffman, who had given the franchise a superior image. No one in baseball took greater or more understandable pride in their organization and city.

In October, the players pleaded guilty to a charge of attempting to possess cocaine. A month later, Wilson, Aikens and Martin were sentenced to a year in prison, fined and put on two-year probation. The court suspended all but three months of the prison terms. Blue's sentencing was delayed until December. These were the first prison sentences ever given active baseball players on drug charges.

U.S. District Magistrate J. Milton Sullivant, in his decision, said, ". . . a professional athlete . . . does occupy a special place in society, and the Court realizes that the life of a professional athlete is not all roses. . . . But all the Court can do is take the totality of circumstances as found in the record in this case and the limitations imposed by the statute and impose a sentence which the Court feels will meet the objectives in this particular case and that is rehabilitation and deterrence to others similarly situated as well as to others that hold you out as a model, a role model, in their lives, particularly the younger individuals."

In our investigatory interviews, all three players admitted the use of cocaine. To his credit, Wilson asked to see me personally in New York. Dignified and restrained, he handled himself well, expressing remorse for his conduct.

Five days after the sentencing, the Executive Committee of the Players Association fired their executive director, Ken Moffett. Ken had been hired to replace aging Marvin Miller in January 1983. Miller was not enthusiastic about the selection. There could be little question that he did not like Moffett's "conciliation" background. The hard line was all that Miller understood in dealing with management—any management. The Player Relations Committee saw Moffett as an improvement on Miller, although they had hardly been charmed by Moffett's role in the 1980 and 1981 negotiations, where they felt his mediation efforts had tilted toward the Players Association. I did not know him very well but felt his low-key, centrist style could help sweeten the too-sour relationship that had long persisted between the clubs and players. Certainly, his appointment prompted me to engineer the selection of Lee MacPhail to succeed the more hard-nosed Ray Grebey as PRC president. As a result, congeniality and cooperation became the hallmarks of the PA-PRC relationship. Moffett and MacPhail discussed a joint drug program, and Moffett admitted the serious nature of the problem—and, more remarkably, recognized that an effective program had to provide for player discipline.

It seemed to me that Miller, behaving like a mean-spirited badger, undermined Moffett. Newspaper reports suggested that Moffett had not been assiduous enough in attending to his duties but no one in baseball's executive ranks considered that anything more than a sham. To make matters clearer, the Players Association cancelled two days of scheduled meetings of a joint committee of players and clubs on drug and alcohol abuse. "If you want to establish automatic penalties," Miller told the Associated Press, "you've stepped way out of line in my opinion." The AP also reported that "union officials had expressed concern that because of Moffett's involvement with the committee, the union might be put in a position of being involved in enforcing punishment against its own members."

Moffett put the blame for his discharge on Miller and identified the drug issue as critical: "There's no doubt Marvin was involved. He's been involved ever since we had that flap last spring. He's saying there's no animosity but he's ripped me to enough people and it's gotten back to me. His fine hand has been involved. For him to say otherwise, he's a liar. Drugs aren't a win-lose type of situation. There are kids who are messed up and need help, and there are ways to do this short of confrontation. You can't go to the mat on every issue. My sense was that management was making an effort to be conciliatory. I felt this was the way to go, instead of to the brink. I think things will now go back to being confrontational. That's wrong, especially in this day and age when there are so many Greyhound situations, so many air-traffic-controller situations, so many National Football League situations. I think it's about time people came to their senses."

For once, somebody on the player side said that messed-up kids needed not only help but discipline. At a Players Association meeting on December 6 in Maui, Don Fehr was named acting director.

At the request of Fehr and Lee MacPhail, who were reviewing the ruins of the joint drug-agreement concept, I put off my disciplinary decisions in the Kansas City cases from the beginning of December until the fifteenth. I had no optimism, however, that anything was in the offing that would help me decide what to do. As to Wilson, Martin and Aikens, I sought the views of Fehr, the league presidents, Barry Rona, who was counsel to the Player Relations Committee, and my own lawyers, Sandy Hadden and Ed Durso. All except Fehr, who thought the jail sentences were excessive, recognized that I had to make a significant move, although Rona warned about the grievance process that was always hanging over my head. Fehr also argued that the club, not the commissioner, had the responsibility for discipline. Fehr well understood the clubs' reluctance to discipline their players. I also reviewed background on the players, which had been furnished by their representatives.

On December 15, the same day that I suspended Steve Howe for the 1984 season, I also suspended Wilson, Aikens and Martin for the year, setting May 15 as a date to review their situation. I put them all on two-year probation following their release from confinement. The probation included mandatory drug testing. In my decision, I said, "It is beyond question that their activities have proven detrimental to the best interest of the Kansas City Royals and of Baseball. Each of these players has failed to conform to the 'high standards of personal conduct' required by his Uniform Player's Contract. The game's integrity and the public's confidence in it are jeopardized."

Miller's comments to the press speak for themselves. To *Newsday* he said: "Ha, ha, ha, the whole thing is funny. Now he's [Kuhn] a federal judge. That's delusions of grandeur to the nth degree. Ha, ha, ha. Bowie is a lame duck with strange ideas. The fact of the matter is that this Swan Song of Bowie is going to be reversed."

To *USA Today:* "Kuhn has made absurd decisions for more than a decade. This is no exception. . . . The notion that somehow he will help matters by taking a swing at people who are already down is about as un-American a decision as I have seen. If it wasn't tragic to the players involved, the whole thing would be comical."

Marvin's cranky remarks suggested a man out of touch with the real problems of the world around him.

By contrast, my decisions in the Kansas City and Howe cases were unusually well received by the press. They were as supportive of me as they were vexed by the criticism that exploded spontaneously from the Players Association. Dave Anderson of *The New York Times,* who rarely had a good word for me, blasted the Association's reaction: "Perhaps the Players Association should be quiet and subdued, too. Instead of attacking Bowie Kuhn, it should be cooperating with him—as the National Football League Players Association did when Commissioner Pete Rozelle suspended several players several months ago, as the National Basketball Association Players Association did in formulating a drug policy with Commissioner Larry O'Brien. Until the Players Association cooperates with Bowie Kuhn and his successor, it will only add to baseball's problem, not solve it."

Darrell Porter, speaking to UPI's Milton Richman, said, "We're no different from anybody else. It's about time we buckled down. You hear guys crying about the invasion of their privacy and their rights, and to me it's a lotta noise. We've gotta become responsible for what we do. We gotta quit worrying so much about our own rights and start doing what's really right for everyone."

Jim Kaat, speaking at Franklin and Marshall College, urged the players to submit to voluntary drug testing to "show the public that we've got nothing to hide. It would be a great step in the eyes of the public," he said, and felt it might enable baseball to recover the "honor" that was lost in the drug scandals.

Jim Murray, the respected columnist of the *Los Angeles Times*, noting the increased difficulty of disciplinary enforcement from Judge Landis's time to the present, gave me strong support: "So, there you have it. In Landis' day, baseball punished its transgressors irrespective of society's view of the matter or its forgiveness. In Kuhn's day, baseball's right to do so is challenged even when society has already condemned and isolated the wrongdoers from its ranks.

"What is going on? Is cocaine addiction a crime on the streets but not in the dugout? Is trafficking in it none of baseball's business unless it takes place at home plate? Is Judge Landis' saving of the game's integrity just an old fashioned notion and not applicable for Bowie Kuhn?

"Say it ain't so, somebody."

The Players Association dutifully filed a grievance. We had a March hearing in Tampa before arbitrator Richard Bloch. A month later, Bloch overruled my season-long suspension, paring it back to May 15. Technically, his decision pertained only to Wilson and Martin, but for practical purposes it also controlled Aikens.

This sent yet another negative signal to our players. That troubled me. But there were positive aspects in that he did sustain the suspension in part and totally upheld my probation and drug-testing provisions. The Players Association grumbled even about that.

I required the three players to meet with me in New York before reporting to their respective teams. I had short meetings with each and warned them that they were on probation and explained what that meant. They assured me there would be no further problems. As I looked into their eyes that day, I believed them. It had been a tough experience; they wanted no more of it.

That left Vida Blue's situation unresolved. In December, Judge Sullivant had imposed the same prison sentence on Blue as on Wilson, Aikens and Martin. At the sentencing, Blue was eloquent with regard to the drug problem: "I'm Vida Blue, professional baseball player, more important, the person. I've let an awful lot of people down and the past few months have really been bad for me, my friends and fans. I regret that it took something this tragic to make me realize that there was something inside of me lying so dormant that was so terrible that when aroused would cause such shame and disgrace to me and my associates. This experience has made me come to appreciate the real Vida Blue, a real person. A person that cares about the opportunity that this great country of ours has given him. I would like to say also to the people of today that drugs in our everyday use, in our society, is very dangerous. It's a very dangerous disease and a very powerful disease. It's made midgets out of giants. It has made bums out of executives and it has made crybabies out of the strongest person. I think drugs in our society in my mind would rank as the Number One potential killer today along with cancer, which is a very deadly disease. And chemical dependency if not checked and controlled can be just as deadly as cancer. . . ."

Blue was always an enigma, from his wondrous debut in 1970 to the day he walked through the prison gate. His fabulous skills seemed to have promised so much more than had been fulfilled. I surmised, incorrectly as it turned out, that the prison gate had closed his career.

Throughout my years as commissioner, I was fated to be involved with Vida. In my early years, I had intervened in the long contract dispute between Finley and Blue. At the midpoint of my administration, I vetoed Blue's sale to the Yankees and then vetoed another sale to the Cincinnati Reds. Now, at the close of my career, the veteran pitcher was testing me one final time.

Released from prison in late March, Blue and his agent looked for a club interested in his services. Some months went by with no takers until the San Francisco Giants in June told him they would be willing to sign him to a Triple A contract, thereby precipitating a confrontation between me and Blue. I was more than mildly annoyed at the Giants for creating a problem where none need have existed. I advised the Giants and the Players Association that any signing was prohibited pending my decision on possible discipline. The Players Association filed the usual grievance and my decision was overturned by Arbitrator Bloch.

I was not going to be deterred. I went to the Federal Correctional Institute at Fort Worth to interview a man named Mark Liebl who had been the principal supplier of cocaine to the Kansas City players and who had been convicted and imprisoned. I suspect it was the first time a sports commissioner had ever "gone to jail" in pursuit of his duties. Liebl told a story both credible and devastating about Blue's use of cocaine, his responsibility for its use by other players and his involving a teenage clubhouse boy in a cocaine party.

On the basis of our full investigation, I suspended Blue for the remainder of 1984. I also placed him on probation for two years with mandatory drug testing. The Association again filed a grievance, but this time they lost out completely. In sustaining my decision, Bloch wrote:

> He [Blue] was far more than a mere passive user or possessor. He was vigorously involved in continuous, heavy use of cocaine. He served as an active connection between other ballplayers who were, or became, users and their supplier, Mark Liebl. He placed himself between the players and the distributor as a liasion, even to the extent of ordering cocaine from the clubhouse. He maintained a close, continuous relationship with a man who was both selling cocaine and giving it away to players brought to him by Vida Blue. The Commissioner accurately characterizes Blue as being at the center—the 'focal point'—of Liebl's spreading involvement with the Kansas City Royals.

My earlier disappointments with the arbitration process were mild compared with my reaction to the result in the matter of pitcher Pascual Perez. Perez, a twenty-six-year-old native of the Dominican Republic, was a fifteen-game winner for the Atlanta Braves in 1983 and a member of the National League All-Star team. He had gone to the Braves from Pittsburgh the year before, and was best remembered for missing a start when he could not find his way off the freeway and into the Atlanta Stadium parking lot. He circled the stadium three times and finally ran out of gas. He had gotten his driver's license that same morning.

He was playing winter ball in the Dominican Republic when he was arrested on January 9, 1984, in Santiago with a half gram of cocaine in his wallet. He told police that he did not know what it was and that it had been given to him by a woman in Atlanta.

A hearing was held in Santiago on January 25, at which Perez gave the following answers to questions:

Q. Why did that girl [in Atlanta] give it to you?
A. She gave it to me as a gift, but I did not know what it had.
Q. That girl that you are talking about, did that girl give it to you in order for you to give it to another person(s), or was it a gift for you?
A. She gave it to me as a gift, but I didn't know that it was that and it was not the amount that was stated, either.
Q. What is the name of the girl who gave you the drugs?
A. I don't know her name.
Q. What was the relationship between you and the young woman who gave you the drugs?
A. We were friends.
Q. How long did you know the young woman who gave you the drugs?
A. I met her in the year 1982.
Q. When she gave you [the packet] didn't you ask her what it was and why she was giving it to you?
A. (No response.)
Q. If you didn't know what it was . . . why did you put it in your wallet and bring it to Santo Domingo?
A. In my haste I put it in my wallet.
Q. How was the substance wrapped?
A. In a little, transparent, plastic bag, you could see it.
Q. How is it possible that you didn't notice when you put it in your wallet?
A. While I was putting everything in hastily, I put it in there.
Q. Pascual, did you know that drugs are prohibited in this country?
A. I knew they were prohibited, but I don't know what drugs are.
Q. Why do you think the police detained you?
A. Perhaps because of egoism, because everybody knows me.

The answers were hardly credible.

On March 23, Perez, who had been in jail since his January arrest, was tried and found guilty of possession of cocaine. He was fined 1,000 gold pesos (approximately $400).

I told John Mullen of the Braves I wanted Perez in New York before he joined the ballclub. On April 14, Perez and his representatives arrived at our offices to be questioned by Harry Gibbs, Ed Durso (our assistant counsel) and Miguel Rodriguez (our Caribbean baseball coordinator, who conducted the questioning in Spanish).

We received many of the same answers Perez had given at the January hearing in Santiago. He had no idea who the woman was, where she lived or what she had given him. We wanted to know if she was a social acquaintance, whether he was part of a trafficking situation, whether there were gamblers involved. But we were given no cooperation by Perez. For his failure to cooperate and for his possession of cocaine, I suspended him through May 15 and placed him on a one-year probation. It was hardly the discipline I thought the situation warranted but it conformed to arbitrator Bloch's handling of the Kansas City cases. Like it or not, I was being practical.

Fehr had called me a few days before to share some thoughts about Perez. By now, Fehr had become acting head of the Players Association. He was bright, and had often provided me with useful ideas. He had also given me a lot of trouble and grief, but that was inescapable if he was going to do his job. As to Perez, Fehr felt he might have been set up and argued that the Santiago authorities made no analysis of the substance in his possession. He felt that Perez's statements in Santiago had been made under stressful circumstances. In short, he did not think I should rely on the Dominican judicial process. I felt that Perez was deluding Fehr and that the substance of the case clearly supported the decision I was about to make.

The day after my decision, Fehr filed a grievance. On April 29, arbitrator Bloch threw out the suspension and the probation, permitting Perez to pitch immediately. He found a lack of evidence that Perez had been involved with cocaine, rejecting the determination of the Dominican court.

The Associated Press speculated that I might be close to "spitting profanities"; they were not far off.

"Considering Mr. Perez's obvious lack of candor," I said, "I find this determination as inexplicable as Mr. Bloch's order of reinstatement. My overall reaction to Mr. Bloch's full decision is that it has done great damage to our drug prevention program. Of course, another contributor to this damage has been the continuing, improvident opposition of the Players Association to virtually all our efforts to deal with this problem."

The press's sympathy did little to alleviate my outrage. With five months to go in my term of office, I was running out of time to find solutions. I knew we had made progress. I knew I had gotten the players' attention with my suspensions, even though some had been modified or overruled. But I had not solved the problem. The heart-breaking part of all this was that it could have been solved but for the resistance of the Association.

There is little evidence of renewed drug abuse after my struggles with players, with their union and arbitrators. The well-publicized 1985 drug trials in Pittsburgh involving twenty-four players all dealt with events from the seasons preceding my suspensions. Maybe a message did get through.

One final chapter had to be written—a joint management-union drug program. MacPhail for the Player Relations Committee and Fehr for the Players Association had been working on it, along with their top people, for months. As I saw it, the key was whether or not a meaningful testing program could be adopted. The Association was adamant; it would not agree to mandatory testing. Lee, who would have preferred testing, believed that even without it a useful program could be put together. So did Fehr. In May 1984, the two men reached agreement on a program that was hinged on a three-man panel of drug experts to consider player cases submitted by clubs and on a reduction of salary for players (like Steve Howe) requiring repeat treatment. Lee urged my support, which I could not in good conscience give. The Players Association's want of concern as to drugs led me to believe that this program was de-signed to delude the public and blunt my assault on drug viola-tions. I doubted their good faith and could not recommend it to the clubs.

I cancelled a major-league meeting scheduled to consider the proposal on May 24. I knew the votes were not there.

Fehr asked to see me. I always saw Don if he wanted to talk. This time he took me by surprise. Normally a man who spoke with restraint, he roared his disapproval of my handling of the drug cases, questioning my motivations, citing the Perez case in particu-lar because he thought the Dominican procedures were a joke, and screamed about my failure to support him and Lee (and the major-league committee that had supported Lee) on the joint drug program. He concluded emotionally, saying he was genuinely de-termined to make the program work and to eliminate baseball's drug problem, but without my support, he said, there would be no program. His speech had taken about thirty minutes. Only Fehr had spoken. He had opened by saying he did not know how to proceed; so he was just going to wade in. That he had done. By stump speech standards, it had been a pretty good show. (Stump speeches are a sort of flea market of ideas, mostly bric-a-brac, but are apt to contain an occasional good item.) Don had included an item that caught my attention, namely his promise of good faith in getting rid of drugs. I said very little when he was through and finished the meeting by saying I would think about it. I later told him I was impressed by his good-faith promise but as to the rest of the baloney I had heard, it was insulting and he was lucky I had not punched him in the nose. I suggested he stop acting like a smart-assed kid and learn some manners. However, I said I would talk to Lee.

A commissioner's skills must include the ability to decline most of the myriad requests he receives, many of which are selfish, crazy or ill considered. My resolve to be negative when necessary was severely tested by our league presidents. I had five in my time—Joe Cronin, Warren Giles, Chub Feeney, Lee MacPhail and Bobby Brown. These were fine, dedicated men, and their requests were hard to turn down.* Lee by now was our PRC director, a job I had strongly urged him to take. He now backed up Don's request because he felt their joint program would work. Lacking faith in the program but having a lot in Lee, I told him I would go along on the condition that a number of changes be made in the program that would commit the Players Association to a more positive attitude toward voluntary drug testing. I also said that when I issued a new and tougher set of drug discipline rules, I did not want the Players Association going out of its way to attack them. Lee and his counsel, Barry Rona, told me they thought the conditions would be acceptable to Fehr. After discussing the situation with Fehr, the Executive Council and the PRC, I called a major-league meeting on June 27. The joint program, which I supported, was adopted by a large majority. There were two dissenting votes.

*When Brown succeeded MacPhail as American League President in 1984, we started the vogue of doctors as league presidents. With the arrival of Dr. A. Bartlett Giamatti as National League president in 1986, the process was complete. Though one was in medicine and the other humanities, it was a nice touch. Actually, I would have preferred their skills to be in psychiatry, but perhaps that was asking too much.

The program had the following features:

- A three-man board of professionals would review cases brought by clubs suspecting players of drug abuse.
- During treatment, the player would get full pay for thirty days, half pay for the next thirty, and then be paid at the rate of the major-league minimum.
- The commissioner could discipline a player convicted of a drug charge, or using or distributing drugs at the ballpark, although the Players Association could file a grievance.

On June 28 I issued my own new set of drug discipline and treatment rules:

- Players convicted of a crime related to the distribution of a controlled substance and those who facilitate the use by others, will be suspended without pay for a minimum of one year and could be declared permanently ineligible.
- Players convicted of or pleading guilty to any crime related to possession or use of a controlled substance and those found in possession of or using any controlled substance on the playing field or premises of a stadium will be suspended for one year without pay.
- Any player disciplined under these rules and later caught violating any of them will be subject to such discipline as in the opinion of the commissioner may be appropriate under the circumstances which could include permanant ineligibility.
- If a player voluntarily seeks assistance for his problem, he will be granted amnesty on the first occasion and not be subject to discipline but will be subject to probation, which could include testing, aftercare and community service.

These rules were much tougher than any we had posted to date. Good to his word, Fehr made no public outcry.

When I got back to New York from the major-league meeting, I called Fehr and congratulated him on the adoption of the program, which the players had approved a month earlier by an overwhelming majority. He asked if I would consider visiting the Association's office to talk about the new drug rules I was about to issue. I strolled over to visit Fehr, Mark Belanger and Gene Orza. Don showed me around the office and introduced me to the staff. He stopped at one point and said, "Bowie, I will never understand why there is such a furor in the press over your leaving. You've been a good commissioner and served for over fifteen years. How many CEOs ever serve so long? I think you ought to be proud of that." Everyone was very cordial—even Mark, who was more heartwarming at shortstop than in a conference room.

It was my first visit to the Association's office since I paid a courtesy call on Marvin Miller the day after I became commissioner in 1969. The press took note of the visit. When asked why it had taken so long, I replied, "No one ever asked me before."

I had my doubts the drug program would work, but given the dreadful nature of the problem, what alternative did we have but to try?

In October 1985, eleven months after I left office, the clubs abandoned the joint program. Since they and Commissioner Ueberroth had not been able to persuade the Association to accept mandatory drug testing, I found it hard to quarrel with their termination of the program. Still, there would be no ultimate solution until the clubs and players found a way to work together.

25

The Casino Conflict

Linda de Roulet, who was president of the Mets in 1979, called me during that season to tell me that Willie Mays, who was a batting instructor for the club, had been offered a contract to do public relations work for Bally's Park Place Casino in Atlantic City. She wanted to know if it was permissible for him to hold both jobs. I replied that I had a real problem with overlapping jobs between casinos and baseball. She said that was all she needed to know at that time. I suspected that my answer did not break her heart. It had not been easy to get Willie to work as the Mets desired, not for Linda or for Don Grant before her, as I well knew. As beloved as Willie was, he was a hard man for the boss to keep on schedule.

I next heard from Al Rosen, who had left the Yankees' presidency to become executive vice president of Bally's. Al was a good guy and a friend. "Commissioner," he said, "I hear you have problems about Mays' coming to Bally's. I assure you we'll keep him away from the gaming operations. Please don't say no right now. Just promise me you'll give it some thought." I told him I was in no rush, but that the chances of my coming out any way but negative were small or none.

At my next weekly meeting with Lee MacPhail, Chub Feeney and Sandy Hadden, I took them through the problem. Much of the business of baseball got done at these "prexy" meetings. We often debated subjects with considerable vigor, but the Mays question was resolved quite simply. None of us saw any way he could have both jobs. There was no debate. We all knew the strong position I had taken on casino questions. When Finley and some of the Braves' officers were revealed to have interests in the Parvin-Dohrmann Company, which owned three Las Vegas casinos, I had directed that they choose between baseball and the casinos.

Del Webb, who with Dan Topping had owned the Yankees for many years until selling to CBS in 1964, came to me in the early 1970s about buying the White Sox. He was the head of Del Webb Corporation, which owned casino operations in Las Vegas. I told him we would love to have him back in the game but only if he was prepared to divest the casino operations. He told me that was not possible but hoped I would reflect on it. He pressed the question subsequently but the answer was the same. He accepted the decision with disappointment but without complaint.

By contrast, Fred Saigh, who had been forced in 1953 to divest himself of the Cardinals when he was imprisoned for tax evasion, was furious when I vetoed his bid to buy the White Sox. He wrote an angry letter that I ignored.

Along with the other team sport commissioners, I had battled state legislatures repeatedly to stop legalized gambling on team sports. We succeeded everywhere but in Canada and Delaware, both of which experimented with sports lottery betting. Both experiments drew litigation from professional sports, the NFL suing Delaware and baseball suing Canada. In both instances, the betting schemes were dropped.

I could see no good reason why I should have one position for Willie Mays and another for Finley and Webb. Nor did I want to undermine my position on legalized gambling on baseball. If our personnel began to work in casino operations, let alone own them, an important support would have been knocked out from under our consistent opposition to legalized gambling. More fundamentally, there was a question of what message Mays' going to Bally's would send to our own people. Were we letting down the bars that had been in place since the time of Judge Landis and the Black Sox? Were we lessening our resolve to support Major League Rule 21, which prohibited gambling on baseball?

If Mays were free to associate with and entertain the big gamblers in Atlantic City, how was I to keep our personnel away from gambling types? We had drummed it into our people for decades that they had to stay away from gamblers. One of the principal activities of my security force was to watch for undesirable associations with our people. Where we found such associations we told our personnel to terminate the relationship. That was common practice. We did

not hesitate to put certain bars and gathering places off-limits if
known gamblers and hoodlums frequented them. I could not have
one rule for Willie Mays and another for everybody else.

In September, Rosen told me that Bally's wanted to go ahead with
Willie. I told him I could not go along with dual employment and
wrote him the following letter:

> Dear Al: September 21, 1979
> I continue to feel that the advice I gave you yesterday regarding
> Willie Mays is good. While I appreciate your efforts to insulate
> him from gambling activities, the fact remains that he would
> clearly represent casino gambling interests. Should he elect to
> go with your organization, then I think he would have to disas-
> sociate himself from his Baseball employment. This would be
> consistent with past precedents. I say this reluctantly because
> I would be unhappy to see him leave Baseball. At the same time
> you are offering him an unusual financial opportunity for a long
> term and I can understand where his personal interests might
> point. Ultimately, it would have to be his decision as to which
> way he wants to go.

By late October, I heard from the Mets that Bally's was about to
announce Mays's employment. Wanting no misunderstanding about
my position, I sent Willie a telegram:

> OCTOBER 26, 1979
> I HAVE BEEN INFORMED THAT YOU ARE ABOUT TO SIGN A LONG-
> TERM CONTRACT WITH BALLY, IN WHICH YOU ARE RENDERING
> SERVICES TO PROMOTE THAT COMPANY'S CASINO GAMBLING
> INTEREST. WHILE I APPRECIATE THE MOTIVATIONS LEADING
> YOU TO THIS ASSOCIATION, IT HAS LONG BEEN MY VIEW THAT
> SUCH ASSOCIATIONS BY PEOPLE IN OUR GAME ARE INCONSIS-
> TENT WITH ITS BEST INTERESTS. ACCORDINGLY, WHILE I AM
> NOT HAPPY AT THE PROSPECT OF LOSING YOUR ACTIVE PARTIC-
> IPATION IN BASEBALL, I MUST REQUEST THAT YOU PROMPTLY
> DISASSOCIATE YOURSELF FROM YOUR CONTRACT WITH THE
> NEW YORK METS.

The telegram was leaked by someone outside my office to the
press and headlines screamed that I was "banning" Mays from baseball. Since that was an egregious misreading of my telegram, which

dealt only with his Mets employment, I sought to clarify the situation with the following release:

> I think there is a clear conflict of interest between working for Baseball and working for an organization which operates gambling casinos.
>
> I would be extremely sorry if Willie Mays chooses to go to work for Bally, but the choice would be completely his and he would make it with advance knowledge of my position on the conflict. There is no implication intended that he has been guilty of any wrongdoing. On the contrary, he has always been a great asset to our game. Nor am I saying he would not be welcome at such events as Old Timers' games. Obviously, he would.
>
> My position is simple: he can continue with us or work for Bally—but not both. I feel certain he has had to wrestle with a tough problem which apparently involves his own long-term financial interests and security.
>
> I would personally be very distressed if he made the choice to join Bally and would still be hopeful that even now he would elect to remain in Baseball.

On the day the telegram was sent, a Friday, I talked to Willie on the telephone and asked him to meet me in my office Monday morning. He arrived at 10:00 A.M. accompanied by his wife, Mae. I had known Mae and Willie since my rookie tour of Arizona as commissioner during the spring of 1969, when she and Willie had dinner with Luisa and me and Joe Reichler. We had talked about all kinds of things that night, including the fact that I was in the Polo Grounds on May 28, 1951, when Mays snapped out of an 0-for-12 major-league batting debut by driving a Warren Spahn pitch over the left-field roof and into the New York night. I was also in the Oakland park when he got his last career hit off Rollie Fingers in the 1973 World Series. He was not picking soft touches at the beginning or end.

I sat in on a Mays performance of a different kind in the 1973 LCS between the Mets and Reds. When the Mets fans, sore at Pete Rose because of his fight with Bud Harrelson, began pelting left fielder Rose with whatever was handy, Sparky Anderson took his team off the field. Chub Feeney asked Mays and other Mets to walk to left field and signal for the crowd to behave. Looking a little shaken at the prospect, they nobly did their duty and in moments the crowd was pacified.

After he became a Met coach, he had a contract disagreement with the team over whether he was spending enough time on his duties. When the dispute percolated into the press, I telephoned Mets chairman Donald Grant and suggested he and Willie meet with me.

"No, no, Commissioner," he said. "I know what'll happen if we do. We'll both be sitting there and Willie will start saying he's sorry and in fifteen minutes we'll all be crying, and I'll take him back and things will be just the same." I laughed at Grant's scenario but persuaded them to come anyway. And his forecast was borne out. In no time at all they were both crying and the dispute was over.

Now, years later, I urged Willie to change his mind, although I realized the hour was late. My effort was in vain. So I told him how deeply I regretted his decision. I also said I would try to find some way to bring him back. As to the headlines saying I had "banned" him, I said that was not so and that he was welcome at any baseball function. I concluded reluctantly that I really could not blame him for making the decision in favor of Bally's. That was so, but in my heart I resented their ability to hire him away. We parted cordially. He walked over to Gallagher's Restaurant, four blocks away, and announced his decision at a noon press conference.

Art Berke of my staff was there and reported to me that "the attitude of the people in attendance was very understanding toward your decision and they were wondering how Willie could ever have thought he could remain on the payroll of the Mets and Bally's." Art was an able fellow and I am sure that his report was accurate. But I braced myself for attacks.

Howard Cosell said the "suspension of Mays from baseball was hypocritical." Like many of his press confreres, he had fallen for the trumped-up notion that Mays had been banned. Even a superior reporter like Howard paid more attention to the headline than the facts. Nor could he understand the distinction between casinos and horse racing, citing the interests of John Galbreath (Pirates) and George Steinbrenner (Yankees) in racetracks. I did not think the horse-racing distinction was either wrong or hypocritical. In the first place, the problems of the casino industry in this country are measurably greater than those in the horse-racing industry. Several months after the Mays press conference, *The New York Times* ran an editorial on the New Jersey casino industry, concluding:

> The scandal unfolding in New Jersey, after only two years of casino activity, shows that gambling is a business so rich, so fast, so powerful and perhaps inevitably so unsavory that it cannot help but undermine government. . . . practically nothing can make casinos worth the risks.

Horse racing had its problems but at least had made an effort to deal with them. The Thoroughbred Racing Protective Association under the leadership of former FBI man Spencer Drayton had done much excellent work to improve the security standards of thoroughbred racing. Baseball before my time had accepted people who were involved in thoroughbred racing, both players and owners. The Galbreath interest in Churchill Downs was one I inherited. I was encumbered by no such historical baggage with regard to casinos. From the first opportunity with Finley and the Braves in 1969, I made it clear that I was drawing a line against overlapping ownership or employment with casinos.

In 1980 I decided to close the door on the future possibility of baseball people owning racetracks—in whole or in part—grandfathering in the existing holdings of Galbreath and Steinbrenner. I wish I had done it several years earlier.

Red Smith had descended on me on this issue, following the same line of horse-racing logic as Cosell. Philosophical bedfellows on this issue, they also thought all Mays would do was "gladhand" or, as Red said, "shake hands, kiss babies and start the peanut race at family picnics." That was naive. Those customers and potential customers with whom Willie would be skillfully drilling golf balls down lush fairways are not interested in the peanut races at the old casino. Not that charming customers is not an honorable American pursuit; it is.

The New York Times fired another sports-page salvo at me with a column by Dave Anderson the day before Red's. Dave said I embarrassed Willie by not talking to him sooner. Actually, that was more like a noodle than a salvo. I had been asked by both the Mets and Bally's about my views and had given unequivocal answers. Willie himself made no inquiry. One way or another he obviously knew the answer.

On the day of Willie's press conference who but Frank Sinatra chipped in with some views as released by his New York public relations firm. He was "outraged" and found it "ludicrous" that I was concerned about Mays's working for a hotel "that happens to have a casino." This was getting pretty funny. He concluded with this good stuff: "Mr. Kuhn told Willie Mays to get out of baseball. I would like to offer the same advice to Mr. Kuhn." I was beginning to learn that fellows who make paid appearances at casinos can get pretty touchy. Anyway, it was enlightening to get Frank's appraisal of my ethics. (By the way, many writers including Shirley Povich, Edwin Pope and Dick Young supported me.)

I made attempts over the years to bring Mays back, hoping to put together a financial package to lure him home. Two clubs and my office might share his services to do public relations work for baseball. Willie and I talked about it from time to time; he was interested. I talked to a good number of clubs but only Bob Lurie of the Giants thought it worth pursuing. Bob was a stalwart. As the years went on, Willie became more and more settled into Bally's, more comfortable with his job and I suspect happy enough to stay put.

When it came Mickey Mantle's turn to enter the glittering casino world, the trail that Mays and I had followed was clear enough. Before 1983 spring training, George Steinbrenner told me Mantle had an offer to work at the Claridge Hotel in Atlantic City, another gambling operation. I told him that the Mays precedent would preclude Mantle from carrying out his contract as a spring training instructor with the Yankees. He accepted the answer without protest. That in itself was something of an upset. I then talked to Lee MacPhail, who was close to Mantle as I was not. I suggested that Mantle might be dissuaded. Lee talked to Mantle and reported back to me that Mantle for financial reasons had made up his mind to take the casino job. He told Lee further that he fully understood he would have to give up his Yankees job. There would be no complaint on that score by Mantle.

Six months after I left office, Peter Ueberroth lifted my restriction on both Mays and Mantle. He and I had talked about their situation a number of times in the preceding year. He wanted to understand my reasoning. The day he announced his decision, he forewarned me. Having gotten to be a pretty good Ueberroth watcher, I was not surprised. Peter has a superior sense of public relations, better than mine. He trusts his own instincts wherever they lead him. Showing "compassion" and "respect" for two of the greatest stars of the game would play well from Montauk to Cypress Point. He concluded by saying he knew that I strongly disagreed with his decision and expected me to say so publicly. I did.

The "Bowie Bans Mays and Mantle" headline still seemed popular with the news media, and indeed, with Willie and Mickey them-

selves. It was not uncommon to read a dispatch such as one filed by
filed by the Associated Press in Denver in June 1986:

> Hall of Famer Mickey Mantle donned the No. 7 Yankee pin-
> stripe uniform for the Denver Dream Old Timers game, his first
> appearance on a baseball diamond since his banishment in 1983
> by then-Commissioner Bowie Kuhn. . . .
> Kuhn banished Mantle from baseball when the former Yan-
> kee veteran accepted a position with a company that owns
> Atlantic City gambling casinos.
> "Since most of my work for that company is for charity
> events, I really felt I should have never been suspended," Man-
> tle said.
> "I guess if Bowie Kuhn was still commissioner, I probably
> would still be under suspension.
> "The lifting of the ban is important to me because now I can
> attend the Yankees' Old Timer's game this year. . . ."

Mantle of course was always free to attend Old Timer's games, as
was Mays. They both knew that.

Over the years after he had left the Mets, Mays grew fond of
saying, "I didn't do anything wrong." It was a strawman he was fond
of punching—a mischievous but essentially harmless exercise. I
imagine it made him feel better. But it was so. He didn't do anything
wrong. Neither did I.

26

Strike Two

U ntil 1981 there had never been a major strike in baseball. Since the origins of major-league baseball stretch back to 1876, it was a remarkable record, perhaps unmatched in North American business history. When the players established a union in 1966 and selected Marvin Miller to run it, that record was doomed.

While the basic origins of the strike were in 1967, connections could be found in 1976 and 1980. The explosive arrival of free agency in 1976 had sent salaries soaring to record highs by 1981. The average salary was $196,500. The industry, which had experienced a series of essentially break-even years through 1979, had a loss of $19 million in 1980, by far the largest in its history. And in my state-of-baseball address at our annual meetings in December 1980 I forecast that 1981 had every prospect of being worse. Moreover, the Players Association was growing so powerful, it threatened to take control of the game away from the clubs. It was an issue over which management was ready to hand-wrestle crocodiles.

Nineteen eighty had seen the adoption of a new basic agreement between clubs and players as the result of negotiations that began in 1979 and ran through May 1980. Everything had been on the table, but the biggest issue was increased compensation to clubs losing free agents. It was the position of management that when a ranking player was lost, the club losing the player should be entitled to receive a player of major-league quality in return from the club taking the player.

There were many other major issues as well, including minimum salaries, benefit-plan contribution, benefit-plan vesting, salary scale, salary arbitration modifications, service period to achieve free agency, reentry-draft modifications and health and safety issues.

In the 1979/80 negotiations, the Players Association faced a new bargainer for the PRC, Ray Grebey. With the retirement of John Gaherin in 1978, the PRC had retained Heidrick & Struggles to handle an executive search for a suitable replacement. The search produced three finalists and the PRC gathered in my office to interview the candidates. Why anybody would want such an impossible job was a mystery, but the PRC was blessed with three excellent men to consider. The unenviable task of the bargainer was to find the balance between the Players Association and Miller on the one hand and twenty-six demonstrably difficult club owners on the other. To make matters worse, the poor fellow was sure to have a commissioner and his staff watching his every move.

Over the course of a decade the difficult job had turned the congenial Gaherin into a crossly suspicious executive who easily might have preferred a ring of grizzly bears to the friends upon whom he relied in baseball. Because I liked Gaherin and had been instrumental in his hiring, I was happy to see him escape to a far, far better world. Not only did he escape, his congeniality returned and persists to this day.

The PRC's analysis of the newest candidates for our special brand of bedlam was swift. Grebey was selected as the nearly unanimous choice of the group. One of the other two finalists was Jack Donlan of National Airlines who, undaunted, became Grebey's counterpart at the NFL. Neither man could have anticipated what rigorous years lay ahead.

Grebey came from a long career in industrial relations at General Electric, which had a reputation for maintaining a tough stance against its unions. Many speculated that he was to be a "hired gun" who was expected to break the Players Association if possible. That was not the fact. The PRC had neither illusions nor aspirations on this score. They were as enlightened and sensible a group as their chairman, Ed Fitzgerald. They hired Grebey because he made a good impression on them, checked out well, and had the experience for the job.

Some of my defenders in and out of baseball who would like to blame the 1981 strike on Grebey argue that I had no involvement in the hiring of Grebey. That is not true. Not only was he interviewed and hired in my very own office, but there is no way he would have been hired without my concurrence. There was no way the PRC was going to hire a man with whom I was uncomfortable even though it was clearly the PRC's final call.

Unquestionably, some owners like Gussie Busch of the Cardinals hoped they could completely isolate me from PRC activities. When the PRC was set up as a separate corporation in 1978, with its own charter and bylaws and with the twenty-six clubs as its only shareholders, I am sure Gussie and his collaborators thought I was isolated. Those who wanted that isolation resented my role in 1976, when I supported the players and ended the owners' closure of the spring training camps. But the clear majority of clubs fully understood that the commissioner and his ability to influence events and people could not so easily be quarantined, nor did they desire a quarantine. The reasons for my behavior during the 1981 strike, as we shall see, had nothing to do with a lack of influence. Perhaps the 1978 corporate change had technically curbed my power, but that was academic so long as I was free to influence the course of events.

The clubs made unusual preparations for the 1979/80 negotiations. These included $50 million of strike insurance, a mutual-assistance fund of $7 million and a stringent discipline system that permitted an owners' discipline committee to fine clubs up to $500,-000 for conduct harmful to the clubs' collective bargaining interests. Quite obviously, they were gearing up for an unprecedented effort to unify the management position as Miller had so successfully unified the players'.

There was quite a furor among the clubs in November 1979 when *The New York Times*'s Murray Chass broke the story of the discipline rule and the mutual-assistance fund. Of the discipline system, one owner said, "It's childish and it's ridiculous; it restricts our freedom of speech." Another executive told Chass it was "collusive—in direct violation of the antitrust laws." Legally, all of that was nonsense. More important, it demonstrated the problem the clubs had in maintaining any sort of unity. They had barely adopted initiatives to control themselves and facilitate their collective bargaining activities, when some seized the opportunity to tell the press the initiatives were unconstitutional and otherwise illegal. The folks in *Alice in Wonderland* would have understood that perfectly well, and so would Miller, who received these gifts like an annuitant's benefits, but to many it was a puzzling form of insanity that gripped certain owners as surely as there were collective bargaining negotiations.

PRC chairman Fitzgerald led his committee and Grebey into negotiation preparations from which emerged the first set of tough demands the clubs had ever made to the Players Association. Foremost among these were free-agent compensation and a salary scale.

The compensation plan stated that if a free-agent player was selected in the November reentry draft by a substantial number of clubs, the club losing him would be able to select a player not on the fifteen-man protected list of the club signing the free agent. This meant that the "losing" club would have an opportunity to get a major-league player in return, although not the quality of the player lost. The clubs saw this as basic "equity." They also saw it as a natural evolution of the free-agency system adopted in 1976 that both sides had recognized as "experimental."

The salary scale would have created a stipulated annual maximum salary for players with less than six years of major-league service. All contracts for such players would be for a single year. Pending the outcome of the negotiations, the PRC asked the clubs to tender these players' contracts for 1980 only.

Collective bargaining began in November 1979 and rolled along quietly into 1980. That was the way bargaining usually went: pretty low-key in the early months as the parties fenced with one another and then becoming strident as the approaching season built the pressure. Since these old adversaries, the Players Association and the PRC, had never learned to trust one another, there was no hope for resolution of problems on a sensible schedule. We always had the painful, highly public trial by collective ordeal. While historical reasons to justify both in their distrust were plentiful, there was little prospect of the animosity's wearing away so long as Miller was in charge.

The Major League Baseball Promotion Corporation authorized a professional research organization to do a March fan study in the major-league markets. The results showed that 43 percent would be "bothered" by a strike; that on specific issues like salary arbitration the clubs' position was heavily favored; and that after hearing the issues, the clubs were felt to be right by a 55 percent–25 percent margin. The most surprising figure to me was the 43 percent who were "bothered." I would have expected a much higher percentage. The fans were probably more tolerant than we thought.

The Players Association was so frightened by the prospect of increased compensation that they truly would not bargain on the issue. They were convinced it would have an adverse effect on the movement of free-agent players. This was a harbinger of the difficulties to come in 1981.

By mid-March, the PRC dropped its proposal for a salary scale in an effort to find an agreement, the Players Association having called the proposal "the greatest obstacle to a settlement." Grebey said, "There is no valid reason why the season should not open on time." Still, as the last week of spring training approached there was no agreement as the Players Association continued to resist compensation and to make demands for benefit-plan contributions that the clubs felt were unreasonable.

From where I stood, the process was going along about as expected. The parties were willing to meet and bargain, with concessions being made here and there. I saw no reason why they could not bargain into the season, if necessary, as we had done in 1976 and as the NFL and NBA had done at other times.

I supported the PRC position on compensation and felt as strongly as any of its members that compensation was necessary for baseball. The PRC liked to talk about the "equity" of the proposal and that was fine. I talked publicly about its "fairness to the fans" who, I felt, should see something a little more like a trade, albeit a badly balanced one, when their club lost a top free-agent player. As a fan, I would have been appalled to see stars walking away from a club with no professional joining the team in return. I was also convinced that compensation would help us maintain competitive balance in baseball.

The Players Association and much of the press criticized me for favoring the owners on this point. I was not about to stay silent simply because I agreed with the owners. If their position was right for baseball, I thought it was my duty to support them and to take whatever criticism might come. Well before the 1979/80 negotiations began, I had met privately with Miller and told him I thought compensation was necessary for baseball in light of our experience with free agency. I also warned him that the clubs were determined on this issue and that he should not misread either their determination or my support. He replied, "Bowie, they'll get compensation over my dead body."

As March wound down with little progress, the PRC elected to bring the Federal Mediation and Conciliation Service into the bargaining. Ken Moffett of that service came to the talks, a role that would occupy him in 1980 and 1981. In time he would succeed Miller as executive director of the Players Association. A patient, quiet man, his drawn visage marked him as the roadrunner he was. He entered the negotiations in Palm Springs, California, but was unable to head off a step by Miller designed to pressure the owners into a settlement. On April 1, Miller announced that the players were striking the balance of the spring training games, which meant that ninety-two games were blotted out. He said the players would open the season on April 9 but would strike if there was no agreement by midnight May 22.

I thought it was an irresponsible and unnecessary move. I would have felt otherwise if the PRC had been refusing to negotiate or make concessions. That simply was not the case. Miller was overplaying his hand without comprehending that the clubs really were determined to make a battle for compensation. Miller thought he could bluff the issue away. This would prove a costly mistake.

As for the PRC's willingness to negotiate and make concessions, I had followed every detail of these negotiations to assure that that was so. My office was thoroughly briefed on every bargaining session and monitored virtually every meeting of the PRC. While it was not the commissioner's job to formulate the PRC proposals, I could assure that they bargained in good faith, a fact that was fully understood, if sometimes resented, by individual PRC members. Keep in mind that as a practical matter the PRC chairman, the league presidents and the league lawyers were at all times closely allied with me and I with them. Given those alliances, my ability to influence the PRC was very great—much more so than some of our archconservatives such as Gussie Busch would have liked.

During April and May, Miller intensified his media campaign. It was his best skill. His striking the last week of spring training and his threat of a strike to come on May 23 needed an offsetting public relations campaign. He developed a series of themes that he worked hard to sell to the media. He argued that the owners' strike insurance and mutual-assistance fund would actually make things "profitable" for them if there was a strike. He said owners were supposedly telling him that they could be fined $1 million for just talking to him. He was sure the owners wanted to provoke a strike so as to "dismantle" the Players Association. He saw the owners as indifferent about an agreement because none attended negotiating meetings. All of this was pure hokum, but much of the press carried it faithfully and many embellished on it, none more than Red Smith and Howard Cosell.

Howard, a difficult man to dupe, went on-air with these comments: "What they now must seek to avoid is the posture of trying to break a union, and they're getting suspiciously close to that posture. There is breakage in the owners ranks, you haven't read about that, but it's true. The basic point is you can't turn back the clock to the 1920s when Pinkerton guards on management's behalf shot down workers before the age of the great trade unions. What will happen here is that baseball will be set back for a decade or more because that union will not be broken. They'll be supported by every great union in America and the rank and file will come to understand it's not what the players make that's at issue it's the principle of union."

Both Cosell and Smith used the phrase "free enterprise" to describe the core issue. Both argued that since court rulings had given the players free agency, it was contrary to the American spirit of free enterprise to modify that free agency with compensation. Smith's May 12 column in *The New York Times* made the point: "If a buyer of designer jeans for Gimbels, having discharged his obligations to that employer, went over to Macy's, Macy's would not be expected to send a buyer of pantyhose over to Gimbels. This is known as free enterprise.

"Nobody gives more pious lip service to the free-enterprise system than the typical owner of a baseball club. But he does not want it operating in baseball. In spite of a whole series of court rulings, he still believes his players are property, and when he loses one he is entitled to compensation."

The philosophy of Smith and Cosell was woefully wide of the mark. The free-agency system had been recognized by players and clubs alike as experimental and subject to change by both sides. Attachment One of the 1976 basic agreement said, "The parties recognize that the provisions of the Agreement concerning player control establish a new dimension in their collectively bargained relationship and, therefore, to a degree must be regarded as experimental." No court decision had pretended to take away either side's absolute right to bargain for change, nor could it. As to free enterprise, labor agreements always abridge the parties' free enterprise. That is what they are all about. Like it or not, that is the system.

On the union-busting issue, I told Cosell he had "fallen into Miller's trap; do you think for a second I would stand by and let the clubs try to destroy the Association? Miller would never protect me on anything but you can be darned sure I would protect him if that ever happened. That is not what is happening. The owners in their wildest dreams don't think they can achieve that. Oh, Gussie Busch might but the rest know the Association will be here tomorrow and ten years from tomorrow. They want compensation and are ready to fight for it. And I happen to think they're one hundred percent right."

Howard, contrary to the impression many people have of him, is an extremely good listener. He listened carefully to me but was not persuaded. I suspect, but do not know, that Howard was being told by an owner that the clubs were trying to "bust" the union. Unfortunately, sources, particularly those that will not be identified, are often wrong.

Cosell and Smith, along with many others, were persuaded by Miller's argument that baseball compensation, like NFL compensation, would destroy the free-agency process. Never mind that the proposal on the table was too limited to have any such effect. It was laughable to think that it would deter a Steinbrenner if he was intent on signing a star free agent. Hungry barracuda would be more easily restrained than George. Moreover, the PRC was prepared to meet the Players Association's concerns through bargaining as indicated by modifications they had already made to deal with questions raised by the Association.

In April, Dave Klein, writing for *The Sporting News*, had dealt with what I would do if there were a long strike:

> At that point, the resolve hardened. It was visible in the commissioner's face. It was the look of a hard, strong man fully cognizant of his authority and options.
>
> "While I don't feel I should step in and force things because I don't look upon this as a bleak and dire crisis, that could change if it began to look as though we were going to get a long and serious strike," he said. "That's when I'd play my hole card."
>
> And what is that hole card?
>
> "I can't say now," Kuhn responded. "In truth, I haven't looked at it yet. I know it's there, and I don't want to use it, but if the time comes, I'll turn it over and play it . . . and accept the consequences."
>
> ". . . But if there is a strike . . . if they leave the field and threaten the season . . . then, of course, that would be the climate for me to act more visibly, more decisively. However, I am completely confident it won't come to that."

My observation that I had a "hole card" (be it the use of arbitration or forcing management to shift its position) turned out to be academic in 1980. (It was not in 1981, when I came exceedingly close to turning that hole card over.)

My telephone was ringing constantly with advice from friends in and out of baseball. Speaker Tip O'Neill, calling "just as a Red Sox fan," said Americans had enough trouble and urged me to shut the adversaries up in a room. Pitcher Jim Kaat told me compensation was designed to wipe out free agency as in the NFL. He urged me to attend the bargaining meetings and to get responsible owners and players into the negotiations. Danny Kaye called to say the issue was "who is to run the game" but urged some "adjustment." John McMullen grumbled that Grebey was no match for Miller and "appealed" to me to get something moving. Ed Williams asked me to help Grebey on the compensation issue and pleaded that the White Sox and Orioles had financial problems. Buddy LeRoux advised that Miller was "patient, patient like Job," betting the owners would not stick together. However, he said, the players were afraid the owners would not "break." There was a lot of other advice but that is a good cross section.

The players had always unified behind Miller. He was an effective leader, taking them where he wanted them. LeRoux noted that the "players stick behind Miller." In press comments, Kansas City's George Brett explained to an Associated Press reporter a practical reason for the players' hanging together: "I can't imagine anybody coming back and saying to the owners he didn't want to strike anymore; anybody who does that is going to spend the rest of his career in the dirt, ducking pitches thrown at his head."

Finally May 22 arrived, with a midnight deadline for a strike. Many went to bed that night convinced the game would shut down the next day. But the working stiffs on both sides were not giving up so easily. They had labored mightily the last two days and now they met throughout the night. At four o'clock in the morning, miraculously, we had a settlement. Milton Richman, in his UPI column, described the process:

> Marvin Miller, spokesman for the players, and Ray Grebey, the owners' representative, both did magnificent jobs. They worked hard, never got any sleep either and didn't quit. Neither did Ken Moffett, the Federal Mediator.
> But it was Kuhn, keeping an extraordinary low profile and

seldom showing himself to the media the first two days before Friday's deadline, who played the key role in bringing both sides together.

Miller had said the way the negotiations were going they were "a waste of time" and that it would take a "small miracle" to reach any kind of agreement. Mike Marshall, Minnesota's militant reliever, said he expected a strike to last at least six weeks.

In the face of all that, Kuhn steadfastly refused to give up. Under the powers vested in him as commissioner, he had to take whatever action he deemed to be "in the best interest of baseball" and he took that literally, meeting with Miller, Grebey, and Moffett, either individually or together, at least a half-dozen times in the past two days. His primary function was to keep them talking, and he succeeded.

"The man played a crucial role," said one club owner.

After arriving at his office at 6:40 Friday morning, Kuhn cleaned up quickly and appeared on NBC's Today Show and when he finished there, he was back at his desk by 7:32.

I was exhilarated. MacPhail, Feeney, Hadden and I celebrated with a festive lunch at "21." We thought we deserved it and perhaps for hard work we did. But there was ticking away in that 4:00 A.M. agreement a time bomb that was scheduled to explode in a year's time and none of the people who had put it there really knew what they had done. With the best of motivations, Miller's idea to isolate the compensation issue with a study committee was incorporated in the agreement. If the committee had not come up with a mutually agreeable approach by February 1981, the clubs could implement their last compensation proposal, which would automatically become part of the formal collective bargaining agreement. The Players Association reserved the right to strike if the clubs implemented.

I think that night we had all gone East of Eden to the Land of Nod. Misled by a few owners like Steinbrenner who felt he would fare better in as free a player market as possible, Miller was convinced he could finesse his way past what he saw as an ownership apt to be lukewarm on compensation in 1981. The PRC was satisfied that Miller's concessions regarding the compensation proposal required him to accept some kind of meaningful compensation in 1981. I agreed with that position.

Miller grossly misgauged the determination of the ownership to battle for compensation. On this issue the PRC and I grossly mis-gauged Miller. Unfortunately, there was nothing left to require his good faith, since all other bargainable issues had been resolved on the morning of May 23. Only one issue, compensation, was left, and nothing to bargain against it.

The study committee was composed of Bob Boone and Sal Bando for the players and Frank Cashen and Harry Dalton for the clubs. These were reasonable people who, left to their own devices, could have resolved the compensation issue. However, it soon became apparent that Boone and Bando were not free bargaining agents and that the committee was a smoke screen.

Had the PRC stuck tight on compensation and taken a strike in 1980, it would certainly have been settled faster than the 1981 strike because there were more issues available for trading purposes in 1980. It is also probable that a better compensation agreement could have been achieved in multi-issue bargaining in 1980. An imponder-able in all this was the question of owner unity. Some powerful clubs were prepared to undermine the PRC. Had there been unity, I am convinced that compensation could have been achieved in 1980 at the price of only a short strike and quite possibly could have been achieved with no strike at all. By contrast, the Players Association never worried much about dissident players. They were powerless against Miller and lost in the shuffle. Moreover, peer pressure to conform was certainly greater among the players. Several dissident owners, however, could wreck the PRC. The simplest way for them to do that was to make the Association and the press privy to PRC strategy. That gave the Association a tremendous advantage in the bargaining process.

By January 1981, to the surprise of few, the study committee had been unable to reach agreement. The PRC announced on February 19 the implementation of the compensation plan. The Association replied on February 26 by reopening the collective bargaining agreement regarding compensation, setting May 29 as a strike date if the matter were not resolved by that time.

Discussions continued throughout the spring, with no progress and no signs at all that the Association was prepared to seriously negotiate on compensation. As the situation turned darker by the day, Ken Moffett was called back into the talks on April 20. Ken was pretty well neutralized by the Association's intransigence on com-pensation. Miller, having convinced the players that compensation would destroy free agency, was taking an uncompromising stance.

There was a memorable diversion on the last Friday of March, when thirty-two Hall of Famers, a handful of baseball executives and I joined President Reagan at the White House for lunch. It was remarkable because this was the largest gathering of Hall of Famers ever assembled. Before lunch I dropped in to see the presidential press secretary, Jim Brady, who was wearing a Cubs cap and was as thrilled as I was to have all these Hall of Famers in the White House. At lunch I sat with the president, who was flanked by Duke Snider and Willie Mays, with Roy Campanella nearby. The president told us that his eyesight had kept him from seeing well enough to play baseball as a child. As a result he concentrated on football, where eyesight was less crucial: "If it moved, you hit it!" As the guests finished their chocolate mousse, he went to the microphone and enchanted everyone with some of his favorite baseball stories, with special emphasis on his role as Grover Cleveland Alexander in the movies. Though he ran way over schedule, he took the trouble to say goodbye to every guest. Three days later the president and Jim Brady were shot outside the Washington Hilton Hotel.

In April and May, the PRC struggled to persuade the Association that the compensation plan would affect neither salaries nor a significant number of players. I was convinced that their arguments were correct. But the Association was communing only with itself, and the more it communed the greater the chamber of horrors it claimed compensation to be. Hung up on outdated trade union dogma about never giving anything back and on his own ego gratification, Miller merely toyed with the issue, apparently confident that patient stonewalling would break the owners' resolve.

The press and my mail began to urge me to do whatever was necessary to achieve agreement. The most popular suggestion was that I "lock" the two sides in a room until they agreed. I could certainly keep the PRC negotiating, even if they were otherwise disposed, as they were not, but I had no power to direct a federally protected labor union to do anything. The ghost of Judge Landis will forever plague sports commissioners. Whatever might have been possible in the 1920s, the scenario was markedly different in 1981.

Miller then tried a diversionary tactic to take attention away from the bargaining. Contending that public statements made by me and certain owners about the financial problems of baseball had made baseball's financial condition a collective bargaining issue, he demanded that the PRC furnish operating statements for each major-league club for the years 1978, 1979 and 1980. When they refused, he filed an unfair labor practice charge with the National Labor Relations Board on May 7, alleging that baseball was not bargaining in good faith. When the NLRB decided to issue a complaint and seek an injunction requiring the PRC to rescind its February 19 action implementing the compensation plan, the dispute moved to the courtroom of Federal Judge Henry Werker. On May 28, the parties agreed that the strike date would be postponed until twenty-four to forty-eight hours after Judge Werker's decision on the injunction. That meant there could be no strike on May 29.

If the injunction were granted, the effect would have been to postpone the strike and the clubs' implementation of compensation for a year. To those who saw putting off the problem as a solution, Miller took on an angelic hue. Forgotten by many in the press was the fact that Miller had scheduled the strike in the first place. Should the clubs successfully fight off the injunction, it would appear to many that they were responsible for any ensuing strike. As we will see, that was exactly what happened.

After a two-day hearing, Judge Werker issued an opinion on June 10 that rejected the Players Association's contentions and found them insincere: "Despite the presentation of a 'compensation' proposal in January 1980 and Miller's apparent knowledge for several years of the losses claimed by club owners, the Players Association first requested financial information from the clubs on February 27, 1981. This delayed request coupled with Miller's expressed opinion that the clubs were not losing money leads to the inescapable conclusion that the proceedings brought before the Board, resulting in the instant action, was not a sincere effort to obtain access to the clubs' financial records, but rather a bargaining tactic by the Association to prevent the implementation of the PRC's proposal."

The judge concluded the opinion playfully with the following four words: "PLAY BALL!!! SO ORDERED."

The court proceeding had backfired, revealing Miller's insincerity. For over a month he had diverted attention away from the bargaining table, tied us all up in legal proceedings and wasted valuable time that could have been used to find a solution. He was hardlining the owners, hopeful that building pressure within the ownership would undermine their resolve to retain the compensation agreement they had obtained in the 1980 bargaining.

Using his infallible touch with the press, Miller, again playing a tactical game, proclaimed that Grebey and I were trying to force a strike. His efforts to restrain the owners by legal proceedings gave verisimilitude to his contention. He renewed his charge that we were trying to break the union. He argued that we had misled the owners into thinking that compensation was assured by the 1980 settlement. Nothing came through more strongly than his point that we were trying to nullify free agency and roll back salaries. His theme that "Kuhn and Grebey" were doing this and that was amusing. Grebey and I were never close during his five years in baseball. The cooperation between us was minimal. My influence in the PRC came from my close relationship with the league presidents, from my friendship with most of the club representatives on the PRC and from my working relationship with the league lawyers, Lou Hoynes and Jim Garner, and PRC counsel Barry Rona. Miller's theory that I was an agent of the PRC had been the keystone of his case before Judge Werker, and the judge had rejected it. Of course, that did not deter Miller, who had successfully been selling that shoddy line of goods for twelve years and was not now to be deterred by a federal court determination to the contrary.

Judge Werker also found that compensation did not present "economic issues" but rather was "addressed to the inequities which flowed from the 'compensation' for 'free agents' as provided for in the 1976 agreement." His ruling should have nullified Miller's argument that compensation was designed to roll back salaries, but it never slowed him up a bit. Good salesman that he was, he continued to find gullible takers.

In a May 30 interview with Cosell and Lee MacPhail, Miller tried out his theory that Kuhn and Grebey were misleading the owners about having compensation assured, but Lee got the last and most telling word:

COSELL: Marvin Miller has charged the owners with wanting this strike. I asked him on what basis. Lee MacPhail will answer.

MILLER: I think that you have to go back to last year. Last year we made a settlement on all of the issues and we postponed this one. On the basis of reliable information apparently both Mr. Kuhn and Mr. Grebey in an effort to sell that settlement told the owners that they had compensation in the bag. I think to those who may have said what do you mean in the bag the players have the right to strike if they don't like it how can that be in the bag. I think they were told we have it don't worry we'll get it. And I think that they realized a long time ago that they could not get it in a good faith bargaining exchange. That the only way they could get it was to stonewall, ignore their legal obligation to bargain in good faith and force a strike. Their hope obviously in a strike is to starve the players out over a long period and in the process break the union.

COSELL: You used the phrase 'on the basis of reliable information.' What is that reliable information?

MILLER: Owners.

COSELL: Directly from owners to you?

MILLER: Directly.

COSELL: Would you care to name those owners?

MILLER: No, I will not name those owners for obvious reasons.

MacPHAIL: Howard, how could those owners be misled when the agreement that was made is in writing and is part of the Basic Agreement? It's right in there to read. Exactly the timing, exactly what happens when, the responsibilities of each party. What each of the parties can do. There's no misunderstanding on anyone's part.

Putting words in the mouths of owners whom he would not name was vintage Miller.

Ever faithful to the Players Association line, Red Smith was sure that compensation was "the opening move in a campaign to nullify the free agent system."

While Judge Werker's decision was pending, Miller came forward with his first proposal for compensation. For months all he had done was criticize various aspects of the clubs' compensation program. That had produced a number of responsive modifications by the PRC. Miller's eleventh-hour proposal called for a pool of major-league players from which a compensation player could be selected. Thus, a club who had not signed a free agent could be tapped for compensation. Clearly unfair, the idea found no favor with the PRC. Murray Chass wrote in *The New York Times* that not all owners had been advised of Miller's new proposal. His source was the usual "unidentified" owner. In fact, a detailed teletype had been sent to all clubs the day Miller made the proposal, as a simple inquiry to the PRC would have revealed.

Now, with Judge Werker's decision in place, Miller had forty-eight hours to decide whether or not to go through with the strike. After bargaining on June 11 and into the small hours of June 12 produced no results, Miller called what became the longest strike in American sports history, a strike on which players had never been given the opportunity to cast a secret ballot, pro or con. It was Miller's strike. Steaming back to my office alone at 1:45 A.M., I was spotted by a passerby who yelled, "Hey, Bowie, what's happening?" I yelled back, "They're out, they're out." I was in no mood for small talk.

I went to my hotel that night not surprised, but deeply saddened and angry. I had lost my usual ability to "leave the work in the office." Luisa noted long intervals between smiles when she saw me at all. I canceled all my travel plans and appearances, cleared my schedule and prepared to devote all of my energies to the disaster that had been visited on baseball.

Miller's strike was an inexcusable miscalculation by Miller of the clubs and me. The clubs, having achieved compensation as part of the collective bargaining agreement, were not going to give it up. It was an issue on which they were prepared to fight if they were forced to do so. It was also an issue where all the equities were on their side. Their compensation program was not going to hurt free agency and would provide more fairness to the experimental free-agency system adopted in 1976. Even if by some unexpected chance it did hurt free agency, the entire agreement would reopen for bargaining in three years' time.

I had said clearly that I thoroughly agreed with the clubs' position because I thought compensation was necessary for baseball. Though I had supported union positions in 1969, 1976 and 1980, I could not be counted on to do it again, barring a prolonged strike that might threaten the entire season.

But Miller was a prisoner of his own ego above all things. According to the press, he had never lost to the owners in collective bargaining and would not now. He loved his press image. Even his perennial critic, sportswriter Dick Young, gave him the nod in his long engagement with the owners. Significantly, this was to be Miller's last negotiation. One more triumph would cap his reputation and humiliate the owners.

The strike was on and we were into what was bound to be a gutter fight. It was the arena where Miller was at his best. But his back-

ground with the United Steelworkers as an economist had not prepared him for a lead role in collective bargaining. As a result, however clever he was at tactical maneuvering, he was not good at the
bargaining table, where he had little sense of timing and virtually
no idea how to close a deal. This weakness was compounded by his
hatred—with all its emotional baggage—of the owners and Grebey.
Thus, it was no surprise that we moved into the arena of insinuations, half truths and outright lies. It beat bargaining on the merits
of compensation.

It was an arena where I was bound to be at a maximum disadvantage. I held what I felt was the most distinguished office in sports,
known for a sixty-year history of protecting the integrity and
honesty of the game. Eddie Chiles later said that what you needed
to counter the likes of Miller was a "junkyard dog." That was neither
my job nor my personal description.

Inevitably I became the punching bag of an important segment
of the press and not just because of Miller's skills. Most sportswriters
were as eager to see baseball return as any other fan. They wanted
to see the commissioner, Zeus-like, step in to quell the interminable
haggling.

I have described the various reasons why I would not step in, but
one bears special emphasis. It was Miller's calculation that the owners would not long stand together against a strike, that their unity
was paper-thin. It seemed to me that unless the clubs took a stand
at some point, the Players Association would forever have its way,
whatever the issue. From where I sat, the industry appeared in
serious jeopardy if management's timid course persisted in 1981 and
beyond. Given free rein, the Players Association would look only to
the financial welfare of the players. There was none of the statesmanship found in the UAW-Chrysler negotiations; there was no
concern for the fans or the ticket prices; there was no bedrock
concern for the game. Not so transient as the players, most of the
club executives, for all their frailties, had a deep sense of dedication
to the game and to the public. Some owners wanted to make money.
But there were easier ways of doing that. It was important that the
clubs retain control of the game.

I hated the strike and had prayed it would not happen. Anyone
who had the faintest sense of my passion for the game would understand that. Anyone who knew my more-than-fifty-year history as a
fan of and romantic about baseball would understand that. So I was
hurt when the press began to pick up Miller's propaganda about my

"engineering" the strike, and was hurt worse when I saw that some of the public was beginning to believe it. How strange that this was achieved by Miller, a man who was not a fan, showed no concern for the fans, and had little sense of responsibility to the public or the game.

The long-term welfare of baseball and the public interest required the owners to take a stand. I was convinced of that, whether the issue was compensation or something else. The issue transcended compensation. But how, in an emotional setting, do you explain to a public, deeply attached to the game and its continuity, that the commissioner had best let the players live with the responsibility for what they had done, that things would be better in the future if they learned now that there was a price to be paid, that future strikes might take short courses or not happen at all? I tried and found no answer. As a result, I took a fearful lashing from the press for allegedly doing nothing. Though far from the truth, the story stuck throughout the strike and lingers today. One of the reasons was a meeting I had with three owners on June 16, five days into the strike.

The night before I had had the unhappy dinner with Edward Bennett Williams that I described at the beginning of the first chapter. The next morning at 9:30 Williams and Steinbrenner arrived in my office with Chiles, who had requested the meeting.

Lee MacPhail was already there. The sun poured through the windows behind my desk, windows through which I had a stunning and consoling view of the west face of St. Patrick's Cathedral. Chiles, who had not been in my office before, began to nose around, inspecting my bathroom and then peeking into the small conference room adjoining the main office.

"Pretty fancy digs," he said, without a smile. His unpleasant tone could not be mistaken.

Dispensing with amenities, Chiles launched into a rambling diatribe against me that embarrassed everyone in the room. Eddie is one of those compulsive speakers who, once he gets rolling, gushes uncontrollably.

"You're sitting here in your fancy office doing nothing," he began. "If you can't figure out anything else to do, you could at least put your desk out on the sidewalk and talk to the fans. It's up to you to do something! But as far as I can see, you're not doing a damned thing. I won't tolerate that! You and Lee MacPhail work for me! I pay your salaries! You're just like any other employees I've got. I tell you what to do, and you're supposed to do it!" The flat Texas voice was full of anger.

I listened with the patience I had acquired after over twelve years on the job. But my surface calm was misleading. I was about as angry as I get. Charlie Finley in his most outrageous, expletive-laden form had never come close to the effect on me of Chiles's outburst.

When Chiles stopped I said, "Are you through?" The tone of the question defied anyone to answer it. "Eddie, you're nothing but a lame-brained old fool. I'm embarrassed for you and I suspect everyone in this room is as embarrassed as I am. You have no appreciation of the distinguished office I am proud to hold or of the traditions which lie behind the major-league baseball structure. If you did, you would know that the commissioner exists to tell the owners what to do and not the other way round. As to the labor situation, I find your remarks nothing short of insulting, and as far as I'm concerned, you can get the hell out of here!"

I then turned to Steinbrenner and Williams and told them that if they subscribed to the nonsense I had just heard from Chiles they could get out, too. Both were conciliatory. They made it plain they did not agree with everything Eddie had said but they did agree that something needed to be done. That was why they had come.

They criticized Grebey and the membership of the PRC and urged new faces. Lee rejected that flatly, saying changes in the PRC could be considered only when the strike had been resolved. They stressed the urgency of the situation. Lee and I assured them we were not in the dark on that point. Williams suggested a solution using multiple amateur drafts or $400,000 as compensation for ranking free agents. We said we would give his ideas to the PRC and Executive Council. Chiles demanded that Williams's suggestions be proposed to the Players Association that very day and railed about the baseball "bureaucracy" when he heard that the ideas would need evaluation by the PRC.

I explained with some care that I did not have the executive responsibility for running the PRC because, as they well knew, the clubs had that responsibility. However, I said, I could use my good offices and influence, which I knew had considerable impact. I also said I could block the PRC if they got out of line. I explained that the three of them and I really came apart regarding the PRC performance. I thought it was good; they thought it was bad.

Williams replied that he was disappointed in my position and leadership. He asked if I would act if I thought the game was "self-destructing." I told him I would undoubtedly find a way but that that was not the situation on June 16.

The meeting ended more amicably than it had started, but the tension was heavy. Moments after they left, Williams alone came back into my secretary's office. He was carrying a plastic sign he had snatched from a secretary's wall down the corridor. It said in bold red letters: PLEASE BE PATIENT—GOD ISN'T FINISHED WITH ME YET. He had signed it "Ed Williams 6/16/81" and addressed it "Bowie." In the dreariest circumstances he never lost his sense of humor.

Unidentified management leaks to *The New York Times* and the *Washington Post* said the purpose of the meeting was to make me understand that a minority could block my reelection in 1982. I assumed the source was either Williams or Steinbrenner. While they had said nothing of the kind to me in our meeting, the implication had been clear enough. Although I had made no decision regarding my availability for another term, I never worried about threats of that kind. My lack of concern sprang from my own hardheadedness and from the fact that I never had needed the job and had an essentially fatalistic view about the dangers of holding it. I had always put my faith in the great majority of clubs who were both decent and supportive. If at some point that was not enough, there was nothing I could do about it.

At this stage I was holding daily telephone conferences with my Executive Council. I reported the morning meeting to them the same day. They were furious at Steinbrenner and Williams. Chiles was dismissed as pretty much a cipher. After reviewing the situation with the balance of the clubs, they released a public statement strongly supporting the PRC, Grebey and me. In an effort to reestablish his credentials with the other clubs, Steinbrenner cabled me and the clubs that he was "supportive" of the PRC and the commissioner. He had certainly come a long way in a day's time.

In covering the three-owner meeting for *The New York Times* and *The Sporting News,* Murray Chass wrote that I had testified before Judge Werker that I "had nothing to do with labor relations." He contrasted that "testimony" with my meeting with the owners that obviously had had a great deal to do with labor relations. The implication was that, to put it politely, my testimony was not candid. In fact, as Murray knew from sitting in the courtroom, I had testified that I was very much involved. A normally capable reporter had become Miller's advocate. Such were the emotions of the strike.

The controversy over that meeting did produce a funny line, and it came, surprisingly enough, from Chiles. Asked if there had been a chin-to-chin shouting match between him and me, he said, "I come up to his belly button. He's six-six and I'm five-nine. I certainly didn't have any chin-to-chin confrontation."

I now intensified my contacts with the PRC and Executive Council. The PRC members were: Chairman Ed Fitzgerald; the two league presidents; Joe Burke and Clark Griffith; Bob Howsam; John McHale and Dan Galbreath. The Council members were: Lee and Chub, Galbreath, Howsam, John Fetzer, Ewing Kauffman, Haywood Sullivan, Bob Lurie, Fitzgerald and Peter O'Malley.

I talked to them in groups and individually. I telephoned them and met with them. They were all spending a lot of time in New York. We worked night and day. The purpose was very simple—to find a solution to Miller's strike. Men like Fitzgerald, McHale, Galbreath, Burke and the league presidents were painfully aware of the urgency of the situation and were willing to consider a wide variety of solutions. Howsam and Griffith were more conservative but were by no means obstructionists. Grebey and Rona and the league lawyers were trying to do the will of the committee. Innumerable possible solutions were evaluated, many of which found their way into the collective bargaining process. At no time was there any thought or hope that the Players Association was going to be broken in this process. On the contrary, we all recognized that Miller had unwisely painted himself into a difficult corner. The question was how to get him out while preserving some kind of meaningful compensation. As the weeks went by, the pressure many of us exerted slowly eroded the compensation provisions on the table.

Williams created a public stir by suggesting that President Reagan ask the parties to put the issue of compensation to arbitration. But the White House responded that "the President has no intention of getting involved in the dispute." Several days later, Ed called to tell me that the idea had come in as a question from sportswriter Peter Pascarelli of the *Baltimore News-American.* However, he was also certain that if I asked the president, he would "welcome" the chance to intervene. Ed also wondered if we were not already at "the point of self-destruct." I did not think that ten days into the strike was such a point.

The bargaining process then moved into the dog days. Occasionally a light breeze from one or the other side would produce some forward motion but not much. The PRC was sticking to its concept of direct compensation, although it was continuing to agree to modifications. Miller steadfastly held that pool compensation was as far as he would go. Both sides were responding to mediator Moffett's calls for meetings. Red Smith was still faithfully espousing Miller's position that a "hard core" of owners was determined to "bust the players' union," and that "Kuhn wanted a strike." He said he found that latter thought on his "grapevine." It was the first I knew that viniculture was among Miller's skills.

The answer was not coming easily. To make matters worse, the National Labor Relations Board proceeding that Miller had instigated was scheduled for a hearing in July, distracting the energies of everyone away from the bargaining table. To further complicate the legal side of things, the Major League Umpires Association sued in Philadelphia to prevent Lloyd's of London from paying the clubs' strike insurance. The Umpires Association hoped that elimination of the insurance would bring a rapid end to the strike and protect the umpires' financial interests. Promising to use Miller as his principal witness, Richie Phillips, general counsel of the Umpires Association, looked to be part of another Miller-inspired diversion.

By July 1, Miller, who had stayed away from the bargaining table since the strike began on June 12, reappeared. His remote-control skills were such that it made little difference whether he was there or not. He attributed his absence to owner criticism of his role in the negotiations. That he was able to pull such a petulant maneuver was another tribute to his ability to charm the press; there was some criticism but it was modest.

Owner unrest was growing for various reasons. Some, like John McMullen, were restless because they were used to a hands-on style of management and wanted to be more involved. Others, like Ballard Smith, felt they did not know enough about what was going on. Then there were Steinbrenner and Williams, who wanted a settlement at any price because they did not see their economic interests served by the PRC approach. George felt compensation worked against his penchant for signing free agents. Lacking the very deep pocket of most owners, Ed saw a long strike simply as more than he could afford. Not surprisingly, there were continuing anonymous owner comments in the press designed to undermine the owner majority that stood strongly behind the PRC. The anonymous sources were saying things such as "the hardliners are adamantly trying to break the union." While this was poppycock, there should have been little wonder that Miller got so much press support for this fantasy. He could say the owners themselves were admitting it.

Williams was always a steady source of information. Two of the most influential players in the union were Mark Belanger and Doug DeCinces, both Orioles with whom Ed kept in touch. I would hear from Ed that Belanger reported the players to be "resolute" and "not about to cave," that they disliked Grebey, that they had a bottom line but would not give it to Grebey. So I would say to Ed, "Get their bottom line and give it to me." On several occasions he did, confident that if the PRC would just make the moves requested, we would have a deal. Then I would go to work on the PRC and get the requested moves, only to have Miller act as if he had been insulted when they came across the table. Ed was amazed.

I also heard from agents like Ron Shapiro and Al Frohman with various ideas for solutions. These and other agents were sincerely looking to help. But it was still too early to move the Players Association because they were convinced they could break the solidarity of the twenty-six–club bargaining unit. There was plenty of reason to think they could do just that. Though I was very critical of Miller's folly in calling a strike, it was hard to fault his bargaining strategy of hanging tough while daily signs increased that owners like Williams, Steinbrenner, Chiles and McMullen were out of step with the majority. By July 7, the din from these men and several others had grown sufficiently clamorous to prompt the PRC to call a major-league meeting two days later in New York.

Held in the Citicorp Building, the meeting was chaired by Fitzgerald as head of the PRC. I was there watching with sharp interest. Except for Williams, who wanted to expedite the process, and McMullen, who disagreed with the PRC struggle for compensation, the malcontent owners behaved like lambs when Fitzgerald asked each club to give its thoughts. It was inescapably clear that the bargaining team was making every effort to find a solution. It was hard to ask more of them. Even Chiles agreed and gave the PRC a vote of confidence.

Though I did not hold a press conference during the strike, I did give in-depth interviews to writers periodically. I wanted to avoid the appearance that I was unwilling to discuss the issues. At the time of the Citicorp meeting, both Peter Gammons of the *Boston Globe* and Joe Durso of *The New York Times* wrote thorough stories giving my account and views of what was transpiring. What came through most markedly was my frustration that the commissioner did not have equal influence over the Players Association and the PRC. I was still haunted by the Landis myth. I did not have the power to direct the activities of a federally protected labor union. Had it been otherwise, there would have been no strike. No sensible person would have permitted the Players Association to strike over the compensation issue. I could not direct the activities of the PRC but I could certainly influence those activities, as I have explained. But why should I influence the PRC to do what in my judgment was not best for baseball? The PRC was clearly bargaining in good faith and showing a willingness to modify its position. In point of fact, I had already influenced those modifications more than I liked.

Congressional pressure mounted. The Senate adopted a resolution proposed by Ted Kennedy calling on the parties to settle as soon as possible. Kennedy wrote to President Reagan urging him to intervene. House Speaker Tip O'Neill and thirteen other congressmen wrote urging me to use my "extraordinary powers" to stop the strike. The moving force behind the O'Neill letter was Georgia Congressman Wyche Fowler, who may have shared the laurels with Tip as the best baseball fan in the House.

Another problem I had was Grebey. He was a bright fellow and knew his profession well but was probably better suited to the day-to-day business world than he was to the penetrating glare of the baseball world. While I believed that Ray was genuinely trying to carry out the policies and directions of the PRC, he brought a feisty, tough style to the bargaining table and press conferences that compared poorly with Miller's unctuous charm. While this comparison may have been unfair to Ray, he and Miller were the chief image makers for the two sides, and Grebey's style was stirring up the critics whether at the congressional, club or press level. And I was hearing from those critics. The right counterpoint to Miller in this type of negotiation would have been the open, disarming style of a Lee MacPhail. (MacPhail succeeded Grebey on January 1, 1984. Grebey's effective transition from baseball to the airline industry in 1984 put him back into the type of setting where his skills were more effective.)

On July 10 I announced that I was cancelling the All-Star Game set for July 14.

As the strike wore on, the issue of service credit complicated the picture. If the players got service credit during the strike, it would count toward their eligibility for salary arbitration, pensions and free agency. Needless to say, the players wanted service credit and the clubs were adamantly opposed. It was a big issue.

On July 15, Secretary of Labor Raymond Donovan flew to New York and talked to the bargaining teams, exhorting them to settle the dispute as soon as possible. It was certainly a sign that the administration was taking an interest above the level of the Federal Mediation and Conciliation Service. I doubted, however, that any level of federal interest was going to affect Miller's stubborn determination to wait out the situation. There were clear signs that players were uneasy, not surprising since they were losing about $4 million per week in salaries. But there was no sign that player unrest could shake Miller's leadership, however quixotic. If he were interested in a settlement, he could have taken the PRC offer on the table at any time without seriously affecting the welfare of the players. As the days went by, I began to wonder if he really had a goal. Was he vainly waiting for the minority owners or someone else to bail him out?

I was listening to an increasing cascade of solutions from owners, agents and my own staff. Steinbrenner told me he had a line to Miller through umpire counsel Richie Phillips. He thought the Grebey-Miller relationship was so bad that they could not reach a solution. I listened to George's ideas and passed them on to the PRC. However, I had doubts about the effectiveness of the Steinbrenner-Phillips conduit, although I kept my ears cocked for any gems that might spring from that source. If it became necessary to negotiate around Grebey, MacPhail would be the most effective. Were the PRC to make such a move, it certainly would undermine Grebey. You simply could not sidestep your chief negotiator without destroying his future utility. Disliking Grebey, George was happy to push him toward any precipice.

By July 16 reports of Grebey's ouster became so widespread that the PRC issued a release stating their confidence in him and saying that they viewed the reports with "disgust and revulsion." At least the rhetoric was colorful. The same day, Grebey told Miller that the clubs were not going to give the players service time during the strike. An angry Miller called that news the "most negative" development of the strike. Miller argued that even suspended players got service time, but he well understood that workers often did not get service time during strikes in American industry. Having already led the players to accumulated losses of nearly $20 million, he was now faced with the danger of costing them service time. No wonder his tone grew more strident.

As both sides dug in on the service-time issue, I was confident that it could be compromised or resolved by arbitration if necessary. It also provided a substantial new issue, not necessarily a bad development in what had been a single-issue negotiation. At least now there was a potential for some horse-trading.

This issue also shed new light on arbitration as a possible solution. The clubs offered to arbitrate service time, a proposal Miller rejected. However, he was willing to arbitrate the compensation dispute, which the PRC would not accept. Miller felt he could not afford to lose on service time and the PRC felt it had already compromised too much on compensation and could not afford to lose more ground through arbitration of that issue. As we moved into the last two weeks of July, I was convinced that arbitration of the entire dispute was the way to go if there was no settlement by month's end. With Fitzgerald in accord, Sandy Hadden and I began to seed that thought in our discussions with clubs. I was confident that either through the PRC or on my own I could create enough pressure to accomplish arbitration, although I thought a negotiated solution was much preferable.

In my staff discussions, I was projecting a settlement by July 30 and we were basing our poststrike plans and scheduling on that forecast. Apart from my seemingly endless daily conversations with the PRC and my Executive Council, I was sorting through a variety of plans for resuming the season. I did not favor picking up the season and running it in normal fashion to the end. I wanted something special, something that could lend some zest to the misbegotten 1981 season. So I gave our administrator, Bill Murray, the job of evaluating different approaches. They included a split season with an extra tier of postseason playoffs. Under this plan, the first-half (prestrike) leader in each division would play the second-half (poststrike) leader to establish the division champion. The LCS and World Series would then follow. A non–split-season approach was for division winners to play the second-place teams in special postseason playoffs. Yet another approach would have a round-robin playoff during the last ten days of the season with all twenty-six clubs involved. And there were variations on these basic formats.

While there was predictable conservative opposition to anything but running the season in normal fashion, I was surprised to find how much press support there was for variations. I even had calls from writers suggesting plans. My biggest surprise came when, during a break in a PRC meeting, Bob Howsam urged me to consider the split-season plan. Bob was normally opposed to tampering with any traditional aspect of the game, but he was also a realist with superior marketing instincts. The more I looked at the possibilities, the more I fastened on the split season. We began to explore its ramifications.

At the suggestion of Labor Secretary Donovan, the negotiations moved to Washington for five days commencing July 20. He and

Ken Moffett persuaded the parties to endure a press blackout during that time. Donovan sat in on the talks. I moved to Washington and brought in my Executive Council as well. The Council had the full power of the major-league clubs. If there was any kind of opening, I wanted them to be there to take advantage of it.

Donovan's move opened the door to heightened criticism of my alleged inactivity. Even the respected Associated Press writer Will Grimsley wondered if Donovan could "put them in a room and tell them not to come out until they've settled their differences, why couldn't Commissioner Kuhn . . . have done the same thing long before this?" Of course, Donovan could not order either party to do anything. All he could do was ask. I, too, had asked them to meet since June 12 and they had done just that with great regularity— unfortunately, without reaching an agreement. That pattern held after five days of meetings with the secretary—no agreement.

Everyone went back to New York and I sent my Council home. During our Washington stay, I had become convinced that Miller would not deviate from his pool proposal, whereby compensation players would come from a major-league pool instead of from the club signing a ranking free agent. He had led the players to believe this could be achieved by patience and waiting for the dissident owners to collapse the PRC. If he had to close down the entire 1981 season, he was prepared to do it and said so.

Sandy Hadden and I had some long talks from which we con-cluded that we had to try to ease the PRC toward the pool or else push everything into arbitration. Though both courses were unsatis-factory to me, they were immeasurably superior to obliterating the 1981 season. For our fans the impact of losing the season was incal-culable. According to my mail they had been more tolerant than one would have expected. Still I did not think we should test their pa-tience much further. In my daily conversations with PRC and Exec-utive Council members I began to talk about the pool concept and why I thought it had become a necessary, if unpalatable, solution. MacPhail was on the same course.

On July 27 Lee had a talk with Marvin Miller. The PRC had reluctantly decided to negotiate around Grebey, a decision he ac-cepted stoically. Miller gave Lee a set of what Lee called "inputs" on all pending issues. Miller told him he would not propose them himself but would fight for them if the clubs accepted them. Lee wrote up Miller's ideas and gave them to the PRC and me. I thought we had the basis for a settlement, as Miller had sensibly blended both PRC and Players Association concepts. The PRC called a major-league meeting in New York for July 29.

The outwardly monolithic house of the Players Association was increasingly showing its seams. More and more players were critical of Association positions or saying they did not know what was happening. The press blackout in Washington had hurt Miller more than the PRC because it shut off his more effective communication system through the press. In print, Miller described the blackout as a "catastrophe." He called a meeting of the Players Association Executive Committee in Chicago for the evening of July 27, the same day he had met with Lee. He emerged from the player meeting saying he had "solidarity," although he was careful to claim no more than a majority of the players behind the Association. By Miller's standards that was a modest claim. As a practical matter, however, Miller had all the control he needed because he dominated the players at the bargaining table and in his Executive Committee.

The owners' meeting was remarkable for its restraint. The PRC was pretty sure it had the basis for a settlement. Fitzgerald and Grebey conveyed that to the clubs. As Ed reported afterward to the press, "the overwhelming consensus was that the clubs want the strike to be brought to a rapid conclusion." That was certainly the sense of the meeting. Ed correctly emphasized that the preferred method was "collective bargaining." They wanted to avoid arbitration, which they knew could be in the offing. That was fine with me.

The meeting had a poignant moment. Major-league meetings have all kinds of moments running the gamut of human emotions, but rarely poignant ones. The Tigers' eighty-year-old owner, John Fetzer, rose to urge harmony and understanding, all very much in character for our revered senior statesman. But then he did an extraordinary thing—he asked each one of us to forgive him for any wrong he might ever have done to us. There was total silence. Perhaps the others realized, as did I, that of all the people in the room who might well have made such a plea, Fetzer least needed to do so. I think he was asking all of us to forgive one another after months of anguish.

Moffett asked the two sides to meet the next afternoon (July 30) in New York and they agreed. The homework done by MacPhail and Miller earlier in the week quickly began to pay off, as Grebey and MacPhail met privately with Miller and Don Fehr for hours in the National League office, not much more than the length of a Mickey Mantle home run from where I was waiting in my Rockefeller Center offices. I was confident that they had a solution to the compensation issue with a hybrid arrangement that borrowed from the philosophy of both sides.

The service-time issue was much tougher. Miller was in yet another corner of his own making. He had told MacPhail he had to have this issue. He was willing to give up his NLRB proceeding, to extend the labor agreement for an extra year, and even to accept in part the clubs' direct-compensation philosophy, but he had to have service time. Many clubs had told me they were adamantly against negotiating away the issue, although they would arbitrate. Miller was afraid of arbitration on this point because politically he could not afford to lose it.

Lou Susman, the Cardinals' attorney, was the most adamant of all. Prepared to sit out the entire season to get meaningful compensation and unhappy with any compromise on that issue, he told me the Cardinals were "inflexible" on service time, and did not even want it arbitrated.

My advice to the PRC was to work within the framework of Miller's compromise or be prepared to face arbitration of all issues. If that meant angering clubs that were adamant on service time, so be it.

While I waited, I kept an appointment with Sister Therese Forker. She was a Catholic nun who had made a career of caring for mentally retarded children, especially those with additional complications like muscular dystrophy. Her dedication was beyond description. Over the years she had interested me in her work. We had spent a lot of time together in schools and homes and in my office with these kids. I had done nothing more rewarding in my time as commissioner. Seeing Sister Therese made me think of those kids. What were our problems compared to theirs?

On into the night and early morning the bargainers worked, moving during those long hours from the National League office to Lou Hoynes's offices at Willkie Farr & Gallagher. That was a good sign because it meant the lawyers were actually putting the agreement on paper, never an easy task. Sandy Hadden and I moved there as well, but not before I gave my Executive Council an encouraging report in a telephone conference. I wanted to be nearby as the final details were put in place. At about 5:30 A.M. on July 31, Moffett advised the press that the strike was over. The season would resume with the All-Star Game on August 9 and regular play the next day. That was it. Well, not quite.

I talked to many people on the telephone that day but my most interesting conversation was with Susman of the Cardinals. He had been threatening litigation if the settlement was unsatisfactory to the Cardinals. After the Finley and Turner lawsuits against me, I had put the clubs on notice that club litigation thereafter would subject them to my disciplinary power. Susman assured me that the Cardinals would not sue. Most unhappy with the settlement, Susman told me that the Cardinals "did not blame Grebey or the professional people." The blame, he said, should be put squarely at the door of the "owners who are screwing up bargaining." For the future, he wanted the PRC and the leagues put under the direct control of the commissioner. In several months, Susman and his client, Gussie Busch, would be ardent allies of some of the very owners who had "screwed up the bargaining"; their target: me.

On Sunday, August 2, I made a quick trip to Cooperstown for the Hall of Fame installation of Bob Gibson, Johnny Mize and Rube Foster. As much as I loved Cooperstown and admired those inductees, I dreaded this day. I was introduced to the crowd of some 7,500 fans by gentlemanly Hall of Fame president Ed Stack. He described my efforts to resolve the strike, only to receive a reaction of boos so thunderous that it may have roused the long-slumbering spirit of the last Mohican wherever it slept in the hills above Otsego Lake. By this time in my career, I could predict the reaction of crowds with an accuracy that would have put vaudeville mind readers out of business. As I flew out of the tiny, forest-rimmed Oneonta, New York, airport, I was glad, for the only time in my life, to shake the dust of Cooperstown, a town about which I am passionate.

Six days after the strike ended, we had a major-league meeting in Chicago. We had to decide whether to ratify the labor agreement and what schedule to play commencing August 10. Ratification was not a problem nor really was the question of scheduling. I had talked to every major-league club and found there was a clear majority of fifteen or sixteen clubs favoring a split season. Five clubs favored picking up the season and simply playing through to the end with the usual postseason play. Four clubs favored other new systems. One or two clubs were on the fence. While picking up had the merit of simplicity, I favored the split season because I thought it put some marketing spice into the balance of the schedule. The split season carried easily when the question came to a vote. Among the negative voters were Cincinnati, St. Louis and Baltimore, who saw parochial disadvantages in the split arrangement. All were strong first-half contenders. Now they would have to start from scratch.

Each viewed me as the villain of the decision and fanned their local press against it.

Notwithstanding criticism of the split season, the fans supported it with good attendance through Labor Day and record attendance thereafter. I think some of the critics were genuinely concerned that the split season would become a fixture. I can recall only one club executive who was so inclined. There was never any intent or thought of carrying it beyond 1981. Still the critics worried. Most fans, players, media and management dreaded change, even temporary change. It seemed to shake their faith in the constancy of things.

The fan support was quite remarkable. If it was good in 1981, it was smashing in 1982, when we set an all-time attendance record. Basically, I think the fans were tolerant because they did not realistically expect baseball to be forever immune to a major strike of this dimension. What industry is?

When it was all over, Grebey said there were no winners or losers. It was the diplomatic and proper thing to say, statesmanlike. In point of fact, there were winners and losers. He and I were two of the latter, at least in a sense. The fans were obvious losers. Fifty days of baseball had been snatched from their summer. Cynics said the fans had plenty of other things to do. True enough, but not in the sense that their alternatives were a substitute for baseball, which is an addiction for those millions of us who love it, an irreplaceable addiction.

Grebey was a loser in the sense that his job in baseball became untenable as a result of the strike. The word "scapegoat" has been used with regard to Ray, and is essentially correct. Without the strike, I have no doubt he would have carried on in baseball had he so wished. However, with Miller moving into a less active role and Moffett coming in as head of the Players Association, the mood on the club side was for change. The fortuitous fact that MacPhail, having retired as American League president, might be available further undermined Ray's position. And so it happened. Ray went out and Lee came in. I took the responsibility of telling Ray that I thought he would be wise to try his hand elsewhere, given the enmity and bitterness that the strike had brought within the baseball family.

MacPhail was the only figure to come out of the strike with his reputation enhanced. His success demonstrates the importance of style and personality in public affairs. He had staunchly defended the PRC position throughout, a sin for which others were pilloried. Not Lee. His unfailingly polite style bore him serenely above the fray where others were battle-axed unmercifully. So strong was Lee's position that when he insisted on unanimous club support in writing for his succeeding Grebey, he got it.

How the players came out is a little more difficult to assess. Miller argued that the settlement was a victory for the "spirit" of the players. Something can be said for that. Led by Miller as a trusting light brigade into the valley of death, they held together much better than the owners. If there was any doubt about their ability to hang tough, and many in ownership doubted it, they resolved that doubt. However foolhardy I may have thought the strike to be, I admired their resolve and, yes, their spirit. I liked to call them the most talented athletes in the world; they certainly had the spirit of thoroughbreds. On the negative side, they were the major financial losers. Miller's folly had cost them nearly $30 million.

It is equally difficult to calculate how it all came out for the owners. They got their compensation, though in a much watered down form. More important, they demonstrated that even in the face of their "loose cannons," as Grebey aptly described the owner dissidents, a strong majority could hold together and stand for something they believed in. Miller's gamble that he could stampede them by a strike was wrong. They, too, had some spirit. Financially, the clubs did poorly in 1981, losing over $50 million. But the figures in 1980 and years subsequent to 1981 indicate they would have lost that amount in any event.

As for Marvin Miller, he had shown he could hold his union together, not an inconsequential feat considering the formidable test he had given the men. By tenacious resistance, he had watered down the compensation plan of the clubs but only at a terrible price to the players and fans. He had brilliantly carried off a propaganda campaign that impugned the ethics and motives of his opponents and heaped the blame for his deeds on them. Lectured by Judge Werker for his insincerity in a court decision on the eve of the strike, Miller turned insincerity into an art form. Guided by an ego that was the North Star of his life, he followed it wherever it led. Fortunately for the players, the path of that star sometimes coincided with the path of their own destiny. In 1981, it did not. He left a legacy of hatred and bitterness between clubs and players that would destructively sour labor relations in baseball for years to come. If he was not the only cause, he was the preponderant one.

Finally, how did I fare in all this? Poorly at best, and that may overstate the case in my favor. Miller's propaganda campaign had its major effect on me. Reading over the press clippings five years later, I realize that the effect was even worse than I thought at the time. I elected to maintain a low profile, exactly as NFL commissioner Pete Rozelle would do a year later when his game was shut down by a strike of greater duration. I considered taking Miller on intensively and publicly but rejected that course for two basic reasons: an already acrimonious atmosphere would only have been worsened to the disadvantage of the bargaining process; the effectiveness of my continuing pressure on the PRC would have been markedly reduced had I gone public with the details. Satisfied then and now that those reasons were correct, I spoke sparingly to the press, but when I did I told them the truth as I saw it, exactly as I had done since I took the job in 1969.

Was my relationship with the clubs impaired by the events of 1981? If anything, that relationship may have been improved. The clubs saw more clearly than most that I was supporting what I thought was right for the game and its public. They deeply resented Miller's efforts to make me the villain in his place. I believe this is why the great majority of clubs stood so firmly behind me in my final challenge.

On the negative side, 1981 generated some minority opposition among the clubs because of the split season. Three contending clubs lost out entirely, never even making the expanded playoffs: Cincinnati, Baltimore and St. Louis. Their gripes were legitimate. Still, a commissioner has to look to the overall best interests of the game. That sometimes means that legitimate club interests have to be sacrificed to the common good. Most owners understood this need for sacrifice even if their special interests lost out in the process. Those three contending clubs elected not to understand and to band together against me. This coalition brought together, among others, Ed Williams of Baltimore and Lou Susman of St. Louis. Not fondly regarded by their baseball peers, they nonetheless understood the rules on the reelection of a commissioner. They knew that four votes in the National League or five among the American Leaguers could kill a commissioner. From his Martha's Vineyard retreat, Williams intoned ominously on the split season: "We were allowed absolutely no input in the decision-making process. It was obvious that the best plan offered was the one by [Orioles general manager] Hank Peters, which would have sent the clubs with the two best records in each division to the playoffs. They had that plan for thirty days to look at, but rejected it without comment and never gave it a chance of being adopted.

"That's nothing new. Those people haven't listened to reason yet. But it is a situation that we cannot allow to continue any longer than necessary. And we will not. At the first available opportunity, we will try to start making some changes."

Never mind that he was 100 percent wrong on every factual assertion he made, he was looking for "change" and I was the target.

The voice of the Cincinnati pitching ace Tom Seaver stood out on the other side of the ledger. He said, "We knew the rules going in. You can moan all you want, but we had our chances."

Finally, one should ask if the nightmarish struggle for compensation was worth the effort. I would like to answer with great certainty that it was. I cannot honestly say that. The better answer is that it *probably* was. With the advent of free agency in 1976, a century after the founding of the National League, the checks and balances of baseball had gone out of whack. Through the long domination by the clubs before 1976, the game had been run as something approaching a public trust, laying aside the kind of cheapskate practices that had contributed to the Black Sox scandal of 1919. The fans had enjoyed honest baseball and the best prices in entertainment. Management profits had been modest at best in an industry that, remarkably for its monopoly status, had operated at a break-even level. For all their faults, the clubs had shown a sense of responsibility for the long-term welfare of the game and the fans. So, indeed, had their commissioners. Free agency threatened that sense. Player agents and the Players Association were concerned only with the financial welfare of the players. There were no other considerations. There was nothing wrong with that so long as they did not control the game. The trouble was that increasingly they did, given the leverage generated by the short supply of major-league talent.

All of this came into focus in 1981, when the clubs sought to protect the modest compensation system they had won in the 1980 negotiations and the Players Association sought to eradicate that system with its June strike. More important than compensation was the need to protect the clubs' control of the game. It might have been forfeited indefinitely had the clubs yielded to Miller's threat and followed the counsel of their dissident owners. I thought it was unlikely that the Players Association would soon again test the vigor with which management would protect its prerogatives. I also thought it was unlikely that either would soon forget the spirit and vigor of the other during those bleak days they had endured in June and July. The brevity of the strike in 1985 (two days), involving as it did issues of tremendous importance to the Players Association and clubs, demonstrated the point. Perhaps we had introduced an era of mutual respect that would benefit the game.

27

The Unraveling

The strike and its aftermath led inescapably to the nine-owner
letter, calling for my resignation, which was shredded on December 10, 1981, at our major-league meetings in Hollywood,
Florida. All that was shredded was paper. The spirit of that letter
was intact. How had it come to be?

Remarkably enough for a business in which almost everything
leaks, the letter had been in existence for ten days without the
press's or my office's getting wind of it. On November 30, the nine
owners met secretly at New York's Grand Hyatt Hotel, less than a
mile from my office, where I was holding meetings with Chub
Feeney and with my Budget and Audit Committee. Beside my diary
entry for that date appear these printed lines:

> If you are patient in one moment of anger, you will escape a
> hundred days of sorrow.
>
> —Chinese Proverb

Patience was going to be a long suit of mine for the next three
years.

Several months after our June 1981 dinner in New York when he
terminated our friendship, Ed Williams had in fact organized the
meeting with the assistance of Lou Susman, Gussie Busch's lawyer
from St. Louis. I learned later that Susman had been secretly campaigning against me since December 1980. Present were Ballard
Smith, John McMullen, Bill Williams, Eddie Chiles, George Stein-

brenner, George Argyros, Nelson Doubleday and Fred Wilpon (both of the Mets), Susman and Ed Williams. Jerry Reinsdorf was invited, but upon learning of the subject matter, declined.

Steinbrenner, who throughout the process would publicly be both on my side and against me, characterized the meeting as "National League inspired. Susman was the organizer, the principal speaker. He did everything. There are guys in our league sympathetic to Susman's position, but it's very much stronger in the National League." George told me privately that Williams was the moving force behind the meeting. It was at the Grand Hyatt that the "Hollywood Letter" was drafted and signed. When the National League met on the morning of December 10, the pro-Kuhn forces carried out their plan of the night before to assail the National League signers. They did so with such vehemence that Susman in a gesture of peace destroyed the letter. One National League owner described the meeting as "a real bloodletting." Both leagues then decided to create a major-league restructuring committee to study the entire administrative structure of the game. It was in part a compromise between the antagonists. The forces in support of me considered it a useful dilatory tactic, providing time to evaluate and probe the strength of my enemies.

The "Hollywood Letter" was leaked overnight to the enterprising Milton Richman of UPI. He asked to see me. Sitting serenely by the pool on the last day of the meetings, I confirmed the existence of the letter but stressed the positive aspects of the restructuring committee, which I called a "positive force for the good of Bowie Kuhn." Milton found me "not uncommonly concerned." He was right. I was surprised myself by my relaxed, even amused, attitude. With the filing of his story after we had all left Hollywood, the subject was out in the open.

Before I left Hollywood, I had a long meeting with Roy Eisenhardt who, with Peter O'Malley, would serve as cochairman on the restructuring committee. I found his attitude constructive. For a new owner, Roy had an exceptionally good feel for the game. He was also supportive of me, dispelling rumors that he might be flirting with the American League mavericks. I also announced the members of the restructuring committee. They were Argyros, Eisenhardt, Reinsdorf, Bud Selig, Steinbrenner and Haywood Sullivan from the American League, and Bill Bartholomay, Charles Bronfman, O'Malley, Ballard Smith, Susman and Bill Williams from the National League.

I spent the next week in New York. It was a memorable one. On Wednesday I had lunch with Howard Cosell, who reminded me that he had warned me several months earlier about Nelson Doubleday's hostility. Howard had made a special visit to my office to tell me not to trust Doubleday, basing this opinion on a conversation he had had with Doubleday the night before. While Nelson was known to wax more lyrical than rational in evening sessions, I had reason to believe that Howard was correct.

On Thursday morning, O'Malley was in the office at 8:00 A.M. Joined by MacPhail, Feeney and Lou Hoynes, the National League attorney, we went over a checklist of every major-league club and developed a strategy for sounding out the dissidents and the doubtfuls. The most interesting decision was to leave Williams to the Executive Council, of which he and Ballard Smith were the two newest members. Experience had shown that membership on the Council always had a salutary effect on a member's relationship with the commissioner.

The next day, I heard from both Bob Howsam and Bob Lurie. Howsam called from Cincinnati.

"Commissioner," he said, "I think things will work out okay here. Don't worry."

Lurie called from San Francisco to report on a lunch with Ballard Smith. Smith confessed that he had been "swept up by Susman and Ed Williams."

Luisa and I closed out the week by taking our mothers, representing 161 years of wisdom, to the Princeton–Ohio State basketball game at Madison Square Garden. Since I particularly relish seeing an Ivy League team beat the mighty Big Ten at anything athletic, I was not too happy when Ohio State pulled away in the second half to beat Princeton. The ladies, enjoying the scene a good bit more than the contest, hardly noticed.

It had been a good week, one full of laughter—an excellent tonic for an embattled commissioner. The weeks that followed would not be the same.

The star of the week, and indeed of the ensuing years, was unquestionably Peter O'Malley. His trip to New York was, as much as anything else, designed to reassure me. It exemplified what would be his selfless conduct as he struggled not only for my welfare but for what he saw as that of the game. I would hear from him every day with ideas, questions, news or just with encouragement. He sought nothing in return, unusual behavior in a game where quid pro quo was a common way of doing business. He was unshakable in his support, rallying the undecideds and firm in his resistance to the dissidents. He even took to supporting revenue sharing, which would hurt him most of all. He did so because he thought it would help my cause. His only concession to self-interest was the suggestion that we ease into it gradually. Like Fetzer and Galbreath, Yawkey and Autry, he believed in the office of the commissioner and believed that for the game to function at its best, the commissioner had to be supported.

Ballard Smith flew to New York to meet me for dinner at 21 three days before Christmas. As I waited for his call from the airport, I reflected on my relationship over the past several years with my newest Executive Council member. The fact was that I had never really gotten to know him well. Perhaps I and some of the owners had been guilty of not taking him seriously enough. His youth (he was thirty-five) had probably been the reason. He had grumbled about my not keeping in touch with him during the strike, and we had exchanged some sharp words over rulings I had made regarding his financial obligations to Willie Montanez. He also resented the $100,000 fine I imposed on Ray Kroc for tampering with potential free agents Graig Nettles and Joe Morgan, even though that fine had prompted Ray to put Ballard in charge of the Padres. Still, I thought he was a bright young man who had a future in baseball.

Ballard brought me two books as an early Christmas gift—Jim Fixx's second book on running and *The One Minute Manager*. Over cocktails, he got right to the point.

"I think I made a mistake signing the letter," he said. "Lou Susman and Edward Bennett Williams were very persuasive. But when I got home from Hollywood, O'Malley and Lurie jumped on me pretty hard. And Joan [Kroc] wasn't very happy about it, either. She likes you. Frankly, I've just plain changed my mind. And I've flown here tonight just to get that off my chest. Whatever differences we've had, I want you to know that I'm now prepared to be one hundred percent supportive."

I was impressed with his candor and touched that he had flown cross-country just to deliver that message. It was the beginning of a strong and lasting friendship. True to his word, he became a fervent member of the Kuhn camp, calling often to share information and offer encouragement. Though Williams lobbied him to return to the rebels, Ballard resisted.

An article by Dave Nightingale in *The Sporting News* stirred up a storm. He quoted an "unnamed owner" as saying "we hoped that Bowie might see the depth of our intent . . . that his future was a fait accompli. If he had gone quietly, if he had quit in December, he probably would have received a nice payoff . . . a big chunk of severance money. But now, if the National League opposition to him holds firm at contract renewal time, it'll be a different story. . . .

"I can't predict for certain that he won't be renewed. He's smart and he's a fighter. He seems to have gone underground lately and he probably has people at work to try and sway enough votes to keep him on the job . . . as he did in 1975 when he nearly lost a renewal vote."

The implication that I could be "bought" enraged my friends. Peter and Ballard called it "indecent to everyone." Eisenhardt was dismayed. Buzzie Bavasi telephoned to say, "Gene Autry says not to worry about those sons of bitches!"

Steinbrenner telephoned Bud Selig to express his disappointment at the article. He said he'd "had a drink with Nightingale," but didn't tell him anything.

Jerry Holtzman of the *Chicago Tribune* became the major media outlet for my opponents. He wrote: "The guess here is that Kuhn will resign sometime before mid-May. Anyway, Emperor Kuhn should be glad he's an American. If this were Russia, he'd be sent to Siberia and all traces of him expunged."

In addition to the idea that I could be bought, a pattern of "dirty tricks" began to emerge through the rumor mills or the newspaper columns. I was pictured as desperate for the job. "Don't kid yourself," said an unnamed owner to syndicated sportswriter Buddy Martin, "[Kuhn] needs the job. And as for that baloney about him going back to his old firm, forget it. They don't want him back."

The rumor mills produced reports that I was in the job for the perks. "Bowie loves the trappings that go with the job," said another unnamed owner to Martin. "The limousines, the expensive restaurants, the bodyguards, the dignitaries, all that glitter. For that kind of money we can get somebody better, somebody who knows how to sell the game, whose image is classier."

The dirty-tricks campaign, which continued and expanded as the confrontation wore on, hardly suggested that my opponents were interested in compromise. That is more obvious to me now than it was at the time.

In February, Smith hosted an Executive Council meeting at the

Kroc ranch in the Santa Ynez Mountains of Southern California. We were missing only Ed Williams, who called me to explain his absence. It was the first time we had talked in months. Considering that by then I was painfully aware that Ed had inspired the campaign against me, it was a remarkably civil conversation. I did not know that Ed's health was deteriorating, nor did he hint at that as we talked. With Williams absent, all present were supporters of mine, including Roy Eisenhardt, who was present as cochairman of the restructuring committee. Essentially it was a love-in, which was good for my morale but bad for any realistic consideration of the guys we were calling "the black hats." By now they included eight clubs (the original nine letter signers minus our host Smith). We counted the Chicago Cubs as a fence sitter and Atlanta as unpredictable—in the style of its owner, Ted Turner. If the Braves and Cubs both tumbled into the black-hat encampment, there would be six National League votes against me. That should have given us more indigestion than it did at the time. Like baseball in the spring, we were inclined to optimism.

Turner was a puzzle. Everybody had a different guess. I received messages saying "Ted loves you" then read in the press that he was a solid opponent. There was no doubt we were antagonists on the superstation issue, which was bread and butter to Ted, but Bill Bartholomay, who spoke for Ted (if anyone could) and was an old friend of mine, said that Ted really was on the fence. I had a typical call from Ted after the California Executive Council meeting.

"How ya doin', Principal?"

"Just fine, Ted. How are you?"

"I hope you've noticed that I'm not linked with those guys going after you; everybody's looking for a scapegoat, but the problems are the owners' fault, not yours."

"I'm glad you feel that way, Ted."

"By the way, I've just been to Cuba to see Fidel Castro, and he'd like to send a team to the United States. Any problem with that?"

"Yes, it is a problem. I really don't think we should play any games with the Cubans unless they are willing to let Cuban players sign professional contracts if they so desire."

"I see, well, any problem if I televise a Cuban all-star game on the superstation?"

"No, that's okay," I said.

The more I thought about Ted, the more I thought he did not want to cast a vote to assassinate the commissioner, but because the superstation issue was critical, he would do so if there was no way to avoid it.

In August 1981, the Cubs passed from the Wrigley family to the Tribune Company, but not until I had extracted from the new owners assurances that they would comply in all ways with baseball's television policy, particularly with regard to superstations. Like WTBS-Atlanta, WGN-Chicago, which carried the Cubs, had become a superstation and WGN belonged to the Tribune Company. I did not want another of our clubs contesting our congressional position against the superstations. Oddly, the National League was sitting on its hands on this question, leaving me to impose conditions on the new owners. So there was one recent source of friction. In addition, Andy McKenna was brought in as club president, and Andy had been a Veeck ally in my successful opposition to Veeck's sale of the White Sox to Edward J. DeBartolo, Sr. Source of friction number two. Finally, the Cubs made Dallas Green executive vice president and general manager. Dallas, like Dick Wagner in Cincinnati, resented directions from the commissioner, and Dallas resented lawyers in general. Wagner and Green saw things only in black and white. During his Philadelphia career, Dallas had chafed over my decisions in a number of cases. Source of friction number three.

Add to the mix Lou Susman's telling McKenna that McKenna ought to be the next commissioner and Anheuser-Busch's negotiating a new long-term broadcasting agreement with the Cubs with greatly increased rights fees, and it had to be a wonder that McKenna was not wearing a black hat twenty-four hours a day.

The fact remained that the Cubs were neither for me nor against me, a situation I attributed to the efforts of Tribune's chief executive officer, Stan Cook, to take a balanced view. I thought that Cook, like Turner, did not want to be responsible for voting me out.

In 1983 I had problems with the Cubs regarding our new NBC-ABC contracts, and in 1984 we had a major confrontation on the issue of lights in Wrigley Field, but none of that had any bearing on the events involving me in 1982.

One day in late February, I learned that Williams had cancer of the liver and was in Memorial Sloan-Kettering Center in Manhattan for radical surgery. I took a cab to the hospital, which was about ten minutes from my office. I arrived to find Ed clad in pajamas and seated in a chair. He looked remarkably well and acted the same. His wife, Agnes, was in the room. She had a quiet, thoughtful style that nicely complemented the ebullience of her husband. He said he felt great and was totally optimistic about his future. That was his nature.

After twenty relaxed minutes, I got up to go. He said he would like to walk me to the elevator. We moved slowly down the hall together, but he needed no support. He looked at me and said, "We've had a lot of problems in the past, Commissioner, but they've been mostly my fault. I have been very mean-spirited. Now I'm going to straighten all that out. You'll see. My actions will speak louder than those words." We shook hands and I left.

Before long there were press reports quoting Ed as saying he had changed his mind and would support my reelection. Indeed, he became a major strategist to that end. And where was I on opening day of the 1982 season? With him in Baltimore's Memorial Stadium.

Only seven letter signers were left, but four still were in the National League. That was enough to beat me—Doubleday, Busch, McMullen and Bill Williams. I decided to confront them all. I saw absolutely nothing to lose. When Ed Williams advised that John McMullen would like to see me, John became the first test.

We had lunch in early April. There was no awkwardness. John talks easily and volubly. He told me straight away: "I'll vote for Bowie Kuhn if that's what it'll take to stop restructuring." He explained that he wanted a strong commissioner and was afraid restructuring would water down the commissioner's powers.

Then he specified his complaints. He was unhappy that I had not cleared Al Rosen immediately in the 1980 casino investigation. He was troubled by player salary escalation, which he called his primary concern. He also observed that there were owners who were "in" and owners who were "out" of the game's mainstream. He thought the "in" owners were appointed to committees. He said I fostered the separation. He complained that he rarely heard from me. And he was not happy about my support of Ray Grebey.

The lunch was cordial though we vigorously debated some of the issues he raised. A man without a coy bone, John was blunt. He made no promises and I sought none. As I described our discussion later, I called it useful but inconclusive.

Though the conversions of Ed Williams and Ballard Smith to my cause had dispelled a lot of press negativism about my chances of success, names of possible successors appeared regularly. Among them were Richard Nixon and Jerry Ford, Supreme Court justices Byron White and Potter Stewart, Henry Kissinger, Senator Tom Eagleton, former New Jersey governor Brendan Byrne (an old friend who came to see me to deny it), Yale president A. Bartlett Giamatti, former players Henry Aaron, Stan Musial, Willie Mays and Jim Bunning, NFL commissioner Pete Rozelle, Eastern Airlines' CEO Frank Borman and baseball executives Lee MacPhail, John McHale, Fred Wilpon, Bob Howsam and Hank Peters. Around my office, checking out and circulating the newest names was something of a parlor game. Even more fun was inventing our own twists, e.g., Yassir Arafat tops dissident list for baseball czar. I saw a newspaper picture of a sleek politician with his head on Arafat's shoulder. With stories that I had been shamelessly politicking for my job in mind, I recaptioned the picture "Kuhn Seen Importuning Dissident Owner" and sent it around to people like Ballard Smith and Ed Williams and anyone else who might see the humor.

The most interesting story of all was that my friend Bud Selig wanted the job. When I heard it the second or third time, I called Bud and told him what I had heard. It was an easy call to make because I was—and remain—as close to him as I was to anyone in baseball. I knew and loved all the Seligs. So I said, "Bud, if this is true, I would be glad to announce my retirement in your favor. My main concern is that the game not fall into the hands of people who don't understand or care for it. If you're interested, tell me." His answer, "Absolutely not." However, it was not the last time I would bring up the subject.

In April, I called Lou Susman.

"I heard you were unhappy that you hadn't heard from me," I said, "so here I am."

"Oh, it wasn't me, Commissioner," he answered. "It was Gussie. He knew you were in St. Louis and was surprised you hadn't called." The reference was to a March appearance I had made at Greenville College in southern Illinois, where President Richard Stephens had conferred upon me an honorary doctorate. TV sportcaster Jay Randolph had interviewed me on local television, so Susman used the incident to imply in his comments to Busch that I had been in St. Louis and was ignoring him. I doubt that Gussie cared one way or the other. But it was an example of the little things Lou did to wear you down. The theme of my acceptance remarks at Greenville College was "From Adversity Comes Strength," taken from St. Paul's second letter to the Corinthians. It was a subject on which I could speak with great conviction.

Susman said, "I've been meaning to write to you—would you be available in New York on May sixth?"

We both noted the date.

The dirty-tricks campaign got worse. Eddie Chiles wrote to all the owners, saying: "One of the rumors [I hear] is that the Commissioner is literally campaigning for re-election to his office much the same as a politician. I hear that he is trying to buy votes by offering all sorts of bribes or inducements to the people whose votes can help him." He later told Ballard Smith that "Steinbrenner conned me into writing."

I first heard of the letter from O'Malley. (Chiles had written "Dear Pete" on his letter, probably the first time that anyone had called him Pete.) O'Malley thought the letter was so bad it might help the cause, feeling that even some of the well-intended dissidents like Bill Williams would be annoyed at the bribery suggestion.

Other comments began to drift in. Roy Eisenhardt thought it was terrible; Selig was aghast; Ed Williams would bring it up with Chiles directly; Haywood Sullivan was mad. Gene Autry wrote a three-page letter to Chiles, saying: "As far as the Commissioner campaigning, I have had occasion to talk with him several times when he was on the west coast, and I can truthfully say he has never asked me for my vote or asked me to campaign for him."

Notwithstanding Chiles, there were positive signs emerging. Ed Williams called to say he was confident he could turn Bill Williams and Argyros around. Steinbrenner called Tom Villante to say he did not like the talk that George was "against Kuhn." He said it was not so.

On April 21, the same day Chiles wrote his "bribes" letter, Doubleday joined me for lunch at my suggestion. We had a freewheeling discussion in which he assured me that his points of contention with me were "nothing personal." He made two major points. He stressed his concern about revenue sharing, which he called "socialism." Since he had bought the Mets for what he considered a big price, he did not see why he should share the benefits of New York with others. He faulted me for my support of revenue sharing, particularly with regard to broadcasting. He also faulted me for not firing Tom Villante after the Mets and Villante had come to verbal blows at the major-league meeting in Arizona the prior November. Tom had challenged the Mets for their indifference to the national television contracts that put critically important revenue in our Central Fund bank account that all clubs shared evenly.

"What are our objectives here?" Tom had asked. "We're doing this for everyone! There's one club in this room that would like to see the Central Fund disappear!"

Frank Cashen, seated next to Doubleday, called out, "Identify that club!"

Tom hesitated, giving his sense of diplomacy a chance to take control.

"Name that club!" Cashen demanded again. "You've made a charge, now substantiate it for all of us!"

Diplomacy lost.

"Nelson Doubleday," said Tom.

I told Doubleday that Tom was a unique asset to baseball, and was liked and appreciated by our clubs. "You can't please everyone," I reminded him. I was not about to please Nelson on that issue.

We talked about a variety of other matters such as our opinions that Steinbrenner was an upsetting influence in baseball, that Turner's superstation was "hurting all the clubs," and finally whether we could get Vice President Bush to visit Shea Stadium for a game. The meeting was certainly a good exchange of views, but I had not changed my commitment to revenue sharing, which was poison to Nelson. He gave no sign of changing his opposition to me.

I learned from an owner that Susman had told him two days before my meeting with Lou that "Bowie's gotta go and if Peter O'Malley wants a war on the issue, he'll get one." He had also said, "Don't worry, we've got the votes."

I invited Lou to join Luisa and me for dinner on May 6. Alternatively, I suggested drinks or a meeting in my office. I could not stand the prospect of having dinner with him and was steering toward a short meeting. I was not certain my patience could take several hours of Susman. He told me that drinks at 5:00 P.M. would be fine.

Over drinks, he said, "I want you to know that I represent the views of Gussie, Fred Kuhlmann [another Cardinal officer and director] and August Busch III [Gussie's son]." Significantly, Busch III was also the chief executive officer of Anheuser-Busch. Susman went on to say, "The Cardinals are discouraged. We doubt there's any solution at hand. The clubs are, and will remain, selfish, with no sense of partnership. We'll lose about one point eight million dollars this year with a two-million attendance. Revenue sharing will not work.

"I think the Commissioner's position is now discredited. We need someone like Potter Stewart to handle our judicial matters. The Commissioner can't both discipline and lead.

"You haven't fired Villante after the fiasco in Scottsdale.

"You haven't gotten broadcasting agreements in place.

"I can't imagine why you'd want to continue; you can make much more money away from baseball. Gussie is personally very fond of you. You've given yeoman service to professional baseball. He's not angry at you for any decisions, fines or labor matters. The labor problems in 1976, 1980 and 1981 weren't your fault."

Then Susman moved into high gear, saying, "Gussie asked Fred Kuhlmann recently if you'd ever done anything in response to our visit last year to see if you could get us into the network broadcasting sponsorships. We had to tell him that Bowie Kuhn has done nothing. We also told him that Anheuser-Busch is now on 'Monday Night Football' because Pete Rozelle got us in and Miller out."

I interrupted him to say that both he and Kuhlmann knew full well that I could not do anything with the current broadcast packages, but that with the concurrence of our clubs I would do what I could when new contracts were negotiated in 1983. He made no response. However, when I pressed the issue by saying that I hoped brewery concerns were not taking precedence in all this over baseball concerns, he dodged the issue by saying, "I shouldn't even have mentioned the brewery matter." Now I knew we had gotten to the crux of the situation.

Like a man composing fugues, Susman wove various themes into the conversation. Listening carefully, I now heard two more major themes. He revealed that Gussie felt I should be "well taken care of financially" if I left the commissionership. He repeated this thought a little later to make sure I had not missed it. Then he said, "Gussie would like to call for a major-league meeting soon to deal with your reelection; you're in a lame-duck situation and that's bad."

He wound up by saying revenue sharing was a very divisive issue, tackling me on what everyone knew was one of my favorite concepts. He also rapped me for using too many law firms, but surprised me by acknowledging that my former partner, Lou Hoynes, was a star performer. It had been my observation over the years that Susman resented Hoynes's excellence, so I was surprised at the concession.

I told him I would discuss the suggested meeting with the Executive Council.

We broke up after an hour and a half. I had learned some very interesting things. If I would get out, a rich golden parachute was available to carry me to my rest. While there was much talk of Gussie's being "upset," the brewery had emerged as a major player in the St. Louis picture. I ruminated on a warning the late Walter O'Malley had given me years before. Because Anheuser-Busch sponsored the local broadcasts of a majority of major-league clubs, he asserted their potential for mischief was enormous, given the leverage those substantial dollar commitments made possible. When I argued that the threat was more theoretical than real, he advised, "Maybe so, but keep your eyes open anyway."

I sent a handwritten note to Gussie the next morning.

May 7

Dear Gussie,

As you know, I met with Lou Susman last evening at "21" and found the discussion very interesting and am only sorry it didn't occur sooner. He said you would like to visit with me in New York before there is any major league consideration of my situation. I would certainly like to see you but would prefer to come to St. Louis. Please let me know if this is agreeable and we will pick a date—hopefully in the near future.

Best regards,
Bowie

I wanted to test the validity of Susman's assertion that Gussie wanted to see me. On May 19, Gussie's secretary called my office in response to my letter. She said, "Mr. Busch is assuming that it's in reference to the problems in baseball. There is no reason for you to come to St. Louis. At the present time, he is not prepared to vote for your reelection. If you feel a face-to-face meeting would be beneficial, he would meet you at a convenient time." I wrote to Gussie and said, "Please let me know your pleasure." There was no answer.

On May 24, Peter O'Malley wrote to Busch about an appointment. He said, "For many years, when problems arose, the Cardinals and the Dodgers always pulled together and it is for this reason that I wish to visit with you."

Gussie's secretary called Peter and said, "Do you want to speak with him about the commissioner?"

"Yes," said Peter.

"Then Mr. Busch says, 'Don't waste your time.'"

Some things were getting clearer.

Not long after my meeting with Susman, I gave a long, ranging interview to Don Markus of the *The Record* in Bergen County, New Jersey, something of a home newspaper for me as a Bergenite.

Reading it over now, I find a line that jumps out at me. I said, "Bowie Kuhn is a pretty good guy and that isn't always the impression the public gets through the filtering process of the media." It was an odd thing for me to say. I rarely indulged in public personal analysis. Perhaps the reelection process was penetrating my thick skin. One thing could not be missed. The press, long my adversary, was beginning to shift to my side. I think they liked the struggling Kuhn better than the imperial one they felt they used to know.

As I was determined to see through these rounds of diplomacy, whether they were getting me anywhere or not, I put Cincinnati next on the list. Some thought it was still a swing vote; others thought they were against me—"in cement." I arranged to fly to Cincinnati to see Bill Williams and his brother Jim.

As Lou Nippert had been before them, the Williams brothers were among the most self-effacing owners in baseball. Along with Nippert they had given the Reds a low-key, gentlemanly leadership that was uncommon in baseball. Luisa and I had known them all and their wives for years and had enjoyed their company. Though I had angered the Cincinnati leadership in 1977 with my decision that denied them Vida Blue, I looked forward to this meeting without reservation.

Two years apart in age, both brothers were in their sixties, both products of Georgetown University. Jim, the older of the two, did little talking the day I visited. Bill, a shy, cautious, conservative man of medium height, was slender, with dark hair and a lined face. He was high-minded and proper in his behavior and speech. The brothers received me warmly.

I opened the serious part of the conversation by asking if they felt, as I had heard, that I was biased against the Reds owing to my ruling on Blue, the 1981 split season, which had hurt them, and Dick Wagner's well-known antagonism toward me. Bill said such rumors were "absolutely untrue." Specifically, he said that Wagner had never talked against me and that Bob Howsam was my friend. I found the reference to Wagner incredible. I had to wonder if I was dealing with men who were going to avoid a personal confrontation no matter what.

Bill went on to say the signing of the Hollywood letter was not personal in any way, that it was merely designed to stop my reelection at Hollywood. He said he would favor my reelection at our regular August meeting if three basic problems could be solved: restructuring, revenue sharing and financial controls on the clubs.

As our meeting moved from their office to the Queen City Club, Bill observed that we needed an enhanced law department and criticized Turner and Steinbrenner for foolish player signings. He thought they should be out of the game. As I flew home, I was convinced they meant well but was fearful they could be manipulated by their dissident confreres. The observation about the law department sounded like something from a Susman script. I made it back to LaGuardia in time for a night game at Shea Stadium.

After a speech at the Coast Guard Academy, I told the press I would not continue if any effort was made to cut my powers. I was consistently drumming that point home and the press was reacting well to it. I was not pulling any punches. The Associated Press's Will Grimsley wrote: "Baseball would do well to keep Kuhn as commissioner although he has been under sharp attacks from some owners and many fans, the latter unfamiliar with his role.

"Assessing Kuhn's tenure objectively, one will find he has not bent over backwards to soft-soap his bosses."

Eddie Chiles, a man for whom I had no great admiration, surprised me at a PRC meeting we both attended by saying in the presence of the committee that he had been wrong to write the "bribe" letter about me and wanted to apologize.

Ted Turner, who did not like the tough stand I was continuing to take about his superstation's carrying Braves games to cable systems across America, had asked me if he could appear before our Executive Council and plead his case. I had agreed. Now he called to say he would be several hours late because he had to testify on cable before Congressman Tim Wirth's committee. Since I had passed up the same opportunity before Wirth because of the council meeting, I chided him a little and suggested he be my understudy before the congressmen. Of course, our positions were diametrically opposed. He said, "Commissioner, I'll be happy to."

Charles Bronfman told me that Doubleday was "set against" me. Nelson was upset about my position on revenue sharing, particularly my campaign to have clubs share a portion of their local pay-television revenue. He told Charles that I "was not budging." Nelson was right. I believed in revenue sharing and was not going to budge for him or anyone else. Charles also told me he had heard from Lou Susman that he was "bitter about the way Bowie treated Anheuser-Busch."

A major-league meeting had been called for Chicago on June 14 and 15 by the Restructuring Committee. Either the white hats or black hats could have put my reelection on the agenda and neither did. Obviously, neither side was sure they had enough votes. I know that my fellows were leery of a vote before acceptance of the restructuring report. O'Malley warned that the opposition might make a direct request that I stand aside. I told him if they did I would refuse on the basis of my wide support and the disruptive effect of a new man at this stage of our affairs.

Another matter came to a head at the same time. The Players Association had sent a series of letters to the clubs and their TV licensees questioning whether the clubs owned baseball television rights and threatening litigation. It was a remarkable claim, since the clubs had always sold their television rights without challenge from the players. After discussion with the clubs at the Chicago meeting, a lawsuit was filed by major-league baseball seeking a judicial determination that the clubs were the sole owners of TV rights. It was hard to believe that Marvin Miller had stirred up yet another crunching engagement with the clubs so soon after peace had been achieved in 1981. I called it "unconscionable."*

As to restructuring, the meetings were a triumph. Roy Eisenhardt's wide-ranging and historic recommendations on behalf of the committee were approved in principle by the unanimous vote of the clubs. I called it "the most constructive day baseball has had in my fourteen years as commissioner." Even though the report was still subject to specific implementation, it was a smashing defeat for those who had sought to water down the commissioner's powers. Significantly, the PRC and Major League Baseball Promotion Corporation were to be brought under the direct control of the commissioner.

The Chicago meetings also increased the number of supportive articles being written by a press corps that seemed increasingly concerned about me now that I had joined the whooping cranes as an endangered species. George Vecsey's column in *The New York Times* was headlined BOWIE KUHN LIVES. The headline on Dave Nightingale's column in *The Sporting News* said KUHN A BIG WINNER IN UNIFIED MAJORS. Ken Nigro, who had once flown across the Pacific with me and the Orioles in 1971, wrote in the *Baltimore Sun,* "It's beginning to look like the commissioner is going to pull off another one of his magic acts. [The dissident] owners obviously discounted Kuhn's counterpunching ability. Not one name has surfaced who could be counted on to do a better job."

But there were developments that made it clear I should not yet

*The clubs prevailed in a court decision that sustained their sole ownership.

aspire to the title of a 1982 Houdini. I lost out on a sensible proposal I put before the meeting to require advance approval of all local broadcasting contracts exceeding three years in duration. A mere five clubs in the National League blocked the proposal, which required a three-quarters vote in both leagues. Since three of those votes were the Mets, Braves and Astros, the episode sent shivers down my back.

After I returned to New York, I heard unhappy news from several owners about the discussion at one of the dinner tables the first evening of our meeting. They said Turner was "vitriolic" because of things I had done to him. "I'm with you boys," Turner had told Doubleday and McMullen. Their impression was that "this thing is cast in stone." One owner had a final bit of information: he said, "Susman wants to be commissioner and has for six months."

Coming from reliable sources, that was rather devastating news. All I had to do was add St. Louis and the ball game was over. Still, I harked back to the advice Cal Griffith had once given me about the unreliability of what owners say. Also, baseball winds have a funny way of swirling.

O'Malley called with a thoughtful observation. He said Ed Williams had been with us for a number of months but had yet to produce a convert. Considering his fabled powers of persuasion, this was odd. We decided to press Ed to focus on August Busch III, CEO of Anheuser-Busch. Both Peter and I were increasingly convinced that August was the key to the St. Louis position.

Andy McKenna called about the possibility that Chub Feeney and I could help the Cubs get lights in Wrigley Field. He said lights would help them on sponsorships "as Anheuser-Busch was very interested in the Cubs," which set off alarms in my head. He pointed out that "Anheuser-Busch has the lowest beer market share in Chicago of any major market—only sixteen percent as against fifty percent in Los Angeles and thirty-five percent in New York." He concluded, "Gussie has made getting the Cubs a personal project." This suggested a tightening relationship between St. Louis and Chicago, hardly good news at this point.

Chub called several days after the Chicago sessions to say that Doubleday and McMullen were requesting a National League meeting to vote on the reelection of the commissioner. This was not the procedure for calling a major-league meeting to consider my reelection, but it was a sure sign that these men thought they had the necessary votes to beat me. Poor Chub, caught between two vying factions within his own league, was in the most delicate situation. I tried not to worsen his problems. I might not survive but I did not want him pulled down in my wake. I suggested to Chub that the major-league agenda was controlled by the Executive Council. If Nelson wanted my election on that agenda, he might as well tell me so and I would put the question to the Council. "Have Nelson call me direct," I concluded, hoping that would take Chub out of the picture. In fact, Nelson and I worked it out with the Council that my reelection would be on the agenda at the summer meeting in San Diego. The Council had agreed with some reluctance because they recognized the ominous importance of Nelson's wanting to vote. But they also recognized that so long as we controlled a majority of clubs, we could table any issue on the agenda if it suited our purpose at San Diego. Upon receiving the agenda news from me, Nelson reacted effusively, "Okay, my friend, I really appreciate that; I appreciate the way you did it. You and I are better friends than you and I realize and I really mean that." When you are commissioner, you have to listen to some remarkable things.

My fellows now began to analyze who would cast the fourth and deciding vote against me. Obviously, three votes were New York, St. Louis and Houston. The feeling was that neither the Reds nor Braves wanted to cast the fourth vote. I learned that Susman was making the same analysis and thought his chances of beating me were only fifty-fifty unless he could get a secret ballot. "Nobody in the National League wants to be the fourth vote," he had said, "including Turner."

Dick Wagner, who according to Bill Williams had never said anything bad about me, told Milwaukee's Harry Dalton in late June that I was "dishonest and unethical." Dick was not really a bad guy but he could be emotional, and a series of decisions from me adverse to the Reds (Blue, Bill Bordley, split season, cable television) had embittered him.*

Ballard Smith reported that Susman came out of the Chicago

---

*Bill Bordley was an amateur pitcher drafted by Cincinnati in 1979 after the Angels had given him assurances that they would meet his money demands if they selected him. Bordley wrote to various eastern clubs urging them not to select him. Buzzie Bavasi of the Angels called some clubs and inquired whether they intended to draft him.

We decided the Angels had violated draft rules and held a special draft. Bordley was signed by the Giants and had a 2–3 career record for them. I fined the Angels $15,000 and awarded two future draft choices to the Reds.

meetings angrier than ever—angry at Chub Feeney because the meeting was "pro-Kuhn," angry at Ballard because he did not call Lou before changing his mind on me, and angry at me because I had let "my friend Charles Bronfman of the Expos sign Gary Carter for two million dollars," because the United States Football League's new TV deal proved my people were not doing their job, because the "Pirates are in trouble, and what's Kuhn doing about it?," because the move to centralized offices in New York City might have a price tag of $400,000 and because he had not been consulted in advance about the television lawsuit against the Players Association. I was learning that Susman's indictment of me was as changeable as the weather around St. Louis. Ballard thought the indictment rehearsed on him would be effective when Susman applied it to Bill Williams.

The Council's gallows humor was growing. During one telephone conference, Haywood Sullivan asked if the Council should recommend me at the San Diego meeting. Ed Williams said if they did, it would have to be unanimous. Ewing Kauffman demurred, saying he was thinking of nominating George Steinbrenner. Feeney closed the conversation by saying, "Good idea, but let's make it a slate of Bowie and George." Laughter.

O'Malley checked with Bill Bartholomay to learn something about Turner's current temperature. He discovered several things. First, that Ted was up the Amazon somewhere with Jacques Cousteau. Ted managed to be interesting even when he was missing. Second, that Bill said Ted was neutral on me. When Peter hoped he was neutral plus, Bill said just plain neutral was pretty good considering that I had suspended him and fought with him over the superstation issue. Several days later I got some additional information regarding Turner's remarks at the Chicago dinner meeting. "I have been waiting for six years to get that SOB because of my suspension," Ted had said, "and I'm not going to miss my chance now." I thought that sounded more like neutral minus than neutral plus.

Bronfman told me he had seen Doubleday and thought he had him "ruminating." They had debated the merits of having an issues-oriented leader versus a business-oriented leader. Charles was a philosopher, believing strongly in the public-trust and public-service aspects of the game. A Bronfman-Doubleday confrontation was like Plato debating Huey Long. Charles cautioned about the importance of avoiding a secret ballot in August. Increasingly, the white hats were concerned that the opposition wanted to hide in the shadows.

Now another member of the press gave me a lift. This time it was John Steadman of the *Baltimore News-American.* He wrote:

> Certainly Kuhn gives baseball an intellectual level of recognition no other commissioner can challenge. There's no doubt he has been particularly fair to the players and maybe this has perturbed his antagonists.
>
> Baseball should realize the goodness and capabilities of the man and, instead of making him battle for survival, reward him with a lifetime contract.

The *Philadelphia Inquirer's* Frank Dolson, who had pounded me steadily over the years, said, "It isn't easy to write these words but here goes, anyway: I hope Bowie Kuhn gets what he wants."

These press comments changed nothing in the balance between my friends and foes but through them I understood how decent the press could be. It was a lesson I had been slow to learn.

On July 29, John Fetzer, John Galbreath and Dan Galbreath flew to St. Louis in the Galbreaths' private plane to see Gussie Busch. Gussie was joined by his son August III, Fred Kuhlmann and Susman. My supporters felt that the two senior statesmen Fetzer and John Galbreath, along with the respected Danny Galbreath, could shake the old brewer's opposition.

Kuhlmann, doing most of the talking for the Cardinals, spelled out what was presented as their collective beliefs—that Bowie Kuhn got high marks as a disciplinarian and for integrity and decency and should be retained, but that a businessman CEO was needed to report directly to the clubs, bypassing the commissioner. The commissioner would handle disciplinary and Washington matters. The visitors insisted that any "businessman" brought into the picture report to the commissioner. The dispute was clearly focused.

There was no possibility that I would accept the Busch proposal.

August III reported the meeting to Ed Williams and Susman did the same for O'Malley. Both O'Malley and Williams thought there was a deal there somewhere. I respected them both as extremely bright and practical men, but I thought it sounded like a rehash of unacceptable ideas. Peter reported a comment by Susman that stuck in my mind. "I like Bowie," Lou had said. "He's great in Washington but he's not flexible. We can't get a good businessman to report to him. He's too much like Landis."

On August 3, Sandy Hadden and I drafted a statement outlining the conditions under which I would remain in office. It included provisions that the commissioner be the CEO of baseball, and report to a twenty-six-club Board of Directors regarding general business affairs.

Between major-league meetings, the Executive Council would have the full power of the Board, and the commissioner's final authority on judicial matters and those involving the integrity of the game would continue.

A Chief Operating Officer for Business Affairs (COOBA) would be selected by the Executive Council to take responsibility for national broadcasting, marketing, promotion, films, licensing, financial matters, long-range planning and office administration. The "COOBA" would report to the commissioner, and in the event of disagreement, either one could submit the matter to the Executive Council for resolution.

I sent the plan to Ed Williams for his continuing discussions with August III. The same day Ed called me and said, "The signs are that they are caving in. They are looking for a way out." However, he was not hopeful about Doubleday. "We'll just have to persuade the others." When Ed received my draft, he called to say it was very fair. Since he did not much like the role of COOBA, he predictably changed the name to COBRA.

With just a couple of weeks until the San Diego meetings, various members of the Executive Council agreed to present my COOBA plan to the balance of the clubs, friend and foe alike. There were numerous meetings and telephone calls. The white hats were willing to accept the plan, although they were not enthusiastic. They found little fault with the present system. The reaction of the opposition was ambiguous or noncommittal.

McMullen and I met at my office, with John saying he would be "going to San Diego with an open mind." But he called some of my staff executives my "Achilles heel" and noted that "everyone's barking up the wrong tree when they speak of revenue sharing and restructuring—the problem is salaries!" He was noncommittal when I described the COOBA plan. He closed by wishing me well. "I mean that," he said.

The same day Bronfman, O'Malley, Doubleday, Susman and Ed Williams had lunch together. Doubleday was the heavy. When Charles urged peace, all agreed except Nelson, who complained of "Kuhn's ego" and attacked my staff. Nonetheless, Peter told me that Susman wanted a deal and that Nelson was his "puppet."

I reported all this to my Council that evening. During the discussion, Bob Howsam said, "Things will be satisfactory in Cincinnati." If Bob was right, the fight was over. The opposition needed five National League votes since no one wanted to cast the fourth and deciding vote. If either Cincinnati or Atlanta left the opposition, the ball game was over. Indeed, Ed Williams described Susman as "terrified to exercise a veto with four votes." I thought Susman was afraid of the consequences to the brewery. Still, I had a feeling ships were passing in the night. Yes, there was a compromise deal available, but I doubted it was one I would accept. The Associated Press's Will Grimsley, thinking the same way, wrote, "Kuhn is almost certain to decline a secondary role."

In an example of more dirty tricks that I found almost too bizarre for belief, Ed Williams told the Council, "Doubleday said that Kuhn has gone to the networks and said 'We'll put the players in green and red uniforms to be more colorful, and we'll shorten the baselines to get more runs.' "

When Ed followed up this news by reporting that the oppostion wanted the commissioner's term limited to four years, Haywood Sullivan exploded. A big, rugged, quiet man with powerful views and a pair of hands that could throttle a grizzly, Sully growled, "Let's have a bloodbath; we're losing our respect and dignity. We're being held hostage. Much more compromise and we'll start losing our friends." It was too bad we could not solve the problem by combat between Sully and some of my foes.

Now the next dirty trick emerged. Word was spread that "somebody" was putting pressure on Bill Williams's clients to get him to support me. None of my supporters believed it. Danny Galbreath called Bill and put it to him directly. Bill replied there was absolutely nothing to it. There was growing anger over that kind of thing.

There was also anger among the black hats. O'Malley had let it be known that he might throw Budweiser out of Dodger Stadium. They had also learned from Bronfman that my supporters had the votes to table the reelection issue if they did not like the way things were going in San Diego, and indeed might table it indefinitely until they got what they wanted.

I had hoped to have a compromise solution by the time we got to San Diego. The situation was murky as Luisa and I took an 11:45 A.M. flight to San Diego. As we flew across the country, you might imagine we were bathed in gloom. The last two years had been brutal. Fortunately for me, Luisa rose above all that. Not that she was complacent about the dirty tricks and ugliness, she was furious, but she did not let it bog her down. There was much more to our lives. We had four devoted children, two great mothers, loving friends, innumerable responsibilities and interests and our churches and our faith. We loved the baseball world but it was far from being our only world. We knew there was life after baseball and that sooner or later we would have to enter it. Besides, ten Susmans would have been no match for Luisa.

On August 17, we had a three-hour session of the Council. They supported the basic COOBA plan with my serving as CEO for four more years (one in my existing term and three beyond). My August 3 proposal had been silent on length of term. Nobody liked the four-year proposal (as opposed to the five- or seven-year proposals that were also discussed), but it was an effort to be reasonable and four years was, after all, the term of American presidents. They also agreed that COOBA could participate in Executive Council meetings and that the commissioner could be removed by a majority of the twenty-six clubs at any annual meeting, concepts I had suggested as both harmless and sensible. O'Malley and Ed Williams were deputized to meet with Susman three hours before the individual league meetings scheduled at 4:00 P.M.

The Executive Council meeting was interrupted when Peter Ueberroth and Dr. Tony Dailey of the Los Angeles Olympic Organizing Committee arrived to make a brief presentation to the Council on what Peter described as "the most elaborate drug-testing program in the world" to be used at the 1984 Olympics. He called it "foolproof testing" and said he hoped to share his findings and encourage its use by baseball, the NFL and the NBA. Peter's presentation was terse, punchy and effective, and we listened attentively.

When the meeting with Susman produced no progress on who would be the CEO of baseball (Kuhn or COOBA), the two leagues convened their separate meetings. The American League adopted the Council's proposal by a unanimous vote and MacPhail, Eisenhardt and Williams left to advise the National League of the action taken. To no avail. The dissidents there were sticking to *their* notion of compromise with COOBA a coequal of the commissioner. It looked as if they had corralled and were holding their five votes. The Council's COOBA proposal had drawn the support of twenty-one of the twenty-six clubs. Like Pickett's charge at Gettysburg, it was our high-water mark.

At the major-league meeting the next day, my adherents did as they had warned: they moved to table my reelection. This led to the formation of a ten-man committee to discuss the reelection issue and to meet immediately during a recess of the major-league meeting. The committee consisted of O'Malley, Bronfman, Doubleday, McKenna, Susman, Argyros, Eisenhardt, Reinsdorf, Sullivan and Ed Williams. The joint meeting had recessed at 11:30, after only a half hour.

The committee met between 11:30 and 2 o'clock and then a delegation with Susman as spokesman came to see me. It included O'Malley, Doubleday, McKenna, Ed Williams and Sullivan. Lou had a surprise. He would agree that COOBA would report to the commissioner but all departments in baseball administration would report to COOBA, with COOBA having the right to hire and fire freely all personnel. This would put COOBA astride all aspects of the game, business as well as integrity and discipline. Susman's solution was well contrived to be unacceptable to me. My rejection of it was further assured by Susman's take-it-or-leave-it presentation. The meeting had been barely polite.

The major-league meeting reconvened. A motion to postpone the election to November 1 was carried 7–5 in the National League and 11–3 in the American. The five National League votes were exactly the clubs we feared had bound themselves together: Atlanta, Cincinnati, Houston, New York and St. Louis.

I told Milton Richman of UPI that, "I'm sorry we couldn't get things straightened out here, but I'm enormously warmed by the great majority of people who have stood behind me and I have every confidence I will come out on top—no matter what the result. I stood on my principles and have nothing to be ashamed of."

Smiling broadly, I told the postmeeting press conference, "Baseball is a complicated game, full of complicated people." I had that right.

Richman predicted I would win and my press support grew even greater. They seemed to like the fact that I would not buy a compromise that would have reelected me but been bad for baseball.

That night Anheuser-Busch hosted a lavish party in San Diego. After some modest debate, Luisa and I decided to go. After all, it was a baseball gathering and we felt we belonged there. Busch and Susman greeted the arriving guests. I imagine they were surprised to see us. Susman later told me that Gussie was truly touched by our presence. When Gussie got up to speak, he made a point of thanking us for coming.

Ed Williams came over and sat beside me. "We're gonna get this thing done, Bowie," he said. "I don't know how we're gonna do it, but I promise you, we'll do it. And I thank you for all the patience you've had with me through all this." I had been listening with my head bowed. When I turned to look at him, tears were streaming freely down his face.

I did not receive a similar visit from Doubleday, who was quoted by Jerome Holtzman in the *Chicago Tribune* as saying, "The day of reconciliation is over." My old friend Jerry was steadily reporting all the bad news about me he thought was fit to print.

A week after San Diego, I was in Chicago to address the American Legion convention. I stopped at Wrigley Field for lunch with McKenna, Reinsdorf and Selig. McKenna expressed the belief that Doubleday was totally controlled by Susman, who could bring him along if we could hammer out a compromise with Lou. He put McMullen down as "hopeless."

"You were only inches apart in San Diego," he said.

We talked about forming another special committee to work on a solution. We agreed to sleep on it.

Soon afterward Tom Villante came into my office in New York to tell me he wanted to open his own sports marketing firm. "If you're doing this to help me," I told him, "I appreciate it, but please don't do it. I don't want you to leave." We talked at length. He convinced me that he really felt he should make the move. It was disheartening. He had made a real contribution to the game, and we had worked well together. I also hated the thought that some would view his resignation as something I had inspired as a gesture to Doubleday.

Dick Young was among the first to write it. I told him in a letter, "I just would never do business that way. Tom can tear up his resignation tomorrow, whether Nelson likes it or not. From his point of view, he is making a wise move. Baseball is the loser."

Dick ran my reply.

Tommy wrote a formal letter of resignation that closed fittingly enough with "Baseball Fever—Catch It. It Lasts Forever."

In its August 30 issue, *The Sporting News* ran an editorial titled "Time for a New Commissioner," with a picture of their candidate, Tal Smith. The editorial inspired more support for me. People from President Jerry Ford to the Japanese Commissioner of Baseball Takeso Shimoda to Tal Smith himself wrote in opposition to the editorial. In a moving display of support, letters came in from leading American amateur baseball figures and from amateur and professional baseball people around the world. I especially cherished the international messages. They were from people with whom I had developed a powerful bond in Asia, Latin America and Europe.

These two letters are good examples of the host of messages received by *The Sporting News.*

Dear Editor:

As a long-time baseball fan, I am writing to let you and your readers know of the high personal and professional regard I have for Commissioner Bowie Kuhn.

Our national pastime is ably represented by Commissioner Kuhn, who stands for the integrity and decency of the game. I know he is effective and highly thought of in Washington, and have been impressed by the generally positive comments I hear from other baseball fans about the Commissioner.

Baseball enjoys a special place in American life, and Bowie Kuhn has done an excellent job in serving as baseball's foremost representative.

Sincerely,
Gerald R. Ford

Mr. Dick Kaegel
Editor
The Sporting News

Dear Mr. Kaegel:

NBC has been in a broadcasting partnership with major league baseball since 1939. We have worked closely with Bowie Kuhn since the day he became Commissioner and we have watched with admiration the success that baseball has enjoyed under his leadership.

It seems to us that of his fine qualities to which you refer in your August 30 editorial—his integrity, his marketing skills, his courage and above all, his unquestioned love of baseball, are directly related to the dynamic growth of the sport during his stewardship.

We hope that those whose decision it is to make will think long and hard about the contributions Bowie Kuhn has made to the game of baseball.

Sincerely,
Grant Tinker, Chairman NBC

At the end of August, Luisa and I turned our backs on the entire scene and flew to Seoul for a meeting of the International Baseball Association. I was there to help advance the Olympic gold-medal cause of baseball. Since Richard Nixon happened to be in Tokyo at the time, I made a special trip to Japan to see him at the request of the Association. We had a long visit at the Okura Hotel during which he volunteered to help in our gold-medal pursuit. Intrigued by the politics of my situation, he asked me for an account, which I gave him. Some time later, when pressed by the media for a candidate to succeed me, he gave a two-word answer: "The incumbent." I liked that kind of brevity.

When we got back to the United States, Luisa and I were immersed in planning for our son George's wedding on September 18. I paid little attention to the subject of reelection; George and his fiancée, Carole, were a lot more interesting to me than Nelson and Gussie.

In the National League West, as fate would have it, the Atlanta Braves were battling the Dodgers for the title. Anyone who thought I might ignore my duties to placate a dissident needed only to watch the developing story in Atlanta. For several months I had been warning Turner in the strongest terms that we were coming to a showdown on his superstation's carriage of Braves games throughout the country, and that if the Braves won the division there could be no carriage of the League Championship Series on the superstation network of WTBS. It was another tough battle between us.

As I recounted earlier, Ted's adamant stand forced ABC and baseball to sue Ted and restrain him by court order. Some way to win votes.

On September 14 in Chicago, Susman, McKenna, Selig, Ed Williams and Reinsdorf got together. Lou aired some new grievances against me, including my trip to Korea and Japan. There was desultory discussion of how COOBA would operate. But Williams in reporting to me on the meeting, said, "We've got to take the destiny of the game out of Lou's hands," describing Lou as "outrageous, a one-man show, feeling his power." Still, Ed said, "we can snare him into a deal."

O'Malley told me that Anheuser-Busch was going to back Turner's effort to get the major-league baseball network package when negotiations got under way in several months. Ted had already announced publicly that he was going after the package. The long arm of Anheuser-Busch, already a major sponsor of the superstation, was reaching further, and in the process I could see Turner being drawn ever closer to St. Louis.

It gave me reason to reflect on my past conflicts with Gussie. In addition to labor matters, where we had rarely agreed, three events stood out. First, in 1976, I fined the Cardinals $5,000 for public remarks by Busch indicating the Cardinals were prepared to spend three to four million dollars to sign Joe Rudi and Rollie Fingers of the A's. This was a clear violation of our anti-tampering rule, which precluded a club from romancing a player under contract elsewhere. I suspect that Busch had never been disciplined before in his long life. Lou Susman called and asked if they could see me in New York to appeal the fine. I saw them in my office.

Polite and apologetic, Busch argued that a fine was inappropriate in light of his long record of good citizenship in baseball. True enough, but the overriding need to enforce the anti-tampering rule in the new era of free agency had greater merit. Though I respected Busch for swallowing his pride through his appeal for relief, I ruled against him. I know that hurt our relationship.

Our second problem came in 1978 when he was part of my Executive Council. The rotation system adopted the year before called for Busch to serve a one-year term. In a touching meeting in his baronial St. Louis home, he told me how much he relished serving on the Council and asked if he could continue.

Making an exception for Busch would have destroyed the rotation system, I had to turn him down. While he accepted the decision gracefully, I knew he was keenly disappointed.

In 1981 came what may have been my paramount problem with Busch. Lou Susman, accompanied by Fred Kuhlmann, came to my office to discuss our network broadcasting contracts with ABC and NBC. They wanted me to use my influence to get Budweiser into the advertising picture, which was then the exclusive domain of Miller Beer. Miller had been an inconsequential factor in the beer market. Acquired and resuscitated by an energetic and imaginative Philip Morris, it had emerged as a threat to Anheuser-Busch's domination.

When I demurred on the ground that this was, as they well knew, a network decision, they countered by arguing that in professional football, Commissioner Pete Rozelle had successfully interceded on Budweiser's behalf.

I told them we would review the situation when new network contracts were negotiated in 1983 but that I had no intention of imposing conditions at a financial price to the other twenty-five clubs, certainly not without their consent. While no threats were made and the meeting was altogether correct, these two attorneys had not flown in from St. Louis to be told I was powerless to help them. Time would make that clear enough.

Later that year I also foiled a bid by Anheuser-Busch to create a package of 52 national cablecasts of Yankees' and Cardinals' games on the ESPN cable network. The deal would have violated our contracts with NBC, ABC and USA Cable. I had no alternative but to say no. I could hear again Walter O'Malley's words of warning about the power of Anheuser-Busch.

When Peter Gammons wrote a story on the team of Doubleday-Busch-McMullen-Turner headlined "This Gang of Four Doesn't Shoot Straight" with Selig as the acknowledged principal source of his information, Steinbrenner exploded in a telephone conversation with Lee MacPhail. George roared that he was voting for me but was not going to "stand for that car salesman from Milwaukee." That was Bud. As to my lawsuit against Turner, he said we were just trying to put pressure on people who opposed me. "I'm going to the Rodino Committee," he said, "and I'm going to talk about how baseball is run." He was refering to Peter Rodino, the powerful chairman of the House Judiciary Committee, which had antitrust jurisdiction. George was threatening to get our antitrust immunity revoked. It was a perfect lesson in the convoluted operations of George's remarkable mind.

Bill Christine of the *Los Angeles Times* tracked down Charlie Finley in LaPorte, Indiana, to probe the wisdom behind what Bill called "his satanical countenance." "Bowie Kuhn is the biggest jerk in the history of baseball," said Finley. "That man alone was reason to get out." I missed Charlie.

Bob Lurie had a very positive meeting with Bill Williams on September 24, a meeting in which Williams volunteered to call Susman and urge him to avoid a bloodbath.

"I'm happy to support Bowie Kuhn," he told Lurie, "and I agree that the chief business officer should report to the commissioner and be in charge of finance." I think that was the real Bill Williams. But the Reds had declined from the glory days of "The Big Red Machine" and Bob Howsam to a struggling, second-class franchise. Anheuser-Busch was putting together a pay-television deal called SportsTime that would include Cincinnati, St. Louis and Kansas City. In addition to being a major regular TV sponsor of the Reds,

Anheuser-Busch, because of SportsTime, was developing an even more persuasive position in Cincinnati.

By the end of September, Selig and Ed Williams had been pretty well convinced by Susman that he had six solid National League votes: Atlanta, Cincinnati, Chicago, Houston, New York and St. Louis. Lou was confidently talking about a "very, very generous" severance for the commissioner and would no longer discuss any compromise involving COOBA. O'Malley was also increasingly concerned about the Cardinals' National League bloc. We discussed alternatives, including the possibility that I might be better off walking away from the whole thing and take advantage of the "severance." Selfishly, that was so, but I warned O'Malley and Selig that if I should get out, they would be at the mercy of the minority in electing a new commissioner. I thought it was far better for the game if I stayed on until a successor was named. O'Malley doubted if that course served my personal interests, but he and Selig liked the idea if I was willing. Peter's concern, a correct one as things turned out, was that I would be criticized by some in the media for hanging on at all costs. I had not come this far to worry about yet another round of criticism of my actions. My goal was to fight off the minority in favor of either myself or of a successor acceptable to the decent people in the game. Peter also worried that the golden parachute might float away. I said that I would take my chances.

I talked to the Council on the telephone about staying on until a successor was named. We agreed to have a meeting of the Council during the World Series to discuss it. I spoke separately to Ed Williams and Ewing Kauffman, who had both missed the Council hookup. "Bowie, don't resign," Ewing said. "I want to keep on fighting." Ed said, "I am one hundred percent for Kuhn to stay on; no way they can elect a new commissioner."

A missing piece of the puzzle now fell into place. O'Malley had learned that Anheuser-Busch had told Susman a year earlier to get rid of Kuhn. Our suspicions were confirmed.

About the same time, a responsible cable-industry source raised with a friend of mine in Washington the possibility that Turner would support my reelection if I would withdraw my opposition to a cable copyright bill pending in Congress. My friend's belief was that the cable source could deliver even though he did not purport to speak for Turner. I told him to ignore it, not even to respond.

On October 10, Luisa and I were in Atlanta for the League Championship Series. We started out in Turner's office in Atlanta Stadium, having a buffet supper and watching the final game of the Brewers-Angels series on TV while waiting for the Cardinals-Braves game to begin. Luisa and I, making what might well be our final postseason swing, had already been to Anaheim, St. Louis and Milwaukee.

The high point of the gathering came when Ted's mother, to whom Ted had introduced me and with whom I had had a delightful conversation, asked me if I worked for WTBS. Ted, overhearing the question, reprimanded her in mock anger. "Mother! Mother!" he said, raising his voice and drawing out the words to convey dismay, "this is the Commissioner of Baseball—you know, the 'one who put me in the slammer for a year!"

The 1982 World Series pitted Selig's Milwaukee Brewers against Busch's St. Louis Cardinals. I found it a fascinating matchup.

The Series began in St. Louis with a night game on October 12. That afternoon, in my hotel suite, we had the appointed meeting of the Executive Council. After Lou Hoynes reported on the details of our victory in the lawsuit against Turner, we had a long discussion on the "status of the commissioner."

Almost everyone had an opinion on how to proceed. The foggy gloom of only two weeks earlier had given way to partly cloudy weather on rumors that Susman had overstated the solidity of his six votes. There was a consensus that efforts should continue to develop a compromise and that, failing a compromise, the reelection vote should go ahead on November 1. If I failed to gain reelection, but had a majority in both leagues, the Council would ask me to stay on through the end of my term in August 1983. If no successor were named by then, the Council would ask me to continue to carry out the day-to-day responsibilities until a commissioner might be elected. The meeting was remarkably upbeat and tough-minded.

I had a telephone conversation with Susman after the meeting. I assumed he had gotten the news that the Council was not folding. He told me that Gussie was concerned about his own credibility, having offered me "three proposals" and all having been turned down. As we talked I perceived that he was focusing on a variation of the plan he advanced at San Diego. Using the title "president" instead of COOBA for the business affairs officer he wanted, he said the president could report to me, with all departments reporting to the president except legal, which *might* report to me. The exception was a sign of flexibility. He said he had "no authority" to bring this up at all as Gussie felt the burden was on my allies to make the next move. We agreed to talk again before the Series ended. I found it intriguing that Susman, who only recently had refused to discuss compromise, was now doing just that. The twists and turns of this never-ending saga were difficult to evaluate but I imagined that the tough attitude being taken by the Executive Council had loosened up the Cardinals' position. We met again two days later in Room 2056, my suite at the Marriott.

Lou told me he wanted peace. He was fearful of deep resentments toward himself, Gussie and Nelson. Anheuser-Busch wanted peace, too.

"I don't want to be the heavy in this; I've only been carrying out the assignment of my client," he said. "I love Gussie like a father."

He tried hard to persuade me that having all departments report to the president would work. He likened it to the arrangement at Anheuser-Busch and the Tribune Company. He said I would control who was selected as president.

"The commissioner and the president would solve problems over lunch regularly," he continued. "If the president wanted to fire someone and you didn't like it, you could fight him. If overall you don't like the president's performance, you fire him. You should make up your mind what you want, call the Executive Council, Gussie and Doubleday together, and sell your idea to them," he concluded. He thought Bill Williams would go along.

"Incidentally, Gussie loves Luisa."

We agreed to talk again in Milwaukee. Though the plan was San Diego revisited, he had suggested quite a lot of flexibility. It began to make some sense and he talked like a man genuinely seeking compromise. It was worth thinking about.

In Milwaukee I told the Executive Council in detail about my discussions with Susman. There was a lot of skepticism. I told them I was not prepared to take a cynical view. He had promised to put some thoughts on paper and get together with me again. I wanted to see what that paper looked like.

Lou and I had more conversations, during which my power to hire and fire the president began to disappear. A four-man owners' committee was now suggested to hire the man. Also, he wanted to put Nelson Doubleday on the Executive Council. The president would have a vote on the Council. Some of this might have been all right, but things kept changing. Though the tone was always friendly and conciliatory, I began to wonder if this was not an exercise to keep the Cardinals and Anheuser-Busch from appearing to be the orchestrators of the scheme to eliminate me. I made some counterproposals, one of which was particularly designed to test Lou's sincerity, namely that my next reelection would be by a simple majority. In effect, that would make me commissioner for an indefinite period. Lou thought that was possible. We were beginning to make some improvements on San Diego.

Along the way, Susman suggested Bud Selig as a possible president. He dropped the thought in very lightly. That could have ended the whole contest. Bud and I could have worked together without difficulty and the clubs liked Bud. I wondered if Susman knew something. But when I checked with Bud, he scoffed at the idea as I thought he would.

On October 22, Susman called regarding the status of our discussion. He told me, "I saw Gussie again—he's tired after the World Series, you know, and his reaction is not as favorable as his initial reaction indicated. I'll be seeing Nelson next week for lunch, and I'll give you a call afterward. Nelson's gonna be tough." It was looking as if the skeptics had been right in the first place.

Three days later, Lou had his lunch with Doubleday in New York City, then came up to my office. "I'm sorry I don't have good news," he began. "I couldn't sell 'our' approach to Nelson or, for that matter, to Bill Williams, who was more adamantly opposed than Nelson. Gussie would have gone along with it, but he's now agreed to support a different approach, which Andy McKenna would also support.

"It has the president reporting directly to the Executive Council and serving as CEO on all business matters. All departments would report to the president except the PRC, which reports to the commissioner.

"The commissioner could not cast votes to break ties on the Executive Council, and both the commissioner and the president would serve three-year terms."

I told Lou it would not work. He suggested I see Andy McKenna and recommended against the Chicago meeting on November 1 unless a compromise was worked out.

Peter O'Malley's reaction to the news of the Susman meeting was very simple. He said, "It looks bad." He was right. Ed Williams said, "Terrible; they're going backward."

Andy McKenna came in to see me the next day. Whereas Susman had led me to believe that McKenna was all for the unacceptable new plan, he came on enthusiastically for the Kuhn-Susman approach. He would go to work strongly in support of it with Susman, Doubleday and Bill Williams. He opposed having a meeting on November 1 unless everything was worked out in advance.

On October 28, my birthday, McKenna called with a present. He said he had bumped into Finley, who had said, "The SOB doesn't have a chance, does he?" Maybe Charlie didn't know that October 28 is the Feast of St. Jude, the patron saint of lost causes.

Two days before the Chicago meeting, O'Malley called to say, "Ed Williams suggests that maybe Lee MacPhail be named commissioner pro tem, and you could immediately be elected president of the American League. When things got better, we could elect you again as commissioner."

"Did you have Mexican mushrooms for breakfast?" I asked.

"I'm serious."

"I'm not about that!"

I could have hugged him for the fraternal spirit of the suggestion (which I had already heard directly from Ed), but we both really knew we could not go in that direction. We also discussed another tabling motion if no solution emerged but we both agreed that was a terrible course. Once was enough. Interestingly, McKenna and Susman were the ones talking about tabling.

As I prepared for the Chicago meeting, to be held the night of October 31, I sat alone and penciled out alternatives. My notes read:

1. Lou plan
2. Business as usual
   A. 100%
   B. Horse
3. X (only if Ex. Council agrees)

When I reviewed them over three years later, they evoke the difficulty of that time. The first alternative was the Kuhn-Susman plan that McKenna and I had agreed on. The second had two possibilities: (a) to make an all-out fight for victory no matter how long it took on the theory that the majority could not be beaten or (b) to remain as commissioner until a suitable successor could be found. I would be the stalking "Horse" for my successor. The third, which I called "X," was to tell the Council I would quit if they thought that would help. Though I could not even write out the word, I did not want them making a fight because of friendship for me.

Luisa and I flew into Chicago's O'Hare Airport on the afternoon of October 31. The Council, joined by Roy Eisenhardt as cochairman of the restructuring committee, met from 6:00 P.M. to midnight in the hotel, except during a two-and-a-half-hour dinner when they were joined by the Player Relations Committee. The Council's members were low-key. I believe we all knew that a five-vote National League bloc would oppose us the next day. The discussion focused on the best course of action to pursue.

It was decided that the election be tied to the Kuhn-Susman plan. Though Susman had helped compose it, I thought it unlikely that St. Louis would now support it. The Council itself was not enthusiastic about this plan but felt it was necessary to seek a compromise.

If the plan lost, we discussed the alternatives as I had listed them in my penciled notes. The alternative of quitting did not even draw a comment from the Council. I had suggested it to them the prior week with the same nonreaction. Needless to say, that was the reaction I wanted. Led by Ed Williams, they decided to go to the "100 percent" alternative if the Kuhn-Susman plan lost, although Selig still harbored the reservations he had when it was first discussed in St. Louis during the Series.

During dinner, Ed Williams as usual found the light-hearted angle. Noting that the waitress had brought Budweiser to the table, he had it taken away and ordered Stroh's in its place.

At daybreak on November 1, Susman called O'Malley and said that Gussie would be willing to meet him, Dan Galbreath and McKenna at the airport when Gussie arrived at 10:30.

At 8:15, Gene Autry called me to say he would like to speak with Gussie, too. I suggested he talk to Peter.

At 9:30, Peter arranged for Selig to meet Gussie in the hotel lobby and take him up to Autry's suite, even if it held up the league meetings.

At 10:00, Ed Williams visited my room. He was comfortable with Kuhn-Susman as long as the Executive Council controlled the identity of the businessman. I said, "Of course."

At 10:30, Chub Feeney came by and said he thought St. Louis would vote yes, but there would still be four negative votes.

At 11:00, Peter called from Butler Aviation and said, "We've had a really good meeting with Gussie and Margaret Busch. Margaret said, 'Believe me, Gussie doesn't want to tear up the National League.'" Gussie agreed to see Autry at the hotel.

A Scots bagpipe band was in the lobby. The press wondered if they would strike up the Budweiser theme when Gussie entered.

Peter called from his room at 11:40 with McKenna, Smith, Lurie, Giles and Galbreath beside him. They had tried a soft-sell approach to Doubleday. His answer was, "Kuhn's gotta go."

Selig was waiting in the lobby for Gussie when the doors swung open and Busch walked in, accompanied by Margaret and Susman. Lou took one look at Selig and physically turned Gussie away, shepherding him quickly out of the lobby. Susman appeared agitated; Selig was shocked.

At 12:30, McKenna reported to O'Malley that Busch had great discomfort with the businessman's reporting to Kuhn. McKenna said Busch joined in the discussion fully and expressed his ideas. Peter said they were going to the National League meeting, where McKenna would propose the Kuhn-Susman plan, which would get seven yes votes. No more.

The National League straw vote was 7–5 as reported to me by Peter at 1:50.

At 2:15, a major-league committee of Peter, Ed Williams, Haywood Sullivan, Lee, Chub, Dan Galbreath and Bill Giles came up to my room and asked my views at this point.

"Based on my continued support from the majority of clubs," I said, "let's get the vote taken."

At 3:00, Feeney called the joint meeting to order, and McKenna moved the adoption of the plan. It was seconded by O'Malley. A secret ballot was distributed to the owners.

Steinbrenner, seated next to Selig, tapped Buddy on the arm with his pen and motioned for him to look at his ballot. Bud looked down and George revealed the word "yes."

At 3:25, Lee called from the meeting room to tell me that the vote went as expected, passing 11–3 in the American League and 7–5 in the National League. I had carried eighteen of the twenty-six clubs but had lost. I was later told that following the meeting Gussie had pounded on a table with his cane, saying, "He should clean out his desk tomorrow!"

At 3:35, the Executive Council met and I was asked to continue as commissioner. Ed Williams had offered the resolution that provided that I continue beyond August 1983 if I had not been re-elected by then. It was Ed who suggested I tell the press I had gotten a 70 percent landslide—and lost.

A large group convened for a press conference. I was asked if I was willing to compromise regarding the businessman and share more power equally.

"No," I said. "I think that would have been wrong. Obviously, I

28

The Bridge to Peter

The next morning, which was Election Day for the "rest" of the country, I did a triple-swing around town, appearing on all three network morning news programs. When I got to my office the entire staff gathered in our conference room.

They had been terrific throughout. Their own jobs were in question, and many of the department heads had come under personal attack in the process. It had been as difficult for them as it had been for me.

There was a lot of gloom in the room. I wanted to give them a report on the events of the day before and give us all a chance to relax together. I told them I did not know where this was all going but that I might still be a candidate to succeed myself. That comment lit up the room. I told them we were going to continue on with our best efforts and would continue to run the commissioner's office at a high level of efficiency.

On November 3, Luisa and I went to Fort Lauderdale and there boarded the S.S. *Rotterdam* for a four-day "cruise to nowhere." I heard not a word about what Doubleday or anybody else was doing.

When I returned, bits and pieces were being offered in the postmortem period. Williams discovered that Susman had "exploded" when he learned, upon entering the lobby, of McKenna's defection: "That's it—no more talk, no more meetings, nothing!" Then he rudely steered Gussie away from Selig. Ed thought Susman had "horsed us all around."

On November 12, the Executive Council appointed a committee to consider and review possible candidates for commissioner. It consisted initially of Selig, Ed Williams, Galbreath, Lurie and Bronfman. Later McMullen, Peter Hardy of Toronto and Argyros were added. The idea was to give it balance. Selig was named chairman, a wise choice, but one that would tend to neutralize his support of me as he went about doing an honest and fair job of screening candidates.

The Search Committee, with great reluctance on the part of some of its members, set out to make a genuine search for a new commissioner. None was more embarrassed by the project than its chairman, Selig. I told him to do his best and not worry about hurting our friendship. That was not going to change. Bronfman called me with a line I loved: "They put me on this damnfool committee to replace somebody I don't want to replace." I urged that they first poll the twenty-six clubs for their recommendations. That did indeed turn out to be the first step.

Baseball's annual meeting convened in Hawaii on December 6, and I greeted a convention of some 2,000 baseball officials and press with what had become my customary state-of-the-game address. I cited 1982 as a "fabulous year" for baseball, but noted that we had financial problems. I knew the gathering expected something more from me, and I concluded by saying:

Over the last fourteen years, I have often been asked why I was prepared to accept the aggravations of the job, given the fact that other career opportunities were open to me.

The answer is simple: I love the game, I love its sights, its sounds, its rhythm, its tradition, even its boisterousness and yes, its people. One does not have to be a commissioner to love the memories of the old scoreboard in Griffith Stadium's right centerfield. The picture of that beautiful old wreck which lies on my desk could lie as easily on a desk elsewhere. I love Fenway Park and Wrigley Field, the Federal League's last legacy to baseball, and Forbes Field, now vanished, where I first saw the National League play, but those recollections follow the man wherever he goes. I love scores of minor-league parks I have seen where the game always seems closer to its origins. I love the timeless records of the game where hitting .300 is as much a standard of excellence today as it was in 1900.

I love the discipline of the Japanese players, which is somehow different in quality from any I have seen. But all of this moves along with the man like the shirt on his back.

In the final analysis it is the people who are the special excite-

oree. This was always a great dinner due to sportswriter Leo Cloutier's leadership. There were a number of kind things said about me
that evening, but I was deeply moved by the words of three active
players—Pete Vukovich, Wade Boggs and Jim Palmer. The 1981
strike had left a gulf between the players and me. For that reason
what I heard had a special poignancy.

"I'd like to express my heartfelt gratitude to Commissioner Bowie
Kuhn for what he has done ever since he has been in this game,"
Vukovich said, "You've had a really tough job, Commissioner,
you've had a rotten going through the years, but you've handled
yourself and the many problems with which you have been confronted with fairness and class."

"I'm comparatively new in the majors," Boggs said, "but in the
short time I have been in it, I must say that I have learned to respect
and admire the great job Bowie Kuhn has done. You've done a hell
of a job, Commissioner, and I really mean that."

Palmer, one of the great pitchers of my era, said, "Baseball has had
five commissioners as its leader in the past sixty-two years, but none
has ever had to face the multitude of problems Bowie Kuhn has in
his fourteen years as its chief. Judge Landis was the first. He was
great because he came at a time when the game was on the brink
of ruin. He was invested with unlimited powers. Kuhn did not have
the same powers, but he accomplished more in the interest of the
sport. He faced mountains of problems, but he never flinched. He
solved them all to the best of his ability. He employed all of his
God-given talents and did a superb job of it."

By January 26, the deadline had passed for the clubs to submit
names. Some had submitted only me. Seventeen clubs submitted
forty-eight names, and Selig and his committee had managed to cut
that down to nineteen. They hoped to trim it to six by February for
discussion at a meeting. John McMullen was furious when he
learned that I was on the list.

While Selig and his Search Committee struggled conscientiously
with their assignment, I had the major project of negotiating new
network contracts along with Bill Giles and Eddie Einhorn. While
I tried to keep in touch with Bud and to advise him where I could
be helpful, the network negotiations were occupying my time, as
were the drug problems.

I was not talking to my old cronies of the 1982 campaign nearly
as frequently as I had during the months that followed the Hollywood letter. It all was beginning to seem like an old movie. But

O'Malley was unrelenting, still planning, calling, hoping that we would find a way. He believed we needed a baseball man as commissioner and I was the only one around who might get the votes—at some point. I told Peter in late January that we really needed a prompt decision. I was beginning to lose my patience, or at least some of it. He counseled patience. He thought baseball was functioning well. "No one could do better," he said.

My name continued to be on the list of candidates being developed by the Search Committee. My old foes, having lost none of their sense of opposition, were not happy. Busch thought it was "tragically regrettable and unfortunate" that I was on the list.

Turner was saying publicly that our network deals, which we were completing in March, might get me reelected. Ed Williams told me our reelection strategy was working. "We're in a new ball game," he said.

During a spring training swing around Arizona, I spent some time with Peter Ueberroth, talking mainly about getting baseball as an official Olympic sport. He was curious about my status and offered his help. I told him I probably knew less than anyone about the subject. We laughed about that.

In early April, the PRC announced that Ray Grebey was resigning. The usual speculation occurred that this would have a beneficial effect on my status. In my judgment, it was of no consequence in my situation. It seemed to me that the dissidents were unchanged no matter what happened. Realistically, once they had voted against me, they feared that if I were renewed I would retaliate against them. That was not the way I was, but that was the way they thought.

The good guys continued to do things for me that were more sweetness than of any practical significance. Gene Autry sent me a resolution of the Angels calling for my reelection. He and Buzzie Bavasi were constantly looking for opportunities to help the cause or perhaps cheer me up. Jerry Reinsdorf called to say, "Be tough and hang in there. The other guys can't elect anybody. Just don't get discouraged."

I was not so much discouraged as the months went by as I was concerned that holding together my loyalists was preventing baseball from finding the superman they knew was out there somewhere. That bothered me.

Reports began to increase that certain owners were turning their support to Bill Simon. There was a man of enormous talent, a potential superman. I told Selig they should seriously evaluate Bill, though I had no idea whether Bill had any interest. By late May he announced he had none.

On April 18 I fined Steinbrenner $50,000 for remarks reflecting on the integrity of the umpires. When I advised him of the fine on the telephone we ended up talking about Simon, whom we both knew well. He agreed that Bill was excellent and then, in one of those conversational switches that only George can make, he said, "If we make a change, we're not going to do as good."

Word reached me that if the eight owners on the Search Committee were asked to vote for commissioner, I would win 6 to 2.

Ed Williams was again talking to August Busch III about supporting me. August would only answer that they were flexible.

I was amazed when Congressman John Duncan wrote to all major-league clubs urging my reelection and saying, "To be perfectly frank, the owners of baseball would be doing themselves a great disservice to select anyone else to be commissioner other than Bowie Kuhn." As a respected senior member of the House Ways and Means Committee, Duncan had a significant voice in the matter.

On May 4, in St. Louis, Fred Kuhlmann of the Cardinals dropped in to see me when I was visiting the offices of *The Sporting News.* I had let Kuhlmann's office know I was in town but had not expected any reaction. He asked if I was open-minded about a solution. When I told him I was, he said he would like to talk to Gussie and get back to me. This all sounded familiar. However, Kuhlmann and I had always been cordial. That put a different face on this discussion.

I had known and liked Kuhlmann since my days as a practicing lawyer. He was a good, steady, reliable man. Cautious to a fault, he was nonetheless a man to be trusted and one who could reach the highest levels of the Cardinals-brewery complex. I never had any question about the decency of his motives or the man himself. He was as different from Lou Susman as a man could be. Not surprisingly, when I heard from Fred, I perked up my ears. Some days later, Ed Williams saw Kuhlmann in Washington and urged his support within the Cardinals-brewery camp. Ed called me to report, "Fred is working for us and hard; he wants to switch the Cards' position and has great influence with young Busch."

On May 10, Kuhlmann and I met in Jacksonville, Florida. We dusted off the old plan that Susman and I had worked up during the 1982 World Series. He wanted to talk to Gussie. He told me that Gussie and Doubleday were very close and both would have to be satisfied.

Kuhlmann and I met again several weeks later in New York. Having discussed the plan with both Gussie and Nelson, Fred said they feared that the businessman would be "thwarted" by me. They wanted some mechanism to prevent that from happening. I suggested that he, Doubleday and I get together. After expressing concern that such a meeting could be counterproductive because of Doubleday's strong feelings, Fred agreed to explore the possibility of setting it up. Fred was obviously afraid of the results if we confronted one another.

Several days later, Hal Evans of our promotion division handed me a note Reggie Jackson gave him at Yankee Stadium while he was there with the visiting California Angels. It said, in Reggie's handwriting:

Bowie
Mr. Commissioner
I hope you stay on as Commissioner because I think you've done one hell of a job for baseball.

Reggie Jackson
6/1/83

The same evening as I left my office I bumped into Ted Turner coming into the lobby. He said he was coming up to see me. We proceeded to have a sidewalk conference leaning on a mail storage box amidst a swarm of homeward-bound office workers who frequently interrupted our talk to shout words of encouragement to me. I was impressed. Whether Ted was too was conjectural, but he asked whether I could win reelection if he changed his negative vote. I replied that I doubted his was the deciding vote at that point but it would certainly help me if he changed. He told me what a good guy I was and how well I had handled things since the past November, when I lost by getting only 70 percent of the vote. He said, "Commissioner, I have enormous respect for you." Did he mean it? Who knows? But when I rolled my eyes heavenward toward the spires of St. Patrick's Cathedral a hundred yards away, his reaction was "I really mean it."

Bud Selig told me that the work of the Search Committee was intensifying. He was traveling coast-to-coast in June 1983, interviewing possible candidates. Apart from straining Bud's energies, this process was quieting the anti-Kuhn forces, who feared that the committee was just a thinly veiled Kuhn front.

I continued to feel for Bud. Many, perhaps most, baseball owners wanted the committee to be a Kuhn front. Instinctively, Bud felt the same way, but he was also a deeply conscientious man who was troubled by the dishonesty of making the committee a farce. Time and again he talked to me about the problem, always getting my encouragement to make an honest search. His was a personality so schooled in diplomacy that he was physically pained by confrontation. Yet no one drew more confrontation than Bud, who because of his decency, open-mindedness and willingness to listen, was constantly barraged by everyone in baseball. He loved the attention but detested the rancor. Still, if the price of being at the hub of baseball's 1983 world was rancor, Bud was willing to pay that price.

Bud was baseball's Henry Clay. Like the great Kentucky statesman, Bud staunchly believed in conciliation as the solution to problems. He had an endlessly patient ear for all colorations of opinion. So infinite was his patience that in successive telephone conversations he could hear out both John McMullen (whom he called "Johnny Mac"), and Eddie Chiles, two of our more voluble spirits. In all the baseball world, only Buddy would not blanch at that assignment. His skills at drawing out and consoling our querulous executives were of such magnitude as to approach those of priest dealing with penitent. Whether he ever offered remission of their sins I have never discovered.

Bud was a Kuhn loyalist. He was also a pragmatist. As the long contest worked its way into the spring of 1983, he began to fear that the National League minority was unshakable. To make things worse, the Chicago Cubs, who had supported me in the November 1, 1982, election, were angered by the terms of the exclusive contract my network bargaining team had negotiated with NBC for Saturday-afternoon telecasts. Andy McKenna argued that NBC could require Cubs games to start at times that were disadvantageous to the club. Though we were able to get some modifications from NBC, the anger persisted. Nor were the Wrigley Fielders happy with my continuing congressional struggle to curb the superstations, a struggle that threatened the growing superstation status of WGN, their sister company in the Tribune family.

Many in my camp felt that time was an ally, but my need to carry out the duties of the office undermined that theory. I antagonized the Cubs and pressed ahead with revenue-sharing plans that further entrenched clubs like the Mets and Cardinals against me.

Selig became more and more concerned that we could not prevail. If that was so, he reasoned, baseball should get on with the

There were other straws in the wind that gave me pause. Bud Selig's list had pretty much boiled down to Peter Ueberroth, James Baker, Bartlett Giamatti and myself. Baker's name was new. As White House chief of staff under Ronald Reagan, he had excellent credentials as a master political strategist. I had met him during the course of my Washington activities and thought well of him. So did others whose judgment I respected. I thought he was not available because of his strong ties to the president. But Bud had all three on the list and probably knew more than I did.

Ueberroth was the most outspoken of the group. He said publicly he was not interested in the job and that they already had the best man possible in Bowie Kuhn. He has told me since that his posture with Bud was very simple: So long as I wanted the job, Peter Ueberroth would have no interest.

My daily conversations with Peter O'Malley were doing nothing to heighten my enthusiasm. Peter, who had spent the last one and a half years spearheading my cause and pumping up my spirits, seemed to be losing heart. He had come to Chicago for the fiftieth anniversary of the All-Star Game in July. While I was attending to the innumerable ceremonial duties that occupy a commissioner at such events, Peter was taking pulses and was unnerved by what he found to be the condition of his principal patient. Three heretofore staunch supporters, Charles Bronfman, Bob Lurie and Danny Galbreath, were being swayed by the World War III argument and, however reluctantly, were beginning to lean toward the possible new candidates: Baker, Giamatti or Ueberroth. In an effort to reinvigorate their enthusiasm, Peter had suggested that the six National League Kuhn advocates (Bronfman, Galbreath, Giles, Lurie, Smith and O'Malley) fly to St. Louis and see August Busch III. The good news was that they had all agreed, recognizing that if the Cardinals joined the Kuhn forces the battle was won, as Cincinnati and Chicago would almost surely follow—and perhaps Turner in Atlanta as well. McMullen and Doubleday were now being ignored as hopelessly lost causes.

As I sat in my Chicago hotel suite and listened to Peter explain all this, I groped for some evaluation of where we stood. I said, "Peter, the St. Louis trip is a long shot and though I like the spunk our guys show by being willing to go, I come out of all this with a very negative bottom line." Peter answered carefully but without hesitation, "You are absolutely right; the odds are now heavily against us."

Under the circumstances, the 8:00 A.M. meeting of the Executive Council in my suite the next morning had unusual significance. Bud

Executive Council as time eroded their resolve; and Lee MacPhail had dealt my cause real damage with his strongly held view that the Council holdover strategy was a mistake. Bud said that Lee's philosophy had become widely known, was even called "the MacPhail approach." That was bad news. It was not much solace to learn that Lee was "painfully" aware of my unhappiness with his activities, nor was it any surprise. Though like Parsifal he was following his conscience, he knew the impact on me and that would disturb, but not deter, him.

While Bud and I were together we received a call from St. Louis, where O'Malley, Bronfman, Lurie, Giles and Smith had met with August Busch III. They felt they had a "good" meeting but I did not like what I heard. August was described as having four basic problems: player salaries; cocaine use by players; Kuhn's desire to continue after losing the reelection vote on November 1, 1982; and the fact that Anheuser-Busch was not involved in network advertising under our expiring contracts with NBC and ABC. As the four men gave their appraisal of the meeting it seemed to me that August was giving them lip service to protect the brewery's existing relationships with major-league clubs. While he had promised to give the possibility of compromise some thought and would talk to his father, I could see little chance that this hard, tough-minded little guy was apt to reverse course in any way that would be acceptable to me. That was how I filtered out the meaning of the words that came across the telephone lines from my friends in St. Louis. Nor was there any question in my judgment that young Busch and the brewery interests were calling the shots in St. Louis. Peter O'Malley had used a line I would not forget, "August never tried to kick the responsibility away from Anheuser-Busch."

I could think of only one good thing about the meeting with Busch: Going there had been a touchingly decent thing for my five friends to do.

Next I learned that the expected switch of the Reds' vote to our side was not occurring. Howsam might be back and Wagner gone, but the Williams brothers were not coming around. Charles Bronfman, after talking to Jim Williams, reported to O'Malley: "No sale." Howsam told O'Malley that St. Louis was the key. On writing off the Cincinnati vote, Peter ruefully reminded me of what his father had told him fifteen years earlier: "Watch out for Anheuser-Busch; they have too much power."

The point was driven home more emphatically when I had one

of my periodic visits from Ted Turner. He said, "Commissioner, if there are vote changes, I would consider changing. I have given my word and I need an excuse in order to change." Reflecting on the fact that Anheuser-Busch was a major sponsor of his superstation network, I had little doubt what change was needed to free Ted's vote. What motivated Ted to talk to me? Was it genuine sympathy for me? Was it a fear that I could get reelected without his support, thereby leaving him on the outside looking in? I am not really sure. As he closed our conversation he said, "I can't tell you how much I respect you for the way you have handled yourself. Real class and dignity. I don't know where we'd get anybody better. People think I'm mad at you but I'm not. In fact, I really like you."

How do you ever know who the real Ted Turner is? Somehow I would like to think it was the one who walked out of my office that night.

Through the difficult, emotional months since December 1981, nobody had kept up my spirits like Peter O'Malley. He had been dauntless, tireless and optimistic in even the darkest moments. During the last half of July 1983, I saw his enthusiasm slowly coming off its hinges. August Busch had come back to Peter with a proposal that I continue for one more year and that the anti-Kuhns be given an equal vote on the Executive Council with my supporters. The effrontery of such a proposal annoyed my friends and shut off any notion of compromise. It was pretty much what I expected, namely, something that had no chance of providing a framework for solution. Busch's "nonproposal," taken together with the continuing fidelity of the Reds to St. Louis, began to sap even Peter's ardor for the cause. He wondered on several occasions if I should consider stepping aside for my own sake. At another point he asked if I would consider acting as an interim commissioner to ease the transition to a commissioner like Ueberroth. He knew I liked Ueberroth as a possible successor. These ideas he lumped under the heading of "the distasteful subject." Basically, Peter was saying that my continuing the battle beyond August 12 was going to bring on an ugly war with the anti-Kuhns, a war that he increasingly questioned our bringing on. He always concluded such discussions with the assurance that he would pursue whatever course I wanted and thought the Council would, too.

The bear market was plunging indeed. As I watched it sink, I knew that a decision was coming that only I could make. The majority would back a holdover beyond August 12, although some were reluctant. Did I want to precipitate the ugliness that would bring on? I could control the decision either way—war or peace. I told Peter I would make no decision before I sat down with the Council on August 2 in Boston. In the meantime, I would talk to my family at Cooperstown.

Seeing that the long struggle was drawing to a climax, I had begun to talk more to my children about the situation and to solicit their advice. I saw a lot of them during July because on many weekends we were together at our summer house in Quogue, Long Island. As we gathered there, I laid out the facts and the options. They asked a host of questions. They were specially interested in what I would do if I left baseball. While they were reluctant to say that any one course was right, I could tell from their questions that they hoped I would find a way to gracefully leave baseball behind. Obviously, Willkie Farr & Gallagher would be my principal activity should I leave. Various consulting opportunities were opening up. I was intrigued by conversations I was having with Burson-Marsteller, the world's largest public relations firm about serving on their senior advisory board. I was also giving serious consideration to writing a book and was satisfied that excellent publishers were interested. The lecture circuit beckoned. I assured my family that these opportunities were attractive, both intellectually and financially. Equally important to me were the opportunities to do more hands-on work in various philanthropic fields, opportunities that had been foreclosed by the intensity of my involvement in baseball, and to work on the international and Olympic aspirations of amateur baseball.

As to writing a book, I had rejected the notion from the very outset of my commissionership, though various people had suggested I do so. Somehow it seemed inappropriate. I had not wavered in that view for a dozen years and made no effort to keep the kind of records which would have speeded such a project. But beginning in December 1981, I began to change my viewpoint. The more dirty tricks I saw, the more it changed. By mid-1983 I had pretty well made up my mind that I owed it to myself and to baseball history to go ahead with a book.

As I discussed all this with my children, they drew me out, probing considerations that had not occurred to me. More than anything else they were doing what family members should do for one another; they were bearing me up through a time that was difficult. They were showing their concern and giving their support. As much as anybody, they lightened my load, reassured me and gave me guidance that would be critical in the days ahead.

As July wore on, I told them that the summer meetings in Boston in early August would provide the forum for a decision. Just before Boston, Luisa and I would be in Cooperstown for the ceremonies installing Walter Alston, George Kell, Juan Marichal and Brooks Robinson as members of the Hall of Fame. During July, I learned from Luisa that all my children were planning to be in Cooperstown. This had not happened in well over a decade. If the last roundup was coming, they were not going to miss it. I was thankful for that.

I imagine I installed more baseball men in the Hall of Fame than anybody ever has or is likely to do. There were over seventy, starting with my opening group in 1969 of Stanley Coveleski, Waite Hoyt, Roy Campanella and Stan Musial to my last in 1984. They were all mine, or so I saw it, and always will be. Those names and all those in between are the sweetest litany I can imagine:

Henry Aaron, Walter Alston, Luis Aparicio, Earl Averill, Dave Bancroft, Ernie Banks, Jake Beckley, Cool Papa Bell, Yogi Berra, Jim Bottomley, Lou Boudreau, Campanella, Happy Chandler, Oscar Charleston, Roberto Clemente, Earle Combs, Jocko Conlon, Roger Connor, Coveleski, Martin Dihigo, Don Drysdale, Billy Evans, Rick Ferrell, Whitey Ford, Rube Foster, Ford Frick, Bob Gibson, Josh Gibson, Warren Giles, Lefty Gomez, Chick Hafey, Jesse Haines, Will Harridge, Bucky Harris, Billy Herman, Harry Hooper, Hoyt, Cal Hubbard, Monte Irvin, Travis Jackson, Judy Johnson, Addie Joss, Al Kaline, Kell, Joe Kelley, George Kelly, Harmon Killebrew, Ralph Kiner, Chuck Klein, Sandy Koufax, Bob Lemon, Buck Leonard, Fred Lindstrom, Pop Lloyd, Al Lopez, Larry MacPhail, Mickey Mantle, Juan Marichal, Rube Marquard, Ed Mathews, Willie Mays, Johnny Mize, Musial, Satchel Paige, Robin Roberts, Brooks Robinson, Frank Robinson, Amos Rusie, Joe Sewell, Duke Snider, Warren Spahn, Sam Thompson, George Weiss, Mickey Welch, Hack Wilson, Early Wynn, Tom Yawkey and Ross Youngs.

Shakespeare never wrote sweeter lines than those.

Amidst the nostalgic swirl of Cooperstown activities, Luisa and I talked to our family about the decision I faced in Boston. CBS's Dick Brescia remarked to me some years later about our family group's hanging together there in the face of all the social and business pressures. "Everyone knew why they were there," he said.

Among our friends in Cooperstown, none was more insistent that I should battle the opposition than Happy Chandler. I lacked the heart to tell him the battle might be over. Apart from my family, Peter O'Malley, Lou Hoynes and Sandy Hadden, I was not telling anybody that. Redoubtable friend that he was, Happy was lobbying the voteless throng in my behalf.

Somehow everything about Cooperstown was supportive, from the fans in the street who encouraged me to "hang in there" to the twenty-five or so Hall of Famers who had returned for the ceremonies. It seemed that everyone in town was on my side. Even Peter O'Malley, who was not normally there, was present to honor Walter Alston. And when I put my hand to tennis, Frank Torre and I won the annual tournament. It was all unreal and I knew it, like a massive, happily numbing dose of euphoria before I faced the reality of Boston.

But the inevitable had to be faced, and all too soon Luisa, Peter O'Malley and I were on a chartered plane flying from Oneonta to Boston. The beautiful summer-green forests of New England could not relieve the leaden sensation in my heart. Peter and I clinically reviewed the picture. Nothing had changed. Cooperstown had been an idyllic dream through which we had both passed only to find the Busches and Doubledays on the other side. As our plane eased into Logan Airport, Peter said he would keep his concerns about the holdover plan to himself during the opening hours of the Executive Council meeting the next morning. Nor would he express them, he said, unless he and I agreed that he should.

In sum, Peter had three reasons for his uneasiness about the hold over. First, it would bring on a bitter internecine struggle. Second, the antis would resort to a character assassination of me. Third, it would greatly reduce any remaining chances of a favorable financial settlement for me.

I had long since cast away caution with regard to his second and third reasons. Besides, my opponents had already done their best (or worst) to undermine my reputation and I thought it had backfired on them. But Peter's first reason left me pondering. There could be a lot to that. The question was whether the game would be hurt more by my yielding to the opposition or by my fighting on against them. In the next twenty-four hours, I knew I would have to sort that out, once and for all.

Arriving in Boston, I learned from my staff that the AP had a story on its wire quoting ABC radio sports as saying that I had already been reelected by a secret vote of the owners. I wished it were that easy.

The council meeting the next morning was uncharacteristically serious, not that they were ever lighthearted affairs, but the usual informality and banter were missing. I had come to listen to them and found they wanted to listen to me. The lawyers spelled out the legal foundation for my holding over at the request of the Council. They had little question that the plan would successfully stand up against any challenge in court. Ed Williams strongly supported the baseball lawyers. He said the matter was open and shut. This brought the Council and myself squarely up against the merits of the holdover plan. Did it make sense for baseball?

I told them I had to make a decision as to which way I would ask them to go. Before I made that decision, I told them, I wanted some very straightforward discussion and expressions of their views. I threw the floor open.

What ensued broke into three categories: those who listened like Peter O'Malley; those who flatly supported the holdover plan like Ed Williams, Gabe Paul, and Haywood Sullivan; and those who were very uneasy about the plan. They included Dan Galbreath and Bob Lurie. No one was more flatly supportive than Gabe Paul. He said, "Bowie, I've been around baseball a long time and they always fight over the reelection of a commissioner; hang in there and fight."

As I listened to the earnest speakers, I asked myself who the real fighters would be if this came to a showdown. Any cause like this needed fighters who would provide determined leadership, who would give the others heart. Whatever his reservations, Peter would be one. Haywood, Jerry Reinsdorf and Ballard Smith would be others. Would Ed Williams be one? He certainly had been an ardent spokesman. Still, I was not sure. While encouraging me to believe that a compromise with the Busches was possible, he had told others there was no hope for one. Nor could I avoid the nagging doubts created by Ed's representation of Anheuser-Busch on certain legal problems, such as the confrontation then going on with the Reverend Jesse Jackson's "Operation PUSH" regarding hiring of blacks by the brewery. Ed was a puzzle. He was always a puzzle. So abstruse is his thinking that I suspect there are times when even he is lost in his own intellectual maze.

There were too few fighters. To be sure, they could probably be persuaded to support a showdown (excepting the two league presidents, who were caught in a political and intellectual bind), but that was not going to be enough in the face of the kind of hardball opposition we would face. Their spirit had been eroded by the long struggle. There was not enough tough spine in the room. To be sure, they wanted me to win, but kind sentiments would not be enough.

They were good guys but goodness without a lot more was not going to get the job done.

As I sat there listening, my heart cracked a little. I had very much wanted to fight against the rule-or-ruin militancy of the minority, to fight for what I thought was right for baseball. Had it been otherwise, I would not have persisted for twenty months since that night in Hollywood, Florida, when Peter had told me about the letter. I could have gone off to an easier and financially more secure life a long time ago.

We took a break and I talked to Peter. I told him I was not going to ask for implementation of the holdover plan. "I'm going to tell the major-league meeting tomorrow that I'm taking my name out of the picture." He asked if I was sure and again said he would go whichever way I wanted. I told him I was sure. That was it. There was a lot more talk that day, but Peter and I had resolved the matter in that little sidebar discussion.

One question remained: Who would be commissioner the day after my term expired ten days hence?

There was no disagreement there. They all felt I should continue until my successor took office, none of us then imagining that would be fourteen months later. I was willing for several reasons. I wanted a hand in determining who my successor would be and in shaping his powers. The most effective place to achieve those goals was from my present chair. Once out of office I knew my influence would be impaired. In addition, as long as I was commissioner, the minority would be less likely to block a new commissioner favored by the majority because the alternative was more of Kuhn.

While my continuation would require a three-quarters vote in both leagues, nobody thought that would be a problem once it was clear that I was removing my name from further consideration.

I closed the meeting and went to find Luisa, who was waiting in our suite. Hearing my account of the day's activities, she was not surprised. It had gone very much as we both expected. Even so, it was not an easy time for the two of us. We were heading down our final baseball road and there was no turning back.

I was up early the next morning to prepare a statement for the major-league meeting. It was short—only 230 words. But it said everything that needed to be said. I read it to Luisa and Sandy Hadden. They said it was all right. I noted that the pencil I had used was Ed Williams's.

I assembled my department heads and told them the news. That was hard. This was not the end they wanted.

At 9:00 A.M. we walked into the major-league meeting. I told them I had a statement. I read it with more detachment than I thought I could muster. It said:

> I have advised Bud Selig as Chairman of the Search Committee that I am withdrawing my name from any further consideration by his Committee. This decision is final, irrevocable and emphatic. I will not review it or reconsider it now or at any time in the future. As I have long endeavored to serve the best interests of this game, I have now concluded that those interests will be best served by the withdrawal of my name. Our profession painfully needs a period of harmony and good will free of the acrimony which has marred our affairs since December 1981. I feel that my decision will advance the prospects of electing a commissioner whom all of you can support and who has the potential to rally together this profession. I promise to give you every assistance I can in identifying and electing and supporting a new commissioner. This decision was not an easy one for me to make as I am proud of the accomplishments professional baseball has achieved during my time as commissioner. Nonetheless I make it without malice or rancor and with a nearly inexpressible sense of appreciation to the executives in this room and the people throughout professional baseball and everywhere in this land who have so faithfully supported me during the trials of these past 20 months. My love and affection for you will never change.

Turning the meeting over to Bud Selig as chairman of the Search Committee, I left the room and held a press conference for a corps of journalists who were as gentle as they had ever been with me.

As I rode down on the elevator, a kid with a baseball cap said, "Do you know who the new baseball commissioner is?" I said, "No, but I know who the old one was."

Incredibly enough, I was commissioner for fourteen months after I threw in the towel in Boston. During the seven months from August 1983 through March 1, 1984, I was reelected so many times that I took to joking with the press that I held the record for most times unanimously elected commissioner in a seven-month period —three. It was true. I also got good mileage by solemnly asking, "Where were the unanimous votes when I needed them?"

But the good humor could not mask the difficulties that lay ahead. If I had hoped when I made my "irrevocable" decision in Boston that my remaining months would be a time of tranquility, I was mistaken. I draw problems as honeysuckle draws bees. And so they came: drug abuse, the worsening transgressions of the superstations, the pine-tar monkeyshines of George Steinbrenner, lightless Wrigley Field and postseason play there and the ever-deepening financial trough into which too many of our clubs were falling.

None of these, however, was as difficult as the task of finding a new commissioner, not that it was one for which I had any direct responsibility. Even so, I was determined not only to influence the result but to assure, if I could, that the new commissioner had the powers and prerogatives necessary to carry out the job. Circumstances played very much into my hands. The anti-Kuhn group was now desperate to find a new commissioner. They were fearful that the passage of time without a resolution could reawaken the slumbering hopes of the pro-Kuhns to have me continue. Make no mistake about it: there were loyalists who had not given up the cause, though I now scrupulously avoided doing anything to encourage them. Given these facts, the anti-Kuhns were not going to quibble over the powers of a new man.

With my withdrawal, Bud Selig had every reason to believe in August that his assignment had been simplified. His committee would sort out the available candidates and pick the best one. Certainly by our December annual meeting in Nashville, the job would be done and a new commissioner elected. Nothing worked that easily in baseball.

Strong currents of support began to develop for different men. There was support for Lee MacPhail as an interim commissioner among some of the veteran owners such as Gene Autry and John Fetzer. Yale's A. Bartlett Giamatti had his supporters, as did James Baker and Peter Ueberroth. All of the latter three, however, had serious obligations—to Yale, the president and the Los Angeles Olympic Organizing Committee respectively. Other commendable names such as Sargent Shriver and Congressman Silvio Conte appeared from time to time, but did not develop the necessary owner support.

As the difficulty of establishing a consensus on any one man became increasingly apparent, so did Selig's renewed anguish. I volunteered to meet with his Search Committee or any of the men they were considering to see if I could help the process. At this point I was as anxious as Nelson Doubleday and Gussie Busch to have a new commissioner selected, and excited to be on my way. I had before me a multifaceted new career in the law, sports marketing, public speaking, writing and public service activities, and I wanted to get on with it. Moreover, every month I lingered around baseball, I ran the risk of looking as if I could not cut the umbilical cord that had bound me for so long to the game I loved.

Then I watched as August, September and October drifted by without a new commissioner and I sensed no real progress from my discussions with Bud Selig. Seeing no way that Ueberroth, Baker or Giamatti could become available, I pushed two names, one new, the other not so new. The new one was Jay Rockefeller, the governor of West Virginia—bright, personable and a baseball fan. I had met him several times along the baseball trail in West Virginia and Washington and liked him at once. Lee MacPhail, who had ties to Jay through Lee's wife, found that the governor intended to finish his term and run for the Senate in 1984 (which he did successfully). Then there was Selig himself. If it was a time for healing in baseball, I liked the idea of Bud, who had the necessary experience and following among the owners to be effective. Besides, we had never had an owner-commissioner, and perhaps the time had come to try one. Clannishly suspicious of outsiders, the owners might give their support to one of their own. Talking to various owners about Bud, I found considerable support, the strongest from Ed Williams.

But there was no support from Bud himself. I could get him to listen, but he was merely being courteous. I even tried to persuade him that his mother Marie and his entire family would take great pride in his being commissioner. True as that was, the answer was always negative.

It was now clear enough that Giamatti was not going to forsake Yale in 1983. Three years later the story was different. Having completed the tasks that had earlier bound him there, he resigned and in short order was elected president of the National League to succeed Chub Feeney, who was retiring in December 1986. I thought the league was fortunate to get this urbane scholar, but much of the sports world was surprised. It so happens that I was attending my Princeton reunion the weekend the story appeared. From all sides I heard the incredulity of my friends who wondered why this onetime Princeton professor and Yale president would take a job in sports. I gave them my best guess: he loves the game with a much greater intensity than you imagine; it's as simple as that. Nobody understands this particular love-virus better than I.

As concerned as I was about finding a new commissioner, there was no avoiding my continuing responsibilities. I was sued by George Steinbrenner in September because of his not-unfounded fear that I might suspend him over his behavior regarding Lee

MacPhail's decision in the "pine tar" matter. Lee had overruled the umpires, denied the Yankees a victory, and ordered a game continued in which George Brett had homered with a bat to which pine tar had been illegally applied. George's wrathful statements about Lee and George's generally recalcitrant behavior prompted me to consider suspending him.

The worsening drug abuse scandal was occupying much of my time. I managed to preside uneventfully over my fifteenth and last World Series, in which the Orioles wrecked the Phillies in four straight after the National Leaguers won the opening game. It was not a memorable series. I rather wished it had been. It sent my mind back to my first Series as commissioner in 1969 when the script was reversed. The Orioles won the first game, only to be decimated in four straight by the implausible Mets. The 1983 Orioles were not implausible, just overwhelming, although I doubt they were as good a team as their 1969 Baltimore counterparts.

I also watched, by no means dispassionately, as Peter O'Malley and Bud Selig structured my final compensation arrangements. I had sought nothing when I decided to step aside, but they were determined that something be done. With the full support of a large majority of clubs they decided that I should receive $50,000 from each major-league club. This was a matter on which the majority could rule. The intriguing question was how my opponents would react. Almost to a man, they were excellent. Doubleday said it should be unanimous and Steinbrenner would have gone higher. Eddie Chiles hoped I would be happy. Several grumbled, but there were few discordant notes. At the end of September, Dick Young accurately broke the story that the total amount was $1.3 million.

As we turned into November, something was plucking at my mind about Peter Ueberroth. A lot of people liked his qualifications. I was one of them. In conversations with Lurie, Selig, O'Malley and others, I found that he was moving up in their esteem. Still, the Olympics were over eight months away. How could he be available? When Ueberroth's office called asking if I could make breakfast at the Waldorf in several days, I thought the plot might be taking an interesting turn.

I called Selig and asked how his committee stood on Peter. The answer was an emphatic "by all means, encourage him." I learned from O'Malley that Ueberroth was seeing a number of owners but was telling Selig that "the best man for the job was still Kuhn." I was sure that Ueberroth knew perfectly well that my withdrawal was genuine.

He and I spent two hours together at the Waldorf's Peacock Alley. If the grueling problems of the approaching Olympics were taking their toll on this man, there was surely no outward sign. He was all cordiality, good humor and vitality. We laughed about the peculiarities of owners. Indeed, show me two commissioners laughing and the odds are strong they are telling stories about owners.

Peter recognized that "other good candidates" were under consideration, but that cast no shadow on his self-assurance. He asked if they really wanted a "leader." I replied that I thought they did and that this could be tested by seeing what new powers they were willing to give my successor. I told him that the job was not worth having unless the commissioner was clearly recognized as the CEO of baseball with all administrative departments reporting to him and unless he could be reelected by a simple majority of all clubs.

But none of this solved the unanswered problem of Peter's availability. When I asked, he said that the Olympics would carry him through October 1984, almost a year away. That was logical enough. The next question was his: "Would you be available to continue as commissioner through the end of 1985?" I was getting my first lesson in Peter's unpredictability. It was by no means my last. 1985! Here we were in November 1983 and Peter was tacking another twenty-six months on to my term. I told him I was not prepared to make any commitment beyond the end of 1983. Undeterred, and I think unpersuaded, he talked about how we could work together in the years ahead.

As our December annual meetings approached, Selig still had no answer. New names emerged like that of Frank Dale, publisher of the *Los Angeles Herald-Examiner*, but my thoughts about Ueberroth grew more insistent. He certainly had his champions among ownership in men like Bob Lurie and George Argyros. The more I watched his style of operation, the more I became convinced that he could handle the job. Of particular importance to me was his cocky self-assurance.

Selig now told me that there would be no decision in time for the December meetings. However, he was confident that by March 1, his committee would have a man. Naturally the question arose as to whether I would carry on an extra two months. I was then intensively involved in trying to resolve our drug abuse problems; several more months would be welcome. Still I had no intention of continuing unless it could be accomplished smoothly. Word was reaching me that some of my foes were anxious to see me on my way. I told Bud they were going to have to be in complete agreement in asking me to stay on. I rather enjoyed imposing that condition. Yet one more unanimous reelection—Bud did his homework and assured me it could be done. And so it was when we got to Nashville.

There I gave my "final farewell address." By this time I was getting quite experienced at that speech and at poking fun at myself. I said, "I've given so many retirement speeches already that I'm beginning to feel like Muhammad Ali." I felt an emotional tug as I welcomed for the last time Toru Shoriki, the owner of the Tokyo Giants. A perennial guest at our conventions and a close personal friend, he exemplified the internationalism of baseball, something which I cherished and had strongly promoted. I then launched extemporaneously into a message that came from my heart. After urging them to get on with the business of selecting a new commissioner, I said:

> "I would urge that Baseball in selecting a new commissioner realize that if he is going to be effective several things have to be so. He's got to be a strong commissioner, strong in several ways. Strong as a personality who will have the necessary courage in the face of relentless problems and pressures to do what is necessary for the good of the game. And he must be a strong commissioner in the sense of the powers he is given, the protection his office is given. It's all well and good to say 'here's a good man, here's a good man to do the job.' But he must have more than that. He must have more than I have had. And if we can achieve the necessary changes, and I think we must—and I think he must insist on it, incidentally—then we can so improve the position of the commissioner that he will be able to face the very tough challenges that I have outlined here in the prior part of my remarks. And I think it's vital that he be empowered to face those challenges. . . . A little look at history will take you back . . . to 1921, when a curly-haired old tough-minded federal judge was about to become commissioner. . . . He said I want more than a legal document. . . . He said I want a moral covenant with ownership to steadfastly support the commissioner. I want a moral covenant by which they say, 'We will stand behind you come thick or thin regardless of what our individual personal feelings might be about its rightness or wrongness. We have given you a tough job and we will stand behind you and we will support you. There will be no knives in your back.'"

I concluded by telling them I loved them. As I looked at some of the faces in that room, I knew that was an exaggeration, but it was apt enough in regard to most.

By way of farewell, they gave me a standing ovation (a department in which I was faring rather better than usual). Whether this was out of conviction or duty, I cannot say—probably something of both. Either way, I was human enough to savor the moment, including the discomfiture of several of my foes who were compelled by decorum to rise and pay me a reluctant tribute.

What I did not savor were the groans of frustration that continued to emanate from Bud Selig. Contrary to my hopes that he and his committee were on the verge of a solution, he told me several days before Christmas 1983: "Right now I have absolutely nothing to surprise anybody with, remember Zale and Graziano battling each other into hopelessness; that's the way I feel." Discouraging as Bud's words were, I could not help but think that between Baker and Ueberroth, they had their man. Believing that the president was not going to let Baker go, I became more convinced that Ueberroth was the answer. I took solace from that. I also took solace from finally disposing of my "pine tar" dispute with George Steinbrenner by imposing financial penalties totaling $300,000. Concerned that he might have been suspended, George accepted with good grace. It was the largest financial penalty in sports history.

The Sporting News gave me a Christmas present three days late by naming me 1983 Man of the Year. I had beaten out Joe Theismann and John Riggins of the Washington Redskins, not to mention Martina Navratilova and Moses Malone. For an old Redskin fan, that was pretty heady stuff. I said I was touched, and I was. More important, I was indebted to publisher Dick Waters, who I suspected was the moving force behind the award.

Selig's activities took a decidedly encouraging turn in January as he and his committee members stepped up their direct contacts with Ueberroth and Baker. There was no longer any question in my mind that both would like to have the job if a way could be found around their other commitments. As they were both men of high quality, I was heartened about the prospects of baseball's future leadership. I noted that both had strong support among baseball owners although for varying reasons. Ueberroth stood out for his charisma, tough-mindedness and business acumen. Baker was a quite different commodity: a Princetonian, lawyer and practical diplomat, a low-key problem solver. Some thought he was closer to a Kuhn model. My guess was that Baker had more support than Ueberroth. Certainly some of the owners were uneasy about Peter's tendency toward unruly independence. It was exactly this quality that I liked best in him.

In the final analysis, the nature of the respective commitments made the difference. Ueberroth was committed through the Summer Olympics but not beyond. Commitments to a president by a man of Baker's quality are not easily put aside. Some indication of the strength of Baker's ties to President Reagan was later demonstrated by his appointment as treasury secretary after the president's 1984 election victory. Ueberroth was getting increasing support from owners such as Peter O'Malley, Joan Kroc, Bob Lurie and George Argyros. With the job in his grasp, Ueberroth told Selig he would not take it unless I would continue through October 1. I loved the audacity of it. I had said I would not stay. My enemies were desperate to get me out of sight. John McMullen as a member of Selig's committee was begging him "not to give us Kuhn again." There were certainly other ways to bridge from me to Ueberroth. The Executive Council could operate baseball for seven months with Sandy Hadden or Lee MacPhail as de facto commissioner. But there was Peter saying, "Without Kuhn, I won't take the job." In a simple, bold stroke, he was showing who was boss and leveraging me into a position from which it would be difficult to say I would not build the bridge to Peter. He called me to say I was the only person who made any sense after March 1 and asked me to stay on. He said, "I trust Bowie Kuhn 100 percent." I told him Luisa and I were leaving for Sarajevo to attend the Winter Olympics for a week and would think about it.

If I should decide to stay, he urged me to tell the clubs to come to me with the votes in hand and say "please." He said any other course would be "flat damaging to you."

Amidst the excitement of the Winter Olympics, Luisa and I found time to talk about staying on. But for Ueberroth's bold handling of the situation, there is no question we would have said no. She asked if he really would decline the job unless I became the bridge. I said, "Dear, I really don't know; all I can tell you is that he has them all convinced he means business, and I've got to tell you he has me pretty well convinced." At this point nobody, including me, wanted to be responsible for shooting down Ueberroth. I also told Luisa that if Ueberroth took a hike, Selig was going to have to start from scratch looking for a new man. To do that to Bud was like a death warrant.

Finally, in Ueberroth we had the man I wanted to succeed me. Not only did he have the prerequisite abilities, or at least most of them, he was a man with whom I felt I could communicate. I did not delude myself that he was a man I could control—neither he nor I wanted that—but I did think I could get his ear. The ensuing years have proven that to be a correct judgment.

So in Sarajevo, the city where the 1914 assassination of Archduke Francis Ferdinand had precipitated The Great War, Luisa and I concluded that the best way to end baseball's great commissioner war was for me to provide the bridge to Peter's succession, assuming it could be done smoothly and properly. That remained to be seen.

Upon our return, O'Malley and Selig urged me to stay on and suggested a prompt joint meeting of the Search Committee and Executive Council to determine whether the necessary "please, Bowie" would be forthcoming. It was a good test, since Doubleday, McMullen and Argyros—three of my opponents—were included. The meeting was promptly pulled together and produced a unanimous request that I continue. The only sour note, I learned later, was a suggestion by McMullen that I agree not to write a book about my baseball career. It was rejected by his peers.

There is a subsequent McMullen story I cannot resist telling. In March 1986, I attended the Dodgers' opening spring training game at Vero Beach against McMullen's Astros. John was there. As I was scheduled to throw out the first ceremonial pitch from the mound, Peter O'Malley asked me if I had any objection to John as the catcher. "That would be fun," I replied. When I strode to the mound, I was surprised to find not McMullen but Mike Scioscia, the regular Dodgers catcher, behind the plate. Peter later told me John had declined the honor after first asking, "How close will Bowie stand?"

I told Bud I would have no answer until I had had an opportunity to discuss the situation thoroughly with Ueberroth. Several days later I took a 9:00 A.M. flight out of Newark for Los Angeles and a three-and-a-half-hour meeting with Peter. We had a relaxed discussion of all the problems facing baseball. He assured me that he would be fair with the people who worked in my office and would discuss personnel matters with me. He repeated his position that he would not take the job unless I continued. The time had come for me to accept or decline. My answer was yes. After working out details of a joint press conference we would hold after a major-league meeting that would be held shortly to elect Peter, I flew back to Newark and was peacefully asleep at home shortly after midnight.

The next day I told Bud by telephone that I had consulted my key constituencies, namely Luisa, Willkie Farr & Gallagher, and Ueberroth, and had decided to stay on until October 1. I could almost hear his layers of concern peeling away. He simply said, "Great!"

The election meeting held in Tampa was an anticlimax. By unanimous votes I was reelected yet one more time and Peter was elected the sixth commissioner of baseball to take office October 1, 1984. More important, all the new powers I had urged upon Peter and Bud were adopted. The new commissioner would be specifically designated the CEO of baseball with all administrative departments reporting to him; his fining power was increased from $5,000 to $250,000; he could be reelected by a simple majority; and he was protected against litigation by the clubs.

The next seven months sped by. Peter spent time in New York and I in Los Angeles. We talked a lot on the telephone. I tried to include him in all aspects of our decision-making process and answered all his questions. Throughout he never intruded in any way on my prerogatives, although he could easily have done so. It was about as good a relationship as two men could have under the circumstances. We maintained our senses of humor with one another. When press critics called him "arrogant and ruthless," he took to identifying himself on telephone calls as "arrogant and ruthless," as though that were his name. We laughed a lot about our mutual problem, although I assured him that he hadn't seen anything yet.

In early August my brother Lou died. He had struggled with leukemia for two years. I had spent as much time as I could with him in Jacksonville, Florida. Ueberroth had thoughtfully sent him an Olympic torch. One of the world's greatest Red Sox fans, Lou hated the thought of my leaving baseball. We talked about that but also about the Red Sox. He loved talking about the Sox. He had the forgiving fatalism and fortitude of all their fans. My brother Lou had a lot of fortitude. He showed it that summer.

Luisa and I were invited by Commissioner Suh of Korean Professional Baseball to attend the Korean postseason play in October. It gave us a nice opportunity to be with old friends in Korea and to gracefully vacate the American stage. On September 27, I finished the massive job of packing up my papers and effects, said my last farewells to my staff, received a cordial farewell call from George Steinbrenner and a visit from Sparky Anderson and Dick Brescia of

CBS Radio Network and did my last press interviews as commissioner. On my bare desk I left a baseball bat inscribed to Ueberroth from me and a pair of swimming trunks I recommended for chilly World Series nights. In several hours we were airborne for Seoul.

It was lunchtime in Korea on October 1 when my term officially ended. Luisa and I were sitting in a small restaurant in the Kyongju Chosun Hotel looking out at beautiful Lake Bomun-Ho. As my watch recorded midnight on September 30 New York time, I raised my glass to Luisa and said, "Free at last." We walked out of the hotel to meet our fellow guests and dear friends Commissioner and Mrs. Takeso Shimoda of Japan. He laughed roundly as he told me he had just heard that the American umpires were going on strike for the League Championship Series. We all joined in the laughter. Peter had told me that changing jobs every so often was a good idea. He was right.

After a brief return to the United States, Luisa and I took off again, this time with the Baltimore Orioles and Ed and Agnes Williams for a Japanese tour. I had urged Ueberroth to go instead of us, but he insisted that we make the trip as his representatives. We went on to Beijing and Shanghai for a series of visits with Chinese baseball and other sports officials. China was of special interest to me as I liked the Chinese and thought they could play an important role in baseball's achieving gold-medal status in the Olympics and in baseball's long-term international growth. I was determined to find a way to help promote baseball there. My subsequent affiliation with Burson-Marsteller as a member of their senior advisory board provided a way to do just that through sports marketing activities in China. Though I was now fading into the history of professional baseball, I wanted to promote the amateur game in China and elsewhere around the world, confident that baseball could in time supplant soccer as the world's most popular game.

The greatest thrill of my baseball career came, oddly enough, two years after I left the commissioner's office. In October 1986 the International Olympic Committee made baseball a gold-medal sport effective with the 1992 Olympics in Barcelona. International Amateur Baseball Association head Dr. Robert Smith called me from Lausanne, Switzerland, with the news. In the joy of the moment my mind flashed back thirteen years to Dublin, Ireland, where I sat in the office of Lord Michael Killanin, then IOC president, and pleaded the cause of baseball. Charming though he was, Killanin told me baseball's task was formidable. He said they didn't really want any more team sports. With hard work, he thought we might make it by the turn of the century, if ever. He also pointed out that baseball had two world associations and needed to pare down to one to have any hope. "Oh yes," he said, "try putting out honest literature; I have a flier from the European Baseball Association that lists Ireland as a baseball country. I happen to know there is no baseball here."

I carried his discouraging message from Dublin to the amateur baseball world. Across continents they lept to the task, in Havana, Tokyo, San Juan, Rome, Managua, Amsterdam, Caracas, Los Angeles and elsewhere. They unified the effort under a single association and named Carlos Garcia of Nicaragua as the first president. That was fitting because nowhere was baseball more beloved than in the Latin American countries. I knew that first hand from my extensive travels in Puerto Rico, Mexico, the Dominican Republic, Venezuela and Nicaragua, and from my knowledge of Cuba and its people. Nowhere had I ever been received more affectionately than in Latin America. My friend Guigo Otero Suro, the Caribbean commissioner, used to say if I ever got tired of the North American job, I should take over as a Caribbean *jefe*. Indeed, my popularity around the world was always greater than at home, a fact which reminded me that abroad I was a promoter and goodwill ambassador, at home a disciplinarian. There was a difference. A story from a September 1986 visit to Tokyo illustrates the point. As I was leaving a luncheon reception given by Sports Nippon, a Japanese executive walked me to the elevator. Using his limited English he said goodbye and then, groping for some additional warm thing to say, gave me this line: "I don't drink Budweiser."

When the Nicaraguan Sandinistas jailed our dedicated friend Garcia, Dr. Smith succeeded him as international president. He organized the final drive that led to the triumph of baseball as a demonstration sport in the 1984 Los Angeles Olympics, and ultimately to the gold medal. That drive included such achievements as bringing the People's Republic of China into the international association in 1980, India in 1985, a baseball complex in Tianjin, China, funded by the Los Angeles Dodgers, baseball as an official international game of China and the beginnings of baseball competition in the Soviet Union in 1986. Dr. Smith's kitchen cabinet of Rod Dedeaux, Peter O'Malley and me scampered around the world and took a happy hand in all of this. Under the sponsorship of AT&T, I was even able to organize in 1986 the first visit ever of a baseball team to the United States from the People's Republic of China. It was exhilarating stuff.

In the several years since Luisa and I walked out of the baseball offices at 350 Park Avenue and headed for Seoul, I have followed Ueberroth's activities with the keenest interest. My offices at Willkie Farr & Gallagher are only two blocks away, and I can almost see Peter's office out of my window in the Citicorp Building. Peter and I talk from time to time, and I keep abreast of baseball developments through my partner Lou Hoynes and other baseball friends. Peter has proven to be the kind of vigorous, assertive commissioner I anticipated he would be. He has established a particularly powerful image in his handling of drug abuse and labor problems with players and umpires. He has gained the respect of the public and press, not an easy accomplishment, as I well know. He has moved Ed Durso and Bryan Burns, two of the best young executives I had hired, into two of the top jobs in his administration. He has followed a distinctly independent line with regard to the owners, trusting his own judgment and instincts more than theirs.

I have supported him consistently with the exception of his handling of the Mays-Mantle cases. His decision that they could hold jobs in baseball while working for gambling casinos was I fear a mistake, albeit a popular one. My reservations on this score are abundantly stated earlier in this book. A sacrifice of principle for expediency, his decision regarding these baseball legends will in my judgment be regretted.

He has remained his own man. He has a drummer who is distinctively his own. He marches where his instincts take him. It is too soon to tell whether this individualistic man with his individualistic approach to the commissionership of this most complex of games will be a long-term success.

Clearly enough Peter came to the job in 1984 with some considerable assets that I did not have when I arrived in 1969. Most obvious among these were a splendid reputation built on his stunning financial and artistic success with the 1984 Olympics and the greatly enhanced powers he was given by the clubs. But I was more fortunate than he was with regard to the basic challenge I faced. Mine was to save baseball from the oblivion into which it was seen to be plunging in the 1960s. It had all the makings of a crusade to save this cherished, hallowed institution from the depredations of the vandals of entertainment. Peter's basic challenge on the other hand was to sharpen the business skills of the game and to increase its revenues, hardly the stuff of crusades or high drama.

Given the nature of my challenge, I was able to create an administration of people who knew and loved the game as I did, people who were thrilled to be involved in its revival. I was able to create an administration of policies that were not so much concerned with the bottom line as with what was best for the game and its great traditions. We involved the minor leagues, amateur baseball nationally and internationally, and professional baseball in the Caribbean, Japan and Korea. They were all an integral part of our crusade. And it all worked. We saw North American college and professional baseball attendance soar from forty to eighty million. We saw baseball become the fastest-growing major sport in the world, and its popularity both nationally and internationally reach an all-time high.

For two years after I left professional baseball, I did not attend any post-season games, out of a feeling that old commissioners do best by simply fading away. Then in 1986, drawn by my fondness for the Red Sox and the bliss of Fenway Park, Luisa and I attended two games in Boston as Ueberroth's guests. I even threw out the first pitch at the fourth game, following Speaker Tip O'Neill, who did the honors the night before. That night I sat with Henry Aaron and talked warmly about baseball past and present. As sentimental as I am about baseball people, I was not prepared for the affection I received from all sides—executives, writers, broadcasters, players, ballpark attendants, taxicab drivers, and most of all, everyday fans in the park and in the streets.

Whatever the problems, whatever the errors of commission or omission, we had wrestled with a lofty challenge and found the way. I could say in the words of St. Paul, "I have fought a good fight, I have finished my course, I have kept the faith."

AFTERWORD TO THE BISON BOOKS EDITION

A baker's dozen years have slipped by since I was commissioner. They have not been altogether good years for the Major League game.

In the half century before me, only four commissioners had served; since, there have been four more. Now that's enough to make an old commissioner feel like an artifact, which is probably irrelevant except to me.

Clearly not irrelevant is this inevitable question: does the revolving door at 350 Park Avenue tell us that the game itself is becoming an artifact? Some say "yes" but here I am, guardedly more sanguine about the future than I have been about the recent past.

I still retain what I at least consider respectable credentials to comment on the game. I remain, as I have been from childhood, an incurable romantic about this unique institution. The long-vanished Senators remain my team, though now they exist only in my imagination and in my enduring faith that they will yet come home. I still talk to baseball people who have the patience to endure my opinions and advice. The print and broadcast media ring my telephone with regularity. The first edition of this book received good notices, my favorite being "so well written as to be almost believable." For me, who suffered "beleaguered" as part of my name, it was high praise.

I remain active on the board at Cooperstown and still shed a tear at the summer ceremonies. I frequently talk to audiences around the country but find their baseball questions these days too harsh for much comfort. There is some evidence that I have retained my wits and that my sense of humor has grown, although my good wife is unsure on both counts. My mother, who inspired my baseball religion, carried on into her ninety-first year and then, with exquisitely felicitous timing, left it all to me.

I practiced law for five years after I left baseball, discovering, as I should have known, that in my case at least you can't go home again. It was a new and tougher profession than the one I had left. I was ill-suited there and left it behind at considerable expense and no remorse. In the last eight years, I have busied myself with consulting, corporate boards, university boards, speaking, writing and volunteer work. I have even campaigned in three presidential races: one win, two losses. But at the end of the day, it's the volunteer work that counts and grows. I spent almost two years as a volunteer in the AIDS wards of St. Clare's Hospital in New York. More recently, I am a volunteer in St. Catherine Laboure nursing home in Jacksonville, Florida, where I try to console the old folks but they in fact console me. Among other things, I read the newspaper highlights to them, replete with personal commentary, feeling all the while like a reincarnation of my favorite New York mayor, Fiorello LaGuardia. My sweet audience includes a ninety-one-year-old former Latin teacher named Fanny, who has grit in a measure that only the truly old can achieve. The other day she said to me, "Aren't you the former baseball commissioner?" When I nodded, she resumed, "I guess I'm supposed to stand in awe of you?" I smiled and said, "Absolutely!" Fanny cried, "Well, I'm not!" Sic transit gloria mundi. Setting me up all the way, she knew a sitting duck when she saw one.

I was succeeded by Peter Ueberroth, Bart Giamatti, Fay Vincent and Bud Selig, in that order. Bud was called "acting." Rarely has an "acting" anything had the durability of Bud, who, more than four years later as this afterword is written, is still baseball's boss.

As appeared earlier in this book, Peter Ueberroth brought a barrel of talent to the job as he had so clearly demonstrated in his years as head of the Los Angeles Olympics. While baseball remained popular under Ueberroth, he was uncomfortable with almost every aspect of it—the owners, the binding traditions, the union and the media. But most of all he grew increasingly scornful of the owners and, with time, they of him. He found the union intransigence as frustrating as those commissioners before and after him. The huge arbitration award obtained by the union against the management on the union's charge of collusive salary arrangements left him little room for maneuver. He was more than happy to be on his way before his five-year term of office came to an end. Peter is an impatient man, perhaps too much so for his own good; he does not like to ride the same horse too long.

The seventh commissioner was Bart Giamatti. The office has never seen anybody quite like Bart, nor has baseball. He was no stranger, having performed as National League president for several years under Ueberroth. He was an exile there, largely removed from the great events of the game. In nearly fifty years of involvement with the professional game, I recall no one as genuinely loved as Bart Giamatti. And this he reciprocated. He was a fan of the game as perhaps only Ford Frick and I had been among commissioners. He believed that organized baseball had a great purpose that transcended other games. As a trustee of Franklin & Marshall College, I asked him to give a commencement address as he was an orator of exceptional quality. He talked about the moral values needed in higher education and of the need to instill values beyond technocracy in young people. This was the way I thought a leader of the national game should sound.

Beset by more serious health problems than most realized and by the Pete Rose case, he survived as commissioner only a few months before his tragic death on a late summer day in 1989. Would he have been a great commissioner? No one can say. He was the most loved. Isn't that enough?

In a state of shock over the death of Giamatti, the owners turned to his deputy Fay Vincent in an uncharacteristic act of sentiment, or so it seemed to me and to many others. There is not much I can say about Vincent as I had not known him before he was commissioner and scarcely did better thereafter. For whatever reason, that was the way he wanted it. An earthquake gave him a bitter test in his first World Series. With no ground rules to guide him, he simply made things up as he went along and handled an impossible situation with aplomb and imagination.

From there, things seemed to go downhill for him. There were more earthquakes in his short tenure, but these were in the boardroom. Though his reign seemed doomed almost from the beginning, his handling of affairs from a substantive point of view struck me as usually correct. His efforts to find rapprochement with the players union made sense. After some initial wobbling, he supported a Japanese bailout of the Seattle Club which stabilized major league baseball in the northwest.

His fatal decision was ordering the Cubs realigned into the National League West. Never mind that the entire National League had opposed the Cubs on this issue. Now most of the clubs, led by the powerful Tribune Company, which owned the Cubs and superstation WGN, turned on him. When the Tribune Company sued him, both Ueberroth and I filed affidavits in his support. It was all too late and Fay resigned.

Vincent was really his own worst enemy. He wanted to be commissioner in the imperial manner of Judge Landis, scything down foes as they got in his road. Among his many skills as thirty-year commissioner of the NFL, Pete Rozelle's great skill was charming owners, networks, press and even other commissioners into seeing things his way. Modern commissioners, in all sports, have at times had to use diplomacy on their irascible constituencies, unleashing the airborne only as a last resort.

What followed was the election of an owner/commissioner, Bud Selig, the boss of the Milwaukee Brewers. Baseball hadn't seen the likes of this since the disastrous rule of the National Commission in the early part of this century, which expired in the ignominy of the Black Sox. That is how we got around to having a commissioner in the first place.

Had the owners collectively lost their minds? My first reaction was to think they had. The owner/leader structure was discredited by our own history. This was not a reflection on Selig, a friend of twenty-five years standing.

Perhaps, I came to think, it might make sense as a temporary measure for one reason and one reason only: to create a level playing field for the then imminent collective bargaining with the Players Association. The players and the media believed, not without reason, that the owners would not take a tough stand. Possibly, they were putting out of their minds the expensive sixty-day shutdown in 1981. An owner/leader like Selig might remind them of 1981 and convince the skeptics that there was equal resolve on both sides of the table. Mutual respect brings about agreements in normal situations. But little is normal in the grand old game of baseball.

Bud did a brilliant job of essentially unifying the owners as no other base-ball leader had done. This was actually brought about by a combination of skill and circumstance. The skill was Bud's collegiality; the circumstance was the increasingly desperate condition of baseball's economics, the essence of which was the relentless increase in player salaries and the financial disparity between the smaller and larger cities.

Any sensible observer knew that something had to be done about the problem and that the solution had to be arrived at by cooperation from both sides of the bargaining table, as had been the case in the NFL and the NBA, where salary caps had been agreed to by the respective unions. But the baseball union is tougher, sometimes to the point of irrationality, than any other, and called the owners' bluff, rebuffed the owner-leaning recommendation of the most respected mediator in the country, misread the owners' gumption and stumbled into a strike as they had in 1981. The strike of 1994–95 and the shocking loss of the 1994 post-season and World Series stunned and soured the baseball firmament as nothing had since the Black Sox. And worse, far worse, the fans were mad at everybody. The Selig solidarity scenario had succeeded too well. After a while, the two combatants, like a pair of brutally beaten prize-fighters, were too mindless even to fall down.

Baseball sputtered back into delayed action in April 1995 when the players mercifully pulled down their strike. Attendance plunged almost everywhere although there were hopeful exceptions in Cleveland and Colorado. Gloom enveloped the game like a dark blanket. Though the strike was over, there was still no labor agreement and no guarantee that everything wouldn't stop again. But two events gave reassurance to the faithful.

The first was Cal Ripken's breaking of Lou Gehrig's record for consecutive games played. In 1939, when the Iron Horse sat down for the first time in thirteen years, we all knew that no one could ever be super-human enough to match Gehrig's endurance. We were all wrong because Ripken did it. He mesmerized the sports world and electrified the general public over a period of weeks as few ever have. And it was an urgently affectionate focus on a man of real character and dedication to the fans of Baltimore.

He hadn't taken the blanket off, but he had lifted it and there was light.

The second was the death of Mickey Mantle. Ordinarily, we are not reassured by death. But Mickey did reassure us, in part by the grace-filled penitence with which he left us and in part because he reminded us he was the Oklahoma kid with beguiling smile and awesome bat who decades after he put down his glove could still touch all Americans tenderly.

There was no salvation yet for baseball. Ripken and Mantle alone couldn't do that. But there was hope.

Major League attendance rose marginally in 1996 but was well short of 1993, the last previous full season. While surprisingly strong new national television deals with NBC, Fox, and ESPN helped with the red ink, the total debt of major league baseball increased. These were still far from the best of times, notwithstanding the continuing emergence of attractive young stars who were pounding balls out of ballparks in extraordinary numbers and a United Nations pitching staff in Los Angeles that inspired an unprecedented search for talent worldwide.

Purists shuddered over an extra tier of playoffs first on display in 1995, partly out of fear of playing the World Series in Green Bay conditions and partly because wild card clubs were included. I thought the experiment a wise one, and in practice it was a clear success. Certain aspects of the game should be sacrosanct, like the playing rules and the role of the commissioner, but that leaves plenty of room for legitimate experimentation. Times they are a-changing, a simple reality of which baseball must take keen note.

Years ago I joined the American League in proposing inter-league play on a limited scale but the National was a fierce stumbling block. You may be sure I was pleased to learn that limited inter-league was made a feature of the 1997 season. I expect another success.

These innovations, expansion into Tampa Bay and Arizona (along with earlier expansion in Colorado and Miami), and a really rousing World Series in 1996 have all set the stage for a baseball resurgence, if the emerging opportunity is seized.

After the World Series, at long last, a labor agreement was achieved. While by no means solving the game's serious financial problems, it did include a small "luxury tax" on overly large club payrolls, with the tax funding a modest amount of revenue sharing for clubs in most need. The great labor war of 1993–96 was over and peace had settled in for five years and, with any luck, perhaps longer. Sound the trumpets!

Sound them too in memory of Jackie Robinson. In 1997, baseball celebrated the fiftieth anniversary of April 15, 1947, when he first took the field for the Dodgers and Branch Rickey stole an incredible march on the other clubs. It was baseball's greatest moment. Perhaps the lustre of Robinson can once again ignite the game. Why not? He was always magic, anyway.

As I write this afterword, the question is unresolved as to whether the game's leaders will do what is necessary to surmount the fearful damage of these recent years. Happily, there is nothing wrong with the fundamentals. The game itself remains the most exquisite of all games. It has an unparalleled run of almost nine months when most of the showtime belongs to baseball, notwithstanding the attractiveness of basketball and hockey playoffs. The minor league and college games have been unscathed by the troubles upstairs and in fact new and unaffiliated minor leagues have been appearing on the scene. Baseball is an Olympic sport that will become more attractive in the future with the infusion of professional players from participating countries and without the likelihood of a "dream team." And, of course, no sport has such a fundamentally strong appeal to family groups nor such rich lore, tradition, humor and storytelling.

Some of the fans have gone away, many never to return, but these marvelous fundamentals are intact.

Baseball has a crisis and more than anything else it is a crisis of leadership. The problem did not begin with the "acting" commissionership. It goes back to the death of Judge Landis in 1944. Restive, almost demeaned under his iron grip, the owners began a process of chipping away at the power of the commissioner. The result was a weakening of the competitive power of the game against the entertainment industry, including other sports. As the effects of this weakening became more palpable during the ill-fated term of General Spike Eckert (1965–68), the ownership resigned itself to a stronger-handed leader. At first they temporized by electing me as a pro-tem commissioner, but then they bit painfully into the bullet and gave me a full seven-year term. I used the powers I was given and redefined them into more than some had intended. The game turned from its doldrums, gained momentum, and reasserted itself as a powerhouse in the entertainment world.

Certainly other factors were at work, but in my judgment, the main factor was the willingness of the ownership to accept leadership. Capable, and in some cases brilliant as they were in diverse ways, they needed leadership to make their partnership succeed. At the end of the day, however much they knew they needed a doctor, they hated the medicine which came in the form of owners being overridden, fined, publicly chastised and even suspended. Most owners were willing to accept that medicine during my sixteen years because we were largely successful, they trusted me and, odd as it may seem, they liked me. A minority did not and they were able to block my reelection. I fought that minority, at considerable personal cost, for several years because I believed that the concept of a strong commissionership was at stake. I have not changed that view.

Make no mistake that much of baseball's strength is a function of public confidence in the office of commissioner. There, they believe, is the genesis of the game's integrity, the assurance that miscreant owners and players will be properly dealt with and the guarantee that franchises will remain stable. However effective their commissioners have been, no other sport has been able to generate this Landis-bred respect for the office. In a stroke, major league baseball could regain much of its lost respect by putting into place a fully-empowered commissioner and letting him lead the game—or her, if Margaret

Thatcher or Elizabeth Dole happens to be available. But they are probably looking for easier jobs like running the United Kingdom or the United States.

Public trust in the national game would surge overnight. Some will say that the money at stake is too huge to give such power to one person. I say the stakes are too high not to do so. And I have a hunch that the largest round of applause just might come from the Players Association, giving rise to the legitimate hope that a real partnership can be forged between the players and clubs.

I envision a national game where the commissioner once again stands for something beyond the ordinary; where the public interest counts; where commercial immediacy can be put aside; where baseball dares to be something more than just another segment of the entertainment industry and where the game is a real model of virtue for the public and for kids in particular. Pure romanticism, cynics will say. I say, dare to try it.

I have now entered my eighth decade. God willing, I will have more to say about the game in the years ahead but this may also be the last and best forum I will have. So in honor of my seven grandchildren who have arrived since I left 350 Park Avenue, let me tell you my wife's favorite baseball story. The setting is a bar in Boston in the cruel winter that followed the Red Sox loss of the celebrated 1975 World Series to the Reds. A Red Sox reliever named Jim Willoughby was removed in the seventh game, after which the Reds rallied to win. In his wintry cups, a man sits at the bar with tears running down his face, inconsolable. A neighbor at the bar leans over and says, "What is it, lad, trouble at home?" The tearful one answers, "They should never have took out Willoughby."

February 1997

Index

Locker, Bob, 82
Long, Russell, 249
Look, 73
Lopez, Al, 423
Los Angeles Dodgers, 6, 22–24, 28, 38,
    39, 158, 164, 169, 186, 205, 234,
    239, 309, 392
Los Angeles Herald-Examiner, 431
Los Angeles Olympic Organizing
    Committee, 388, 428
Los Angeles Times, 254, 314, 394
Louis, Joe, 24
Louis, John, 50–51
Lowe, Mary Johnson, 291
Ludtke, Melissa, 299–300
Lupica, Mike, 271
Lurie, Bob, 211, 212, 244, 249, 252–53,
    254, 259, 329, 351,
    Hollywood letter and, 8, 11
    Kuhn as holdover commissioner and,
        405, 417–20, 425
    Kuhn's 1982 reelection campaign
        and, 368, 369, 394, 401
    replacement of Kuhn by Ueberroth
        and, 430, 431, 434

McAndrew, Jim, 62
McCarthy, Joe, 220
McCarthy, Tommy, 299
McCarver, Tim, 74
McCormack, John, 57–58
McCovey, Willie, 60
McDonald, Arch, 292, 293
McDonald, David, 75
McDougall, Don, 190, 191, 192
McEnroe, John, 273
McGarr, Frank, 182, 184, 262
McGovern, Hugh, 299
McGraw, Tug, 62
McGregor, Scott, 205
McHale, John, 8, 29, 31, 41, 45, 48–49,
    86, 143, 145, 148, 156, 163, 177,
    195, 206, 351, 374, 416
McHale, Patty, 406
Mack, Bill, 242
Mack, Connie, 26, 175
McKenna, Andy, 372, 382, 389, 390,
    392, 398–99, 401, 404, 412
McLain, Denny, 25, 67–73, 237
MacLaine, Shirley, 263
McLendon, Gordon, 180
McMullen, John, 47, 235–36, 339, 352,
    405, 408, 412–19, 434
    Hollywood letter and, 6–7, 10
    Kuhn's 1982 reelection campaign
        and, 373, 382
McNally, Dave, 155–58
MacPhail, Larry, 4, 179–80, 423

MacPhail, Lee, 4, 29, 31, 55, 67, 104,
    140, 163, 166, 173, 177, 192–94,
    196, 198, 205, 206, 207, 216, 242,
    245, 246–49, 277, 312, 319–20, 329,
    344–45, 355–64, 434
    Hollywood letter and, 7, 8
    Kuhn as holdover commissioner and,
        416, 418, 428–30
    Kuhn's 1969 election and, 33
    Kuhn's 1975 reelection and, 145–49,
        151
    Kuhn's 1982 reelection campaign
        and, 374, 388, 394–402
McRae, Norm, 72
Maddon, Bill, 301
Maddox, Elliott, 72
Maglie, Sal, 19
Magnin, Cyril, 189
Major League Agreement, 9–10, 120,
    182, 197, 207
Major League Baseball Promotion
    Corporation, 32, 66, 67, 205, 334,
    381
Major League Franchise Committee,
    189
Major League Players Association
    (MLPA), 29, 41, 46, 50, 60, 68, 73,
    74–84, 139–42, 154–65, 166, 170,
    172, 178, 275–76, 298, 304–14, 315,
    318–19, 322, 331–65
    Executive Committee of, 80–81, 82,
        358
    1969 strike of, 3–4, 40
    1972 strike of, 106–8
    1981 strike of, 331–65
Major League Rule 12, 45–47
Major League Rule 21, 43, 120, 324
Major League Umpires Association, 352
Malone, Moses, 433
Mantle, Mickey, 20, 39, 51, 73, 150,
    329–30, 423
Manush, Heinie, 15
Mansfield, Mike, 191
Marcus, Don, 378
Marichal, Juan, 423
marketing of baseball, 38, 51–52,
    170–71
Markus, Don, 378
Marquard, Rube, 423
Marriott, Willard, 96
Martha, Paul, 215
Martin, Billy, 143, 150, 298
Martin, Buddy, 370
Martin, J.C., 62
Martin, Jerry, 311, 313, 314–15
Martinez, Tippy, 205
Mathews, Eddie, 21, 52, 121, 122, 423
Matthews, Gary, 259–60
Mauch, Gene, 143